D0898929

Quality Enhancement in Developmental Disabilities

Quality Enhancement in Developmental Disabilities

Challenges and Opportunities in a Changing World

edited by

Valerie J. Bradley, M.A.
Human Services Research Institute
Cambridge, Massachusetts

and

Madeleine H. Kimmich, D.S.W.
Human Services Research Institute
Tualatin, Oregon

·P A U L·H·
BROOKES
PUBLISHING CO ®

Baltimore • London • Sydney

Paul H. Brookes Publishing Co.
Post Office Box 10624
Baltimore, Maryland 21285-0624

www.brookespublishing.com

Copyright © 2003 by Paul H. Brookes Publishing Co., Inc.
All rights reserved.

"Paul H. Brookes Publishing Co."
is a registered trademark owned by
Paul H. Brookes Publishing Co., Inc.

Typeset by Integrated Publishing Solutions, Grand Rapids, Michigan.
Manufactured in the United States of America by
Versa Press, East Peoria, Illinois.

All case studies in this book are based on the authors' actual experiences. In all instances, names have been changed; in some instances, identifying details have been altered to protect confidentiality.

Purchasers of *Quality Enhancement in Developmental Disabilities: Challenges and Opportunities in a Changing World* are granted permission to photocopy the individual exercises in this volume. None of the forms may be reproduced to generate revenue for any program or individual. Photocopies may be made only from an original book. You will see the copyright protection at the bottom of each photocopiable page.

Michael W. Smull, author of Chapter 7, retains all rights on Exercises 2, 3, 4, 5, 6, and 7.

Library of Congress Cataloging-in-Publication Data

Quality enhancement in developmental disabilities : challenges and opportunities
    in a changing world / edited by Valerie J. Bradley and Madeleine H. Kimmich.
       p.   cm.
    Includes bibliographical references and index.
       ISBN 1-55766-626-1
    1. Developmentally disabled—services for—United States.   2. Developmentally
disabled—care—United States.   3. Developmentally disabled—social networks—
United States.   4. Social work with people with disabilities—United States.   5. Social
service—United States—Quality control.   I. Bradley, Valerie J.   II. Kimmich,
Madeleine H.

HV1570.5.U6 Q83   2003
362.1′968—dc21   2002034239

British Library Cataloguing in Publication data are available from the British Library.

Contents

About the Editors

Valerie J. Bradley, M.A., Human Services Research Institute, 2336 Massachusetts Avenue, Cambridge, Massachussetts 02140

Ms. Bradley has been President of the Human Services Research Institute (HSRI) since its inception in 1976. She has a master's degree from the Eagleton Institute of Politics at Rutgers University. Ms. Bradley has directed numerous state- and federal-level policy evaluations that have contributed to the expansion, enhancement, and responsiveness of services and supports to people with disabilities and their families. She helped to design skills standards for human services workers and conducted a study to translate the experience with decentralization in Scandinavia to an American context. Ms. Bradley was also the project director of a national evaluation of self-determination. She currently co-directs a national project on performance measurement and is Principal Investigator of a national technical assistance center for quality assurance, funded by the federal Centers for Medicare & Medicaid Services. She co-edited *Creating Individual Supports for People with Developmental Disabilities: A Mandate for Change at Many Levels* with John W. Ashbaugh and Bruce C. Blaney (Paul H. Brookes Publishing Co., 1994). Ms. Bradley was the Chair of the President's Committee on Mental Retardation from 1994 to 2000.

Madeleine H. Kimmich, D.S.W., Human Services Research Institute, 8100 Southwest Nyberg Road, Suite 205, Tualatin, Oregon 97062

Dr. Kimmich has been Senior Project Director at the Human Services Research Institute (HSRI) since 1987. She holds a master's degree and a doctorate in social welfare policy from the University of California–Berkeley. Since 1976, Dr. Kimmich has been engaged in evaluation research and policy analysis of public social services programs, specializing in child welfare and developmental disabilities. She has assisted numerous states in designing and implementing systems reform, outcome measurement systems, and quality assurance efforts. She has evaluated a variety of state child welfare and developmental disabilities service systems. Dr. Kimmich is currently leading a multiyear evaluation of Ohio's Title IV-E Waiver Demonstration Project, which adopts a managed care approach to increase the efficiency and effectiveness of the state's child welfare system. She co-authored a book on family-driven managed care for children and family services, entitled *Partnering with Families to Reform Services: Managed Care in the Child Welfare System: A Primer on Family-Driven Managed Service System,* with Tracey Field (American Humane Association, 1999), and she has contributed chapters to several books on quality assurance for people with developmental disabilities.

About the Contributors

John Ashbaugh, M.B.A., is Vice President and Director of U.S. Operations for Danic Technology, Inc. Mr. Ashbaugh has directed the deployment of Danic Tools software and services in the United States. Danic Tools is an integrated, enterprise-level, person-centered information system for developmental disabilities and other human services agencies that may be run on a network or over the Internet. Prior to this, he was Senior Vice President at the Human Services Research Institute (HSRI), which he co-founded in 1976. His focus was on the planning, design, analysis and evaluation of management systems at the federal, state, and service agency levels.

Sarah Basehart, B.A., is Assistant Director of The Arc of Maryland, where she coordinates the Ask Me!℠ Project, a statewide quality-of-life survey. Under the direction of Ms. Basehart, participation in the project has become a statewide requirement for all state-funded developmental disability provider agencies. She works closely with the project and supports the training of 40 project interviewers, all of whom have developmental disabilities.

Madeline Becker, M.A., is Director of Quality for the Vinfen Corporation. Ms. Becker has a master's degree in psychology and is currently completing her doctoral work in human development. She plans, develops, implements, and coordinates agency-wide continuous quality improvement, risk management, and outcomes management programs and analysis, as well as reports on program and agency data for Vinfen. In addition, she oversees all regulatory compliance and accreditation processes and the development, revision, and implementation of policies and procedures for the organization.

Gordon Scott Bonham, Ph.D., is President of Bonham Research. Dr. Bonham has been the researcher on the Ask Me!℠ Project since its inception and has conducted numerous needs assessments and program evaluations in the area of disabilities during his 30 years of survey and social research experience. He has a doctorate in sociology, and he has conducted research at Towson University, the University of Louisville, and the National Center for Health Statistics. Dr. Bonham serves on the Board of The Arc of Baltimore and chairs its Quality Assurance Committee.

Denise M. Brown, M.S., is Vice President of Program Services at The Association For Independent Growth, Inc. (TAIG), a multi-faceted provider of day and residential services in the Philadelphia metro area. She has spent more than 20 years supporting people with mental retardation and related developmental disabilities. Ms. Brown's experiences include university-related training on disability issues and government management of disability programs.

Joseph R. Bucci, M.S., has been President of The Association For Independent Growth, Inc. (TAIG), a multi-faceted provider of day and residential services in the Philadelphia metro area, since 1985. He is an executive management professional with more than 30 years of expertise in directing community-based supports for individuals with developmental and mental health disabilities.

Tina Campanella, M.A., is Executive Director of the Quality Trust for people with developmental disabilities in Washington, D.C. Previously, she was Vice President of The Council on Quality and Leadership in Supports for People with Disabilities. Ms. Campanella has been responsible for the development of The Council's training, consultation, and other learning resources to support quality improvement in services and supports for people with disabilities. She played a key role in the design and development of The Council's *Personal Outcome Measures,* published in 1993, and developed support publications that help organizations to become more focused on personal outcome achievment.

Guy Caruso, Ph.D., is Western Coordinator for the Institute on Disabilities, Pennsylvania's University Center for Excellence in Developmental Disabilities at Temple University. Dr. Caruso is a technical advisor to Pennsylvania's Independent Monitoring for Quality Program, in which consumers with disabilities, their family members, and interested others interview people receiving services through the Pennsylvania Office of Mental Retardation about aspects of their lives. Since 1975, Guy has been an active member of the Normalization/Social Role Valorization network, conducting training and PASS/PASSING evaluations. He has been involved in a number of leadership development, strategic planning, and systems change projects primarily in New York, Pennsylvania, and Louisiana.

Richard Cohen, J.D., is Executive Director of the Disabilities Rights Center, Inc., the federally designated Protection and Advocacy Agency for New Hampshire. He has been a practicing attorney for 30 years, principally in the area of disabilities rights law. He was counsel to the plaintiff class in *Garrity vs. Gallen,* a suit that ultimately led to the closure of Laconia State School, making New Hampshire the first state to operate a system of services for individuals with disabilities without a public institution. He subsequently served as a federal and state court monitor around the country over class actions involving deinstitutionalization and community placement, rights of students with disabilities to a free and appropriate public education, and improvements to states' child protection systems.

Elizabeth Couchoud, B.A., is Health Insurance Specialist at the Centers for Medicare & Medicaid Services (CMS), part of the U.S. Department of Health and Human Services. She has a bachelor's degree in psychology from George Mason University, with a focus on child development. During her career in the Survey and Certification Group of the CMS, she has focused on improvements in the survey protocol and surveyor training for the program for intermediate care facilities for people with mental retardation (ICFs/MR) and the development of quality indicators for programs that serve beneficiaries who have developmental disabilities.

Dale L. Dutton, M.S., is responsible for the Business Development for the Employment and Community Services Unit of CARF . . . The Rehabilitation Accreditation Commission. He is a dedicated advocate for community-based, inclusive support services for individuals with disabilities and the parent of a young adult with Down syndrome who is currently thriving in a combination of supported living and supported employment in California.

Celia S. Feinstein, M.A., is Associate Director for Training and Technical Assistance at the Institute on Disabilities at Temple University. She has been at the Institute for more than 20 years. She currently directs 12 projects including the Pennsylvania Waiting List Initiative, the Independent Monitoring Project, Monitoring the Well-being of Pennhurst Class Members Living in the Community, Equal Justice for People with Mental Retardation, Competence and Confidence: Partners in Policymaking, and the Philadelphia Quality Improvement Initiative.

Robert M. Gettings, M.A., has served as Executive Director of the National Association of State Directors of Developmental Disabilities Services (NASDDDS) since the organization opened its first headquarters office in 1970. He has written and lectured extensively on the impact of federal legislative and administrative policy and helped many states solve a variety of service delivery problems over the years. A Life Member of the American Association on Mental Retardation, Mr. Gettings was recognized by the National Historic Trust on Mental Retardation in 2000 as 1 of 36 major contributors to the mental retardation field during the 20th century.

Timothy C. Greusel, L.S.W., has been Director of the Quality Enhancement Support Team since 1994 and has worked in a variety of positions in the disabilities field since the 1960s. Prior experience includes direct contact work; residential and day supports program management; training, technical assistance, and consulting with Therapeutic Concepts, Inc., and Copeland and Associates; and program and project management with the Pennsylvania Office of Mental Retardation and Temple University's Institute on Disabilities.

Gail Grossman, M.S.S.A., is Assistant Commissioner for Quality Management in the Commonwealth of Massachusetts Department of Mental Retardation. Ms. Grossman has a master's degree in social service administration from Case Western Reserve University. She has 30 years of experience in planning, developing, and evaluating services for individuals with mental retardation. Her work in legislative and legal advocacy, direct services, and state administration has focused on developing and strengthening services and supports for individuals in the community. In her current position, she has helped to develop the state's outcome-based survey and certification system and is currently developing the department's integrated quality management and improvement system.

Catherine Hayes, M.A., is President of H&W Independent Solutions, Inc., a training and consulting firm for disability and related issues. She has more than 25 years of experience and has worked in many settings, serving as Manager for Continuing Care Services and Team Leader for intermediate care facilities for people with mental retardation (ICFs/MR) at the Centers for Medicare & Medicaid Services (CMS). She has worked as a manager, trainer, and quality enhancement coordinator, and she is past Director of the Epilepsy Foundation of America's Training and Placement Program (TAPS). Ms. Hayes is a lifelong volunteer and served as President of the Huntington's Disease Society of America, during which time she published an editorial on genetic testing in *The New England Journal of Medicine.*

Amy Hewitt, Ph.D., is Director of Interdisciplinary Training and Research Associate at the University of Minnesota, Institute on Community Integration, Research and Training Center on Community Living. Dr. Hewitt has more than 20 years of experience and an extensive background and work history in the developmental disabilities field. She directs several federal and state research, evaluation, and demonstration projects in the areas of direct support staff workforce development and community services for people with disabilities. Dr. Hewitt is a national leader in workforce development and community supports for people with developmental disabilities. She is Founder and past Co-Chair of the National Alliance for Direct Support Professionals. Dr. Hewitt is the current Social Work Division Chair for the American Association on Mental Retardation.

Geoffrey P. Jones, M.B.A., is a consultant clinical psychologist working with offenders with learning disabilities in Kent, England. He has worked in the disability sector in the United Kingdom and Australia since 1976, mainly as a clinical psychologist, trainer, and consultant. From 1992 to 2001, Mr. Jones was Director of E-QUAL Disability Consultants in western Australia. He maintains a keen interest in service quality and the participation of people with disabilities in decision making.

Linda Joyce, M.Ed., J.D., is Team Leader for intermediate care facilities for people with mental retardation (ICFs/MR) at the Centers for Medicare & Medicaid Services (CMS). Ms. Joyce has a master's degree in educational administration and a juris doctorate, and she is licensed to practice law in Vermont and the District of Columbia. She has worked in the field of mental retardation and developmental disabilities in both the public and private sectors, at the state and national levels, and as a private consultant. In her current position, she addresses national issues that affect people living in ICFs/MR including regulatory interpretation and implementation, policy design, and strategic planning initiatives.

Rosemary Lawn, Dip. OT, has worked in the disability sector in Australia and New Zealand for more than 24 years as an occupational therapist, employment services manager, trainer, quality monitor, consultant, and evaluator. She has worked with a variety of disability agencies, including those that provide early intervention, employment, accommodation, recreation, advocacy, education, and training. From 1992 to 2001, Ms. Lawn was Director of E-QUAL Disability Consultants in western Australia. Many E-QUAL projects have supported the voices of people with disabilties in the context of service quality improvement.

Cristine Marchand, M.S., is Executive Director of The Arc of Maryland. Ms. Marchand has worked in disability rights at the state, national, and local levels since 1976. She has developed successful state legislation in Maryland around supported living, education rights, system reform for people with developmental disabilities on waiting lists, and helping youth with disabilities make transitions.

Leena M. Matikka, Ph.D., is Director of Research at the Finnish Association on Mental Retardation. Dr. Matikka has been involved in the field of intellectual disabilities since the 1970s and is considered a leading expert in her field. She has published articles and several reports on quality of life and the quality of services provided for people with intellectual disabilities. She is a fellow of the International Association for the Scientific Study of Intellectual Disabilities.

Dorothy Mullen, R.N., M.S.N., is a consultant in developmental disability–related health, safety, and quality assurance and improvement activities. Ms. Mullen has more than 25 years of experience in the field of developmental disabilities and has served in a variety of clinical and administrative senior management positions during her tenure with the Massachusetts Department of Mental Retardation. Prior to her recent retirement from the department, she held the position of Assistant Commissioner for Quality Management, with responsibility for the Home and Community-Based Services (HCBS) Waiver and the development of several new systems to improve health supports, strengthen safeguards, and more fully integrate quality assurance and improvement structures.

Marcia Noll, R.N., M.S.N., is Director of Health & Clinical Services for the Connecticut Department of Mental Retardation, where she oversees and monitors the quality of health and clinical services provided directly and indirectly by the department. With more than 25 years of experience in the field of developmental disabilities, Ms. Noll administers several quality assurance systems including the department's mortality review, medication certification for unlicensed personnel, psychotropic medication and restraint monitoring, and health standards development. She has led initiatives to improve incident reporting and develop professional job performance standards. She is presently leading the department's Focus Team on Aging, a project initiated to develop a vision and recommended action plan for serving older adults.

June E. Rowe, C.A.G.S., is Senior Project Director at the Human Services Research Institute (HSRI). Ms. Rowe has a certificate of advanced graduate studies in rehabilitation counseling from Northeastern University. She has worked for more than 20 years in services for individuals with developmental disabilities, particularly in developing community-based services in Massachusetts for individuals who had previously lived in state institutions or with their families. Ms. Rowe has done extensive work in developing quality management and improvement systems using person-centered and organizational outcomes. She is Project Director of a national technical assistance center for quality assurance, funded by the Centers for Medicare & Medicaid Services.

Barry Schwartz, M.Ed., L.M.H.C., is Senior Vice President for Mental Retardation Services at Vinfen Corporation. He leads a team that currently provides residential and day supports to more than 500 individuals and 165 families in Massachusetts and Connecticut. As a member of Vinfen's Executive Team, he champions a focus on internal and external consumer-, innovation-, outcomes-driven continuous quality improvement. Mr. Schwartz has a master's degree in counseling and has been creating and administering community-based supports for more than 30 years. He serves on several nonprofit boards and provides consultation to many organizations.

Julie F. Silver, M.M.H.S., is Project Director at the Human Services Research Institute (HSRI), where she conducts research, evaluation, policy initiatives, and demonstrations concerning the human service workforce; the quality of services and supports for people with disabilities; and the structure, implementation, and function of service systems. Ms. Silver has directed studies of quality enhancement and advocacy processes for systems under court monitoring, and she currently directs efforts in several states to identify quality-of-life concerns among system constituents. Ms. Silver was the lead author of the *Plan to Enhance the*

Direct Support Workforce in Massachusetts and of the Relationships Course for the College of Direct Support, a web-based education program for direct support professionals. Ms. Silver holds a master's degree in the management of human services from the Heller School at Brandeis University.

Gary A. Smith is Senior Project Director at the Human Services Research Institute (HSRI), where he directs several disability-related projects. Prior to joining the HSRI, he served for 14 years as Director of Special Projects for the National Association of State Directors of Developmental Disabilities Services (NASDDDS), where he specialized in Medicaid-related policy topics related to underwriting the costs of community services for people with developmental disabilities, furnished technical assistance in more than 40 states, and was instrumental in launching the Core Indicators Project. He also held other senior state government management positions in Colorado and Illinois, with a focus on human services.

Michael W. Smull is Director of Support Development Associates and also consults with agencies, regions, and states on learning how to do person-centered planning, implement the plans, and make the organizational changes needed for successful implementation. He has been working with people with disabilities for the past 30 years, and he has had extensive experience in nearly all aspects of developing community services. He founded two community agencies; helped a number of agencies convert from programs to supports; and helped states, regions, and counties in changing their structures to support self-determination. He has also worked to help people leave institutions and most recently was a consultant in the closure of Fairview Training Center in Oregon. He has written extensively on issues relating to supporting people with challenging behaviors, person centered planning, and the challenge of changing our system to one that will support self-determination.

Roger Stortenbecker, B.A., is Administrator for the Office of Aging and Disability Services in Nebraska, which includes the Developmental Disabilities System. He has been working with people with developmental disabilities since 1977. Mr. Stortenbecker previously worked in direct support and management positions with the Lancaster Office of Mental Retardation for 12 years.

Sarah L. Taub, M.M.H.S., is Senior Research Associate at the Human Services Research Institute (HSRI). She currently serves as Project Manager for the Core Indicators Project, a national effort to develop performance indicators for developmental disabilities service systems across states. Prior to joining HSRI, Ms. Taub provided direct services to adults with developmental disabilities and worked as a special education teacher. She holds a master's degree in management of human services from the Heller School at Brandeis University and a bachelor's degree in psychology from Cornell University.

Marianne Taylor, M.A., is Senior Research Associate at the Human Services Research Institute (HSRI). Ms Taylor has directed and worked in projects in the areas of workforce development, education and training, family support, quality enhancement, community inclusion of older people with disabilities, and the evaluation of supported living programs and other Medicaid waiver services. Ms. Taylor's work in direct support workforce development is based on the understanding that the quality of life for people who use community-based services is intrinsically and inextricably linked to the quality and competency of those people who support them. Ms. Taylor directs the Pathways from Classroom to Credentials Project to study the predictive validity of various staff assessment processes. Ms. Taylor is currently working on developing the STARS curriculum for training direct support professionals in the 12 competency areas of the Community Support Skill Standards.

Jan Tøssebro, Ph.D., is Professor of Social Work in the Department of Social Work and Health Sciences at the Norwegian University of Science and Technology. Dr. Tøssebro has a master's degree and a doctoral degree in sociology. Since 1987, he has been deeply involved in disability research and has also acted as a member of a Public Committee on Disability Policy. One of his main research responsibilities has been the evaluation of the closure of institutions for people with intellectual disabilites in Norway, including a follow-up 10-year report. Another important research area is a longitudinal project on growing up with disabilities in which a sample was followed from early childhood through adolescence. He is currently the editor of *Scandinavian Journal of Disability Research* and a member of Norway's National Committee on Research Ethics in Humanities and Social Sciences.

Foreword

This volume is a timely resource for everyone in the field of developmental disabilities concerned with the quality of services and supports. Its title, *Quality Enhancement in Developmental Disabilities: Challenges and Opportunities in a Changing World,* could not be more apt. Unlike the first wave of deinstitutionalization and community service development in the 1970s and 1980s, which was spurred largely by institutional reform litigation that affected some institutions and not others, the new wave of community service development promises to be broader and more comprehensive. This wave is fueled first by the broad and systemic responses by the federal government to enforce the decision of the U.S. Supreme Court in *L.C. v. Olmstead* (119 S.Ct. 2179). The Supreme Court interpreted the Americans with Disabilities Act (ADA) of 1990 (PL 101-336) and found institutional placement to constitute a form of discrimination against individuals on the basis of disability, if the segregation is unnecessary in the opinion of qualified professionals. As a result of the proactive approaches by federal agencies, most state governments are engaged in efforts to develop plans that examine their institutionalized populations to identify people who no longer need to be confined. Second, waiting list lawsuits, brought under the Medicaid statutes in several states, seek the development of additional community services for tens of thousands of people with disabilities who remain unserved or underserved in the community. In some ways, these developments create the same types of pressures for state governments to expand their community services as the institutional closure or downsizing cases did in years past.

In the first wave of deinstitutionalization, efforts at developing quality assurance strategies suited to the community services were subordinated in the rush to meet court-ordered deadlines. As this volume attests, we have now had the time to assess what worked and why and, just as important, what did not work and why. The authors, many of whom are veterans of the court cases in various capacities, describe lessons learned and offer the reader a veritable banquet of new ideas, strategies, and practical pointers on how to develop quality enhancement programs that set and reinforce high expectations for quality of life and consumer satisfaction, while also providing strategies for monitoring health and safety.

Of course, the environment in which community services are being developed in this second wave has also changed substantially. Since the 1970s, expectations changed from simply relocating people into group homes in the community to integrating people through person-centered planning approaches. Public policy now squarely embraces a recognition of and respect for autonomy and self-determination, a development unimaginable in the more paternalistic era of the 1970s. As a result, the complexity of frontline jobs has changed significantly from the heyday of the era of intermediate care facilities for people with mental retardation, when all that was asked of staff was to comply with detailed and prescriptive regulatory mandates.

The title of Chapter 1, "New Building Blocks of Quality Assurance," captures a snapshot of where the field stands after more than a quarter century of radical transformation of service systems across the country for people with developmental disabilities. Along the way, the reader is treated to a wonderful, concise history of the evolution of both the services system and the role of quality assurance through the years. We have struggled mightily to vanquish the stark horrors of Willowbrook, Partlow, Pennhurst, and dozens of similar, if less infamous, institutions across the country. We have succeeded in replacing them with a spectrum of opportunities for community living that were unimaginable when the reform movement first started. But the challenge of ensuring quality—of balancing self-determination and safety—persists. As Michael W. Smull puts it, "Happy and dead are incompatible. Alive and miserable are unacceptable." He reminds us that it is as vital to know what is important *to* the person as it is to know what is important *for* the person.

Many troubling signals have drawn attention to emerging problems in community services. Not only have these problems been cropping up often enough to be a matter of concern within the field, but they have also been the subject of media attention. *The Washington Post* won a Pulitzer Prize for exposing widespread breakdowns in Washington, D.C.'s community-based mental retardation system. Similar stories have appeared in many states. When such stories appear, one reaction is to minimize them because they are not typical. We believe we are doing well in many respects, and part of what makes these stories news is that they are unusual, but performance is uneven. There is a constant tension between efforts to produce quality and excellence for a few and the pressure to provide less for many. But even when there is no pressure, we are challenged in our ability to transform lofty statements of policy and philosophy into day-to-day reality for the people we serve in the community. The challenges lie not only in the inherent difficulty and complexity of harmonizing competing policies and values, but also in the environment in which we must execute policy—a work environment increasingly characterized by low pay, high stress, and high turnover of employees who exist at the fringes of the labor market reserved for those without higher-level skills.

In the transition from institutions to community, the security and longevity of public employment has been traded in for high turnover of minimum-wage jobs in the private sector. In the 1980s, in my testimony before Senator Lowell Weiker's Subcommittee on Labor and Human Resources, I noted that direct care staff are expected to have the wisdom of Solomon, the patience of Job, and the compassion of Florence Nightingale, all for the wages of a janitor. In the ensuing years, the challenges have become even greater as increasing responsibility has been delegated to the frontline staff in order to balance competing interests in safety and self-determination, often without adequate staff training, supervision, and support.

Notwithstanding all of these shortcomings and challenges in supporting front-line workers, which are discussed by Marianne Taylor, Amy Hewitt, and Julie F. Silver, independent assessments of the quality of services and satisfaction often produce reassuringly high scores, as Celia S. Feinstein and Guy Caruso report. Scorecards can inform the reader, but they can also mask complex realities.

In the area of safety and freedom from abuse and neglect, where performance scores generally tend to be high, even if we were able to achieve a 99% standard of perfection, the remaining 1% would represent approximately 3,600 people, or more than the total number of people with developmental disabilities in residential programs in each of 22 states. Due to the very size of service systems, even a very small rate of failure can affect large numbers of people. So determining where to set the benchmarks is a critical consideration for public policy, as is developing procedures that examine individual cases regarding safety.

No discussion of quality assurance would be complete without a discussion of the reporting and investigation of incidents of abuse and neglect. All too often, as in many of the stories reported in the news media, this function is the Achilles' heel of the service system. Inadequate attention to the design and operations of this function creates an environment of collective innocence rather than individual responsibility. Richard Cohen guides the reader through the process of developing an effective system to perform this critical function, with plenty of practical suggestions drawn from his wide experience. The central point of ensuring accountability for each incident will not be lost on the reader.

What I have observed in examining the performance of large systems trying to implement policies supporting choice and self-determination is that the performance is highly variable. Programs accomplish remarkable things for some people, yet other people struggle to get access to minimal services and supports to ensure their health and safety. In looking more closely at the reasons for variations in performance, it is my preliminary impression that such policies work better for some people than for others, and the reason for this has less to do with the nature of individual needs or aspirations than with the allies and supporters the person has.

In much of the recent discussions about the tension between self-determination and risk, there has been an inadequate recognition of the different challenges that service systems face regarding two generally different groups of consumers of services. One group of people have recently entered the adult service systems and already have a network of family, friends, and peers who support and advocate for them. The second group of people were living in institutions for a long time and are now trying to adjust to community settings where they have been recently placed. The needs and challenges that each group presents are quite different.

In large part due to the success of public policies such as special education, a whole generation of individuals with disabilities is entering adult service systems with a network of families, friends, and peers and with the experience of having grown up in their communities, without ever having experienced the separation and severing of bonds that come with institutionalization or out-of-home placement. For this group of adults making the transition into the adult service system, the challenge for government and support agencies is to support and nurture the network that exists, to allow it to transform itself and adjust to the changing needs of the young adult, and to continue to play a vital role as a support and safeguard for the individual with the disability. How well government and support agencies meet these challenges can influence the ease and extent to which each person's network of family, friends, and peers can be supportive; however, in most cases, this network will be available regardless, due to the nature and strength of the bonds that have been maintained over the lifetime of the young adult. These bonds also ensure a degree of personal vigilance over the services and supports provided and continued personal advocacy on behalf of the individual. When I ran the Protection and Advocacy System in New York, I noticed that the most insistent and incessant demands for our advocacy services came from families. State regulatory and licensing agencies have had the same experience.

The second group of people being served in the community is composed of people who were placed in the institutions many years ago and have now been placed into a variety of community settings as the role of institutions has declined. For a significant number of people in this group, who have been in institutions for a long time, family ties have withered away because of death, distance, the passage of time, or other unique circumstances. These people now find themselves without personal allies or the type of nurturing network that typically supports young adults. They lack the benefit of personal vigilance and personal advocacy from such allies, and should they need the assistance of government monitors, regulators, or independent advocates, they are significantly disadvantaged in gaining access to these resources.

The challenge for government and support agencies is to create a network of support and safeguards for each individual from scratch, to build durable community connections, and to maintain this new network. For this group of people, the success or failure of the community experience is highly dependent on the quality of paid staff, case managers, support coordinators, public guardians, monitors, regulators, and advocates; and the quality of these staff is highly dependent on the effectiveness of agencies in organizing, supervising, monitoring, and sustaining the systems. Many critical governmental functions that serve as safeguards have been eliminated or privatized in the process of downsizing, rightsizing, and reinvention, leaving them mired in conflicts of interest.

Quality assurance systems are ultimately engaged in holding up a mirror to allow the service system to see itself as it is and to prompt progressive cycles of improvement in performance. Reliable information about systems performance is a critical tool for advocacy for resources and reforms to address shortcomings. Sarah L. Taub, Gary A. Smith, and Valerie J. Bradley discuss the use of performance indicators to monitor performance at the state level. John Ashbaugh guides the reader through the steps of building a management information system (MIS) infrastructure.

Robert M. Gettings draws on his remarkable breadth of knowledge to help the reader understand the essential building blocks of a comprehensive statewide quality management program. He will save legions of administrators and advocates countless hours of misspent energy by declaring forthrightly that "adequate financial resources . . . are by no means the only determinant of service quality." He focuses on doing things that are within an administrator's control, rather than lamenting conditions that are not.

Both the casual reader of this book and the serious student will find ideas and perspectives that will challenge them to think more deeply about the challenge of ensuring quality in a changing world.

Clarence J. Sundram
Special Master, United States District Court
Albany, New York

Quality
Assurance
and
Enhancement
in Flux

This section explores the major shifts that have occurred in quality assurance since the 1970s, as the field has moved from prescriptive regulations and processes to a persistent focus on consumer outcomes. This shift has set *quality* loose from the limitations of a strictly defined set of standards to be an ever-changing core in continuous quality improvement efforts, in which the definition of *good quality* varies over time and across individuals and in which the mechanisms to assess its presence keep evolving. Chapter 1 sets the stage.

Chapter 2 reflects on the state of the art in 1996, when the Health Care Financing Administration (now the Centers for Medicare and Medicaid Services [CMS]) funded a comprehensive study of outcome-based quality assurance efforts in all state developmental disabilities (DD) systems. The review shows that quality assurance can indeed "move beyond traditional regulatory compliance and token consumer satisfaction, to judge system performance in terms of the experiences of individuals served." All of the major tools of quality assurance—certification, consumer survey, volunteer monitoring, continuous quality enhancement processes, and safeguards for consumer health and safety—have undergone substantial changes to make them more outcome-focused and connected to the experiences of individuals receiving services and

1

supports. The Massachusetts case study highlights integration of consumer outcomes into the licensure process, and the Pennsylvania case study emphasizes the crucial role that staff play in ensuring positive outcomes for consumers and thus the importance of attending to the quality of the work environment for staff.

Chapter 3 presents a brief history of the accreditation movement in the United States, noting especially the challenges posed by the rise of consumer-directed services and supports and self-determination initiatives. Like all quality assurance activities, the process of accreditation is redefining itself to help providers make the transition to a new role in supporting individuals with developmental disabilities.

To complement the consumer-outcome focus of this section, Chapter 4 describes how a focus on personal outcomes, in the collective, guides overall organizational improvement. Having greater clarity about the outcomes that people expect from their supports and services enables the organization to better support people. When organizations include people receiving supports in the discussions of needed internal changes and then enter into dialogues with all participants, they demonstrate their commitment to continuous learning and the value they place on the views of all stakeholders—especially the people receiving supports and the staff providing those supports. The case study about Philadelphia's Quality Enhancement Support Team further underscores how individuals' experiences in receiving services and supports can be analyzed to directly inform systemwide policy and practice.

CHAPTER 1

New Building Blocks of Quality Assurance

VALERIE J. BRADLEY

The first words from *A Tale of Two Cities,* "It was the best of times, it was the worst of times," may be overused, but they do capture the current state of services and supports to people with developmental disabilities (DD) and their families in the United States. On the one hand, inclusive community options continue to expand, and the number of people in large congregate facilities continues to decline (Prouty & Lakin, 2001). A robust self-advocacy movement has emerged, and a national organization—Self-Advocates Becoming Empowered—is flourishing. Person-centered planning is at least an aspiration in virtually every state, and the choices made by people about their homes and with whom they share their lives have increased (see Chapter 13). On the other hand, there has been a spate of newspaper articles about preventable deaths (Altimari & Hamilton, 2001; Bennish & Beyerlein, 2002; Fallis, 2002; Richissin, 2002); problems with recruitment and retention of staff have compromised the effectiveness of many community supports (see Chapter 15); and although states have expanded community services, long waiting lists are the norm as demand for residential services remains strong across the country (Smith, 1999).

Given these two competing and conflicting dynamics, the challenge is to preserve and support the burgeoning empowerment of people while ensuring that reforms proceed in an intentional fashion. Clarence Sundram was one of the first in the field to articulate these tensions:

> I think we have tended to be seduced by the power of the new application to people with disabilities of old ideas of equality, choice, autonomy, and inclusion to the point that we have relied more upon hope and belief than upon good judgment and careful planning to help make these ideas a reality. (1994, pp. 8–9)

Failure to adopt a multilayered strategy has led to flawed reforms, such as the "dumping" of individuals with mental illness from state institutions. In

1978, Bradley made the following observation, which continues to resonate today: "In the past, the failure to put deinstitutionalization in a systematic framework among equally important goals for reform has in fact resulted in only partial and, in some instances, detrimental change" (p. 60). This book provides a framework for a thoughtful consideration of the task at hand—to provide an integrated system of safeguards that anticipates individual risk while supporting individual choice.

HISTORICAL OVERVIEW

The adoption of quality assurance systems after World War II began in earnest with the intervention of the federal judiciary to remediate conditions in public institutions. These cases, premised on a right to treatment or a right to habilitation, included remedies that prescribed standards for public facilities that had previously been only weakly regulated by the states. Prominent cases included *Wyatt v. Stickney, New York State Association for Retarded Children and Parisi v. Rockefeller, Welsh v. Likens,* and *Davis v. Watkins.* As Bradley reported in 1978, these standards tended to concentrate on the rudiments of custodial care:

> The standards set forth in these decisions are very extensive in scope and are quite detailed. They reach into every facet of institutional life and beyond, including intake, physical plant, nutrition, staff number, distribution, shift schedules, training, resident care and treatment, record-keeping, etc. (p. 142)

The next wave of evolutionary change in quality enhancement took place as the community system gained more confidence and as targeted behavioral, instructional, pharmacological, and other therapies began to show promise in assisting people with DD in gaining new skills and adapting to new environments. The result was the creation of highly specific "process" standards intended to embed promising developments into routine practice. This change was apparent in state standards for individual habilitation plans (IHPs) that dictated the format of the plan, the composition of the planning team, and the levels of measurement of goal attainment. Concentration on treatment strategies and planning concerns were especially evident in the design of the original regulations governing the conduct of intermediate care facilities for people with mental retardation (ICFs/MR).

As providers became more sophisticated, services and supports less facility-based, and residential arrangements less standardized, many in the field began to chafe under the constraints of more rigid and prescriptive standards. Criticisms of the ICF/MR standards persisted into the 1990s (Boggs, 1992; Holburn, 1992; Kennedy, 1990; Shea, 1992; Taylor, 1992). Tecla Jaskulski (1996) summarized these concerns in a report to the Health Care Financing Administration (HCFA):

- Compliance does not equal quality.

- The standards are not focused on outcomes.

- The processes that are reviewed are not sufficiently linked to desired outcomes.

- The yes/no dichotomy (i.e., in or out of compliance) ignores individual differences.

- The adversarial approach of the survey creates an atmosphere of fault finding.

- There is no focus on continuous quality improvement.

- The survey process itself is intrusive in the lives of people with mental retardation.

The dissatisfaction with prescriptive process standards led to an exploration of ways to build outcomes into quality enhancement assessments. An early examination of the multiple facets of quality enhancement noted, "Outcome measures are generally seen as the most telling measures to use and as the ultimate basis for legitimizing other approaches to measuring service quality" (Ashbaugh et al., 1980, p. 17). However, the discussion went on to note that "in our analysis of twenty-two quality assurance systems . . . few concentrate on outcome measures, and some have no client outcome measures at all" (p. 90).

The initial construct that characterized consumer outcomes focused on the acquisition of skills or the achievement of goals. Functional scales, such as the Scales of Independent Behavior (Bruininks, Woodcock, Weatherman, & Hill, 1984) and the Vineland Adaptive Behavior Scales (Sparrow, Balla, & Cichetti, 1984) were used to ascertain whether people's functional and adaptive abilities had improved. This form of "outcome measurement" was driven by the objectives set in individual plans that reflected professional expectations. By the early 1990s, the adoption of norms such as choice and empowerment shifted the outcome perspective from the IHP team to the individual. Rather than focus primarily on improvement in adaptive skills (or reduction in maladaptive behavior), the criteria for the effectiveness of services and supports placed increasing emphasis on outcomes valued by the individual (Bradley, 1994).

A dramatic example of this shift in focus can be seen in the substantially revamped standards published by the Accreditation Council on Services for People with Disabilities (ACDD, 1993). Instead of using 817 process standards (in areas such as advocacy, information and referral, individual records, and plan coordination), the ACDD (1990) proposed a streamlined set of 10 "outcome measures for people," and four sets of performance indicators for organizations. The consumer outcomes were (ACDD, 1993)

- Personal goals
- Choice
- Social inclusion
- Relationships
- Rights
- Dignity and respect
- Health
- Environment
- Security
- Satisfaction

SIGNS OF CHANGE

That quality enhancement "gyroscopes" are undergoing change is apparent from shifts in assumptions, expectations, and approaches to monitoring. A review of these changes reveals the subtle and not-so-subtle influences that are reshaping the configuration of public DD systems and the concrete manifestations of such shifts.

Changes Rooted in Community Norms

Quality benchmarks are no longer pegged to institutional care. In other words, success is more than just creating a system that was better than a state facility—a norm that was present in the deinstitutionalization studies of the 1970s and 1980s (e.g., Conroy & Bradley, 1984). The bar has been set much higher, and there is some momentum to compare outcomes not just with the outcomes of other people with disabilities but also with those of members of the general population (see Chapter 12). Nerney made an eloquent plea for such an approach:

> Public policy leaders need to adopt a different definition of quality. This new definition must rest on expectations for individuals with disabilities that mirror the expectations all other members of this society have for themselves. Current quality enhancement systems are normed on disability programs and services; rather, quality should be normed on aspirations that all human beings have—not on satisfaction with human service environments and interventions. (2001, p. 3)

Changing Expectations

Another factor shaping emerging quality norms is the change in the expectations of the current generation of families and people with disabilities. One of these changes has to do with the advent of self-determination and consumer-directed services as priorities among self-advocates and young family members. An evaluation (Agosta, Silver, Heaviland, & Bradley, 2000) of the Robert Wood Johnson Foundation self-determination projects included a component aimed at the perceptions and involvement of self-advocates in the demonstrations. When asked what *self-determination* meant, some of the responses from people with disabilities included

- I am a person like all people: My life is my own.

- I speak for myself. I speak up. I stick up for myself.

- I make my own choices.

- I am the boss of my own life.

- I make my decisions in my own life.

- I do for myself… and not depend on others so much. (p. 4)

These strong statements telegraph a change in the locus of power vis-à-vis the dominance of professional judgment. The sentiments also indicate that quality is not a standardized commodity but a flexible notion heavily influenced by the person receiving services and his or her family and friends.

Movement Away from Prescriptive Standards

In line with changes in the service system and assumptions about how services and supports should be provided, several states have revamped their licensing and certification processes to reflect a more person-centered focus. Massachusetts, for instance, has combined its licensing provisions with survey and certification and developed the Quality Enhancement Survey Tool (QUEST) (see Case Study 1). QUEST eliminates some of the more rigid elements of licensing including such things as stair height and staff–client ratios. In their place, the state developed an approach that relies heavily on the experience of people receiving supports. Other states—such as New Hampshire, Vermont, Colorado, and Oregon—followed a similar path.

Emphasis on Enhancement

Most of the energy expended in the DD field since the 1970s has gone into expanding community services and relocating individuals from institutions to community homes and supports. Many states are now all but out of the custodial care business (e.g., Vermont, New Hampshire, Minnesota, New Mexico,

Rhode Island), and some have turned their attention to building the capacity and stability of community systems.

Dissemination of Information

The number of stakeholders concerned about services to people with DD in the public sector has grown as community services and supports have proliferated. This fact, paired with the move to empower families and people with disabilities, has put increasing pressure on state agencies to provide information about the performance of the service system in a timely and accessible fashion. Some states, such as Michigan, have for several years published "report cards" on the performance of their community mental health centers. Wyoming routinely publishes the results of its licensing reviews on the state's web site. Other states, such as Colorado, have made consumer outcome data available statewide. These steps are the beginning of an effort to make systems more transparent and to respond to the increased need for information by families and people with disabilities making choices among providers.

Involvement of People with Disabilities and Their Families

The self-advocacy movement coupled with an emphasis on choice and self-determination has spawned a more "democratic" quality enhancement system in many states. Whereas quality enhancement has traditionally been the purview of state bureaucrats and accreditation entities, people with disabilities and their families have become increasingly involved in performance oversight. Specifically, consumers have been involved in the design of consumer surveys in Maryland (see Chapter 8) and New Hampshire, and people with disabilities and their families are part of independent monitoring teams in Pennsylvania (see Chapter 9).

CONTEMPORARY CHALLENGES

Contemporary challenges to reaching outcome goals include cracks in the foundation of the community system, struggles with inherited technological resources, decentralization of services, expansion pressures, self-determination's blurring of the locus of responsibility, and case manager overload. The following sections explore each of these challenges in further detail.

Cracks in the Foundation

In spite of the extraordinary and positive changes that have taken place in services and supports for people with DD and their families, cracks are beginning to emerge in the façade of the community system. Evidence of these cracks can be seen in alarming newspaper articles and in the results of reviews conducted by the Centers for Medicare & Medicaid Services (CMS) of state Home and

Community-Based Services Waiver. A review of 13 state waiver reports found that states were severely lacking in several areas, which can be grouped in the following major clusters of citations (Rowe & Taub, 2002)[1]:

- Provider capabilities, including staff training/workforce development issues and the development of more coordinated and effective systems to monitor providers

- Service planning and implementation, particularly in the area of increased choice among providers and services

- Participant safeguards, with health and medication taking the lead

- Systems monitoring and performance, in particular the development of cohesive quality management/quality improvement systems with more specific data collection and dissemination protocols

The disturbing subtext in many of these reviews is the occurrence of decidedly avoidable incidents, such as falls and medication errors, that can be directly traced to inadequately trained direct support staff. The crisis that exists in the recruitment and retention of direct support staff (see Chapter 15) and the increased decentralization of the system have exacerbated these problems and have necessitated a review of the basic protections and safeguards that states have erected for people with DD.

Struggles with "Legacy" Technology

A multilayered, integrated quality enhancement system has to be built on the collection and analysis of data. Attempts to create such systems in the past have been taxed with overweening ambition, inadequate management information systems, and cumbersome data collection protocols. As a result, the systems degraded in time, and providers—who rarely saw useful feedback—became reluctant, if not hostile, respondents. Since the creation of these faulty systems, technology has moved forward rapidly, and the widescale ability to enter, transmit, and analyze data electronically is within reach (see Chapter 14). States such as Pennsylvania have taken bold steps to integrate this technology into their quality enhancement systems so that uniform data can be collected statewide, in addition to being available for analysis at the local level.

Challenges of Decentralization

Some states are better situated to the creation of integrated quality management systems—specifically, states such as Massachusetts, Connecticut, and Rhode Island that manage community services through substate offices staffed

---

[1]This analysis was prepared by the Human Services Research Institute (HSRI), under contract to The Medstat Group, Inc., CMS Contract No. 500-96-006, Task Order No. 2. Prepared for the Centers for Medicare & Medicaid Services.

by state employees. In these states, the goal of uniform data collection (with respect to incident management) is more in keeping with the operational style and history of the system. In states that have traditionally managed services through highly decentralized county or local nonprofit entities, such as Wisconsin, Virginia, and Pennsylvania, the task of creating an integrated network of data collection is much more difficult.

Expansion Pressures

Public DD systems also face pressure to expand services and supports to serve people on waiting lists and to accommodate the spirit if not the letter of the *Olmstead v. L.C.* decision. Prouty and Lakin (1999) estimated that approximately 63,000 people nationwide were waiting for services and that systems would have to increase by more than 18% in order to meet their needs. Law suits and assertive advocacy have forcefully made states more aware of this persistent gap in services. The state of Florida, for example, is committed to expanding services to an additional 2,400 people. The state of Massachusetts is obligated to serve a comparable number over the next several years based on the requirements of a recent court settlement. The service expansion illustrated in these two examples places stress on systems—stress that is exacerbated by staff shortages and state budget shortfalls.

Self-Determination and the Blurring of Distinctions

The advent of consumer-directed services has created an even more diverse and idiosyncratic service system. Although the core of services in most states is group homes and other traditional residential arrangements, the number of atypical arrangements is increasing. The levels of support and the extent of professional services in these residences vary widely. People in such settings may live with a paid roommate, may live with their families with support, or may rely on sporadic, rather than 24-hour, support. For state quality enhancement officials, these settings raise the question of who is in and who is out of the formal quality enhancement system. If an individual is receiving only 6 hours of support per week, should his or her residence and the supports he or she receives be licensed? Should they be certified? If an individual falls in his or her own apartment when staff are not present, should this be reported as part of the incident management system? There are no simple answers to these questions.

Case Manager Overload

Case management, the "thin blue line" of DD systems, is stretched to the limit in several states around the country. Theoretically, the role of case managers is to provide support for individual planning and to assist in brokering services; however, these functions have been increasingly combined with heavy doses of paperwork related to state regulation and the management of Home and Community-Based Services Waivers. HSRI reported to the North Carolina state legislature that case managers estimated that they spend at least 50% of their time on paperwork and provider auditing (Bradley et al., 2001). This is not an isolated report. As these pressures have risen, case manager turnover has also become a problem. In one service agency in Texas, the case manager turnover reached 100% in one year (Semple, Bradley, & Ashbaugh, 1998).

Case managers are, in essence, being asked to carry out functions that are more suited to accountants and auditors, yet they are recruited on the basis of their skills as human services workers. This conflict in roles not only compromises their ability to ensure person-centered planning and supports but also undermines their ability to work as frontline monitors.

THE JOB OF PUBLIC AUTHORITIES

The trends and challenges noted in the previous sections led to a revised set of expectations for the conduct of quality enhancement in the DD field. Robert Gettings, Executive Director of the National Association of Directors of Developmental Disabilities Services, advanced nine functions of an emerging quality enhancement framework (see also Chapter 11):

- *Protecting consumers:* The capacity to effectively monitor the physical safety and security of individuals with disabilities who are enrolled in publicly funded programs.

- *Service planning:* The capacity to develop comprehensive, individualized service/support plans and to ensure that all prescribed services and supports are delivered in a timely, effective manner, in accordance with the terms of each individual's service plan.

- *Safeguarding rights:* The capacity to protect the rights of all individuals applying for or enrolled in publicly funded DD programs and services.

- *Overseeing providers:* The capacity to ensure that all providers of community services and supports meet the qualifications and other operating standards and requirements established by the state.

- *On-site monitoring:* The capacity to monitor the overall performance of the service delivery system.

- *Ensuring financial integrity:* The capacity to ensure that public funds are disbursed and managed in an accountable manner, that fraudulent transactions are detected and investigated, and that the responsible parties are punished.

- *Monitoring physical and mental health:* The capacity to monitor the health status of all individuals with DD who receive publicly funded long-term community supports and to ensure that these individuals have access to appropriate, high-quality health and mental health prevention and treatment services.

- *Screening consumer satisfaction and outcomes:* The capacity to obtain structured feedback from individuals and families, as well as comparative data on system-wide performance (both longitudinally and across jurisdictions) in areas deemed critical to achieving overriding systemic goals.

- *Ensuring quality improvement:* The capacity to initiate a continuous cycle of activities designed to address weaknesses in the service delivery process and improve service outcomes.

To accomplish these aims, which reflect the suggested multilayered approach, states need to improve and enhance the precision of current quality enhancement techniques while exploring the application of new performance monitoring practices.

EMERGING PRACTICES

Several practices are emerging that attempt to address these aims and develop a multilayered approach. These practices include establishing performance indicators, developing health and wellness initiatives, and investing in quality management.

Performance Indicators

One area in which new techniques are necessary is monitoring the overall performance of state systems from a macro-level point of view. As systems have become more complex and decentralized, ascertaining whether services and supports are meeting public policy and individual expectations has become much more difficult for state administrators and providers. The use of performance indicators is one robust method of assessing trends and spotting potential problems (see Chapter 13). Performance indicators are much like the gauges on a car that tell you how fast you are going, how much gas you have left, and whether the engine temperature is too high. In the field of DD, performance indicators can tell administrators whether the mission of the system is being achieved, whether people are safe and healthy, and whether the infrastructure of the system (e.g., staff retention, turnover) is sound. The criteria for the selection of performance indicators should reflect the following:

- *Major organizational or systemic goals:* Outcomes must be directly relevant to the central mission of an organization.

- *Issues that can be influenced by the organization or system:* Outcomes should reflect activities that are within the control of an agency to affect so that their measurement contributes to organizational improvement.

- *Fact validity:* The outcomes chosen should be relevant to the major concerns of the constituencies served by the organization or system.

- *Directional qualities:* Indicators should represent change over time.

- *Rates or sentinel events:* An indicator or an outcome is usually expressed as a rate or a proportion (e.g., the number of people employed full time over all people receiving vocational supports).

- *Associated standards:* Many outcome/indicator systems include a standard or a goal for the attainment level of each element. For instance, 75% of people express satisfaction with their living arrangements.

Health and Wellness Initiatives

Health issues, always a concern for people with DD, have become even more prominent. As more and more people are living in communities, the weaknesses in generic health supports have become apparent, as noted in the discussion of trends in waiver reviews. The Office of the U.S. Surgeon General (2002), in the report *Closing the Gap: A National Blueprint to Improve the Health of Persons with Mental Retardation,* documented the shortcomings of medical and health supports for people with disabilities. To address these issues, several states have designed innovative ways of supporting health and wellness. In Pennsylvania, local health care units have been established to provide training and consultation to local health providers and to assess trends in areas such as medication use. Massachusetts has instituted a risk management process that promises early detections of health issues, and California has developed a statewide health and wellness network.

Quality Management

Since the late 1980s, states and providers have embraced the notion that quality enhancement should be a complex system of approaches (Bradley & Bersani, 1990). Yet, the notion of *quality management*—the use of quality data from multiple sources to track performance, improve services, and remediate systemic problems—has only recently gained currency. Several states, such as Connecticut, embarked on a form of quality management as part of their response to a court order (Bradley, Ashbaugh, & Allard, 1989). As part of their Quality Assurance Plan, Connecticut's Department of Mental Retardation officials used data on incidents, investigations, and licensing findings to conduct monthly reviews of regional performance. The city of Philadelphia (as part of the ongoing *Halderman v. Pennhurst* case [Silver et al., 2001]) formed a quality management committee composed of key managers to review incident reports, investigations, case management monitoring, data from the Quality Enhancement Support Team (see Case Study 3), and other sources of quality data. Based on the biweekly reviews, staff used the data to respond to red flags. Other states, such as Massachusetts, are in the process of instituting a quality management process that will link key quality indicators across current quality enhancement functions (see Case Study 1).

IMPORTANT NEXT STEPS

Community services and supports are now the primary way in which people with DD are served. Although public institutions and large residential settings still exist in some states, the number of people living in these settings is declining. The job ahead is to ensure that the promise of the community imperative is realized. For those who have spent years in the struggle to create institutional alternatives and to promote the empowerment of people with disabilities, there must be a candid assessment of what remains to be done to ensure that the foundation that has been built continues to be stable and strong. In order to ensure such stability, the following should be considered:

- *Place the individual at the center of any examination of quality.* The individual's experience and response to services and supports should be the window through which quality is observed.

- *Enlist the assistance of consumers and families.* The creation of quality monitoring approaches—whether at the state or the provider level—should incorporate the participation of people with disabilities and their families both in the design and the conduct of oversight.

- *Use the shared experiences as citizens and community members as the norms for quality.* Methods should be found to move beyond assessments of an individual's experience of the service system to an exploration of values and goals shared by all people.

- *Build on emerging technologies.* The ability to transmit, analyze, and disseminate information through computer networks improves daily. The challenge will be to harness these technologies rather than allow them to create roadblocks.

- *Disseminate information.* Quality information is everybody's business. States and providers should make performance information available through a variety of venues, including web sites and reports, accessible to a range of audiences.

- *Manage quality.* Information about quality does no good if it is not used for system improvement or viewed in conjunction with other sources of information in order to provide a three-dimensional picture.

- *Build rigor into reporting systems.* Every state, regardless of the way it is organized, must develop uniform reporting and investigation protocols. Allowing information on critical incidents and other important events to remain at the local level and subject to local discretion should be a thing of the past.

- *Reassess roles and responsibilities of case managers.* Case management as currently configured is on the verge of collapse. Unless this role is reinvented and administrative functions are stripped off to more appropriate entities, the myth that case managers are the first line of defense in a quality enhancement system will be just that.

- *Expand an understanding of person-centered planning.* Case managers and others who participate in individual planning need ongoing support and training regarding the creation of true person-centered plans. As Michael Smull notes in Chapter 7, the plan is truly the key to ensuring that the individually tailored safeguards are in place.

- *Increase the status and pay of direct support professionals.* The heart of the system of services and supports for people with DD is the contribution made by the direct support professional. Failure to address the national crisis in recruitment and retention will without a doubt compromise the gains that have been so painfully and slowly achieved. We ignore this problem at our peril.

CONCLUSION

The following chapters provide a range of ideas and experiences that display the types of innovations and progress that are being made across the country to meet the very real challenges posed both by our successes (e.g., self-determination, person-centered supports) and by our shortcomings (e.g., inadequately trained staff). The examples were chosen in order to show that integrated and multi-tiered quality enhancement efforts can succeed. They are also offered with a certain urgency, given the promise that public systems and providers have made to people with disabilities and their families regarding the primacy of community membership and supports.

REFERENCES

Accreditation Council on Services for People with Developmental Disabilities (ACDD). (1990). *Standards and interpretation guidelines for services for people with developmental disabilities: National quality enhancement program.* Towson, MD: Author.
Accreditation Council on Services for People with Developmental Disabilities (ACDD). (1993). *Outcome-based performance measures.* Towson, MD: Author.

Agosta, J., Silver, J., Heaviland, M., & Bradley, V.J. (2000, December). *Year two impact assessment report: Focus on self advocate perspectives.* Cambridge, MA: Human Services Research Institute (HSRI).

Altimari, D., & Hamilton, E. (2001, December 3). How did they die? The state won't say: Answers lie buried with the dead. *Hartford Courant.*

Ashbaugh, J.A., Bradley, V.J., Allard, M.A., Reday, M., Stoddard, S., & Collignon, F. (1980). *Assuring the quality of human services: A conceptual analysis.* Cambridge, MA: Human Services Research Institute (HSRI).

Bennish, S., & Beyerlein, T. (2002, February 3). There are deaths that are preventable. *Dayton Daily News.* Retrieved February 6, 2002 from http://www.activedayton.com/ddn/local/0203mrdd.html.

Boggs, E. (1992). Getting into the jet stream. *Mental Retardation, 30*(3), 178–180.

Bradley, V.J. (1978). *Deinstitutionalization of developmentally disabled persons: A conceptual analysis and guide.* Baltimore: University Park Press.

Bradley, V.J. (1994). Evolution of a new service paradigm. In V.J. Bradley, J.W. Ashbaugh, & B.C. Blaney (Eds.), *Creating individual supports for people with developmental disabilities: A mandate for change at many levels* (pp. 11–32). Baltimore: Paul H. Brookes Publishing Co.

Bradley, V.J., Ashbaugh, J.W., & Allard, M.A. (1989). *Quality assurance audit of services to persons with mental retardation in Connecticut.* Cambridge, MA: Human Services Research Institute (HSRI).

Bradley, V.J., & Bersani, H.A. (Eds.). (1990). *Quality assurance for individuals with developmental disabilities: It's everybody's business.* Baltimore: Paul H. Brookes Publishing Co.

Bradley, V.J., Smith, G., Taylor, M., Taub, S., Heaviland, M., Simon, S., Cooper, R., Gerowitz, A., Hitzing, W., & Rader, R. (2001, November). *Today's choice, tomorrow's path: An evaluation of the system for people with developmental disabilities in North Carolina.* Cambridge, MA: Human Services Research Institute (HSRI).

Bruininks, R.H., Woodcock, R.W., Weatherman, R.F., & Hill, B. (1984). *Scales of Independent Behavior.* Allen, TX: DLM/Teaching Resources.

Conroy, J.W., & Bradley, V.J. (1984). *The Pennhurst longitudinal study: A report of five years of research and analysis.* Philadelphia: Temple University Developmental Disabilities Center and the Human Services Research Institute.

Davis v. Watkins, 384 F. Supp. 1196 (N.D. Ohio 1974).

Dickens, C. (1993). *A tale of two cities* (Everyman's Library Series). New York: Knopf.

Fallis, D.S. (2002, January 1). Report questions mental facilities' handling of deaths. *Washington Post.* Retrieved February 13, 2002 from http://www.washingtonpost.com/ac2/wp-dyn?pagename=article&node=&contentId=A51975–2002Jan15

Holburn, S. (1992). Rhetoric and realities in today's ICF/MR: Control out of control. *Mental Retardation, 30*(3), 133–137.

Jasckulski, T. (1996). *Analysis of the application of the active treatment definition* (unpublished report). Available from the Human Services Research Institute (HSRI), Cambridge, MA.

Kennedy, M.J. (1990). What quality assurance means to me: Expectations of consumers. In V.J. Bradley & H.A. Bersani (Eds.), *Quality assurance for individuals with developmental disabilities: It's everybody's business* (pp. 35–45). Baltimore: Paul H. Brookes Publishing Co.

Nerney, T. (2001). *Filthy lucre: Creating better value in long-term supports.* Ann Arbor: Center for Self-Determination.

New York State Association For Retarded Children and Parisi v. Rockefeller, 357 F.Supp. (E.D.N.Y. 1973), order entered as NYSARC.

Office of the U.S. Surgeon General. (2002). *Closing the gap: A national blueprint to improve the health of persons with mental retardation: Report of the Surgeon General's conference on health disparities and mental retardation.* Rockville, MD: U.S. Department of Health and Human Services, Public Health Service.

Olmstead v. L.C. (98–536) 138 *F.3d* 893.

Parisi v. Carey, 393 *F.Supp.* 715 (E.D.N.Y. 1975).

Prouty, R.W., & Lakin, K.C. (Eds.). (1999). *Residential services for persons with developmental disabilities: Status and trends through 1998.* Minneapolis: University of Minnesota, Research and Training Center on Community Living, Institute on Community Integration.

Prouty, R.W., & Lakin, K.C. (Eds.). (2001). *Residential services for persons with developmental disabilities: Status and trends through 2000. A report providing statistics on persons with developmental disabilities in state, non-state and Medicaid-funded residential programs in the United States for the fiscal year ending June 30, 2000.* Minneapolis: University of Minnesota, Research and Training Center on Community Living, Institute on Community Integration.

Richissin, T. (2002, February 13). Progress on health probes promised: State official testifies on investigative plans. *The Baltimore Sun,* p. 5B.

Rowe, J.E., & Taub, S. (2002). *Trend analysis of CMS regional office waiver reviews* (unpublished paper). Available from Human Services Research Institute (HSRI), Cambridge, MA.

Semple, A., Bradley, V.J., & Ashbaugh, J.W. (1998). *Service coordination and a person-directed system: Implementation issues in three local authorities.* Cambridge, MA: Human Services Research Institute (HSRI).

Shea, J. (1992). From standards to compliance, to good services, to quality lives: Is this how it works? *Mental Retardation, 30*(3), 143–147.

Silver, J., Bradley, V.J., Taylor, M., Kimmich, M., Breedlove, L., Butterworth, J., Cohen, R., Hitzing, W., White-Scott, S. (2001). *An evaluation of Philadelphia's quality assurance plan.* Cambridge, MA: Human Services Research Institute (HSRI).

Smith, G. (1999). *Closing the gap: Addressing the needs of people with developmental disabilities waiting for supports.* Alexandria, VA: National Association of State Directors of Developmental Disabilities Services (NASDDDS).

Sparrow, S.S., Balla, D.A., & Cicchetti, D.V. (1984). *Vineland Adaptive Behavior Scales.* Circle Pines, MN: American Guidance Service.

Sundram, C. (1994). A framework for thinking about choice and responsibility. In C. Sundram (Ed.), *Choice and responsibility: Legal and ethical dilemmas in services for persons with mental disabilities* (pp. 3–16). Albany: New York State Commission on Quality of Care.

Taylor, S. (1992). The paradox of regulations: A commentary. *Mental Retardation, 30*(3), 185–186.

Welsh v. Likens, 373 *F.Supp.* 487 (D.Minn. 1974).

Wyatt v. Stickney, 344 *F.Supp.* 373 and 387 (M.D. Ala 1972 aff'd sub.nom).

CHAPTER 2

Trends in Quality Assurance and Outcome Monitoring

MADELEINE H. KIMMICH

In 1995, the Health Care Financing Administration (now known as the Centers for Medicare & Medicaid Services [CMS]) contracted with Human Services Research Institute (HSRI) to assess states' use of outcome-based quality assurance (QA) approaches in their service systems for people with developmental disabilities (DD). QA encompasses both quality control activities, which ensure that service systems meet a minimum "floor" of quality, and quality enhancement (QE) activities, which ensure that service systems continue to improve over time. HSRI's study of state QA approaches examined both types of activities.

After surveying all states' QA activities, HSRI focused on the seven states with the most developed outcome-based systems. It soon became evident that these leaders employed similar arrays of outcome-focused QA mechanisms, yet each state system had evolved in a unique way. This chapter presents the findings from HSRI's study (Bradley et al., 1996), identifies the major tools and processes being used to assess and enhance consumer outcomes, and discusses the relative merits of each principal approach. Several common themes and lessons on how to address particular implementation difficulties emerged from the study.

The two case studies that follow this chapter highlight different aspects of the study findings. Case Study 1 describes the efforts of the Massachusetts Department of Mental Retardation to move toward an outcomes-based QE program, beginning with an individual-focused approach to licensure that does more than ensure minimal quality. Case Study 2 presents The Association For Independent Growth (TAIG), a private service provider in the Philadelphia area that emphasizes the importance of enhancing the work environment to support and nurture staff as the foundation for improving consumer outcomes. Both case studies demonstrate the need for ongoing modifications to quality control and enhancement activities in order to meet the ever-changing demands of the DD service arena.

OUTSTANDING QUALITY
ASSURANCE EFFORTS IN SEVEN STATES

In 1995, seven states—Colorado, Massachusetts, Missouri, New York, Oklahoma, Oregon, and Utah—led the way in reforming their approach to quality to ensure that the provision of services and supports to individuals with DD would lead to enhanced consumer outcomes. Each of these state DD agencies—an independent department in two states and a division or subdivision in the other five (see Table 2.1)—demonstrates a primary commitment to assessing and enhancing outcomes for individuals. As the following discussion indicates, these states offer proof that QA can move beyond traditional regulatory compliance and token consumer satisfaction to judge system performance in terms of the experiences of individuals served.

Primary Outcome-Focused Quality Assurance Mechanisms

All of the study states had one or more QA mechanism that focused on achievement of valued consumer outcomes (see Table 2.2). The most common types of processes included 1) certification-type surveys, in four states (more of the

Table 2.1.   Locus of responsibility for developmental disability (DD) services

State agency	Location within the bureaucracy
Missouri Division of Mental Retardation and Developmental Disabilities	Department of Mental Health
Oklahoma Developmental Disabilities Services Division	Department of Human Services
Utah Division of Services for People with Disabilities	Department of Human Services
Oregon Office of Developmental Disabilities Services	Mental Health and Developmental Disabilities Services Division, within the Department of Human Services
Colorado Developmental Disabilities Services	Office of Health and Rehabilitative Services, within the Department of Human Services
Massachusetts Department of Mental Retardation	Cabinet-level
New York Office of Mental Retardation and Developmental Disabilities	Cabinet-level

Some names and locations have changed, as state bureaucracies have reorganized.

Table 2.2. Outcome-focused quality assurance mechanisms

State	Mechanism	Year began	Primary responsibility	Used in intermediate care facilities for people with mental retardation (ICFs/MR)?	Description
Colorado	Colorado Progress Assessment Review (COPAR)	1986	Developmental Disabilities Services (DDS), private firm	Yes	Longitudinal evaluation of service outcomes based on interviews with consumers and primary support staff
Massachusetts	Quality Enhancement Survey Tool (QUEST)	1993	Department of Mental Retardation (DMR)	No	Enhancement-oriented site survey focused on individual consumers
Missouri	Certification survey	Piloted 1995	Division of Mental Retardation and Developmental Disabilities (DMRDD)	No	Enhancement-oriented site survey by diverse team, focused on agency as a whole
	Missourians Advocating for Individuals with Developmental Disabilities (MOAIDD)	Pre-pilot	MOAIDD	No	Citizen monitoring visits done in alternate years of certification survey
New York	Consumer Outcomes Management Plan and Agency Self-Survey (COMPASS)	Piloted 1993–1994	Division of Quality Assurance (DQA)	Optional	Quality improvement system includes management planning, self-survey, and outcomes review
	Consumer/Advocate Review and Evaluation (CARE)	1993	Developmental Disabilities Council	No	On-site review of residential programs (observation and interviews) by consumers, families, and advocates in programs that volunteer

(continued)

Table 2.2. (continued)

State	Mechanism	Year began	Primary responsibility	Used in intermediate care facilities for people with mental retardation (ICFs/MR)?	Description
Oklahoma	Quality Assurance (QA) Survey	1990	DDS Division (DDSD)	No	On-site assessment of agency compliance with AC standards and DDSD contract standards, done by DDSD staff, including observation, interviews, and records review
	Oklahoma State University (OSU) Consumer Assessment	1990	OSU	Yes	Longitudinal assessment of individual consumers, including interviews with the consumer and the primary support person, and home observation
	Oklahoma Advocates in Monitoring (AIM)	1991	Tulsa Arc	No	Citizen monitoring of community residences done by local Arc parents and consumers, including interviews and observation
Oregon	Residential Outcomes System (ROS); started out as the Valued Outcome Information System (VOIS)	1994 (VOIS: 1985)	Office of Developmental Disabilities Services (ODDS), University of Oregon	No	Individual-based outcome monitoring system, including assessment, service planning, and implementation, completed by direct care staff

State	Program	Year	Agency	Citizen monitoring	Description
	Oregon Advocates in Monitoring (AIM)	1991	Oregon Arc	No	Citizen monitoring of selected community residential settings done by local Arc volunteers (parents, consumers, and other citizens)
Utah	Quality Enhancement Outcomes Survey	1991	Division of Services for People with Disabilities (DSPD)	No	On-site assessment of agency compliance with outcome standards, based entirely on observations and interviews with individual consumers
	Consumer feedback surveys	1995	DSPD	No	Consumer interviews used as a supplement to quality enhancement surveys
	Volunteer monitoring	1980 (Utah State Developmental Center), 1990 (community)	Mental Retardation Association of Utah (MRAU) initially, now DSPD	Yes	Citizen monitoring in all residential settings by parents, including observations, consumer interviews, and parent telephone interviews

states have such surveys, but not all are strongly outcome-oriented); 2) consumer survey approaches, in five states; and 3) citizen monitoring efforts, in five states. One state, New York, had a comprehensive QE system, and other states were moving in that direction (e.g., Massachusetts). The consumer outcomes focus was fairly new in all the states, with only the Colorado Progress Assessment Review (COPAR) and Oregon's Valued Outcomes Information System (VOIS), the latter of which is a predecessor to the more recent Residential Outcomes System (ROS), used before the 1990s.

Beyond these basic commonalities, the states varied considerably in how heavily they relied on outcome-oriented QA tools. Although all of the outcome tools were focused in some way on enhancing outcomes of consumers and assessing the process of reaching the desired outcomes, few of them actually assess the achievement of the outcomes. Massachusetts not only rates achievement of consumer outcomes but also uses these measures to determine whether a provider is licensed.

Another important difference across the study states was the degree of commitment by the state DD office to promoting outcome-focused QA as a preferred approach over more traditional regulatory compliance techniques. Several of the states embraced outcome-oriented QE over any other approach (e.g., Colorado, Oklahoma, Massachusetts, New York), and a few fostered a focus on organizational enhancement parallel to their existing quality control focus, in terms of systems to support consumer outcomes (i.e., Missouri, New York, Oregon).

Certification Surveys   Several of the seven states profiled in the 1996 report based their program survey processes on the standards set by The Accreditation Council for Persons with Developmental Disabilities (now The Council on Quality and Leadership in Supports for People with Disabilities, or The Council) or The Council on the Accreditation of Rehabilitation Facilities (CARF). In 1996, Oklahoma was using The Council's process standards, and intended to make a transition to a hybrid outcomes model drawing on The Council's then newly revised outcome standards; and Utah borrowed heavily from The Council in building its outcomes survey. Other states (Colorado, New York, Massachusetts, and Missouri) have created their own outcome-oriented survey processes, modifying their licensing standards accordingly. The Missouri and Massachusetts processes are very labor intensive—Missouri's certification process can take from 2 days to 2 weeks to complete, Massachusetts can take from 1 week to 10 weeks.

Self-assessment was used as an alternative to state agency monitoring in only two states, Colorado and New York, and only for selected agencies (in New York, all Consumer Outcomes Management Plan and Agency Self-Survey [COMPASS] participants). Several of the other study states had self-assessment processes, but these did not substitute for an on-site visit by the state DD office team.

Consumer Survey Approaches   Several of the study states have developed consumer survey tools to assess consumer outcomes. University-based researchers in Colorado, Oklahoma, Oregon, and Utah have played key roles in the design. The Oklahoma, Colorado, and Oregon tools were used longitudinally and have been generating data for several years, providing an important resource for studying effectiveness. A key distinguishing characteristic among the consumer survey instruments was the locus of responsibility for measurement. An external entity conducts the surveys in Oklahoma and Colorado, and the Oklahoma survey was also analyzed and refined by an outside group (Oklahoma State University); data-gathering was provider-based in Oregon; and only in Utah were the consumer surveys handled by DD office staff.

The consumer survey tools were generally used only in community residential settings, although Colorado's COPAR and Oklahoma's Longitudinal Survey are done with people in all settings. In nearly all the states, the public intermediate care facilities for people with mental retardation (ICFs/MR) were exploring ways to use a modified version of the state's consumer survey tool, so such practices will likely become more common in the future.

External Volunteer Monitoring   Five of the study states (Missouri, Oregon, Oklahoma, New York, and Utah) used some form of external volunteer monitoring. Although key informants in each state saw the activity as valuable, citizen monitoring receives varying levels of financial and official support and occupies a somewhat precarious position in many state QA systems. This is in part because of the difficulty in mounting a system that relies on volunteers, in part due to a lack of stable funding and in part because of an ambivalence in these systems regarding the authority that should be vested in citizen reviews. The experience in these states suggests that, to survive, citizen monitoring requires 1) advocacy sponsorship, 2) paid coordinating staff, 3) a commitment to citizen monitoring, 4) stable funding, and 5) systematic training of volunteers.

Continuous Quality Improvement Mechanisms   Focused attention to overall organizational enhancement, as exemplified in continuous quality improvement (CQI) efforts, varied considerably among the study states, although it was recognized as a crucial process in enhancing consumer outcomes, especially as QA responsibilities are increasingly delegated to regional DD offices and to providers themselves. Missouri and New York made the most dramatic commitment to CQI approaches; indeed, Missouri put organizational change at the heart of the state-sponsored certification process. Oregon also devoted specific resources to fostering organizational change, but such activities were not mandated.

Health and Safety Safeguards   All of the study states have taken the movement toward consumer outcomes seriously and have made modifications in their approaches to ensuring basic health and safety in community residences and in ICFs/MR. Minimal health and safety surveys have begun to focus less on documentation and more on observation and interviews, both with staff/primary support people and with consumers. This shift did not reduce attention to safeguarding health and safety; rather, it made the efforts more clearly targeted on specific risk situations. Several states added "red flag" checklists to their QA mechanisms (e.g., Oklahoma AIM, Utah's QE survey).

As of 1996, the incident reporting process remained a weak link in many states, with little oversight at the state level and varied attention given by local officials. Some states were swamped with insignificant incidents, making them unable to respond promptly and thoroughly to serious incidents or to step back and identify underlying systemic problems (e.g., staff training, supervision, environment). Chapter 5 offers guidance in establishing a workable incident reporting and response capability.

The two case studies that follow this chapter offer a close look at the evolution of QE thinking and behavior in two contrasting environments—a large state DD agency and a moderately sized private service provider. The accounts highlight the necessity of remaining open to continuing critiques and refinements and the importance of listening to stakeholders—especially consumers and staff—as QA reforms are developed and implemented.

Implementation Challenges

The major challenge to the implementation of an outcomes-focused QA system is broadening the attitudes and expectations of providers and surveyors who are still conditioned to regulatory compliance and professional decision making. This is well illustrated in the two case studies that follow this chapter. In laying the foundation for an outcome-based system, developers must come to grips with organizational development issues, especially clarifying the role of staff in the new environment of quality enhancement as well as quality control.

Several expected challenges did not materialize as significant issues in the study. One anticipated concern was that states, in their rush to measure outcomes, would lose control over basic health and safety. None of the states abandoned their focus on health and safety but rather balanced it with a new or expanded look at consumer outcomes. Another expected problem was that states would lose the support of key stakeholders. To the contrary, state DD offices focused on good communication with the field; they included other stakeholders in planning and design efforts; and they lessened their punitive and prescriptive role (especially in Oklahoma and Colorado) in favor of creating partnerships to enhance quality.

EMERGING THEMES FOR THE FUTURE

Findings from the study of outcome-oriented QA systems and the profiles of Massachusetts and TAIG signal clearly that even the most enhancement-oriented state systems are not resting on their laurels but rather are assertively pursuing better ways to ensure that individuals with DD attain their desired outcomes.

As QE continues to evolve, several themes are likely to receive increased attention.

Increased Reliance on Self-Assessment

In many of the study states, reliance on self-assessment approaches is increasing. This practice is born of necessity—shrinking resources at the state level—and a strong commitment to collaborative QE. Given state budget constraints throughout the United States, the use of self-assessment in lieu of some aspects of formal monitoring can stretch QE resources and reward outstanding providers that have demonstrated a commitment to quality; however, it will be critical to establish some threshold health and safety review process to ensure that a basic level of quality is in place first.

Training Surveyors

Most state QA officials emphasized the importance of training surveyors to use new outcome-based instruments and to apply techniques of observation and interviewing. In New York, Colorado, and Massachusetts, surveyors received special training on the survey tool. It is equally important to *untrain* staff who are accustomed to traditional licensure reviews that look at paperwork and very specific characteristics of the facility in order to enhance staff's skills in obtaining information through interviews and observation of consumer–staff interactions. In particular, surveyors may need assistance in developing approaches to interviewing consumers with more significant communication limitations in order to ensure that these individuals are equally represented in consumer outcome findings.

Organizational Development

Many of the QA systems reviewed by HSRI included either implicit or explicit attention to organizational enhancement in provider agencies. Given the significant changes that many organizations must initiate in order to manage services in a more outcome-oriented fashion, the inclusion of an organizational development strategy is an essential ingredient in any state QA reform effort. New York's COMPASS program is an explicit example of an organizational development approach combined with an outcomes focus, and Pennsylvania's State Transformation Project (see Case Study 2) is another such endeavor.

Ensuring a Citizen Voice in Quality Assurance

Citizen monitoring of programs serving people with DD is a facet of many of the QA systems reviewed by HSRI. Citizen monitoring has the benefit of extending scarce monitoring resources and providing multiple perspectives, especially those of families and people with disabilities; however, as noted previously, the citizen monitoring process requires substantial coordination and support, which many states have found difficult to sustain, much less expand. Nonetheless, state DD agencies remain committed to obtaining the perspectives of families, consumers, and ordinary community members, whether by using an independent citizen monitoring process, by including lay people on state survey teams, or by teaming consumers or family members with professionals as they observe residential and employment settings.

Importance of Stakeholder Consensus

Central to the evolution of outcome-oriented QE systems in the seven states reviewed was involvement of key stakeholders—people with disabilities, families, direct care staff and managers of provider agencies, and policy makers. Similarly, TAIG's internal reform in Philadelphia was driven by expressed concerns of direct care staff, those closest to the individual being supported. Stakeholder groups brainstorm about needed changes, review plans, and reflect on information gathered through the outcome monitoring process. This trend will only become more dominant, creating tension in state agencies because of its demands on limited time and resources but providing invaluable support for agreed-on reform efforts.

REFERENCE

Bradley, V.J., Ashbaugh, J., Brown, L., Kimmich, M., Mulkern, V., Raab, B., et al. (1996). *Analysis of outcome-based quality assurance systems.* Cambridge, MA: Human Services Research Institute (HSRI).

The Survey and Certification Process

THE EVOLUTION OF QUALITY ASSURANCE IN MASSACHUSETTS

JUNE E. ROWE AND GAIL GROSSMAN

To understand the evolution of monitoring and oversight systems in Massachusetts, one must view them in the context of changing trends in service delivery. In the 1970s, a group of families and advocates successfully sued the Department of Mental Health for conditions judged to be inhumane in the state schools serving individuals with mental retardation. The resulting consent decrees precipitated major changes in the development of community-based residential programs specifically designed to serve individuals leaving the state schools. On a more limited basis, these programs also benefited individuals who were living at home with their families and young people who were graduating from special education residential schools who generally did not have a family or home to which they could return.

To ensure that providers met minimum standards of health and safety and to avoid repeating the conditions in the state schools, regulations and procedures were developed to license residences and day programs. Licensing set baseline program standards to protect individuals' rights, health, and safety. Minimal in orientation, the standards were fairly prescriptive in requiring such things as staffing patterns, staff credentials, and physical and environmental conditions. Although licensing served an important function, this was somewhat diminished by the focus on process: licensors primarily reviewed the physical conditions and the provider's paperwork but generally did not observe individuals in their day-to-day lives as part of the survey. The emphasis was on the processes the provider had in place, not service quality or the impact of the services on the quality of individuals' lives.

INTRODUCTION OF OUTCOME-BASED, QUALITY-OF-LIFE EVALUATION PROGRAMS

During the early 1990s, the Department of Mental Retardation (DMR) began to introduce new quality enhancement programs to evaluate the quality of services that people received. (Services to individuals with mental retardation were provided through the Department of Mental Health until 1987. At that point, the DMR became a separate state agency.) In 1991, as a requirement of the consent decrees, the DMR implemented a family citizen-monitoring (FCM) program. Through the highly successful FCM program, one or two citizens accompanied by a DMR staff person would visit residences and evaluate the quality of the services. The citizens used a tool measuring quality-of-life outcomes, such as community participation, relationships, health, and safety. DMR also developed an outcome-based program evaluation process that involved a team of people, including DMR staff and citizens to evaluate residential, day, and respite programs. Although DMR managers received FCM and program evaluation reports, these quality enhancement processes had little or no clout. Providers faced no consequences if they did not make changes in response to the issues raised in FCM or program evaluation. Licensing remained the sole monitoring process with authority to effect change, and providers made every effort to come into compliance with its requirements.

USE OF OUTCOME-BASED QUALITY-OF-LIFE EVALUATION AS THE BASIS OF LICENSURE

Although DMR attempted to integrate the information from FCM, licensing, and program evaluation, the efforts met with little success. Among the other challenges, sophisticated computerized data collection systems did not exist to facilitate that integration. Although these processes related information about single homes or work places, they did not provide information about whether the provider as a whole was able to provide good services across all critical domains in an individual's life.

In 1993, DMR decided to combine the functions of FCM, licensing, and program evaluation into a single system and developed a tool that used an outcome-based process to measure quality. The new system was intended to integrate activities that, until that point, were separate licensure and service enhancement functions. Staff from DMR, individuals, families, and providers engaged in a year-long planning and development process. During the year, provider groups and advocacy organizations had the opportunity to offer broad-based input. In January 1994, DMR implemented its survey and certification (i.e., licensing) process. Implementation folded together the FCM, licensing, and program evaluation activities into a single certification process. Prior to start-up, DMR staff who had supported these separate functions received intensive training in using the new process and tool. DMR also developed a computerized data system to report on both individual and provider outcomes and to track service improvement.

THE SURVEY AND CERTIFICATION PROCESS AND TOOL

The survey and certification process uses a tool called the Quality Enhancement Survey Tool (QUEST), which measures quality-of-life outcomes in the following areas:

- Rights and dignity
- Individual control
- Community and social connections
- Personal growth and accomplishments
- Personal well-being (health, safety, and economic security)

In this survey tool, each quality-of-life area has from three to five outcomes, with a total of sixteen individual outcomes. Six of these are flagged to denote safeguards that are critical to an individual's rights, safety, health, and funds. Many of the requirements contained in the flagged outcomes are based on the DMR regulations and serve as a foundation for determining if the outcome is rated as being achieved. In addition to the quality-of-life areas, the survey tool has a section on organizational outcomes that focuses on the provider's systems to safeguard individuals, support and train staff, and foster ongoing organizational learning, growth, and change.

In preparation for conducting a survey, DMR develops a computer-generated sample of individuals served by the provider. The sample size is based on the total number of individuals served and is both representative of and proportional to the discrete types of services it offers. A team comprised of DMR staff from the survey and certification unit conducts the survey, with each surveyor on the team responsible for reviewing the services of approximately five individuals. Citizen volunteers, primarily individuals or family members not associated with the provider being surveyed, are also recruited to participate in the survey.

Surveyors use three primary approaches to review the services of each individual in the sample and to rate each of the quality-of-life outcomes: 1) observation of the individual, 2) discussion with individuals and key people in their lives, and 3) review of documentation such as the individual support plans, medication charts, behavior plans, and restraint reports. Once team members complete the individual surveys, they rate each quality-of-life outcome as "exceeds," "achieved," "partially achieved," or "not achieved" for each individual in the sample. The level of certification (from 2 years with distinction to decertification) is based on the cumulative ratings for the services and supports of the individuals whose services were reviewed during the survey. The level of certification (and license to operate) is issued to the provider as a whole for all of the services and supports to individuals with mental retardation and not to each program location, as was the case with the original licensing system.

The team presents the survey results in two ways. First is the service enhancement meeting where the provider, survey team, and DMR representatives discuss the overall trends and patterns in services derived from the individual surveys and organizational review. Meeting participants are encouraged to share ideas that will further enhance the quality of services that individuals receive. Second, the team prepares a written provider certification report that includes a narrative on each quality-of-life area and the organizational outcomes along with specific commendations, suggestions for service enhancement, and areas needing improvement. In addition, the team prepares a report for each individual who participated in the survey, highlighting the impact of the services on his or her quality of life.

CHANGES IN SURVEY AND CERTIFICATION

Not surprisingly, the survey and certification process has come under intense scrutiny and criticism since it was implemented. Although some providers welcomed the new system, others were more comfortable with the traditional licensing system, which only measured the providers' processes for safeguarding individuals but did not review how these processes affected individuals' lives. Providers and other constituent groups were also uncomfortable with using quality-of-life outcomes as a basis for licensure. Some groups believed that DMR was not placing enough focus on health and safety in the new process. Others felt that differences in the way individual survey staff rated the quality-of-life outcomes led to inconsistent and subjective conclusions. Finally, some groups felt that the survey process was labor-intensive and took too much time to complete.

Since 1994, DMR has improved the survey and certification system on the basis of surveyor experience and in response to critiques. Once again, DMR sought input and involvement from all key stakeholders including individuals, families, providers, and DMR staff. They participated in focus groups around the state to discuss specific aspects of the survey process and tool. Information from these sessions was particularly helpful in targeting areas for change. DMR conducted several inter-rater reliability studies to ascertain the consistency among surveyors in rating the outcomes. A consultant to DMR conducted a factor analysis to determine if some of the outcomes were measuring similar items. As a result, DMR made the following revisions to improve the process:

- New worksheets were developed as a guide for survey staff in order to ensure consistency in their review of critical aspects of health and safety.

- Additional weight was given to scores on the flagged outcomes so that they could affect the providers' level of certification.

- An electronic "help desk" was developed to increase consistency of practice statewide and to provide guidance on the survey process and interpretations on specific outcomes.

- Interpretative guides were included in the survey tool, and later, additional guides were disseminated to provide a more in-depth discussion of particular outcomes and how they were to be rated by the surveyors.

- A number of outcomes were combined to make the process more efficient and effective. Some ineffective outcomes were eliminated, and the total number of outcomes was reduced from 35 in the original tool to 16 in the current version.

- Several modifications made the process more "user friendly" to providers and to DMR managers. For example, 1) streamlining the survey report made it shorter and easier to follow; 2) an executive summary was added that gives a short description of the provider's strengths and areas to consider for service improvement; 3) the provider began to receive a draft of the certification report in advance of the service enhancement meeting, which allowed the provider more time to digest the findings so that the meeting could focus more constructively on how the provider used the survey results to improve services to individuals.

In March 1999, DMR finalized and implemented these changes. Providers responded quite positively to the revisions in the survey and certification process. Most liked the changes in the survey process and the written certification report. However, many providers still find the process too labor-intensive and the results too dependent on surveyor subjectivity. In addition, some operations managers internal to DMR have at times disagreed with the levels of certification given to particular providers. Some believe that the survey process is not sufficiently critical of a provider's shortcomings, and still others find that the process is too punitive, holding the provider accountable for issues outside of its control.

FUTURE DIRECTIONS IN MASSACHUSETTS QUALITY ASSURANCE

Survey and certification is DMR's most public and formal quality assurance process. Because it is used to license the provider, it receives a great deal of attention from various stakeholder groups. Since July 2000, DMR has been involved in a strategic planning process to develop an integrated approach to quality assurance. This more comprehensive and diverse system will integrate information already being collected from a number of venues, including survey and certification, human rights, investigations, risk management, mortality, and critical incidents. Survey and certification will thus continue to provide DMR managers and other stakeholders with vital information, but it will be part of a much larger picture of the quality of services provided to individuals in the DMR system.

Developing an Internal Quality Enhancement System at the Provider Level

A PENNSYLVANIA CASE STUDY

JOSEPH R. BUCCI AND DENISE M. BROWN

Pennsylvania's mental retardation system is entering a period of unprecedented change. These changes hold great promise for people with mental retardation and their families and present providers of services and supports with many challenges and potential opportunities. Historically, the quality of services in Pennsylvania, as in most other states, was driven by state licensing regulations and was tied to standards that focused on process. These standards grew out of national accreditation efforts of the 1970s and 1980s and litigation that has occurred since then. During the 1990s, while regulations continued to direct the system, state and local levels began to focus on outcomes of services. This focus has redefined quality and redirected Pennsylvania's service system. As a result, service providers have had to implement new strategies to attain agency effectiveness.

During 1999, the Pennsylvania Office of Mental Retardation (OMR) launched its State Transformation Project to foster a more consumer-driven, responsive system that will meet the needs of a greater number of people. The project—driven by OMR's Multi-Year Plan, waiting-list litigation, and a recent review by the Centers for Medicare & Medicaid Services (CMS)—is built on several principles:

1. Self-determination must be reflected in all service approaches and provision of supports.

2. The service system must be guided by high-quality management practices and high-quality improvement efforts based on specified indicators and outcomes.

3. The system must use new business processes and information systems.

4. System capacity must expand, and staff recruitment and retention must be addressed in order to serve more individuals.

This project sets the stage statewide for providers to prepare for a more competitive marketplace in which people with mental retardation and their families control their own service dollars and select their own providers. Providers need to be able to demonstrate creativity and flexibility and need to provide high-quality services on the basis of outcomes specified by individuals. Although these expectations may prove challenging, the transformed system will allow successful providers to function in a less standardized and less punitive system, and it will present many opportunities for expansion.

The provider marketplace in Philadelphia has been particularly subject to change. For decades, Philadelphia has been actively involved in significant litigation regarding people with mental retardation and their services. Most notable is the Pennhurst deinstitutionalization case that began during the 1970s. Driven by active litigation in this case, during 1994, Philadelphia created the Pennhurst Management Team to address issues of compliance with the court order. A great deal of attention was focused on meeting the needs of Pennhurst plaintiff class members and on enhancing service quality. Specific areas of focus included person-centered planning, meeting individual health care needs, enhancing case management, developing incident management strategies, and supporting agency training and technical assistance efforts. Although expectations of the county have proven demanding for providers, the result of these expectations has been the development of agency infrastructures aimed at addressing the needs of all individuals supported—Pennhurst plaintiff class members and those who are not part of the litigation. During 1997, the Pennhurst Management Team launched a major initiative with The Council on Quality and Leadership in Supports for People with Disabilities (known as The Council) to begin the move from a strict compliance orientation to a more progressive quality improvement approach. This transition coincided with Philadelphia's early efforts in self-determination. As a result of these initiatives, in 1999, all Philadelphia providers were required to develop formal quality improvement plans.

ONE PROVIDER'S RESPONSE

Founded in 1985, The Association For Independent Growth (TAIG) exists to support people with disabilities to be successful in every endeavor they choose and in every situation they encounter. The goal of TAIG is to be the agency of choice by providing innovative and high-quality services that achieve the outcomes its consumers select through a staff that wants to work at TAIG and shows respect for the organization, each other, and all those served.

Since 1997, TAIG has had a formal quality improvement function. In accordance with the directives of the City of Philadelphia and professional practice, TAIG has focused on achieving outcomes as defined by The Council by creating a formal, person-centered planning process; this process identifies quality-of-life objectives as determined by those being served and their teams. To date, ongoing outcome interviews and feedback from funding sources indicate that TAIG has increased its effectiveness in supporting individuals in attaining desired goals and, subsequently, higher levels of satisfaction with support provision.

At the end of the 1990s, TAIG began to expand its quality improvement focus. An agency-wide situational analysis was conducted to assess TAIG's readiness to respond to the State Transformation Project, its ability to use new business practices and information systems, and its ability to participate in anticipated systems' growth to address a growing waiting list. The analysis clearly indicated that if TAIG wanted to attain its mission consistently, it would need to concentrate on the second part of its vision: an energized, productive, professional work force.

Indeed, TAIG's analysis confirmed national and local studies completed in Pennsylvania. In the midst of planned expansion and systems change in the state, the Pennsylvania OMR identified the issue of staff competence and retention as a serious roadblock to success. In February 1999, the Pennsylvania Legislative Budget and Finance Committee reported a 42% average turnover rate among mental retardation providers. The crisis is especially acute among direct care and frontline supervisors, the very employees who are the cornerstone of any quality enhancement initiative. Nationally, the *Wall Street Journal* ("Work Week," 2001) cited a poll conducted by the Gallup Organization that found that nearly 20% of workers surveyed met its definition of "actively disengaged"; that is, they complained that they do not know what is expected of them, do not have the materials to do their job, do not have a best friend at work, and cannot get the attention of their supervisor. Furthermore, disengaged workers miss more days of work and are less loyal to their companies.

Through more than 100 interviews conducted by an external consultant, TAIG staff expressed similar views. They cited lack of respect, input, and communication as impediments to job satisfaction and teamwork; however, despite unsatisfactory work relationships, staff almost unanimously indicated that they work at TAIG mainly because of the consumers. Although staff turnover remained constant at 15%, the overall agency vacancy rate increased to 18% because of difficulties in finding staff for new consumer services.

The TAIG Way

In response to staffing problems, since 2000 TAIG has expanded its quality enhancement activities to include a re-engineering process, which ensures that the company is not only consumer-oriented but is also a place where people want to work. Called "The TAIG Way," this corporate culture change process aims at building and maintaining a nurturing, rewarding, productive work environment within which all staff work in unison and focus all efforts on TAIG consumers.

"The TAIG Way" aims to redefine the company's culture by clearly delineating standards of professional behavior and breaking down territorialism and departmentalization. First, by setting team objectives and identifying and eliminating victim behavior (e.g.,"I couldn't do it because . . . ."), accountability and teamwork have increased. Second, by assisting employees in understanding basic communication styles and cultural diversity, staff relationships have improved. Last, retention rates have risen by adding training in customer service, problem solving, meeting participation, and management, and by identifying and preparing successful staff for advancement. Among TAIG's most important corporate changes are 1) the addition of corporate coaches, 2) a staff needs assessment, 3) the Book of Accepted Conduct of TAIG Staff (ACTS), 4) identification of individual workers' communication styles, 5) identification of team objectives, 6) a Leaders' Club, 7) the buddy system, 8) a tool to guide the "perfect meeting," 9) consumer focus groups, 10) the brown bag lunch, and 11) reality-based training.

Corporate Coaches   Outside consultants complete assessments, provide individual coaching to employees at all levels of the organization, and are available to just talk. In addition, they assist the president in developing and managing the change process. Over the years, multiple consultants have been used as TAIG has evolved. The consultants' prior corporate experience has been directly related to their success at TAIG.

Staff Needs Assessment   By participating in one-to-one confidential interviews, staff at all organizational levels receive feedback regarding work attitudes, relationships on the job, and specific job responsibilities.

The Book of Accepted Conduct of TAIG Staff   ACTS gives specific guidelines for professional behavior and outlines how to professionally participate in workplace activities with an emphasis on delineating accountable behavior versus victim behavior. ACTS tells how best to take responsibility for actions on the job, understand how to stop blaming others, be honest, understand the scope of control, and create a victim-free work environment.

Communication Styles   Identifying home-based communication styles (e.g., pleaser, controller, promoter, pragmatist) helps improve the way staff communicate with each other and increases open communication and mutual respect. Individuals identify their own style of communication based on specific definitions and characteristics related to each style, as defined by TAIG.

Team Objectives   Multilevel management work groups operate as a team to solve problems and to engage in performance evaluation centered around the achievement of specific objectives. Staff rise and fall together on the basis of objective outcomes.

Leaders' Club   The Leaders' Club, a comprehensive 12-month management training program, grooms specific staff for advancement and upward mobility in the agency, preparing them to move into key management positions.

The Buddy System   Members of senior- and middle-level management team up to give each other instant feedback, to critique each other's job performance, and to exchange "big picture" ideas.

The Perfect Meeting   Managers use a specific tool to critique meetings and to ensure good time management, professional facilitation, an appropriate agenda, and a defined meeting purpose.

Consumer Focus Groups   TAIG managers hold regular meetings with a cross-section of consumers to identify what they like, what they do not like, and what TAIG can do better.

Brown Bag Lunch   All staff can participate in a monthly noon luncheon and talk in an open forum about anything and everything, from external topics, to internal issues and concerns. It is an opportunity to communicate openly with others and to continue the push for mutual respect and better communication.

Reality-Based Training   Reality-based training is a straightforward approach to understanding problems, problem solving, and practicing conflict resolution. This initiative uses role play of specific situations taken directly from the workplace. The role players are selected from all levels of staff through an agency-wide "casting call."

Although "The TAIG Way" is still in its infancy, initial results have been quite positive. Reassessments of staff one year later indicated that the processes put in place have resulted in a more professional, open, friendly work environment. Direct-care staff and frontline supervisory staff now feel that senior management is more supportive and receptive to their needs and those of their consumers. Several respondents stated that the implementation of "The TAIG Way" was the main reason they have remained at TAIG.

As "The TAIG Way" matures, new strategies are constantly being developed to incorporate staff feedback and better meet their needs. For example, TAIG has found that staff training must be interactive and fun and must focus on real work issues. One outcome has been the creation of the "TAIG Role Players," which are modeled after the popular reality-based television shows. Using scripted role play that targets real workplace situations, the audience is challenged by a facilitator to understand and solve the role-playing situation presented. The role players are real TAIG employees who have developed defined characters in their roles, making TAIG's reality-based training both compelling and entertaining. Most interesting, this training approach provides a nonthreatening environment in which staff identify with the role players and situations and fully exchange ideas and perceptions. Furthermore, employees have been able to generalize agreed-on solutions to interactions with consumers in their daily lives.

CONCLUSION

Quality enhancement, as defined by meeting consumer outcomes and producing high consumer satisfaction, cannot occur within the provider system without a stable, knowledgeable, satisfied workforce. In Pennsylvania, the State Transformation Project cannot succeed unless providers successfully recruit, retain, and train staff to have the competencies to flourish within a diverse, multi-faceted, con-sumer-focused marketplace. The success of TAIG, signifying the presence of high-quality services, is inextricably tied to its workforce. Just as consumer satisfaction is an important measure of quality, so must employee satisfaction be a measure of agency vitality. TAIG believes that quality enhancement activities must focus on employee outcomes as well as those of the individuals being served.

REFERENCES

Pennsylvania General Assembly, Legislative Budget and Finance Committee. (1999, Febru-ary). *Salary levels and their impact on quality of care for client contact workers in commu-nity-based MH/MR programs: A report in response to House Resolution 450.* Harrisburg: Author.
Work week. (2001, March 13). *Wall Street Journal*, p. A1.

CHAPTER 3

Accreditation in an Era of Self-Determination

DALE L. DUTTON

The notion of a nationally recognized accreditation body for health and human services first began with the formation of the Joint Commission on Accreditation of Hospitals (JCAH) (which later changed to the Joint Commission on Accreditation of Healthcare Organizations [JCAHO]). Actually, there was some movement to establish national standards for health care and patient safety in the United States before the JCAH was formed from two organizations in 1951. However, the success of JCAH paved the way for the development of accreditation approaches in other areas, including rehabilitation services. In the mid-1960s, with some staff support from JCAH, several major provider organizations joined to form the Commission on Accreditation of Rehabilitation Facilities (CARF, known now as CARF...The Rehabilitation Accreditation Commission) with an initial focus on the quality of sheltered employment facilities for people with mental retardation and other developmental disabilities.

The Council of Accreditation of Services for Families and Children (COA) was formed in 1977 by the Child Welfare League of America to focus on the quality of private agencies serving children and youth and has subsequently expanded to include agencies providing behavioral health and other services. By the early 1980s, another group split off from JCAH and formed the Accreditation Council for Persons with Developmental Disabilities (ACDD), known now as the Council on Quality and Leadership in Supports for People with Disabilities or simply The Council. The purpose of ACDD was primarily to accredit congregate residential settings. (Note: Current organizational names and contact information for these accrediting bodies are listed at the end of this chapter.)

These accrediting bodies, and others that developed during these years, helped raise public awareness of the need for external monitoring to ensure the health and safety of individuals with mental retardation and developmental disabilities and to protect them from exploitation. Typically, the marketing for accreditation was aimed at public funding agencies responsible to taxpayers, and the mantra was quality assurance, uniformity of service delivery, and personal well being. Standards in these early accreditation systems were very prescriptive and tended to set minimum expectations for the provision of services, as they were aimed primarily at minimizing potentially abusive practices in institutional and congregate settings.

THE REVOLUTION IN ACCREDITATION
PRODUCTS, SERVICES, AND STANDARDS (1994–1996)

During the early to mid-1990s, accreditation for mental retardation/developmental disabilities (MR/DD) programs and services began a transformation from quality assurance products and services to a focus on the person receiving the services. Instead of examining the quality of the program, programs adopted a guiding question, "Are you [the person receiving services] better off today than you were?" This was accomplished by moving away from very precise, prescriptive standards to statements of outcomes or results. At the same time, accreditation site surveys began to look at the lives of people receiving services to see if the people receiving services were satisfied as a result of the services delivered.

This move was more than just a re-definition of terms—it changed the very nature of accreditation. It also re-educated an otherwise staid and mature industry about the expanding expectations and introduced them to a future envisioned by people with disabilities, their advocates, and their families. Accrediting bodies found themselves developing new products and services through a field-based environment. They were applying quality improvement technology from the world of manufacturing to human services. Quality needed to be built in, not inspected out, and the "delight" of the customer was a measure of that quality. The consumers of services (and their families) began to be thought of as the primary focus, as customers whose wants and needs should drive supports and result in satisfaction.

The work of moving from a very prescriptive, standardized, sanction or deficit-oriented process to a consultative, quality enhancement model was neither an easy nor quick task and, indeed, continues to evolve today. As a rule, accreditation only directly influences service providers every 2–3 years when the team makes an on-site visit. Given the shift to a quality enhancement mode, the first survey often just establishes a baseline from which the provider is expected to advance during the tenure of the accreditation award and their on-going relationship with the accrediting body.

In a field accustomed to licensing, sanction-based accreditation, public disclosure of deficits, and the potential effects of that information on local fund-raising capability, these early moves met with some resistance. Accrediting bodies devoted a great deal of time, energy, and resources to training and orientation, together with resources and information aimed at helping organizations move to a more consumer-centered perspective. Health and safety aspects of service, while still very important, were joined by satisfaction, quality of life, and service improvement measures and observations.

Service delivery requests and expectations changed rapidly as well. The success of community employment during the late 1980s was continuing. This, coupled with the first waves of young adults leaving educational environments in which they experienced integrated education as a result of the 1975 implementation of the Education for All Handicapped Children Act (PL 94-142) and, later, revisions such as the Individuals with Disabilities Education Act (IDEA) Amendments of 1991 (PL 102-119), brought individuals and families with radically different expectations into public MR/DD systems. Consumers, advocates, and families began to question the quality of congregate settings for employment, day activity, and residential support. Traditional service models and their funding agencies were under question, as were the accrediting bodies that had been issuing them seals of quality.

THE EVOLUTION IN ACCREDITATION PRODUCTS AND SERVICES (1997–1999)

Changes in accreditation benchmarks should remain ahead of the current field practices in order to enhance provider quality and to avoid merely codifying the status quo. That the changes in accreditation have influenced the behavior of the system is evident as provider organizations and funding agencies are changing to respond to enhanced expectations. Some large facility-based service providers have initiated new divisions with community-based services. New programs of service funding have been developed, some as pilot programs, to serve at least a portion of the disability population—often aimed at the new entrants from school programs. Accreditation for service coordination, transition from educational support and settings to adult systems, and assistive technology were unknown until the late 1990s. New accreditation emphases have necessitated new methods to determine quality and an increase in the participation of people with disabilities, their families, and advocates in the definitions of what was good and what was desirable.

During the early to mid-1990s, more than 1,000 MR/DD provider organizations had been accredited. These providers had experience with a prescriptive, process-oriented system that relied heavily on documentation and the medical model of "fixing" people. The attempts at uniformity of service delivery flew in the face of the rising tide of individualization and increasing requests from individuals and their families for more understanding of their needs and expectations.

The challenge was threefold: change the basic definition of accreditation, focus the standards on high-quality service and delivery, and introduce the revised accreditation products and services to service provider organizations, surveyors, funders of service, and—most important—primary and secondary consumers. Some accreditation bodies began earlier than others, but generally between 1993 and 1997, accreditation stopped emphasizing inspection and began focusing on collaboration and quality improvements.

With the right products and services matching increasing calls for accountability and results, requests for accreditation grew in astonishing numbers—doubling the number of accredited organizations and services—between 1995 and 2000. A factor in this growth was certainly the emergence of many newer, smaller support service providers, as well as several very large ones with aggressive growth policies. An increase in community-based residences and job programs produced many more and smaller delivery sites.

WHERE WE ARE NOW

Today's accreditation products and services are used in many ways. In some locations, external accreditation replaces governmental licensure or certification regulation—in total or in part (deemed status). Several states use the information gained by site survey observation as an agenda for training and technical assistance to providers. Some consumers, advocates, families, and referral agents use accreditation in their selection of providers.

The relevance of these changes has been contested in relation to the environment of self-determination with individualized funding, where free-market forces should drive competition and survival of a provider system that has not enjoyed universal appreciation. However, the fact remains that today's provider organizations employ and train hundreds of thousands of qualified, dedicated professional service staff that will continue to be needed, regardless of programmatic or funding shifts. Indeed, this new accreditation definition and framework for service delivery is helping provider organizations prepare for, accommodate, and survive the competition and marketing required by self-determination, workforce development initiatives, Ticket-to-Work, and similar funding mechanisms through a focus on their consumers and the relevance of their services.

Accrediting bodies are focused on refining and marketing the "value added" component of an accreditation framework based on quality enhancement, customer-driven services, and stakeholder satisfaction. Accreditation and the ongoing consultation relationship between the provider and the accreditation entity provide a business management framework for the effective and efficient delivery of high-quality services for people with disabilities. This relationship and the current emphasis on enhancement are similar to what is seen in good commercial and business enterprises. External quality recognition systems used in businesses are providing methodologies for alignment of accreditation standards and services with higher systems of quality. Examples include the International Organization for Standardization (ISO) 9001 conventions for product and service uniformity and the Baldrige Criteria for Excellence. In order to look at the relationship between these business-oriented models and accreditation and the ways in which they address quality assurance and quality enhancement, it is important to consider the purpose and delivery model of each.

ISO 9001:2000

ISO 9001:2000 is the current version of an international convention aimed at ensuring that the consistency of a product or service meets the specific requirements of a consumer. Requirements might include specifications of such things as materials, color, purity, and delivery times or locations. The idea is that every item or service purchased will be consistent or indistinguishable from every other item and will match the purchaser's specifications precisely.

The ISO convention standards rely heavily on the organization's documentation of prescriptive, precise procedure and process, and they required certification site visits to compare what an organization has written down about how it creates a certain thing with what actually happens. The 2000 version contains standards in four major process areas—management responsibility, resource management, product realization, and a section that covers measurement, analysis, and improvement. The standards are very product oriented, though they could also be compared to a professional service, such as accounting, in which an established uniform ethical practice guides individual services. The ISO standards apply more to accreditation standards for individualized planning and services. They describe a product or service quality assurance system.

ISO auditors are paid to work with an organization until full compliance is reached and certification of the organization's adherence to the convention is established. Once an organization is certified, the award is renewed or continued by auditor visits every 6 months. Organizations currently certified in the 1994 versions have 3 years to move to the streamlined 2000 standards using this audit/inspection mode. Accredited human services organizations report that ISO certification often offers enhanced paid work opportunities to their site-based and community-contracted employment services.

Baldrige Criteria for Excellence

The Baldrige Criteria for Excellence have more to do with customer relationships; they focus on the experience a consumer has with a vendor of products or services. The criteria are used to analyze the organization's ability to exceed a consumer's expectations in the business relationship, in addition to its ability to meet product specifications in a consistent manner. The criteria are very nonprescriptive and ask an organization to describe and demonstrate its culture of doing business. The criteria focus on people—employees and consumers—and how they interact to address the needs of both parties.

Baldrige awards are annual competitions, with relatively few actual awards but with many organizations completing entry applications as a means to adopt and internalize the criteria to help them become more productive, competitive, profitable, and stable. Entry applications are written documents that address an organizational profile—leadership, strategic planning, customer focus, information and analysis, staff focus, process management, and organizational performance—a specific description of how that organization's business is conducted.

Written applications are reviewed, for a fee, by individual and team examiners and rated as potential examples of excellence in class. Current classes include manufacturing, service, small business (less than 50 employees), education, and health care. Comparisons of the specific criteria for each of these classes show them to be almost identical with one another, with variations of terminology suited to the consumer audience (e.g., vendor, designer, manufacturer, customer, stockholder, student, family, patient).

If the potential for an excellence award is great enough, a site visit is offered to the organization at additional cost. Organizations not seeking the award may drop out at this point, and each written application receives detailed formal written feedback from a team of trained examiners. Many organizations report this to be a very valuable and cost-effective consultative external observation of their attempts to excel in customer service. As the Baldrige criteria are management, administration, and organizational monitoring for improvement, they relate to accreditation, organizational, and outcome management standards. They describe an overall business quality improvement or quality enhancement system.

Today's accreditation products and services offer both quality assurance and quality enhancement elements to customers, as both are important aspects of doing business (any business) in today's competitive, consumer-focused environment. Variations of the focus on quality assurance versus quality enhancement in the standards among specific accreditation bodies reflect the differing needs of their various consumers and stakeholders.

Accreditation has an additional, primary focus on enhancing people's lives as a result of the accredited organization's activities: human services first, product consistency and consumer relationships next. Accreditation standards look at such things as health and safety considerations at the service site; realization of the desired outcomes of people receiving services; and involvement of their participation in the planning, delivery, and evaluations of the services to be accredited. These are important items not specifically identified by either ISO or Baldrige.

In addition, a positive relationship forms with the accreditor's external surveyor team, and consultation focuses on quality indicators and quality improvement activities. This provides a business framework for human service delivery that remains very viable in a rapidly changing environment. Often, it is the accrediting body's consultation and referral to additional training, technical assistance, or peer linkage that provides the opportunity for improvement.

WHAT HAVE WE LEARNED ALONG THE WAY?

Important differences between the terms *quality assurance* and *quality improvement* have emerged, as well as some basic needs to identify provider qualifications, best practices, and predictors of consumer satisfaction. Also, the importance of external, impartial contributions to the body of knowledge concerning publicly funded human services has been acknowledged.

In late 2000, the U.S. Department of Health and Human Services, Health Care Financing Administration (HCFA; now known as Centers for Medicare & Medicaid Services [CMS]), issued the *HCFA Regional Office Protocol for Conducting Full Reviews of State Medicaid Home and Community-Based Services Waiver Programs.* This set of regulations became the standards that determine the federal funds to be used in long-term service delivery to people with MR/DD in community-based settings across the country. This protocol requires each individual state to define *quality assurance* and to delineate the responsibilities that qualified providers must assume in order to use federal funding, as requested in Home and Community-Based Services (HCBS) Waivers in the United States.

Because HCBS monies account for a very large percentage of the funding for services nationally, state MR/DD officials have tended to reach out to additional entities, such as external accreditation, to provide a partial share of the risk in their individual systems of monitoring. This partnership also imports potential training and organizational development frameworks into the existing state's systems of service delivery.

The Developmental Disabilities Quality Coalition (DDQC), a national association of consumer advocates, provider associations, federal agencies, and accreditation organizations, has released a position paper outlining organizational principles and primary operating components considered necessary for a comprehensive, state-wide quality management program (DDQC, 2001).

Moving past the questions of adequacy of funding for services, the DDQC position paper clearly reinforces the necessities of quality enhancement, the attention to health and safety issues in a community service delivery system, the protection of consumer and family rights, ethical practice and financial integrity, and internal provider oversight. Also addressed are comprehensive individualized service planning and delivery; resultant satisfaction and quality-of-life improvements; and the introduction of a very important element—sufficient public information concerning services, providers, and funding to allow for informed choices among providers and service delivery options.

In addition, new initiatives such as self-determination, individualized funding, cash and counseling, and Ticket-to-Work mandates all shift control of the expenditure of resources to the primary consumer and families. As a consequence, they will need and expect information and knowledge regarding the quality of services that has not typically been present in the past. In order to be wise shoppers, consumers and families will want to know about provider capacity, service availability, past service accomplishment, comparative cost effectiveness, consumer satisfaction, and other information that is vital to informed decision making.

WHERE IS ACCREDITATION HEADED?

Although the present service delivery system seems to be growing more diverse and complex, at the same time, it is simpler in some regards. Consider the following new ways of doing business:

- Some consumers with individualized funding now control what is purchased, from whom, where, and when. In many ways, this is a retail, rather than a wholesale, marketplace. Consumers are now shoppers who demand quality on their terms and have the ability to move their purchasing power to another vendor at will. Some consumers are now hiring their own direct service professional staff.

- Support services are being purchased from for-profit, nonprofit, corporate, and noncorporate entities that range in size from large to individual. Some services may more closely resemble service coordination than traditional support services.

- New services, such as fiscal intermediaries and recruitment of personnel, are being requested. New staff competencies and flexibility are being requested—and satisfied.

Consider the impact of these changes on traditional providers. There are no longer any guarantees! Not so long ago, when an individual was referred into a provider's service delivery after leaving an educational support system, there was an implied guarantee of funding for that individual's service needs (at some level) forever. Increasingly, providers must compete in an open marketplace with no assurance of year-to-year (or in some cases, month-to-month) income streams.

Such direct marketing calls for new skills, historical data on outcomes (i.e., past results of services), and predictive information on changing demographics and trends in order to compete in this new retail world. Furthermore, there is new competition (perhaps for the first time) and new organizational structures and functions to consider:

- Service brokerage: The identification, qualification, training, and placement of direct service professionals

- Fiscal agents: Assisting in the financial matters of life

- Service coordination: True independent advice and assistance with informed choice options for lifestyle, health and safety, and support desires

- Advocacy: At the local, regional, and national level to enhance and protect the rights of people with diverse needs

Marketing ability, fiscal strength, and flexibility become prime determiners in the survival of today's traditional provider organization or service delivery system. What are the quality indicators of such a provider or system? What does accreditation of such a provider or a system indicate to the consumer? Or to the funding source?

Accrediting bodies are continuing to refine the importance and value of their new accreditation products and services. Accreditation in the 1970s and 1980s celebrated services that were specifically defined, often as a program. In the new order, it may be within an organization's capacity to respond to any individual's needs and wants that determines an accreditation outcome. Indeed, recent standards developed for networks, one-stop career centers, and workforce development services examine administration rather than the services themselves. It is clear, however, that the process must provide ongoing, independent, impartial information for all parties in this increasingly complex and, at the same time, very individual and personal human services arena.

The accreditation seal on the wall may continue to indicate to state funding and referral agents that both the accrediting body and the provider are partners in an overall quality enhancement system. It may provide a portion of the definition of a *qualified provider* in that state. It may indicate that services are provided in a consistent quality improvement framework (á la Baldrige and ISO 9001:2000), in which customers and stakeholders determined the quality of the transaction to their specifications and an alignment to the community in which they take place.

To the provider, their potential consumers, and competition, accreditation may well answer several questions.

- How well do you accommodate the needs of your consumers?

- How well do you market your services (outreach)?

- How well do you measure the quality of what you provide, and have you built in the important perspectives of individuals and their families?

- How well do you ensure staff competency?
- How well do you prepare for adequate organizational service capacity?
- How well are you tracking results data and using outcomes information?

In order for accreditation to remain relevant in a world influenced by self-determination and consumer and family-driven services, it will have to provide:

- Competitive marketing advantages
- Outside, experienced peer observation and consultation
- Functional outcomes management systems for quality improvement
- Tools for staff unity and professional development
- Linkages to field resources for organizational development and service improvement
- Updates on changes in the service delivery environment
- Venues to ensure adequacy of public information concerning services

WHAT'S NEXT?

Self-determination and individualized funding are still in relatively embryonic stages in most states. As the movement grows, it will not create new services but a totally new service environment. The potential results in terms of positive outcomes in the lives of consumers, as well as the service system, seem very promising. Yet, there is much to be learned as implementation grows. Although implementation has mainly been limited to pilots and small demonstrations in most states, some directions for future learning seem clear:

- For consumers and families: Continuing to learn to be wise shoppers and how to gain access to the information and support services they need

- For existing service providers: Continuing to learn about new business models, a new or renewed focus on consumers and families as paying customers, and strategic planning toward change to new ways of doing business

- For accrediting bodies and their competitors: Continuing to refine products and services to help providers make the trip from "here" to "there" and survive the journey!

- For funding sources: Continuing to refine the quality assurance and quality enhancement of an oversight management system that will protect consumers as well as public funding from potential abuse or misuse

- For us in the field: Continuing to learn and grow. The fact that you are reading this book suggests that you are a leader with vision, probably a survivor, and certainly a dedicated advocate!

Congratulations and stay tuned! As the title of this book says, this is a "changing world."

REFERENCES

Developmental Disabilities Quality Coalition (DDCQ). (2001). *Building a comprehensive quality management program for public developmental disabilities service systems: Organizing principles and primary operating components.* Available from DDCQ, 1010 Wayne Avenue, Suite 650, Silver Spring, Maryland 20910.

Health Care Financing Administration (HCFA), U.S. Department of Health and Human Services (DHHS). (2000, December 20). *HCFA regional office protocol for conducting full reviews of state Medicaid Home and Community-Based Services Waiver programs* (Version 1.2). Retrieved May 30, 2002, from http://www.hcfa.gov/medicaid/proto1-2.pdf

RESOURCES

For more information, history, and current accreditation opportunities, contact:

CARF...The Rehabilitation Accreditation Commission
4891 East Grant Road
Tucson, AZ 85712
Telephone: 520-325-1044
Fax: 520-318-1129
http://www.carf.org

The Council on Accreditation of Services for Families and Children (COA)
120 Wall Street, 11th Floor
New York, NY 10005-3902
Telephone: 212-797-3000
Fax: 212-797-1428
http://www.coanet.org

The Council on Quality and Leadership in Supports for People with Disabilities (The Council)
100 West Road
Towson, MD, 21204
Telephone: 410-583-0060
Fax 410-583-0063
http://wwwthecouncil.org

Developmental Disabilities Quality Coalition
1010 Wayne Avenue, Suite 650
Silver Spring, Maryland 20910
Telephone: 301-565-5471

The Joint Commission on Accreditation of Healthcare Organizations
    (JCAHO)
One Renaissance Boulevard
Oakbrook Terrace, IL 60181
Telephone: 630-792-5000
Fax: 630-792-5005
http://www.jcaho.com

International Organization for Standardization (ISO)
1 rue de Varembé, Case postale 56
CH-1211 Geneva 20, Switzerland
Telephone: + 41 22 749 01 11
Fax: + 41 22 733 34 30
E-mail: central@iso.ch
http://www.iso.ch

Baldrige National Quality Program
National Institute of Standards and Technology (NIST)
Administration Building, Room A600
100 Bureau Drive, Stop 1020
Gaithersburg, MD 20899-1020
Telephone: 310-975-2036
E-mail: nqp@nist.gov
http://www.quality.nist.gov

CHAPTER 4

Personal Outcomes
and Organizational Change

TINA CAMPANELLA

The success of personal outcome measurement has changed the concept of quality in human services. The emergence of practical approaches to applying person-centered principles in quality measurement and program design has assured that the developmental disabilities field will continue to move away from what was previously thought of as business as usual. More and more, *quality* is being defined by the people receiving supports and services. The field has moved from sole reliance on professionally defined criteria for quality in services to working in partnership with people in order to design supports that will enable the people to achieve the outcomes and goals they define as most important. As a result, stakeholders now expect that organizations will respond to what is important for people seeking support.

Focusing on personal outcomes helps organizations to be person-centered because the outcome measurement process produces an understanding of how each person defines and prioritizes issues in his or her life. Engaging people in active discussion to learn about their preferences and needs brings each person's unique perspective into focus. Through interacting with the person and learning about his or her quality-of-life experiences, staff are able to define an effective process for the organization to respond to the person's need for support. Such a listening process yields benefits not only for the individual but also for the organization as a whole. Just as understanding each person's unique perspective serves as the foundation for planning individual supports, so too understanding the collective priorities of the people supported and the issues that are most important to them enables the organization to appropriately modify and improve its support process.

But data is only one aspect of the learning and change process. Data on personal outcomes cannot produce a scorecard that tells the organization exactly what to do. The information must be used thoughtfully, considering the possible ways the organization may need to change in order to make the best use of its resources in support of people.

Although human services organizations intellectually recognize that organizational change is a necessary part of doing business, fundamental change is nonetheless very difficult to accomplish. Many forces strongly resist change; their reservations range from innate fear and lack of vision, to more concrete concerns about financial viability and the necessity of making the particular change. The limited number of employment organizations who have shifted resources away from sheltered work to community employment is witness to this difficulty.

This chapter explores a variety of issues affecting successful change efforts. No single strategy will be effective in all organizations. Each organization is a unique grouping of people and resources, located in a unique community. The most critical variables in a successful change effort are 1) clarity of mission and values, 2) a learning culture, and 3) decentralized decision-making.

MISSION AND VALUES

The first step for many organizations in approaching change is to explore the agency's mission and values. Most organizations have developed statements of purpose and mission, but how these statements are used in the management of organizational performance varies significantly. Many organizations fail to ask the hard questions about the effectiveness of their mission, such as "Do staff members understand the mission?" and "Can people describe how they contribute to making the mission come alive?"

A mission statement answers the basic question of purpose for the organization: "What are we here to do?" The values are the beliefs and commitments that guide how the work is done. An organization's mission and values keep people within the organization working collaboratively toward the same purpose. An understanding of the organization's mission and values provides staff members with a common framework for assessing performance. In reviewing the success of service and support efforts, staff will ask not only whether things went as planned but also whether they produced an outcome consistent with the mission and reflective of organizational values. For example, if the mission is to help people to find meaningful work in the community, staff must measure the progress of their efforts based on the number of people who have reached or are moving toward this goal. With a clear mission, staff can also make critical support decisions, such as who can benefit from the supports and services offered. Values like "partnership with people" and "respect for individual difference" speak to how an organization wants to conduct its work. Staff can use the values to ask the question "Are my actions a reflection of our shared values?" Without clarity of mission and values, staff tend to rely on successful implementation of processes and procedures to measure success instead of looking at results for people.

Being Mission Driven

Being mission driven requires a collaborative process of clarifying assumptions and expectations. One community organization, recognizing the need to refocus and clarify its mission and values, devoted 2 days to bringing together people who were being supported, direct support workers, managers, and key community leaders to talk about what was most important. Initially, the group worked in pairs and small groups, listening to each other express thoughts about what was most important to them. Using words and pictures, this information was then shared with the larger group. What emerged were common goals and shared commitments to each other. People being supported were provided a forum to participate meaningfully with staff in identifying organizational priorities. This new partnership was used to guide the organization's ongoing transformation and reexamination of how it does business.

Mission and values have been used collectively as an effective quality management tool in many businesses that are industry leaders. Southwest Airlines is widely recognized for delivering great service at low cost in a fun, people-friendly way. These principles not only direct the airline's marketing campaign but also serve as the foundation for all management and internal processes. They guide every aspect of how the organization functions, including how people are hired, how work is completed, and the definition of the desired customer experience.

It Is Not About Us

Grounding organizational change in personal outcomes focus requires staff to acknowledge that the quality of life for people being supported cannot be controlled by the provider of services. People with disabilities experience the same ups and downs in life as everyone else. Although an individual's quality of life may be influenced by support activities, that person's life experience may improve or decline despite the best support efforts of people in the person's life.

Recognizing that accountability to people does not guarantee that everything will be perfect is a prerequisite for being an effective support organization. Accountability requires that support providers commit to gathering and using all available information about the person to guide decisions about service actions. Decisions are made with the person and his or her family being fully informed about options, benefits, and consequences. Support providers must also know the limits of their own resources and practices and be sure to convey these limitations to the people and their families seeking support. An honest dialogue about expectations and goals sets the stage for a cooperative support relationship.

In implementation, staff may need help to identify which of their old service assumptions will not work anymore. Some old beliefs are in direct conflict with supporting the outcomes that people want to attain. For example, staff who emphasize safety and health over everything else may not be open to hearing other priorities from people. Support workers need a framework to begin the process of re-evaluating the impact of their actions on the life experiences of the people they support. Following are examples of specific principles some organizations have used to redefine expectations for service and support inter-actions and to guide staff in working with people toward outcomes.

The Person Sets the Agenda   Traditionally, professionals have iden-tified individual's service needs. People being supported were invited to meet-ings to hear what had been identified as important for them. At best, the person's role was limited to one voice among the many. Focusing on outcomes for people requires just the opposite. The person sets the priorities and the pro-fessionals listen. Professional expertise is a tool to enable people to clarify and explore their personal goals, not to set those goals.

It Is More Important to Be Respectful and Responsive than to Always Do Things the "Right" Way   In the past, staff followed specific processes and procedures in the belief that these would lead to positive out-comes for the person. Unfortunately, this focus on the perceived correct process often left little room or time for individualization. Best practice now asserts that the most important characteristic of good service is to listen to the person and to respect the person's perspective and experience. Staff then use their understanding of the person to guide their recommendations for supports. If conflicts arise between standard practice and what the individual wants, staff are urged to seek assistance in resolving the situation.

Listening Is an Important Skill and Activity   The ability of staff to communicate with and learn from each person they support is central to the quality of the supports they provide. Support staff must be willing to hear sug-gestions from people who are being supported and actively seek information from each person about his or her individual needs and services. The interper-sonal skills needed for establishing relationships with people are as important as professional skills. All training and support for staff must emphasize this new priority. The time that staff spend with the person, engaged in active ex-change, is as valuable as other kinds of activities.

As an organization makes the transition to an outcomes-focused mission and person-centered values, staff may feel overwhelmed by the breadth of changes confronting them. They may also feel that the shift in practice casts a negative light on the work they did in the past. It is essential to support staff in the change process, with supervisors providing specific direction and working with staff around real issues that they have experienced with people being sup-ported. One community organization adopted such an approach to launch their change effort. They targeted training efforts at the supervisory staff, redefining their role as mentors, coaches, and facilitators of change. Supervisors were taught to identify ways that they could be a resource to support staff in implementing a person-centered focus and in problem solving when barriers were encountered. For a full year, all staff meetings included an agenda item that focused on difficulties with implementing the new principles. Staff were encouraged to bring issues to the meetings and to seek out supervisors whenever they needed support. This process facilitated open dialogue about the challenges involved in changing support practices and relieved direct support staff of sole responsibility for decision making. Staff reported that the partnership enabled them to feel more confident about their role in supporting people on a daily basis.

EMBRACING CONTINUOUS LEARNING AND CHANGE

Creating an organizational culture that values and practices learning as a way of doing business takes intentional nurturing. Every organization is a product of how its members think and interact. If an organization desires to change its old patterns of operating, it must learn—at an individual, group, and organizational level—to think and interact differently. The learning organization establishes routines, interactions, and activities that promote and encourage both individual and group learning.

The use of outcomes places both individual staff and organizations in learning situations. For staff, it means learning about oneself and one's own values, assumption, and beliefs. Then, staff can learn from people with disabilities what results they want from receiving supports and services. This individual learning about people with disabilities is distinctly different from assessment and evaluation, although assessment may be used as a learning tool. It requires staff to spend time sharing experiences with people, so they develop an understanding of each person's priorities and preferences.

The organizational dimension of learning builds on what is learned by individuals. Using data from interviews concerning outcomes, organizations can examine the ways people think and act collectively. Having greater clarity about the outcomes that people expect from their supports and services enables the organization to better support people. Organizational cultures that value learning share three primary characteristics: they systematically gather data, they openly discuss organizational performance, and they make learning fun.

Conscientious Information Collection

Organizations typically collect a variety of performance data, addressing 1) compliance with external requirements from local, state, and federal authorities or 2) internal needs relating to financial performance, staff turnover, medical needs, use of behavioral interventions, abuse and neglect, and so forth. Conscientious information collection means that an organization looks at all of the performance information it collects and makes conscious decisions about what is needed. Data collected without a purpose uses time and resources that could be devoted elsewhere and does not contribute to organizational learning.

Organizations focused on learning prioritize the data that they need to understand the effectiveness of their supports. Information from the people being supported is of primary importance. Data are collected through interviews with people and their stories of challenge and success. Data collection can be numerical, indicating the number of people who have achieved certain outcomes in their lives. This type of data is useful for identifying trends across the organization; for example, a recurring issue might be that lack of support for individual choice or limited access to a variety of options for meaningful work is a barrier to desired employment outcomes. Such an issue would then become a target for a specific change initiative.

Data may also be anecdotal and story-based. To guide thinking about changes needed, teams of people leading organizational change have found it very useful to focus on the issues facing one or two individuals. For example, in one organization, interviewers collecting data on outcomes for people also wrote up a summary of the main challenges each person confronted. One story seemed to symbolize the type of changes needed for the organization: The person being interviewed had summed up her feelings at the end of the process by saying, "My life would be better if I could just go out to the movies when I want to, with whomever I want to." Team members discussed why this could not happen and discovered, in the process, a number of organizational practices that presented barriers. They found that the patterns of staff support available to this woman did not allow for spontaneous leisure decisions—activities had to be planned ahead, or they did not happen. They also discovered that procedures established for accountability and safeguarding funds resulted in the woman having access to only a small amount of cash at any one time. Other challenges were uncovered, including transportation barriers and lack of supports for personal autonomy. By addressing the issues for this one woman, the team was able to work through a variety of issues that cut across many organizational systems in a practical, concrete way. Changes made in support of this one person could then be generalized to making the system work for others.

Open Dialogue

Many organizations find it challenging to create management processes that include staff throughout the organization as well as people receiving supports. Decision making often comes only from the top. Promoting honest dialogue about performance issues requires real inclusion.

One strategy that organizations have used effectively to open communication and broaden active participation is to delegate responsibility for managing learning and performance to a group that represents the diversity of the organization, with limited or no involvement from management staff. Representatives from different operating sections and different levels of the organization are included. The group reports to the top executive but is charged to work independently, to examine critically how effectively the organization is working to achieve the mission. This strategy creates a safe way for people throughout the organization to communicate about needs for support and change. It is easier to communicate concerns to colleagues than to the boss. As staff members see their ideas and concerns taken seriously, they build the confidence needed for open participation and begin to see themselves as valuable contributors in the change effort.

Having Fun with Change

Change is not typically seen as comfortable and fun. People are understandably afraid of the unknown and wary of the risks associated with changing patterns of doing business. Much of the resistance comes from a lack of understanding about why change is needed. Developing organization-wide strategies that combine learning and change with fun and celebration is a great way to minimize apprehension and to include everyone in the process.

Replacing traditional learning activities in the classroom with activities that are both fun and experience-based is both a practical and productive strategy to support change. A training coordinator at a large community organization created an "Outcome Scavenger Hunt" that encouraged staff to find examples of people who were experiencing positive outcomes. Instead of implementing this in the classroom, she met with groups of staff at their places of work. At each meeting, staff discussed a group of outcomes, and then participants were given guidelines for learning about whether positive outcomes were present for the people they supported. In follow-up meetings, staff presented what they found, discussed issues, and then collectively decided which story represented the best example of what positive outcomes could mean for the people they supported. The process produced enthusiasm and energy around supporting people, made learning specific and concrete, and created the foundation of a peer support network for excellence in supports.

Celebration of accomplishment is another often-neglected strategy in creating and sustaining momentum for change. Taking time to acknowledge and celebrate achievements is frequently overshadowed by the urgency to move on to the next challenge. Organizations that invest the time to spotlight and celebrate their accomplishments gain in two important ways. First, they provide recognition and reinforcement to staff members that their efforts are valued and appreciated. Second, the celebration builds commitment to sustain the changes over time. Celebration of accomplishments elevates the efforts from just another job well done, to a source of pride and reflection of organizational culture.

Celebration can take many forms. Large meetings of staff, parties, and awards dinners are typical venues for celebrating. Organizations have found many other ways to spotlight and cheer their accomplishments: 1) having contests that encourage staff to nominate a colleague for recognition; 2) documenting individual successes through pictures, words, or other creative means; 3) designating one staff member to find examples of employee excellence and accomplishment; and 4) taking the celebration to the employee. These kinds of surprise celebrations not only put the spotlight on achievements but can also be used to directly reinforce the kind of individual actions that the organization values most. Whatever strategy is selected, the act of celebrating is a valuable tool to keep people focused on what is most important.

WHOLE SYSTEMS CHANGE

Achieving the goal of person-centeredness in an organization requires fundamental change that will touch all operating systems. Organizations that succeed in making significant improvements in the outcomes for people they support find they must transform many of their traditional activities to be in line with customer expectations and needs. Although senior management must take an active role to guide and direct the organization in efforts to be person-focused, the process of change must involve everyone throughout the organization. Quality in support is measured by the organization's response to each person being supported. This responsiveness reflects the integration of technical knowledge about support processes with the values of the support role. Ultimate success in being person-centered comes from building organizational capacity for learning, problem solving, and change, which enables the organization to respect the unique needs of each person seeking support.

Role of Direct Support Staff

Human resources are one of the most critical variables to achieving high quality in the service organization. Direct support staff must have the knowledge, skill, and authority to respond to customer needs as they change during the support process. Policy and procedures can never provide the detail needed to ensure that the support process is individually responsive to each person. Staff need ongoing training and feedback from managers. So critical is the "people" element in service quality, many experienced managers believe that no organization can succeed in person-centered supports without designing strong systems to take care of the people providing support (Dykstra, 1995).

Current approaches to staffing and training in human service programs emerged during an era of great emphasis on safety and consistency of services. The role of the direct support worker was to implement programs developed by professionals. Direct support workers were expected to follow specific guidelines under the direct supervision of professional staff and managers. In today's environment, direct support workers need broad and diverse skills. They often work independent of direct supervision and must have the basic skills to make decisions about the supports people need.

With the onset of the workforce development crisis in the late 1990s, organizations began rethinking all aspects of their human resource strategy. Efforts to quantify the costs associated with high levels of staff turnover produced strong motivation for change. Some of the key questions managers are asking about their human resource systems include

- Does the recruitment and hiring strategy bring forward qualified and interested applicants? Does the organization only hire people who are qualified?

- Do the job descriptions provide direction and guidance to staff on key performance and role expectations?

- Does the organization pay people equitably? Are people recognized and rewarded for performance? What benefits do people value most?

- Does the organization have systems that support people to learn and grow in critical performance areas? What performance areas are most critical? Does the organization have processes that promote ongoing learning and performance improvement?

- Is the organization explicit about its values? Is the organizational culture and structure consistent with these values?

As organizations address these questions, practices are slowly beginning to change. Approaches to hiring more frequently include people with disabilities as part of the screening and decision-making process, in recognition that there needs to be a good fit between people and the workers who support them. Staff hiring and staff orientation processes include an emphasis on values and mission in order to ensure that people who get hired are open to embracing the organization's vision for the future. More of the training process is occurring on the job, with supervisors and lead staff serving as facilitators, in recognition that skill transfer from the classroom requires support. Finally, revised job descriptions are explicit about the expectation that employees will support outcomes for people.

Building Functional Leadership

Building the capacity for leadership throughout the organization is another element that characterizes person-centered organizations. Since the 1980s, the role of manager and leader has changed dramatically. Emphasis has shifted from control, thinking, and acting to vision, communication, and nurturing capabilities. Senge proposed that the manager in this new framework might be better described as a "researcher or designer" (1990, p. 299). The manager's primary responsibility is to promote understanding of how the system works and to support employees in learning new ways to use resources to produce desired results. Attention shifts to helping people think critically about issues, rather than controlling staff behavior. This allows leadership to emerge throughout the organization.

This new leadership mandate begins with the principle that employees should be supported in the same manner that they are expected to support people with disabilities. Using the same values of individual respect and involvement, the manager who is concerned with achieving outcomes for people works to understand the range of unique circumstances that workers experience in their personal lives to which the organization needs to respond. Just as staff learn by listening to the people they support, leaders also ask questions, listen, and observe without assumptions about what they will find or what should be. Through dialogue and interaction, managers discover opportunities for improvement and change in organizational supports for staff.

Leaders model the values of the organization in order to make them come alive for the staff. Commitment to learning and change as an organization is demonstrated by top management. Managers more concerned with maintaining control cannot promote the flexibility needed to be responsive to people. Only by showing the willingness to listen and learn through daily interactions can managers promote this kind of service for people with disabilities.

Leaders of excellence do not feel compelled to know everything. Their role is to set the mission that directs the implementation of person-focused supports. This helps staff to define the organization's role in the lives of people and to emerge as leaders on their own. Managers cannot take responsibility for making decisions about the details of service interactions; however, they are responsible for the big picture. The manager's job is to provide the resources and supports for staff to assess and support individual outcomes. It is also the manager's role to ask questions and prevent the organization from returning to comfort and complacency with accomplishments.

CONCLUSION

Successful organizational change requires deep commitment to learning about the best ways to provide support for people being supported by the organization. No single path will work for all organizations. Fundamental change in the work of the organization occurs through the coordinated and sustained efforts of all stakeholders. The challenge faced by each organization is to use principles, examples, and colleagues to guide their learning about what does and does not work in different situations. Developing an organizational culture of learning and change cannot be forced but will emerge from long-term efforts to establish inclusive processes. Ongoing organizational improvement is fueled by continued examination of how effective the organizational processes are at supporting people to achieve what is most important in their lives.

REFERENCES

Barker, J.A. (1992). *Paradigms: The business of discovering the future.* New York: Harper Business.

Block, P. (1993). *Stewardship: Choosing service over self-interest.* San Francisco: Berrett-Koehler Publishers.

Dykstra, A. (1995). *Outcome management: Achieving outcomes for people with disabilities.* Homewood, IL: High Tide Press.

O'Reilly, C.A., & Pfeffer, J. (2000). *Hidden value: How great companies achieve extraordinary results with ordinary people.* Boston: Harvard Business School Press.

Senge, P. (1990). *The fifth discipline: The art and practice of the learning organization.* New York: Bantam Doubleday.

Schon, D.A. (1983). *The reflective practitioner.* New York: Basic Books.

Philadelphia County's Attention to Personal Outcomes

TIMOTHY GREUSEL

In 1985, the parties in the landmark *Halderman v. Pennhurst* litigation entered into a final settlement agreement. This agreement has played an important role in establishing the rights of people with disabilities to live, learn, work, and spend their free time in the community. Less well known, perhaps, is the fact that the final settlement agreement also provides a framework of quality enhancement activities to ensure that plaintiff class members' supports and services are consistent with the various provisions of the settlement and best practice, contemporary standards of service provision.[1] One of the activities that the final settlement agrees on is an annual evaluation of the quality of class members' home and day supports and services.

In 1993, motions for contempt were filed against the Commonwealth of Pennsylvania and Philadelphia County, alleging that various provisions of the final settlement were not implemented according to the agreement. After holding hearings, the court ruled that the Commonwealth and the County were in contempt. Various orders were issued to re-establish compliance. One of the areas of noncompliance addressed by the court was related to annual monitoring of class members' services.

In an effort to secure current and future compliance with the final settlement, Philadelphia County decided to proceed in a new direction with the task of annual monitoring. Philadelphia County has historically contracted this task to an outside organization. The Quality Enhancement Support Team (QEST) was created in May, 1994, by Philadelphia Mental Retardation Services (MRS) to conduct the

---

[1]The process described in this case study generates a substantial amount of detailed information that is used to improve the quality of people's lives; however, this process is somewhat more time consuming, labor intensive, and consequently, more costly than traditional systems that monitor quality. Although many facets of the process are applied to evaluating quality of supports throughout the Philadelphia service delivery system, the full process described in this case study applies only to those people who are members of the Pennhurst plaintiff class. For clarity, they are referred to here as "class members."

annual evaluations of class members' supports required by the final settlement decree.

The parties to the final settlement recognized that it was necessary to shift the focus from evaluating compliance and noncompliance to examining the outcomes for class members. Although answers to questions directly related to final settlement compliance remained important, new questions related to actual support outcomes for class members began to take center stage.

In 1995, MRS embarked on the development of a comprehensive quality assurance plan. This effort sought to create a blueprint to continuously improve the quality of class members' supports and services. One of the major steps in this plan was to develop a set of standards that could be used in the design, implementation, and outcome measurements of both existing and new supports and services. These standards became known as the Everyday Lives Standards (see Table 4.1).

To move away from a compliance-based monitoring process to one that evaluates individual class member success and areas where improvement could be made, QEST and MRS collaborated on the development of an annual evaluation process that is proactive, useful, and user friendly. This entirely new effort was designed to shift 1) the orientation from detection to prevention, 2) the process from adversarial to collegial, and 3) actions from problem resolution to the discovery of success and problem anticipation.

The new quality enhancement effort centers on the belief that each and every class member is unique. Each person who needs and wants support brings a set of very personal expectations, hopes, dreams, and requirements that, in turn, become a separate and unique test of the system's ability to respond.

Table 4.1.   Everyday Lives Standards

All class members have a plan, and it is being followed.
People have opportunities to make choices.
People have support for the choices that they make.
People have opportunities to interact and be included.
People have the chance to be heard.
People live in homes that are safe.
People have protections from harm.
People have good health care.
People have opportunities for privacy.
People have support to obtain and manage personal possessions and resources.
People who want jobs have them.
People have opportunities and support to pursue things they like to do.
People have access to coordinated supports.
People have access to a system that promotes quality and is continuously improving.

KEY PROCESSES

QEST began its initial efforts by developing a pool of subcontracted evaluators who are professionals in the field of disabilities. Each subcontractor has many years of experience providing direct supports and services in the Philadelphia County system, and each fully supports the new quality enhancement effort. The QEST annual evaluation process has three distinct components: record review, person and staff interviews, and direct observation of supports.

Record Review

The first stage of the evaluation process is an extensive review of each class member's record. The reviewer conducts a documentary analysis, examining the substance and basis for each class member's plan of support (see Table 4.2). In Philadelphia, this is called the individual support plan (ISP). In conjunction with the new continuous quality improvement system, MRS also undertook a 2-year effort to restructure the support planning process. This effort resulted in one of the most significant large system conversions to a person-centered planning approach in the United States.

Person and Staff Interviews

The second stage of the review process consists of an interview with the particular class member and the team that provides supports and services (see Table 4.3). During this team meeting, the reviewer engages the group in a wide-ranging discussion regarding the design and outcomes of the supports in place. The reviewer seeks information and evidence of each person's success since the last review and any challenges that have developed in providing or receiving needed and desired supports. The reviewer facilitates this discussion so that each member of the team has the opportunity to share his or her unique perspective about the class member's supports and the resulting outcomes. The reviewer is able to corroborate the information shared by team members, based on the prior record review.

Table 4.2. Elements of the documentary analysis done by Philadelphia's Quality Enhancement Support Team (QEST)

Assessments
Class member and team-identified support needs and preferences
Personally desired goals and objectives of supports in the individual support plan (ISP)
The context in which these were established and are currently implemented
Evidence of personal success or obstacles related to the services in place

Table 4.3.   Individuals interviewed by Philadelphia's Quality Enhancement Support Team (QEST)

The class member, if he or she chooses to attend or participate
Family members and friends
Residential support provider staff
Day support provider staff
Therapy support provider staff
The supports coordinator
The advocate (if applicable)
The QEST reviewer

In some respects, the reviewer duplicates part of the ISP process but uses an outcomes focus rather than a planning focus. For example, the reviewer discusses supports in various life areas that are important, desired, or needed by the class member. This information is then compared to the plan of supports actually in place. The degree of consistency with the ISP and the design of the support configuration can be determined, as well as the results of the person's and the team's efforts. This phase of the annual evaluation process seeks to determine whether planning has properly captured what matters most to the class member, whether the support access is consistent with what the person wants and needs, and the extent to which efforts have been successful or enhancement considerations could be made.

Observation

The third stage of the review process is direct observation of class member supports and services. This provides an avenue to affirm the work that the class member and the team are doing and to directly corroborate the interpretation of outcomes presented in the record and the team interview process. Using a standardized protocol, the evaluator enters the information acquired from the record analysis, team discussion, and direct observation. The protocol creates a record that is used for analysis and internal QEST quality control.

IMMEDIATE FEEDBACK

At the conclusion of the information-gathering process, the evaluator prepares a written leave-behind report that provides information about three aspects of the class member's support configuration: compliance concerns, service domain scores, and team commitments to action.

Compliance Concerns

The leave-behind report identifies issues related to legal guarantees provided to class members. It indicates whether any aspect of the class member's supports

constitute risk to the mandatory, nonnegotiable requirements of the final settlement decree. Because the annual review process is still part of long-standing litigation, this information provides the team and Philadelphia County with immediate information regarding the congruency between a class member's service
configuration and the basic guarantees of the decree.

Service Domains

The heart of the leave-behind report is a list of 23 major support and service domains available to each class member, indicating whether each is a part of the
class member's configuration (see Table 4.4). Each applicable domain receives a
designation of acceptable, unacceptable, or not applicable. However, unlike many
quality enhancement efforts, the reviewer does not decide this alone—the determination is based on a facilitated consensus process. The reviewer and the team
discuss what designation should be given, based on the knowledge of the team
and the reviewer. Typically, the team and the reviewer agree on each designation
because everyone in attendance has heard the same discussion and has had access to the same evidence. Discussion continues until consensus is achieved. In
the rare event of a deadlock, the reviewer makes the designation and notes the
disagreement.

Team Commitments

The third part of the initial leave-behind report is a recording of team commitments. In traditional monitoring, the evaluator typically identifies the successes
or problems at hand and then proposes solutions or directs the agency that is
being monitored to fix what is wrong. In the QEST process, because enhancing
quality is the goal, the team is vested with the responsibility to identify and resolve problems. Implementation of enhancement or corrective action is much
more likely to be effective when the solution is devised by those who carry it out.
In response to an identified issue, the team may propose specific action; this commitment is recorded by the team on the leave-behind report.

Table 4.4.   Examples of service domains used
in the leave-behind report

Medical supports
Transportation
Day activities and supports
Vocational supports
Therapy
Recreational/leisure time
Supports coordination
Advocacy
Staff supports

To ensure that team promises are fulfilled, several processes occur: 1) the QEST review is scheduled in advance of the class member's annual ISP meeting; 2) the supports coordinator follows up through ongoing, regularly scheduled monitoring; and 3) the supports coordinator's supervisor oversees a response process. By doing this, any promises made to enhance or adjust support quality can be included in the yearly planning process, with regular, follow-up evaluation and management oversight.

SUMMARY DOCUMENTATION

QEST develops several products that summarize the individual reviews, for use by those responsible for class members' supports and services: a narrative report, a qualitative-to-quantitative data conversion, and a cumulative database.

Narrative Report

The evaluator prepares a full narrative report of each person's support and service outcomes and chronicles how life has evolved for each person. Each subsequent year's report continues the story, presenting the current support configuration for each person and analyzing what these services mean to the person and how they work. This approach provides the reader with a frame of reference to understand successful outcomes that are occurring in a person's life and a context for the ways in which quality can be enhanced. In addition, the main narrative summary report iterates any promises made to the class member at the time of the team discussion. Following the descriptive text, the reviewer also answers a series of standardized questions that provide further analysis of the class member's supports.

Data Conversion

In the course of a year, QEST reviewers write approximately 6,000 pages of narrative describing the outcomes of 500 class members' supports. To make this large body of information useful at the management and administrative levels, QEST designed a process through which all of the qualitative information is converted into countable data. The resulting database can then be analyzed for trends and patterns over time, or it can be used to provide specific snapshots of the overall system as it works to deliver quality supports. The narrative written by the reviewer that describes support outcomes, celebrates achievement, or discusses barriers to success is similarly translated into a set of common themes that are known to contribute to class member achievement or that are obstacles to support success.

Cumulative Database

Narrative information has been converted into quantitative data for all class members since 1994. QEST's cumulative database currently contains not only this information but also sections of the leave-behind reports, in particular, compliance-related information and service domain scores. Internally, QEST maintains a comprehensive quality control process that ensures the integrity of the information presented in the narrative report and the translation of this information into the data system. The raw information entered into the working protocol serves as the evidentiary foundation for both the narrative summary and all subsequent database information, and the data is subject to rigorous internal scrutiny.

Summarized information generated from this database is used in numerous ways by the county:

- The executive staff level established the Management Information Group to evaluate macro-level trends and patterns. For example, system weakness emerged in the area of supports for people to obtain and maintain employment. MRS addressed this by developing a master employment plan for class members and the responsible agencies, which has resulted in a tripling of the number of people who have found and sustained competitive employment.

- The county's Risk Management Unit analyzes information for issues related to health and safety concerns. The county is then able to support targeted agencies with specific collaborative plans designed to better address class members' needs in this area.

- Supports coordination reviews QEST-generated information for ways to enhance service quality and to resolve particular issues. Resulting activities are tracked.

- Provider agencies receive various data runs that provide necessary information for their annually required quality enhancement plans. These plans and their successful implementation are in turn included in the contract performance criteria between the agency and the county.

- Perhaps the most important use of this information occurs at the team level, where team members can take steps, on a day-to-day basis, to improve and enhance each individual's supports and services.

The database also serves as an ongoing information resource to answer particular systemic questions as they arise. For example, a key factor affecting class members' living conditions is the neighborhood in which they live. A county official may want to know whether any trend indicates that a provider is experiencing issues in a certain neighborhood. An administrator of a large agency serving many people may want to know how to enhance the quality of people's lives in terms of the neighborhoods where they live. Relevant information can be rapidly obtained from the data system. If someone requesting this information also wants to know the detail of one or a group of class members' experiences or outcomes, they can then return to the individual narratives and read the full text.

CONCLUSION

The information acquisition, analysis, and reporting that constitutes the QEST/MRS review process ultimately provides a snapshot of what it is like for Pennhurst class members to receive supports and services, and it illuminates both successful outcomes and areas in which challenges might exist. Although designed to serve the needs of plaintiff class members in a class action settlement, this quality enhancement system can be duplicated in any system, large or small, in which stakeholders are committed to continuous improvement of service.

The QEST process is based on the premise that services exist to meet individually desired and needed life outcomes with the intent of supporting and promoting independence, health, safety, social inclusion, and a valued personal lifestyle. Continuously striving to include these standards in people's supports and having access to information about the outcomes of this effort over time at both the personal and organizational levels are the foundations for continuously enhancing and evolving quality in the Philadelphia system that serves Pennhurst class members.

REFERENCE

Halderman v. Pennhurst, No.74–1345 (E.D. Pa. 1977).

Health and Safety Issues

This section discusses ways to ensure the health and safety of individuals with developmental disabilities in an increasingly open service delivery environment. That is, how can an agency meet the challenges that arise when people choose to live in more diverse, dispersed, and decentralized living situations? In each of the chapters, protection of individual well-being is juxtaposed with quality enhancement—the ultimate goal of which is to instill best practices to make people safer.

Chapter 5 highlights three states' mortality review processes notable for their applicability to a decentralized service arena. Few state developmental disabilities (DD) systems consistently or systematically gather data on the deaths of people they serve; these three states not only gather comprehensive information but also analyze it for patterns and use the insights to improve systemwide practice. Nebraska's system is unique in being an interagency effort; Massachusetts has approached mortality review as part of a larger quality management and improvement initiative; and Connecticut has dealt with the issue for the longest time, revising its death review recently to focus on particular cases—people who live independently or who receive self-determined services. "The fundamental goal [of all these systems] is consistent with self-determination—to make individuals safer in the lives they choose to lead" (Chapter 5). Running throughout the state case studies is the knowledge that mortality reviews will become increasingly important as people live in more dispersed settings and come to rely primarily on direct support professionals and local generic health systems.

In contrast to more punitive activities, the profiled state systems seek to support and encourage staff to be open about sharing information and concerns surrounding the death of people they serve, so that strategies to prevent future unnecessary deaths can be developed. Using the information for systems improvement is crucial, not only to foster better services and supports currently but also to inform future service activities: "As the service population ages, health needs expand, and service models evolve, data obtained from mortality reviews will play an increasingly important role in . . . strategic planning."

Chapter 6 takes a detailed look at incident reporting systems, outlining the basic components and alerting the reader to structural, administrative, and management issues pertinent to establishing and operating the system. An effective abuse and neglect investigation system encompasses four core components: reporting, intake and screening, investigation, and remediation. With these elements in place, a public DD system can not only deter wrongful or neglectful conduct but can also lead to improvements in policy and practice to reduce victimization in the future.

Chapter 7 offers a fresh look at ensuring health and safety for individuals with developmental disabilities: integrating person-centered planning precepts into decisions about how to keep an individual safe and happy. The chapter begins with the provocative statement, "Happy and dead are incompatible; alive and miserable are unacceptable." It proceeds to challenge those who support individuals with developmental disabilities to be open to the idea that someone's everyday life can be filled with things "important *to* the individual" as well as things that are recognized as "important *for* the individual." The end result can be a richer *and* safer life. Included are numerous training exercises designed to give direct care staff a deeper practical understanding of ensuring an individual's safety within the context of a personally meaningful day-to-day existence.

CHAPTER 5

Procedures for Investigating Deaths in the Developmental Disabilities System

THE EXPERIENCE IN THREE STATES

MADELEINE H. KIMMICH, MARCIA NOLL,
ROGER STORTENBECKER, AND DOROTHY MULLEN

Until fairly recently, mortality review has not been in the forefront of state quality assurance activities. Most states do not routinely explore the causes of individual deaths, nor do they systematically examine trend data concerning those deaths. In general, state developmental disabilities (DD) systems do keep track of deaths as incidents and appropriately investigate cases of alleged abuse or neglect. This pattern, however, is beginning to change. As increasing proportions of the service population live more independently in dispersed settings, it becomes more difficult for state policy makers to know intuitively whether certain living situations, certain providers, or particular population groups face greater risks of death. This chapter describes the efforts of three state DD systems to establish a mortality review process that works in a decentralized service arena. These approaches enable state administrators to learn systematically from their own experiences of deaths of people they serve. This systematic process then allows them to take clear steps to reduce the likelihood that these patterns continue.

One state, Connecticut, has been reviewing deaths for 15 years, gradually fine-tuning the system; the other two states, Nebraska and Massachusetts, have more recently begun a death review process. Nebraska established its review process on an interagency basis from the start. In Connecticut, the Department of Mental Retardation (DMR) instituted a two-tiered process in 1987, which served them well for nearly a decade. It identified many practice areas needing attention both locally and statewide. DMR did not, however, become complacent with its well-operating system; in the mid-1990s, DMR went through a thoughtful process of revising its mortality review process in order to better focus its resources on cases needing closer attention.

In 1992, Nebraska Health and Human Services (HHSS) established an interagency death review process in order to examine patterns in the circumstances surrounding the death of any service recipient with developmental disabilities. Using this information to develop training, they seek to reduce preventable deaths, and to enhance providers' knowledge of best practice and prevention.

Massachusetts began its mortality review process in 1998, as part of an extensive quality management and improvement system. In collaboration with the University of Massachusetts Medical School, the Massachusetts DMR has begun to analyze its mortality data, using the findings to guide service improvements.

These three states take the mortality review process several steps forward, showing the importance of educating state and local policy makers and service providers about patterns evident in the situations surrounding client deaths, and making a firm commitment to ameliorate the situations that appear to increase the likelihood of client deaths. In all cases, the fundamental goal is consistent with self-determination—to make individuals safer in the lives they choose to lead. Each state has established a thorough and precise process for investigating the deaths of people with developmental disabilities and uncovering trends, not to punish so much as to enhance systems for the benefit of future service recipients and their families.

A CONNECTICUT MODEL

The Connecticut DMR developed and implemented a mortality reporting and review system in 1987, as part of the department's changing focus from an institution-based system to a community-based service model. The purpose of the system was to review the quality of health care, overall care, and quality of life for people living in both community and institutional settings. Connecticut's 1985 consent decree involving the downsizing of one of the state's large institutions, Mansfield Training School, resulted in major changes in department leadership, direction, philosophy, and mission. DMR and private agencies rapidly developed community day and residential programs to meet the needs of people moving from institutions, nursing homes, and other settings, including family homes. DMR reorganized into six decentralized regions, and for each region, a managerial-level registered nurse (Director of Health Services) position was created. The Director of Health Services for each region is responsible for the development, coordination, and oversight of community health services. These regional health service directors play a key role in the Connecticut mortality review system.

Table 5.1.   Living arrangement of adults and children served by the Connecticut Department of Mental Retardation (DMR) (N=14,023)

Type of living arrangement	n	Percentage
Independently	280	2%
In family home	6,451	46%
Receive individual supports	421	3%
In a DMR operated, funded, or licensed program[a]	6,170	44%
In the residential program of other state agency[b]	701	5%

[a]The types of residential services available for people include community living arrangements (CLAs), community training homes (CTHs), individual supports (IS), residential schools (RS), and supported living (SL) services.

[b]Includes Departments of Public Health, Mental Health and Addiction Services, and Children and Families.

Dimensions of Today's System

The Connecticut DMR currently provides services through a decentralized administrative model consisting of five regions, each headed by a regional director who works under the direction of the commissioner and deputy commissioner. The department currently serves more than 18,460 people—4,440 children in the birth-to-three system and 14,023 adults and other children. Of the 14,023 adults and children served, the majority (51%) live independently, live in their family homes, or receive individual supports. The rest of the people served live in DMR operated, funded, or licensed facilities or programs (44%) or in facilities or programs operated by other state agencies (see Table 5.1). Of those 44% who receive residential supports from DMR, 35% live in DMR operated programs, and 65% live programs operated by private, not-for-profit, and for-profit agencies that are funded or licensed by DMR or by the Department of Public Health (DPH).

Nature of the Mortality Review Process

Connecticut DMR's mortality review system relies on the prompt reporting of deaths. The department's policy requires the immediate reporting of the death of any person who is a client of the department or any individual who is monitored in the department's mainframe system (see Table 5.2). For example, when a person's death is confirmed by a physician or other authorized person (e.g., a registered nurse per the Nurse Pronouncement statute and regulations), the person's program manager or case manager immediately notifies the DMR regional director, who completes and forwards a death report to the DMR central office. If the person received residential supports or services, the DMR mortality review process is initiated. If the person did not receive residential services from a DMR operated, funded, or licensed provider and did not live in a nursing facility, no further action is necessary unless abuse or neglect is alleged. Cases involving an abuse or neglect allegation are referred to the appro-

Table 5.2.   Population covered by required reporting in Connecticut

People receiving residential services

People living at home or receiving individual supports

Children receiving birth-to-three services

People living in nursing facilities, including people who do not have
mental retardation but for whom the DMR has oversight
responsibility under the Nursing Home Reform Act of 1987
(PL 100-203)

priate agency (e.g., Office of Protection and Advocacy, Department of Children and Families, Department of Social Services) for investigation, and to local or state police, if appropriate. Deaths of children under the age of 18 are reported to the Office of the Child Advocate for an additional independent review.

Where DMR responsibility includes medical care, the mortality review process is always involved. Connecticut DMR policy requires a mortality review after the death of every person for whom the DMR had direct or oversight responsibility for medical care (see Table 5.3). For example, the department would review the death of a person who received supported living services that included assistance with medical care. However, a review would not be done for a person who received limited supports (e.g., case management assistance with finances) if the department had no involvement with the person's medical care; similarly, for people who were placed in nursing homes directly from home by their families with no DMR involvement, no DMR mortality review would be conducted.

The purpose of Connecticut mortality review process is to review the person's health care, overall care, and quality of life; to identify and resolve issues and concerns; and ultimately, to improve the quality of care and quality of life in the future for others. Although the primary focus is not to punish or discipline the responsible party, reviews may result in referral to appropriate authorities for further investigation and/or action as warranted.

Original Process   The original mortality review process implemented in 1987 involved a two-tiered review system: initial review by a Regional Mor-

Table 5.3.   Mandatory mortality review populations for whom the Connecticut Department of Mental Retardation (DMR) has medical responsibility

A person who lived in a DMR-operated, -funded, or -licensed program

A person who received residential supports and services if the
department assisted with the person's health and medical care

A person who lived in a nursing home or residential care home if the
person was placed directly or indirectly by the department

A person who was placed in a nursing home from a DMR-operated,
-funded, or -licensed program

Table 5.4. Membership of the Regional Mortality Review Committee (RMRC) and Medical Quality Assurance Board (MQAB)

Membership of the RMRC	Membership of the statewide MQAB
An assistant regional director	A community physician (internist)
The director of health services	A medical examiner from the Office of the Chief Medical Examiner
The director of case management	
The regional health service director or Southbury Training School (STS) medical director serves as chairperson	Representatives from the Department of Public Health (DPH) and the Office of Protection and Advocacy
	The Department of Mental Retardation (DMR) director of quality assurance
	A DMR regional director of health
	A DMR director of case management
	The STS medical director
	The central office director of health and clinical services serves as chairperson

tality Review Committee (RMRC), followed by a statewide Medical Quality Assurance Board (MQAB) review. Composition of these committees differed somewhat, with the membership of the statewide group being much more extensive (see Table 5.4).

Regional Mortality Review Committee Process   Each regional review process was initiated by the person's case manager as soon as possible after the person's death by requesting and obtaining consent for release of information from the person's next-of-kin. The case manager then began the process of obtaining the required documents for the mortality review packets (see Table 5.5) He or she then forwarded the mortality review packets to the regional committee chairperson, who distributed them to regional committee members for review prior to the scheduled meeting. The regional committee process included a review of the submitted documents plus an oral presentation provided by the deceased person's case manager, program managers, and other appropri-

Table 5.5. Required materials for mortality review packet

A copy of the death certificate
A health summary
Physicians' orders, notes, and physical exams
Laboratory and diagnostic tests
A case management summary
The autopsy report
Hospital discharge summaries
Case management notes, residential notes, and logs (from the past 3 months)
The most recent plan of service

ate staff. Following each presentation, the committees documented their findings and actions on the Regional Mortality Review Form and forwarded the form, with the mortality review packet, to the MQAB chairperson.

Medical Quality Assurance Board Review   In a process similar to the regional review, for each case, the MQAB chairperson sent the packets to MQAB members for review prior to the next scheduled board meeting. The regional health service director originally responsible for the local review presented the details of the case, including the outcome of the local review. Following the presentation and discussion, the MQAB documented its findings, actions, and recommendations on the MQAB form. Within 30 days of the board meeting, the MQAB chairperson presented both regional and MQAB findings and recommendations to the commissioner for approval or further action. Following the commissioner's approval, the RMRC chairperson (i.e., the regional health service director) took responsibility for implementing board recommendations, follow-up, and tracking. Examples of possible board actions and recommendations included

- Requests for additional information from providers, physicians, or hospitals

- Requirements for policy and procedure review and revision

- Referrals to appropriate licensing bodies (e.g., DPH) for investigation

- Requirements for training or retraining staff

Responses to recommendations and actions were submitted to the central office health service director (the MQAB chairperson) for review at the next MQAB board meeting.

Changing the Process   By the mid-1990s, the department's mortality review process was ready for reform. In its nearly 10 years of operation, the process had tended to review the deaths of older individuals and individuals whose deaths were anticipated due to diagnosed terminal medical conditions. Although the reviews had led to identification and resolution of many systemic care issues, department managers expressed concerns about the time and resource demands of the process. In response, the commissioner appointed a committee of interested parties and constituencies to review the existing policy and to make recommendations for revision. This work group determined that the process was a valuable quality enhancement tool that should continue, with a few process changes. DMR piloted the recommended changes and made subsequent revisions.

The 1997 revisions streamlined the review process, while maintaining a high standard for quality reviews and follow-up actions. The changes did not affect the actual review process—the RMRC would continue to review all deaths where applicable using the same process described previously. However, six key changes were made:

1. RMRC could either close a case or refer the case to the MQAB for further review.

2. MQAB would review all cases referred by the RMRC and a minimum of 10% of the cases closed at the local level as a quality assurance audit.

3. All cases reviewed by the local committees would be reviewed by the MQAB chairperson.

4. Two additional required members were added to the RMRC to address conflict of interest issues—a health professional not associated with DMR and a person serving in a client advocacy role.

5. MQAB membership would be expanded to include the DMR director of investigations.

6. In particular situations, the regional committees were required to refer cases to the MQAB (see Table 5.6).

Annual data since 1997 show that the MQAB actually reviews between 20% and 25% of cases closed at the local level. The quality assurance audits have revealed no concerns about the quality of the local review, and decisions to close a case at the local level have met policy standards. Although the review process is still both time and resource intensive, it continues to be a valuable vehicle in identifying critical care and systems issues, particularly in light of the changing service paradigms and quality enhancement initiatives.

Supplemental Processes   In conjunction with the implementation of the original mortality review system, Connecticut developed and implemented two unique supporting processes: an agreement with the Office of the Chief Medical Examiner (OCME) and the department's policy on obtaining autopsies. In 1987, the OCME agreed to be the responsible agency for reviewing deaths

Table 5.6.   Situations requiring Regional Mortality Review Committee (RMRC) referral to the Medical Quality Assurance Board (MQAB)

The death involved an allegation of abuse or neglect.

The case was accepted for autopsy by the Office of the Chief Medical Examiner.

An autopsy was performed.

The death was sudden or unexpected.

The person died unexpectedly because of causes unrelated to a previously diagnosed medical condition (e.g., the person was hospitalized for a certain condition, but the cause of death was unrelated to the admission diagnosis).

The regional committee findings or recommendations were significant and may have statewide significance.

The regional committee was unsure about whether to refer the case to the MQAB.

Table 5.7.   Criteria for cases receiving autopsy

A sudden or unexpected death

A death involving an earlier accident or trauma

A death involving questionable contributing factors

Any case in which the cause of death is not due to a previously diagnosed condition or disease

Cases involving an allegation of abuse or neglect

of all DMR clients who were subject to mortality review. If the OCME declined a case due to jurisdictional issues, the department's autopsy medical advisory went into effect. This advisory directed regional managers to conduct autopsies on all people subject to mortality review. In 1991, the autopsy medical advisory was revised to limit autopsy requests to cases meeting one or more specific criteria (see Table 5.7). The DMR pays the cost of autopsies it requests if no other funding mechanism is available. Although autopsy costs can present budget challenges, the information obtained is often critical in determining whether quality-of-care issues affected or caused the person's death. When families have refused consent for autopsy in these type of deaths, the MQAB is often unable to determine whether acceptable standards of care were provided.

Achievements of the Mortality Review Process

The mortality review process has identified and addressed agency/facility-specific issues as well as statewide systemic issues, resulting in improved quality of care in both community and institutional settings. Systems improvements have included

- Revisions to record transfer systems

- Staff training initiatives for areas such as signs and symptoms of illness, emergency responses, medication administration, and seizure management

- Development or revision of protocols and procedures for respite care services, supported living services, end-of-life decisions, nursing delegation, and medication administration

Areas of Special Concern   Mortality review findings have revealed a wide array of critical issues, leading DMR to make many specific system improvements. Among the key issues are response to health emergencies, quality of documentation, staff knowledge, and skills of acute care personnel.

Medical Emergencies   The MQAB has frequently found situations in which staff have called the house manager or agency nurse prior to calling 911 when an individual was exhibiting life-threatening symptoms such as difficulty breathing. In these cases, the MQAB action routinely is to request the agency's policies and procedures for health emergencies. Upon review, if agency procedures instructed house manager or nurse notification prior to a 911 call, the agencies were required to revise their policies to include clear guidelines detailing the types of health emergencies for which staff must call 911 prior to any other notification. If agency policies already met this requirement but staff had not acted accordingly, the Board would require documentation of staff re-training.

Quality of Documentation   Quality of documentation is a concern among both direct care and professional staff. Nursing documentation often fails to meet standards of nursing practice. Direct care notes are often poorly detailed, include subjective information, include information about other individuals (raising confidentiality issues), do not provide clearly detailed objective information, and contain illegal corrections such as *cross outs, erasures,* and *white-outs.* Improper, incomplete, inaccurate documentation about any aspect of care is a vehicle for potential harm for the people who are served. When the documentation involves health information, the risk of harm is increased.

One example of documentation issues involved Sue, a woman in her mid-fifties who died from a massive coronary. Direct care notes indicated that Sue had complained of chest pain for 2 nights. Staff notes indicated that she was yelling and complaining and would not go back to bed. Staff attributed her complaints to behavior and included derogatory descriptors. There was no indication that the nurse was notified until Sue was taken to the emergency room (ER) by the house manager. The ER physician directed staff to have Sue see her primary care physician the next day for follow-up treatment. Sue's physician diagnosed indigestion, ordered an antacid, and instructed staff to bring her back if symptoms persisted.

The nurse's notes did not indicate that a nursing assessment was conducted or that staff were given any direction or training on observable signs and symptoms of heart disease. Staff notes did not indicate that the nurse was notified regarding the outcome of the physician visit. Staff notes continued to document Sue's behaviors (e.g., yelling, complaining of pain) for several more days. Squeezed between the lines of two other nursing notes and dated the day Sue suffered a cardiac arrest was a note saying the nurse had called the physician reporting Sue's symptoms but that he had failed to return her call. Unfortunately, because the nurse's note was not done according to acceptable nursing documentation standards, the nurse's note was subject to suspicion. Was the physician actually notified or did the nurse try to cover up her inaction?

Sue went into cardiorespiratory arrest that night, several days after she began to exhibit symptoms. Direct care notes did not provide any information about the events preceding, during, or following Sue's cardiac arrest. The MQAB review found that hospital ER records noted a diagnosis of Stage II heart block with a recommendation for physician follow-up. Because the Board could not determine whether Sue's physician was aware of the diagnosis (due to the nurse's improper notation), the case was referred to the DPH for further investigation. The DPH investigator was also unable to ascertain whether the physician was ever notified and recommended follow-up action regarding the improper documentation.

MQAB actions included retraining for direct care staff on signs and symptoms of illness, proper documentation, and respect and dignity principles. In addition, the agency was required to develop and implement nursing documentation standards and to provide documentation of training for nursing staff. Reviews identifying similar documentation issues are handled in a similar fashion in that staff retraining is required for all agency-specific cases involving documentation issues. Also, the MQAB found that documentation was a statewide, systemic issue for which the department responded by developing and implementing Nursing Documentation Standards that provide best practice standards for nurses. Direct care documentation training was revised and enhanced.

Lack of Staff Knowledge   Cases that identified lack of staff knowledge in signs and symptoms as well as person-specific health information have been a major concern for the MQAB. Sue's story provides one example. In another case, staff providing support for a man with paraplegia (paralyzed below the waist), an in-dwelling urinary catheter, and chronic urinary tract infections did not know the signs and symptoms of acute kidney infection (i.e., fever and change of level of consciousness). This information was critical for staff who were caring for a person who could not feel increased pain or pressure or experience urinary frequency. Without this information, they did not know that his increased lethargy and confusion could be due to a severe kidney infection, and they did not think to check for an elevated temperature. They were unaware of any problem until he lost consciousness and died several hours later. An autopsy revealed that he had an overwhelming kidney infection and sepsis.

In another case, documentation showed that Tamika, a 50-year-old woman who lived in her own apartment and received supported living services, had experienced several severe asthma attacks over a period of about 4 months, all requiring hospitalization. No nursing services were provided by the agency or obtained from a community nursing agency. Staff who were not certified to administer medications were trained to administer asthma medications via nebulizer by a manufacturer's representative. Medication administration records revealed months of medication errors that included wrong medications and wrong dosages due to transcription errors and misinterpreted physician orders. Care following hospitalizations was not well coordinated with the primary physician and pulmonologist. It was clear that staff did not understand the seriousness of unstable asthma and medication regimen accuracy. Even after Tamika's death, staff thought she had died from a heart attack and were stunned to learn that autopsy results identified status asthmaticus as the cause of death.

Subsequent to MQAB findings, the agency hired nursing support for the individuals receiving supported living services, completed health assessments for each individual, and trained staff in medication administration per DMR policy. At about this same point in time, the department was revising supported living service protocols. This and other similar cases reinforced the need for departmental policy changes that included 1) health assessments for use in planning for people referred for supported living services and for people currently receiving such services, 2) self-medication evaluations, and 3) staff certification in medication administration if staff were directly involved in medication administration (e.g., they poured and gave medications to people). Health service needs identified during a person's planning processes would be provided by agency staff or community services.

It is important to note that although all of the examples identified serious issues, the reviews did not and could not conclude that the deaths were directly caused by or were the result of the identified care issues. In some cases, the board felt that although the care provided may have affected or influenced the outcome, it could not be identified as the cause of the deaths. In all cases, appropriate corrective actions were taken, resulting in improved care in the future for others.

Major Care Concerns   Mortality reviews have also revealed major care concerns in acute-care hospitals and long-term-care facilities that are licensed by the DPH. Referral to the DPH for investigation has resulted in licensing citations, fines, and referrals to physician and nursing licensing boards for investigation and further action. For example, one hospital was cited and a nurse disciplined for failure to follow postoperative procedures that resulted in the death of an individual following a routine eye surgery. In the recovery room following surgery, Joe went into respiratory arrest due to tracheal occlusion caused by his unusually large tongue. The recovery room nurse failed to follow hospital procedures for postoperative monitoring and did not discover that he was in respiratory arrest. When Joe's respiratory arrest was discovered, attempts at resuscitation failed.

In another case, a hospital and physician were cited for failure to follow clearly defined protocols for the use of an experimental drug being tested in the treatment of end-stage esophageal cancer. Documentation revealed that Michael, a man in his mid-sixties, received several extra doses of medication that far exceeded the experimental protocol. Although Michael had terminal, end-stage cancer, the medication overdose clearly caused his death. Despite hospital actions taken following an internal review, the MQAB reported the incident to the DPH for further investigation. The hospital was cited, and the physician was disciplined.

In addition, long-term-care facilities have been cited and fined by the DPH for care issues such as poor pain management, untimely responses to health status changes, inadequate documentation, poor quality of care, delayed care, and other similar issues.

Other System Improvements   Since 2000, the mortality review process has identified several additional areas requiring systems and process revision or development: response to sudden and/or unexpected deaths; eating, diet, and nutrition concerns; bed side-rail and mattress safety; and improved linkages to the abuse/neglect system. Several of these merit some further explanation.

Sudden and/or Unexpected Deaths   Reviews of cases involving sudden and unexpected deaths of a few individuals revealed that current systems had not provided adequate and timely interventions by either the department or the provider agency. If the death had involved an allegation of abuse or neglect, appropriate investigations had been completed. But this did not occur in all cases. Because the mortality review process occurs several months after a person's death, quality-of-care questions raised by the review were difficult to determine months after the fact.

In response to system inadequacies, DMR developed and implemented a new statewide procedure. The procedure requires that agencies clearly define processes for immediate notification to the DMR regional director, for securing the environment and records, and for conducting a preliminary investigation including police involvement. This new procedure works in conjunction with the department's procedure for obtaining autopsies either by the OCME or through hospital pathologists, as previously described. Regional managers are responsible for working with families to obtain the required consent for autopsies not performed by the OCME.

Nutrition and Safety Concerns   Another important quality of care issue is staff training and agency policies and procedures in the areas of nutrition, diets, physiological eating disorders, bed side-rail and mattress safety, and personal care. Major concerns in these areas were identified following a few untimely and tragic deaths due to choking, entrapment by improperly installed side-rails, and two drowning deaths that occurred during bathing. In response to these concerns, the department took immediate action. To address nutrition and eating concerns, the department developed protocols and procedures to identify people with dysphagia and other physiological eating disorders. In addition, a statewide workgroup comprised of people from various constituencies (e.g., parents, managers and clinicians from both DMR and private agencies) identified issues and recommended actions, such as development of 1) standardized diet manual and training modules that will be available on the DMR web site; 2) new-employee, ongoing, and person-specific nutrition training; and 3) standardized food consistency charts and descriptions. These recommended actions are currently in various stages of development and implementation.

Concerns with mattress and bed side-rail safety prompted the immediate development and implementation of procedures requiring routine assessments of and corrective actions for special mattresses (i.e., water and air: proper filling and temperature), side-rails, side-rail padding, appropriate mattress size and compatibility (for the bed and the person), physical maintenance (e.g., loose or missing screws, worn or faulty wires), and other bed-safety issues.

The department immediately responded to the two drowning deaths by requiring that all agencies review, revise, and develop personal care protocols for every individual based on the person's care needs. They also required agencies to provide plans for implementation, including documentation of staff training. (Note: The two drowning cases occurred in different agencies within about 2 months of each other. In both cases, timely police investigations, which included autopsy reports from the OCME, led to the arrest of the two staff members responsible for the individuals in their care. One person was charged with negligent homicide and the other with second-degree manslaughter. Both cases were pending trial as of 2002.)

It is extremely important to note that of the reviewed cases with quality-of-care issues and concerns, only 10% involved people who received services from DMR operated, funded, or licensed facilities or programs. An additional 6% of cases with quality-of-care concerns involved people who lived in nursing homes licensed by the DPH. Data shows that since implementation of the revised system in 1997, approximately 55% of reviewed cases were closed at the local level, indicating that no care concerns were identified. Of the remaining 45%, the MQAB found relatively few quality-of-care issues for most people who received services in DMR operated, funded, or licensed facilities or programs. The examples detailed in this document represent the most significant and serious examples of mortality review findings.

Conclusion

As Connecticut continues to review, revise, and develop quality enhancement systems, DMR will need to re-define the population for whom the mortality review process applies. Currently, people who live independently or who receive self-determined services would not be included for mortality review. This was appropriate in the beginning years of self-determination. As the system continues moving toward a self-determined service model, this may not continue to be appropriate.

Overall, the Connecticut mortality review process has proven to be a valuable method of identifying and resolving issues of basic health and safety. It remains an important tool among a cadre of new and changing quality enhancement initiatives. The process has led to identification of critical care issues and has resulted in quality enhancement initiatives at the local agency and regional level and at the statewide, departmental systems level. Data on immediate and contributing causes of death will be valuable for disease prevention and health promotion initiatives. In addition, as detailed data categorizing MQAB findings, actions, and follow-up activities becomes available through a newly developed MQAB database, DMR will be better equipped to identify high-quality programs and services. Finally, as the service population ages, health needs expand, and service models evolve, data obtained from mortality reviews will play an increasingly important role in the department's strategic planning.

NEBRASKA

The Nebraska Health and Human Services (HHSS) agency established an interagency Death Review Committee in April, 1992, for the first time providing data regarding deaths of Nebraskans with developmental disabilities. Staff from the Department of Services and the Department of Regulation and Licensure make up the committee. Committee membership includes representatives from the Developmental Disabilities (DD) System; Health Facilities Standards, Protection, and Safety; a physician; and a nurse. The stated purpose of the committee has been widely publicized within Nebraska's DD services system:

> The Committee will review information submitted by providers of services relative to the death of people with developmental disabilities, and whose services are funded by the State of Nebraska in an effort to determine trends or individual situations which may indicate training and education needs and to provide information to service providers regarding best practices and prevention.

Many quality assurance activities exist in Nebraska's DD system. Most are aimed at sampling the quality of habilitation, consumer and family satisfaction, protection and safety, health and well being, handling of consumer finances, utilization, and a host of other indicators. Random samples for review are pulled from active service records and are limited to people served by a given provider. None of the files in these reviews include people who have died while being served by HHSS. The Death Review Committee fills an important niche in an overall quality assurance plan by reviewing all deaths, across all providers. Prior to the establishment of the Death Review Committee, each death was treated as a discrete event. The committee review and statewide data allow for identification of trends or patterns that may not otherwise be recognized.

Death Review Process

The Death Review Committee establishes uniform, consistent reporting of deaths of people with developmental disabilities receiving services in community-based developmental disabilities (CBDD) services and intermediate care facilities for people with mental retardation (ICFs/MR). Based on review of reported deaths, the committee identifies prevention strategies and provides feedback and technical assistance to service providers. The committee identifies the need for change in the system of services and supports or upgrades to regulation, policy, or state legislation. The committee does not investigate criminal activity, abuse, neglect, or medical malpractice. If necessary, the committee makes referrals to the proper investigating authority.

Prior to the creation of the Death Review Committee, deaths were not consistently reported to HHSS. Information reported was typically limited to date, time, and location of death. Cause of death and circumstances leading up to the death were seldom included in the reported information. As the service system grew to include more people receiving services and more service providers, the inadequacies of informal reporting became more apparent. Service providers new to the service system were unaware of the informal reporting process. Reporting deaths did not necessarily have the same priority among providers. Knowing the time, date, and place of the death provided nothing more than information to end the service authorization. With the formalized process, reporting has become routine and reliable. Reports include enough information to allow for a meaningful review.

Presently, all deaths are reported using the standardized notification process developed by the committee. All CBDD service providers and ICFs/MR are required to report the deaths of people receiving services from their agency. The services coordinator reports deaths of people receiving services coordination only. Provider contracts, rules and regulations, and provider agreements support the requirements for provider reporting of deaths. Although there is no specific statutory authority for this, lack of statute has not been a barrier because service providers recognize the potential benefits of learning from the statewide review of deaths.

The death review process includes six main steps (see Figure 5.1). Primary responsibility rests with the HHSS protective services coordinator. In the preliminary report, the coordinator must include 1) the name of the deceased, 2) time of death, 3) the service provider's name, and 4) a brief description of the circumstances surrounding the death.

The full Death Review Committee meets each month to review recent deaths and to receive updates on pending cases. When committee members receive initial notification of the death, each member collects relevant information to bring to the committee meeting, such as related incident reports, medical records, or previous service quality concerns cited by state agencies. The discussion among committee members is not rushed. Each member is allowed ample time to ask questions and provide their perspective and concerns.

The "Notification of Client Death" form is a key document. It includes a host of information about the deceased (see Table 5.8). When necessary, the

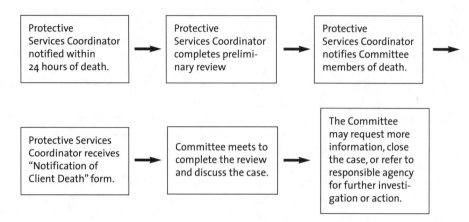

Figure 5.1. Six steps of the death review process in Nebraska.

committee contacts provider staff, hospital staff, or medical staff for additional information about the death. Over time, the information collected has been expanded to include information about the deceased's specific activities in the 24-hour period preceding death, as well as staff activities and involvement for the 24-hour period prior to death, at the time of death, and immediately following death.

The committee members have access to a wide variety of information sources that can be pertinent to the committee's work. Autopsies have provided useful information to assist the committee in determining cause of death. Due to expense and refusal by families and guardians, autopsies are not routinely completed. Death certificates have provided little information that can be used by the committee to develop learning and prevention strategies. As necessary, committee members review individual program plans, service coordination monthly contact notes, and service monitoring records. Direct support staff logs and incident reports often fill in blanks that more formal medical reporting does not include.

Such data can provide valuable insight into causes of death. Direct care staff records and reports in some cases note behavior changes that may later be linked to medical conditions or illnesses. The early symptoms of a bowel obstruction may appear very similar to symptoms of the flu. In some cases, the committee has reviewed the physician's orders, nursing notes, hospital records, police reports, and ambulance records. In some cases, the supplemental information gives a more complete explanation of the acute medical treatment, which in turn gives some insight into the cause of death. This is especially important when autopsies are not available. The committee may request additional information because of inconsistencies in diagnosis, medical conditions,

Table 5.8. Information included on Nebraska's
"Notification of Client Death" form

Name
Gender
Age
Address
Residential supports
Day supports
Diagnosis
Medical conditions
Medications
Medical history
Recent illnesses
Recent hospitalizations
History of abuse or neglect
Date, time, and place of death
Staff on duty at time of death
Staff activities and interventions just prior to
    and following the death

medications, treatment, medical history, gaps in time frames, or vague or incomplete information. The request typically comes from the committee member agency best suited to make the request. For example, the state Medicaid agency may request ICF/MR or hospital records under the reporting requirements of the Medicaid provider agreement; or the DD system may request information from the CBDD service provider under the reporting requirements of the service provider contract or regulations.

Using the Death Review Information to Improve Practice

Knowing the specific cause of death has led to development of specific staff training, especially in prevention. For example, bowel obstructions and choking, although not identified as leading causes of death, are preventable problems. As mentioned previously, the symptoms of a bowel obstruction may appear very similar to the symptoms of the flu. Certain diets, eating habits, or medications can increase the risk of a bowel obstruction for certain people. With this information, service providers and direct care staff are able to identify people who may have higher risk and seek prompt medical diagnosis and treatment when early symptoms appear. People with swallowing disorders may be at greater risk for choking. For these people, meals are prepared and served with heightened awareness. Staff are trained in advance to handle choking emergencies.

Reviewing events and care immediately preceding and following a death has yielded important information. The Death Review Committee has reinforced the importance of training direct care staff to follow established emergency medical procedures. Information reviewed by the committee revealed that when staff are not familiar and comfortable with the service provider's emergency procedures, they might contact their immediate supervisor to determine if 911 rescue should be called. The supervisory staffs are stretched very thin and are not always immediately available. Needing to check with someone else before calling 911 can cause critical time delay. The need for training and technical assistance extends beyond medical conditions of people receiving services. The committee has discussed the opportunity to provide information and training that may help family members, roommates, staff, and others cope with the death of a loved one.

The Death Review Committee keeps a database of all deaths reviewed. Data collection began with the committee's first review in April, 1992. The committee collects and reviews the data and reports them to the National Core Indicators Project. (The National Core Indicators Project is an initiative of the National Association of State Directors of Developmental Disabilities Services [NASDDDS] and Human Services Research Institute [HSRI], funded through state contributions. See Chapter 13 for more information.) In being part of the National Core Indicators Project, the committee is able to review Nebraska's performance on certain data elements in the context of data from other states. Figure 5.2 presents an example of the tracking record. The column titled "Referral date" records referrals to other agencies for further action, such as a referral to the DD system for technical assistance to the service provider. The information from the tracking record is entered into a simple database to allow the committee to query the data. In the majority of cases, the committee conducts its review and closes the case, with no further action necessary. Comparison of committee data on deaths of people with developmental disabilities with HHSS vital statistics data on deaths of Nebraska's population in general indicates no significant differences in cause or rate of death: Most frequent causes of death in both populations include heart disease, cancer, and cerebrovascular disease (stroke). Despite the lack of contrast with overall population death trends, the data gathered by the Death Review Committee serves a valuable purpose. By observing patterns in the data, the committee is able to inform policy makers and providers about factors that could reduce future deaths of people with developmental disabilities.

The work of the Death Review Committee has led to the provision of much needed technical assistance to those in the field. The committee as a group has prepared relevant written materials, including correspondence and information on best practices. More detailed and specific training and technical assistance needs have been met by individual committee member agencies. For example, one prevalent issue noted by the committee was inadequate com-

ID number	Age	Sex	Provider	Date of death	Date of notice	Cause of death	Place of death	Autopsy re-quested	Autopsy com-pleted	Com-mittee review date	Date addi-tional infor-mation requested	Referral date	Status

Figure 5.2.   An example of a data tracking record for deaths.

93

munication between the consumer, support staff, and medical personnel during the provision of medical care. After the committee shared its observations and recommendations with service providers, many providers altered their practice around medical appointments, now sending the staff person who best communicates with the consumer.

Conclusion

The demand for services and supports is changing. People with developmental disabilities and their families desire services and nonspecialized supports, not necessarily provided by traditional community-based service providers or ICFs/MR. In the new, innovative service delivery environment, death review will become increasingly important. As service delivery systems change to meet consumer demand for more flexibility and autonomy in provider selection, data collection methods will need to change also. Collecting data from a large number of single-consumer, single-service providers may prove to be a considerable task. Feedback and technical assistance methods may also need to change to reach the new generation of service and support providers. Traditionally, the committee has been able to reach large numbers of direct care staff within a short time frame, by coordinating training events or sending several copies of written materials to the limited number of service providers. As providers increase in number and variety, the committee will need to monitor the effectiveness of multiple communication methods in order to ensure that all service providers are reached. Ultimately, the Death Review Committee's purpose will remain the same, but its process will look very different.

MASSACHUSETTS

Recent quality assurance initiatives at the Massachusetts DMR began after a period of intense public scrutiny and criticism of the department's performance in ensuring an appropriate level of consumer safeguards. The Massachusetts legislature, the media, and a variety of advocacy groups all made it clear that DMR needed to take a hard look at some of its systems, particularly those that affected the health and safety of individuals supported by the agency. Tracking, review, and investigations of deaths was one of the specific areas cited.

The newly appointed commissioner took the criticism very seriously, making a public commitment to address all of the issues identified. He convened a management review committee, with both internal and external components, and embarked on a major management review and system improvement project, with mortality review identified as one of the areas needing improvement.

Several other factors converged to influence the effort to enhance the quality of DMR's safeguard systems. The department was involved in two areas of litigation. One related to individuals on a waiting list for DMR services, and another related to individuals residing in nursing homes and seeking DMR community residential services. The DMR community system has already seen significant expansion; as a result of the litigation, the growth rate will be even greater, stretching the capacity of existing oversight and quality enhancement structures. At the same time, the Centers for Medicare & Medicaid Services (CMS, formerly the Heath Care Financing Administration) created a new and more stringent process for overseeing the services funded through the federal Home and Community-Based Services Waiver program. The new review process requires states to have a strong and demonstrably integrated quality assurance system in order to ensure the health and welfare of individuals receiving waiver services.

DMR's effort to strengthen death reporting and review processes has, by necessity, been incorporated into a system-wide approach to quality enhancement. The accelerating growth of the community system and the looming new federal waiver requirements also made it clear that the department would require external support and collaboration to achieve its goals. As a result, the department began a major strategic planning process, with consultation and facilitation provided by the University of Massachusetts. The department also joined the National Core Indicators Project and entered into a long-term health and clinical services partnership with the University of Massachusetts Medical School (UMMS).

As a result of this significant management effort, DMR has produced a Quality Management and Improvement System (QMIS), designed to draw together relevant person-centered and organizational information. The system uses new and existing oversight mechanisms and more effectively integrates the work of a wide variety of quality enhancement processes in order to provide data-based guidance for service improvements. The QMIS is grounded in the recognition that quality assurance processes must balance the dual responsibilities of keeping people safe and supporting individuals to realize self-determination and independence. A key component of the QMIS, the DMR Mortality Review System includes a two-tiered process for reporting and reviewing deaths of individuals supported by the department.

Mortality Review Process

In 1998, as the first step in strengthening the department's tracking and review of deaths, DMR established the Mortality Review Committee. The committee is composed of clinical, legal, administrative, and investigative staff from the department and external representation from the Department of Public Health and the Governor's Commission on Mental Retardation. The Mortality Review Committee's initial charge was to develop a mortality review system that provided 1) analysis and comparison of mortality data, 2) prevention initiatives, 3) organizational learning, and 4) integration of mortality data with other safeguard data to support data-based quality enhancement initiatives.

The majority of deaths within the DMR system are anticipated, are the natural outcome of disease and aging, and occur in an attentive and caring environment. A small number of deaths require investigation of the possibility of abuse, neglect, or omission. Regardless of the cause of death, valuable information for improving health supports and program oversight systems can be gathered through a broad review of the circumstances surrounding the time of death. The Mortality Review Committee identified the need to create a clinical review process to gather that information not currently available through the existing Death Reporting and Investigation Systems. To address this goal, the committee developed the DMR Protocol for Reporting and Clinical Review of Deaths, which defines a two-tiered process for death reporting and mortality review.

Death Reporting   All deaths of people with mental retardation who are 18 years and older and deemed eligible for supports from DMR are reported to the Investigations Division within 24 hours after DMR staff become aware of the death. A variety of reporting requirements are in place for notification of other DMR staff, the Disabled Persons Protection Commission, law enforcement, and in specific circumstances, the district attorney, the medical examiner, and other state agencies. Oral notification is made to the investigations agency, followed by a DMR Death Reporting Form that is submitted electronically. Internal, external, or criminal investigation is initiated for the small number of death reports that meet criteria related to abuse, neglect, or omission.

Mortality Review   Within 30 days of the death, a clinical review is conducted by a regional registered nurse or doctor for any individual who met any of these criteria:

- He or she was receiving at least 15 hours of residential supports funded or arranged by DMR.

- He or she was receiving residential supports certified by DMR.

- His or her death occurred in a day support program funded or certified by DMR.

- His or her death occurred in a day habilitation program.

- He or she died while in transportation funded or arranged by DMR.

A three-page Mortality Review Form is completed by the regional registered nurse or doctor, reviewed and signed by the regional director, and submitted to central office within 30 days of the death. The DMR Mortality Review Committee reviews each form and recommends additional review or action as necessary.

Using Data

As part of DMR's health partnership with UMMS, the university prepares an annual analysis of DMR's mortality data and a report on findings and recommendations related to causes and predictors of mortality and identification of risk factors and prevention strategies. Because the DMR clinical review process was not initiated until 2000, the first mortality report, which covered 1999, was limited in scope. Nonetheless, the review provided the opportunity for UMMS to critique the existing mortality review system and make recommendations regarding consistent standards for collecting future mortality related data.

Although the findings prior to 2000 are limited, the analysis determined that causes of death for individuals served by DMR have been fairly consistent with those for the general population. However, in two areas, death rates were higher than the national averages: 1) deaths from pneumonia and 2) deaths from sepsis and renal disease. Neither of these contrasts is surprising; the prevalence of swallowing disorders and a variety of health problems experienced by many individuals can lead to frequent aspiration pneumonia, and in the case of sepsis and renal disease, the early signs and symptoms of these medical conditions may go unnoticed among people who are more frequently beset with health issues or whose cognitive disabilities are a barrier to the accurate reporting of symptoms.

The Mortality Review Committee also spent some time studying the issue of choking and aspiration in order to identify common risk factors and prevention strategies. Initial findings revealed that these individuals tend to have low body weight, are nonambulatory, require specialized diets or tube feedings, are in fair or poor general health, and have several medical diagnoses. Through the UMMS health partnership, more work will be done to identify specific prevention strategies for individuals with this and other health problems. The UMMS partnership will also assist the DMR in refining its clinical review process to ensure its effectiveness in identifying and responding to individual and system issues.

Conclusion

Massachusetts DMR is satisfied with the progress to date in improving its internal systems for mortality reporting and review. Maintaining a focus on system improvement can be a challenge, and sorting out the complex issues around individual lifestyle choices and compliance with treatment recommendations requires thoughtful attention. Additional challenges emerge when reviewing the actions of the external, generic health care system or individual health care professionals because of the difficulty in obtaining detailed information from entities outside the DMR system.

In a culture that often views death as a medical defeat and in a public environment that often seeks to find fault when serious incidents occur, the DMR Mortality Review Committee seeks to support and encourage staff to be open about sharing information and concerns surrounding the death of people they serve. In this way, both DMR and its service providers can improve their ability to prevent unnecessary deaths and to promote quality supports for individuals at the end of their lives.

CHAPTER 6

Best Practices
in Abuse and Neglect
Reporting and Investigation

RICHARD COHEN

Investigation of incidents of abuse and neglect is a crucial component of quality assurance and enhancement. This chapter introduces the elements and components necessary for an effective and efficient investigation system. The material focuses on incidents of abuse and neglect against people with disabilities served or supported by programs or services operated, funded, certified, or licensed by government agencies, including private providers. The alleged abuse and neglect may have occurred in traditional settings such as total care institutions, community living arrangements, or day programs, as well as in community-based or generic situations, such as places of employment. The common denominator for the type of incident and investigation discussed is the involvement of a caregiver in the alleged abuse or neglect. The alleged perpetrator may be a direct or personal care/support staff, professional staff, a member of management, a private or public agency itself, a foster parent, a family member, a health professional, or an organization.

Although this material applies primarily to organizations and systems with a primary mission of serving people with disabilities, it may be of interest to a broader audience because many of the concepts and elements are appropriate to other contexts, including 1) investigation of abuse and neglect in the child protection system and acute care settings, such as hospitals or nursing homes; 2) investigation by law enforcement of charges of physical or sexual abuse against children or adults with disabilities; 3) investigations of alleged human or civil rights violations committed against people with disabilities; and 4) other incidents that affect an individual's well being (e.g., self-injurious behavior, unexplained injuries).

As used in this chapter, an abuse and neglect investigation system encompasses four core components: reporting, intake and screening, investigations or other disposition or resolution, and remediation. The operational definition of abuse and neglect used reconciles most state-to-state variations and has been adapted from the Massachusetts Disabled Persons Protection Commission (DPPC) (M.G.L.c.19C Section 1 and its implementing regulations). Under this definition, four types of caregiver conduct are reportable:

- An *intentional act,* which is defined as willful and deliberate and includes what is commonly characterized as physical, emotional, verbal abuse, sexual abuse, or use of excessive force or restraint

- A *reckless act,* which is defined as an act of indifference to the consequences that are likely to follow (e.g., leaving someone unattended where it is foreseeable and likely that the person will put him- or herself in danger)

- A *negligent act,* which results from the failure to exercise that degree of reasonable care of a person of ordinary prudence under the existing circumstances in view of the probable danger or injury, examples of which would include nonintentional failure to provide for basic nutritional, acute, or chronic health needs and medication errors

- *Omission,* which is a failure to take action to protect or provide for basic needs and a form of neglect

Although serious physical or emotional injury must accompany these acts in order to trigger a report to DPPC, in many other jurisdictions or contexts these acts are prohibited and reportable if they cause any degree of harm or merely pose a threat of harm. Acts of retaliation against reporters are also prohibited and reportable in most jurisdictions.

This chapter highlights the major operational, management, structural, and policy issues relevant to establishing and maintaining an investigations system, but it is not intended to give step-by-step instructions on conducting an investigation The chapter examines the need for an investigative capacity, provides an overview of the components of an effective investigations system, and addresses some key structural, administrative, and management issues.

NEED FOR INVESTIGATIONS CAPACITY

An abuse and neglect investigation capacity is important for four reasons. First, the prevalence of abuse and neglect committed against people with physical, emotional, or cognitive disabilities has been and continues to be high. These high rates generally have roots in the devalued status of people with disabilities, their vulnerability, and the propensity of certain types of people to prey on or exploit that vulnerability.

Second, the necessity for an investigations system arises from the nature and impact of abuse and neglect. Although harm or trauma to a person who has been abused can range from mild to severe and lifelong, no amount of abuse or neglect should be tolerated. The first rule should always be to prevent abuse and neglect, but when that does not happen, an effective investigations system should prevent reoccurrence. No matter how good other aspects of a person's life are, quality of life is compromised if a person's personal safety or well being cannot be ensured.

Third, and clearly related to the second point, is the role and responsibility of public and private administrators and management in investigating serious incidents. Incident investigation provides managers with a tool to determine what has happened and why, enabling them to develop and implement corrective and preventive actions.

Fourth, the investigation itself, and specifically the investigation report, is a salient source of information for a number of critical purposes:

1. Providing an authoritative, impartial, accurate, and recent account of the abuse or neglect incident

2. Guiding development and implementation of corrective plans to address the incidents or conditions

3. Providing information for use in a variety of administrative or legal processes or proceedings that may occur as a result of the incident (e.g., personnel disciplinary actions, licensure proceedings, contested abuser registry proceedings, criminal proceedings)

4. Providing information for preventing subsequent abuse or neglect, not only with regard to the individual or setting but also on a systemwide basis

5. Providing information for managers, quality enhancement personnel, licensors, consumers, and families to evaluate the quality of services and consumers' quality of life

Generally, information from an investigation that is disseminated beyond the individual principals is presented in summary, redacted, or quantitative form in order to prevent disclosure of private or confidential information.

An investigation is never an end to itself but should lead to outcome and change. The overriding purpose of an abuse and neglect investigation process is to learn what truly happened, document it, correct it, learn from it, and prevent reoccurrence in the future. For the investigations process to be effective, however, two essential values must be held paramount and embedded in organizational culture. The first value is the commitment to seeking the *truth* about what *really* happened. Abuse and neglect investigations, especially high-profile ones (e.g., allegations of rape, death by neglect), receive much attention, bringing pressure for certain investigative conclusions. An investigator should never be influenced by such pressure.

The second essential value is *zero tolerance* of abuse and neglect. This must be firmly embedded in the mindsets of all staff, consumers, and other stakeholders. It also must undergird each element of the investigations process. Without it, an incident may be overlooked, not reported, or given inadequate treatment in the investigations and remediation process. With a broad and deeply held commitment to zero tolerance and with appropriate operational elements and practices in place, incidents of abuse and neglect will be addressed seriously, and investigations and corrective plans will be done thoroughly and professionally.

CORE PRACTICES AND PROCEDURES OF AN INVESTIGATIONS SYSTEM

Generally, an investigation of abuse and neglect will have five somewhat overlapping components or phases:

- Immediate and initial steps, including reporting

- Intake and disposition, including assignment of the investigator

- Conduct of investigation and investigation report or other resolution

- Corrective actions

- Appeals and grievance process

Immediate and Initial Steps

Table 6.1 outlines the tasks normally required in the initial stage of investigation and who is traditionally responsible for each task. Other people could be added or substituted, including volunteer community members, relatives, or the consumer him- or herself, depending on the circumstances. Although many issues arise related to the initial phase of an investigation, including the order in which the steps are taken and the need for treatment or remedial action, the following discussion focuses on just the issue of reporting.

Reporting   Three points about reporting are worth emphasizing. First, some systems do not require staff to *directly* report abuse or neglect to external authorities. For example, in Philadelphia, a staff person who witnesses abuse or neglect of a person with mental retardation is only required to report it to the vendor's designated staff person (DSP), who is then responsible for making the external report. Although most people carry out their responsibilities, it is best to mandate both internal and external reporting by any person employed by the provider, as well as other professional and paraprofessional workers.

Second, the criteria for external reporting should be clearly differentiated from internal reporting. Virtually every incident, no matter how minor and re-

Table 6.1.   Immediate and initial steps of an investigation

Initial steps	Person(s) responsible
Immediate assessment for injury	Direct support staff and supervisor or designated staff person (DSP)[a]
Provision of treatment for physical or emotional injury	Range of personnel, depending on injury
Preservation of evidence, as applicable: • Securing the scene • Physical exam or rape kit • Taking immediate statements from the victim and any direct or eyewitnesses (i.e., fresh witness statements) • Filling out incident report • Taking photographs (e.g., the scene, bruises)	As applicable, direct support staff, supervisor, DSP, investigator, police, medical personnel
Reporting • Should be done immediately in case of serious or ongoing abuse and neglect and within 24 hours for all other types • Should report both internally to the supervisor, management, or the DSP and to any external agency that has jurisdiction	Person(s) having reasonable cause to believe abuse or neglect occurred
Risk assessment (i.e., what is the likelihood of abuse or neglect reoccurring or continuing during investigation)[b]	Management, DSP, investigator, police
Immediate or initial protective or remedial actions to ensure that the person is safe and free from neglect[b]	Supervisor, management, DSP

[a]A Designated Staff Person (DSP) is used in the Philadelphia mental retardation system. By policy, each vendor must have a DSP who is trained to carry out particular investigative functions. Assuming the DSP has adequate training and can competently execute such a system, the vendor may rely more heavily on its internal operations to carry out the initial steps, with external investigative entities then ensuring that the initial steps were properly carried out.

[b]Assessing risk or putting in place protective actions may involve making private residential arrangements, which may or may not receive government support. Court orders may have to be obtained to perform these functions when 1) abuse or neglect is suspected, 2) the person is not capable of making or acting upon informed decisions because of lack of mental competence or being in a coercive situation, or 3) investigating authorities cannot gain access otherwise.

gardless of whether it affects the welfare of an individual, should be reported internally because the management needs to know and be able to act. However, reporting to external authorities should focus on those situations in which there is reasonable cause to believe that the abuse and neglect standard of the jurisdiction has been met. (A jurisdiction may also require as a matter of course external reporting of other serious incidents, regardless of whether they may be linked to abuse or neglect.) The following definition is adapted from the reporting standard of the Massachusetts DPPC. *Reasonable cause to believe* means "a basis for judgment that rests upon specific facts, either directly observed or obtained from reliable sources, which support a belief that it is more likely than not that abuse and neglect has occurred" (Massachusetts Rules and Regulations, 118 CMR 2.00). In policy and practice, and therefore in training, this definition should be accompanied by a clear message that, in close cases or when staff are unsure, they should err on the side of reporting or at least contact the outside authority to determine whether the matter is reportable.

Third, as the previous points suggest, abuse and neglect reporting can be complicated. Indeed, in many states, staff or providers may have to report to different or multiple agencies, depending on the type of incident. For example, in Massachusetts, if a person with mental retardation dies in a mental health wing of an acute care hospital (e.g., as a result of abuse or neglect involving restraint), reports potentially would have to go to the DMR, Department of Public Health, Massachusetts DPPC, the Protection and Advocacy (P&A) agency, local or state police, the medical examiner, and CMS (HCFA), in addition to reporting internally and to a DMR regional office. When uncertain, a mandated reporter should report to all entities on a reporting chain to which he or she may have a responsibility to report. The best systemic solution is a centralized hot line (regionwide or statewide) to receive calls, which in turn would make the other notifications. An adequate alternative is to streamline the process as much as possible and to provide a handy graphic or flow chart outlining the reporting responsibilities. It can be used as a training tool, disseminated throughout the field and to other stakeholders (e.g., to families), with more detailed background material available in policy and procedures or a manual. Figure 6.1 is a model chart that briefly outlines reporting responsibilities for all incidents affecting consumers. A similar graphic can be designed depicting the multitiered procedures required for reporting deaths of consumers.

Intake and Disposition

After a report of suspected abuse or neglect is made, the next action most people think will follow is an investigation. This is not necessarily the case, even when the report is made to law enforcement. There generally is and needs to be an intake and screening process to determine whether the matter warrants an investigation (and by whom) or whether other options are more appropriate. The range of options or dispositions and related activities are set out in Table 6.2. These options and activities are inherent to any incident investigation system and should be adapted accordingly. However, the list here is based on a model in which the report of abuse and neglect is made to an external authority charged with screening, investigating, or otherwise resolving or overseeing such activities. The external authority could be a licensing, contracting, or funding agency such as a department of developmental services or

All incidents pertaining to individuals served, injuries of unknown origin, and medication occurrences shall be reported and handled through the incident reporting and remediation process.	Staff observing →	Ensures that the consumer is protected and fills out an incident report
And if the incident or condition harms or places an individual at risk due to abuse, neglect, or illegal, dangerous, or inhumane conduct, Department of Mental Retardation (DMR) investigations must be notified.	Reporter →	Notifies the Regional Senior Investigator
And if the person's injury is serious and is believed to be a result of caregiver abuse or neglect, then the Department of Social Services, Disabled Persons Protection Commission, Executive Office of Environmental Affairs, or the Department of Mental Health must be notified.	Reporter →	Notifies the applicable external agency
And if there is a human rights issue or violation:	Complainant →	Seeks resolution through the human rights process

Additional or special procedures apply when there is:

• Suspected sexual assault	Staff observing →	Initiates sexual abuse protocol and notifies law enforcement
• Reason to believe a felony was committed	Staff observing →	Initiates sexual abuse protocol and notifies law enforcement
• A death	→	Multitiered reporting procedures followed depending on the type and cause of death

Figure 6.1. A model chart of responsibilities for all incidents involving consumers.

Table 6.2. Intake, screening, and disposition steps

Activity or disposition	Comment
Assigning each intake a sequential, public log number	A uniform sequential logging system is important so that every intake can be accounted for, regardless of what the ultimate disposition is.
Making sure that initial and immediate activities were or are being done	The intake person does this by reviewing faxed or emailed documentation, and when necessary, making follow-up calls by having the investigator do an onsite confirmation
Making generally one (but sometimes more) of the following dispositions:	Like the previous step, the intake person should be able to rely on the documentation for disposition but must make follow-up calls (e.g., to the reporter or collateral contacts) if necessary
1. Assignment of investigator(s) from the unit or agency	
2. Resolution without investigation in which the key facts are agreed to, such as when a documented confession from the perpetrator has been obtained as part of the incident review process, during the disciplinary process, or during the early phase of the investigation	Sometimes the time involved in resolving a case in this manner amounts to a mini-investigation, raising the question of whether this resolution method should just be folded under the investigation disposition. However, the advantage of a discrete disposition is that a prompt timeline can be imposed (e.g., 1–2 weeks versus 1–2 months)
3. Designate or rely on provider investigation: • When it does not appear to be abuse or neglect • When, based on predetermined criteria of severity, frequency, nature of incident, and track record of provider, the provider investigates less serious abuse or neglect cases	
4. Defer to another agency to investigate when it is the more appropriate agency to handle the investigation in the first instance (e.g., law enforcement, Department of Public Health, Child Protection Agency)	
5. Make a referral internally or externally when the allegation does not constitute abuse or neglect but requires resolution from another department or agency or through an ombudsman or compliance officer (e.g., human rights violation, program deficiency)	

Activity or disposition	Comment
6. Investigation or referral not indicated when: • On its face, the allegation does not constitute abuse or neglect and does not warrant other action or is frivolous in nature • The allegation has been properly investigated previously and no abuse or neglect was found	Generally, few cases are screened out entirely. Usually some other disposition is more appropriate (e.g., referral). Moreover, the intake person should follow up if he or she thinks details may be missing in the report, particularly if it is made by a consumer with communication or cognitive impairments.

mental health, or an agency inside or outside the human service umbrella, whose sole or primary responsibilities is investigations, such as the Massachusetts DPPC. In Table 6.2, comments about the dispositions and related activities are set out in the right-hand column. Of the many issues that could be discussed here, perhaps the most problematic one concerns incidents of consumer-to-consumer abuse.

Addressing Consumer-to-Consumer Abuse   There is frequent confusion about whether consumer-to-consumer incidents should be treated as a programmatic issues, as incidents, or as matters to be fully investigated. This section outlines principles and guidelines to address this issue. Consumer-to-consumer abuse often has a relationship to caregiver neglect, particularly in group settings in which the conduct is often foreseeable and preventable. Historically, incidents of physical or sexual abuse or assaults between consumers, prevalent in institutional settings, went largely unaddressed. Continuing ambivalence about how to address this problem stems largely from the failure to more clearly define what constitutes consensual sex and related concepts. Because that issue is beyond the scope of this chapter, this discussion addresses incidents in which consent was not given.

A threshold question generally presented is whether these incidents should be reported to investigations as possible incidents of caregiver neglect. If the incident amounts to abuse by one consumer against the other while receiving services from a provider or paid caregiver, the incident should be reported, regardless of whether the incident can be attributed to caregiver neglect. This is the case for at least three reasons:

1. The injury and trauma that results from physical, sexual, emotional, or verbal abuse is just as serious whether the perpetrator is a caregiver or another individual receiving services.

2. Although incidents of this type may *not* be foreseeable and preventable by staff, in most cases the conduct is foreseeable, raising at least the specter of staff neglect.

3. A report should be made in consumer-to-consumer incidents because it
    enables intake personnel to make the finer determinations and appropri-
    ate disposition.

Several guidelines may be useful in addressing this area. All policies and
procedures and training should clearly indicate what constitutes consumer-to-
consumer abuse and that it is reportable in the same way as any other forms of
abuse. In addition to the standard considerations in abuse investigations, several other topics should be addressed in consumer-to-consumer cases:

*   Has the consumer complained of or engaged in similar behavior previously,
    and, if so, has the provider or responsible staff taken all reasonable steps to
    prevent reoccurrence? *Reasonable steps* may require immediate deployment
    of additional staff while more long-term or permanent solutions are being
    developed. They might also necessitate training of staff on a new interven-
    tion to ensure that staff implement the new steps properly, and evaluation
    of whether the new approach is doing what was intended.

*   Even if a particular occurrence was not foreseeable, did staff handle the sit-
    uation appropriately? Could they have prevented an escalation to an actual
    assault? If not, did they intervene promptly to prevent further assaultive or
    abusive behavior or injury?

The answers to these questions may be hard to ascertain at intake. If so, the situation warrants an investigation.

Conduct of Investigation and Investigation Report

Table 6.3 briefly outlines the basic components of an abuse and neglect investigation. (The reader is referred to the "Quality Standards of Investigations"
[1997] developed by the President's Council on Integrity and Efficiency for
further information on the elements of an investigation and investigation report, including a discussion on the importance of investigation planning and
timeliness. The standards may be accessed at www.ignet.gov/pande/standards
.html) The narrative that follows provides further detail about two of the components that frequently give agencies and personnel the most difficulty—interviewing witnesses with disabilities and preparing an investigation report.

Witness Interviews   Too often the practice is not to interview meaningfully or at all people who have significant (or not so significant) emotional,
cognitive, or communication impairments. Although there are instances when
meaningful interviews cannot be conducted, they are far rarer than many assume. Augmentative and alternative communication systems are becoming
more common for people with limited or no verbal communication and greatly
enhance the reliability of the interview. Developing ad hoc augmentations for
purposes of the interview in consultation with people who know the individ-

Table 6.3. Components of investigating abuse and neglect

Investigation plan—Generally written and revised as necessary, setting forth
- The issues to be addressed, including identification of underlying causes
- The elements of the alleged offense
- The activities necessary for the investigation to include the witness to be interviewed, the location and/or identification of documents to be reviewed, and other items and tasks listed below, as applicable

Witness interviews

Documents to be obtained and reviewed

Physical evidence (tangible items material to the allegation such as restraints in an excessive restraint case)

Demonstrative evidence (evidence that depicts what happened, such as photos of scene or bruises, scaled diagrams of scene)

Review of applicable laws; regulations; codes; and professional, licensing, or accreditation standards, policies, and procedures

Forensic, expert, or consultative resources or needs (e.g., medical examiner, other forensic or medical expert, behavioral intervention expert)

Use of extraordinary or unusual investigative techniques (e.g., subpoenas, undercover operations[a], unannounced views or visits)

Preparation of the investigation report (see Table 6.4 on components of an investigation report)

[a]Generally, undercover operations are left to properly trained law enforcement personnel.

ual or with a communication specialist is also possible. Facilitated communication, though still controversial, can be used. For ad hoc systems or facilitated communication (as well as for augmentative systems generally, where needed), the investigator should assure him- or herself that the mode of communication is accurate and reliable based on prior reliability checks or through checks set up for purposes of validating just the investigative interview. Even if the admissibility of the person's testimony in court may be questionable, such testimony may be given weight in an administrative forum or may help an investigator develop leads or rule out theories, possible perpetrators, and so forth. Not interviewing people who have disabilities also feeds into predators' perceptions of the vulnerability of people with disabilities. One of the reasons often cited as why individuals with disabilities are subject to predation and neglect is that predators assume (unfortunately correctly) that people with disabilities will not be considered reliable witnesses. Thus, effective interviewing has the practical effect of enhancing an investigation and may have a broader or indirect deterrent effect.

The Investigation Report   The *investigation report* is a central vehicle to pull together and document the investigation and other preceding steps. Table 6.4 sets out the generally accepted components of reports. All aspects of the investigative report need further discussion. However, because the conclusion is the bottom line in the investigation report, providers on whom a report

Table 6.4.   Components of an investigation report

Title or cover page
List of information (e.g., witnesses or consultants interviewed; documentary, physical, or demonstrative evidence relied on; dates of site visits)
Applicable laws, regulations, and professional standards or literature relied on (optional—can be cited in the narrative)
Statement of actions taken to date
Issues or questions presented (optional)
Findings of facts, citing evidence relied on
Conclusions about whether the allegation of abuse or neglect was substantiated and by whom
Recommendations

is filed may go first to that part of the report. It reflects a logical, deductive process of distilling the facts and interview information into a decision about whether abuse or neglect occurred.

A few points should be emphasized with regard to conclusions. The conclusions can be framed in several ways, depending on the facts and type of incident or conditions. Three of the most common methods are presented in Figure 6.2. These illustrations offer insight for providers not only about how to approach reports of their own internal investigations but also about how to think through the incident that occurred, prior to providing information to external investigations.

Corrective Actions

Corrective actions are generally necessary not only after a finding of abuse or neglect but also when the findings or additional findings otherwise indicate a need. Depending on the type of case, the determination of corrective actions can be straightforward or quite complicated. The corrective phase has three functions or purposes: 1) to remedy any harm to the person who experienced the abuse or neglect, 2) to take action (corrective or punitive), and 3) to prevent recurrence of the same or similar incidents toward the person and others. The following are components or standards recommended for development and implementation of effective corrective action plans:

1.   Thorough and clear investigation reports on which to base corrections (and an informal or formal process for management to seek clarification from the investigator to ensure an accurate understanding of the findings or conclusions)

2.   Understanding and application of the purposes and functions for corrective actions

Illustration 1

- Ms. Smith was responsible for supervising resident Mr. Jones.
- Her supervisory responsibilities required that Ms. Smith constantly watch Mr. Jones or keep all doors locked.
- Ms. Smith's failure to properly carry out her supervisory responsibilities, as more fully described in Findings 3–10, permitted Mr. Jones to leave the home, enter the pool, and drown.
- It is found (or concluded) that Ms. Smith's omissions constituted neglect, and her neglect resulted in Mr. Jones's death. Neglect against Ms. Smith is thereby substantiated (or confirmed or found).

Illustration 2

Neglect contributing to resident Jones' death is substantiated against Executive Director Doe based on the following:

- His agency was cited 2 months prior to Mr. Jones's drowning for failing to erect a fence around the pool.
- Although no time frame was given for correction, based on the citation and the nature of the population he was serving in the house (see findings 1–4), Mr. Doe should have acted promptly to erect a fence, which then would have prevented the drowning.

Illustration 3

Neglect is also found against the department's licensor, Ms. Johnson, for her failure in her September 29 licensing visit to raise and document a red flag concerning the lack of the fence. She did not specify a prompt timeline for correction or follow up to ensure that the fence was erected as required by of licensing regulations 123 and 789(a).

NOTE: While each illustration is somewhat different, each references the relevant facts (albeit in summary form or by referencing paragraph-finding numbers) that relate to each element of the allegation. Given the facts in this hypothetical situation, all three individuals were found neglectful, and a conclusion was then explicitly made.

Figure 6.2.   Three common methods of framing conclusions of investigations.

3. Understanding and application of standard plan format components, including clearly stated actions or activities, timelines, specification of people responsible, and monitoring strategies

4. Development of actions, particularly in the personnel area, that are fair, that are not arbitrary, and that are consistent with good management and human resource principles

5. Investigation of system breakdowns requiring remediation. Regardless of whether an investigation delineates underlying causes, management should be analyzing for system breakdowns requiring remediation. This is the case at the provider level and in applicable departments of oversight agencies

6. An appropriate system of monitoring to ensure that the corrective plans are fully implemented and are having their intended effect and to identify those that need to be revised

Table 6.5 offers a range of possible actions, adapted from a list set forth on the Massachusetts Department of Mental Retardation public logs. They are not intended to be exhaustive but are provided to illustrate the range of options available to providers and state agencies.

Appeals and Grievance Procedures

Fundamental and constitutional principles of fairness and due process require that there be a vehicle for the person alleging abuse and the alleged perpetra-

Table 6.5.   Possible corrective actions for abuse and neglect

Employee discipline (e.g., reprimand, reassignment, suspension, termination)
Restitution
Relocation of the consumer
Staff training
Policy review or change
Individual service plan (ISP) or program review or revision
Therapy or services to the person who experienced the abuse or neglect
Consumer supervision or staffing change
Quality enhancement review
Revocation or nonrenewal of the contract or license
Full or partial provider decertification
Referral to law enforcement
Referral to the licensing/certification board
Change in the individual's competency status or guardianship
Referral of the consumer to an advocate or another agency
Offer or provision of in-home services or out-of-home services

Source: Massachusetts Department of Mental Retardation (1996) public logs.

tor to contest the outcomes of investigation reports and remedial actions. The precise process and when it is triggered will vary depending on a number of factors, including the laws of the state, collective bargaining agreements, and so forth. The range of possibilities include 1) appeal within the provider agency to the oversight state agency, to an arbitrator (e.g., when collective bargaining rights apply), to the civil service commission, or to an administrative law judge who may hear license suspension or revocation appeals of a provider or professional and 2) a process for an individual to contest the entry of his or her name on an abuser registry.

STRUCTURAL AND MANAGEMENT ISSUES

Central to a good investigations system are two issues: the organizational structure chosen for conducting the investigations and the ways in which the investigations system is supported by the larger organization.

Deciding Which Agency Should Investigate

Two questions predominate concerning which agency should investigate alleged abuse or neglect when there is potential multiple agency involvement: 1) should an investigation be conducted (or led) by an investigator internal to the organization in which the abuse occurred or should it be conducted by an external entity; and 2) should a more generic agency (e.g., child or adult protective services) conduct or lead investigations versus a more specialized unit or agency (e.g., funding or licensing agency of the provider where the abuse occurred). Failure to address these issues can lead to jurisdictional rivalry, unnecessary multiple investigations, unnecessary delays in completing the investigation, the wrong agency conducting the investigation, and contamination of testimony of people subject to an "initial" interview on multiple occasions.

Common sense dictates that the agency best equipped to conduct the most efficient and thorough investigation and to affect the best remedy should be the one to investigate; however, because investigation entities develop or are added over time without sufficient attention to addressing overlapping and multiple jurisdiction, it is not easy to determine the best entity. Even when it is, that does not ensure that the appropriate agency will conduct the investigation. The following six factors and principles should be considered in deciding who should conduct an investigation, from the perspective of building or reforming the system as a whole and in terms of what is the best single intake decision.

Capacity and Competence of the Agency   As a general rule, the interest, commitment, and track record of an agency should be considered in addressing the multiple-agency investigation problem. For example, generic adult protective agencies in some states have little experience or training in investigations of abuse or neglect of people with disabilities in DD systems. Although it may be necessary under mandatory reporting laws to report abuse or neglect of adults with disabilities to such agencies, a provider or specific human service agency having jurisdiction would be wise to conduct its own investigation. However, where abuse may amount to criminal conduct, police should be involved even if they have little experience; they should receive training to inform and sensitize them on the issues unique to people with disabilities and human service systems.

Role and Purpose of the Investigation   The purposes for which one agency requires an investigation may not be adequately served by another agency's investigation. Agencies responsible for direct services need to know not only what happened but why, in order to determine appropriate corrective or personnel action. For example, a police report or a P & A agency report may not provide the necessary information or even be accessible at the appropriate time. Conversely, a P & A agency may be looking at other issues that would not be covered in a provider or police report or even in a state agency investigation report. In general, however, licensing agencies and provider agencies should have sufficient mutuality of interest that either may rely on the other's investigation.

When more than one agency is compelled to conduct an investigation because of differing needs, the agencies should conduct a joint investigation. If that is not possible, the two investigations should still be coordinated, with one identified as primary and the other as supplemental.

Authority of the Entity   As a general rule, the agency conducting the investigation should have authority to carry out all aspects of the investigation (e.g., interview all witnesses; access records, including personnel records; conduct announced and unannounced site visits; acquire and hold physical evidence and original documents). Although the provider clearly has that authority, the provider may not necessarily be the best entity to conduct the investigation.

Conflicts of Interest or Bias   It is not always a conflict of interest when an agency investigates abuse or neglect occurring within its organization or an organization it licenses or funds. Situations exist, however, in which actual or perceived conflict makes it prudent to have another agency perform an investigation (e.g., high-profile cases that appear to be part of a pattern of abuse, cases in which the allegations point to culpability of senior staff). If stakeholders or the public strongly perceive a bias or conflict, no matter how impartial and thorough the investigation is in reality, findings may not be widely accepted. It is important to keep in mind that an agency that is external is not immune from bias or conflict. Given the often political and even partisan environment in which human services agencies operate, external agencies are not immune from particular agendas and bias.

Nature of the Incident   Who conducts an investigation should also depend on the nature of the incident, its severity, and its frequency. Certain classes of offenses generally demand an external investigation:

- Cases in which the harm resulting from the abuse or neglect is severe (e.g., fractures, burns)

- Cases in which the conduct of the alleged perpetrator was willful, intentional, or reckless, as opposed to unintentional or as the result of simple neglect

- Cases in which there is a pattern or recurrence of injuries, even if they are minor

Although the nature of the incident may have some appeal as a sole criterion, it should not be considered without regard to the other factors. Providers or agencies that have good track records in investigations can be considered even in serious cases.

The Status of the Alleged Perpetrator   Although the primary focus of this chapter is abuse or neglect committed by caregivers employed or connected with service providers, two other categories of perpetration raise particular issues in determining the appropriate investigations organization. The first category is composed of natural caregivers who are not connected to the human service system, such as parents, guardians, relatives, or individuals who have assumed a caregiving role (e.g., a friend or another individual, with or without the informed consent of the person with disabilities). One of several agencies may be appropriate to investigate caregiver abuse or neglect in these situations—an agency that serves the individuals who have the same or similar disabilities or a generic adult protective services agency. Whichever agency has sole or chief responsibility, it is important that the investigators or protective service workers have

1. Additional training to deal with these situations. Risk assessment skills are particularly critical.

2. Clear general authority to investigate these cases

3. Specific authority to carry out necessary functions immediately and promptly (e.g., entering the home, interviewing the alleged abuser, seeking and obtaining protective or other court orders when there are site or interview access problems, intervening when there is a refusal to accept voluntary services for children or for adults who are potentially incompetent, intervening when a possible coercive situation exists)

   The second category of potential abusers are individuals who do not have a caregiving status toward the person who experienced the abuse or neglect. It could be someone who is known to the person or a stranger. Generally, if the acts amount to criminal conduct, then the matter should be referred to law enforcement. For either of the two categories of alleged perpetrators, investigations should determine whether any action or omission on the part of paid caregivers, including state personnel (e.g., case managers) contributed to the abuse (e.g., failure to heed early warning signs). An investigation could be warranted on that basis.

Two Proposals

To address the factors discussed above, two arrangements appear to be the most viable: a single, generic agency or a hybrid external–internal investigation system.

MODEL 1

One investigative or protective service agency performs all investigations involving caregiver abuse and neglect, which may either be

- Wholly generic and covering children, older adults, adults with disabilities, or a combination of children and adults
- A single specialized agency that investigates all reported alleged caregiver abuse and neglect cases against individuals with disabilities

The investigative agency should have its investigations audited by a private or public sector organization periodically to ensure quality and impartiality, much in the same way that agency budgets and finances are periodically audited.

MODEL 2

All cases of alleged abuse or neglect are reported to an external agency, which may be a funding, licensing, generic or disability-oriented investigation or quality assurance agency. (This is in addition to staff reporting within a provider to ensure, among other things, the initiations of initial or immediate actions.) Intake personnel make dispositions from the types of options listed in Table 6.2. Except in the minority of cases in which deferral is warranted, investigations would be assigned either to the provider responsible for the facility in which the alleged abuse or neglect occurred or to an external agency. The assignment would be based primarily on two criteria: the track record of the provider and the nature of the reported incident.

These two criteria interact in several ways. If the provider had demonstrated excellent capacity on serious cases, then the provider could be assigned most or all of the investigations. Conversely, an agency that had a mediocre track record would not receive any cases, unless on limited investigation assignments over time, they began to demonstrate enhanced commitment and competence. To err on the safe side, the "trial cases" could be ones in which the external agency is also performing an investigation.

To address possible pervasive incentives, agencies that had a poor track record, requiring the external agency to do the investigation, would be penalized monetarily for all or a portion of the time the external agency spent on investigations that normally would be handled by the provider. To determine the capacity and competency of the provider agency to conduct investigations, random audits of a sufficient number of provider investigations would be conducted to determine their quality and impartiality. Similarly, the external investigative entity should have its investigations audited as per Model 1.

Under either model, deferral by the external agency would still be necessary to other external or sister agencies (e.g., public health, adult protective services, state police, medical examiner), and protocols or interagency agreements should be developed accordingly.

Advantages of Each Model   Each proposal can theoretically work if designed and operationalized properly. The advantages to Model 1 are

1.   Uniformity of investigations across the service delivery system(s)

2.   Cost efficiency

3.   Uniform quality

The potential disadvantages include timeline compliance and loss of specialization. In addition, although this type of model may be the purest and addresses the internal and external debate, it has the disadvantage of often being difficult to institute because one has to effectively consolidate any number of pre-existing units or agencies into one. Massachusetts and New Hampshire have unsuccessfully attempted such an approach. Their experience suggests attention to two key issues:

•   The larger the agency and the more removed it is from the field, the greater its problems will be with timeline compliance and growing case backlogs.

•   Excellent training and some degree of specialization within such a model is necessary to counteract the expertise that is lost when smaller, more categorically focused agencies are consolidated.

The advantages to Model 2 are

1.   Provider investigators encounter fewer problems in gaining access (e.g., scheduling interviews) and performing timely investigations than government agencies.

2.   It is consistent with the sound management principles of keeping the investigative and remedial functions at the level of first accountability (i.e., the entity responsible for caring and serving individuals).

3.   It can be implemented without a major overhaul of government agencies or relationships.

4.   It frees up government and independent investigators to concentrate on more serious or repeat problems.

The disadvantages of Model 2 have been noted in the description of the model— the disincentive for an agency to develop capacity to do its own investigations. Empirical research evaluating the efficacy of these and other models is greatly needed to better answer these and other concerns.

Organizational Supports Needed for an Investigations System

The management and support functions that need to be in place for a successful investigations operation are those found in any successful private or public sector professional service or human resource-intensive organization: a comprehensive set of policies and procedures (as a manual), a sufficient number and mix of staff, appropriate training, consistent and accessible supervision, and a reliable and comprehensive management information system (MIS). Although all of these topics are equally important, several aspects of staffing and training are highlighted in the following sections.

Staffing Investigations   The number and, to some degree, the type of staff necessary to perform investigation and ancillary functions will vary depending on the nature and size of the organization and volume of cases. Sufficient numbers and types of staff must be available to address all functions of investigations, including

- Intake, with the capacity to receive calls 24 hours per day

- Ability to address serious emergency situations (e.g., ability to be immediately on the scene in case of a suspicious death)

- Investigator caseloads of no more than 20–30 investigations per year when the caseload is made up of primarily serious and complicated cases

- Supervising investigators who are responsible for supervising no more than six investigators in order to properly perform the supervising functions

- Staff to develop or review and monitor the corrective actions (the functions of which may be done by the provider or the non-investigations departments of the agency)

Training Topics   Several key topics are frequently overlooked in the training of investigative staff: the core values in developmental disabilities, basic writing and interviewing skills, and training by outside experts.

- All investigations staff should receive training in core quality-of-life values and rights, similar to training generally provided to all agency or provider staff. It is essential that investigations staff adhere to the basic axiom that people with disabilities have the same quality-of-life needs and rights as all people.

- Often overlooked in preservice and subsequent training are basic skills in report writing and interviewing, especially for people with communication, cognitive, or emotional impairments.

- Outside professionals or experts (e.g., police investigators) can be an important part of the overall training curriculum for investigation staff, as long as their presentations are clearly linked to the other material being presented. Sometimes, it may be preferable for staff to take certain advanced courses from other agencies (e.g., police academies).

Extent of Training   In addition to ensuring that certain topics are covered in the training of investigations staff, the extent of training that should be required of all staff should also be considered.

- The length, depth, and breadth of required training should depend in large part on the prior experience of a newly hired employee. A minimum of 1 week is generally needed for an individual with prior experience in investigations, and 2 weeks is needed for someone with little or no experience.

- Preservice training should be followed with strong on-the-job-training and follow-up formal training after 3–6 months on the job.

- Investigators should be required to participate in continued in-service or continuing education based on individual professional development plans; such an individualized approach is challenging to implement and may be partially replaced by a preset curriculum for particular types of advanced training (e.g., training on police investigation processes).

CONCLUSION

Developing a strong system for investigating incidents of abuse or neglect is a challenging task. Zero tolerance for abuse and neglect should be firmly embedded in the culture of human service systems as well as in society as a whole. An investigation should never be seen as an end to itself but as a critical element to deter wrongful or neglectful conduct and also to learn from and prevent victimization in the future.

CHAPTER 7

Helping People
Be Happy and Safe

ACCOUNTING FOR HEALTH AND
SAFETY IN HOW PEOPLE WANT TO LIVE

MICHAEL W. SMULL

Happy and dead are incompatible; alive and miserable are unacceptable.

The perception persists that developing and implementing a person-centered plan requires that professionals honor choice and ignore issues of health or safety when they conflict with choice. This is not the case. Part of the power of good person-centered planning is that it offers a more effective approach to looking at issues of health and safety. A key concept is the relationship between what is important *to* and what is important *for* people; helping people have more of what is important *to* them makes them more willing to work with staff on what is important *for* them. When issues of health and safety are complex and when they are rooted in the person's disability, using what is important *to* the person as the context within which problem solving occurs can increase the person's quality of life, while still helping him or her to stay healthy and safe. Knowing how to do this is the first of three related skills that help staff (those who plan, manage, or provide services to support people with disabilities) in moving toward the lives that people want, while accounting for issues of health and safety.

The second skill is the ability to look at what is happening in the life of a person using services at any moment in time and to determine what is and is not working from the perspectives of each of the key stakeholders. Doing this provides a framework for problem solving that has embedded in it two of the key principles of negotiation: everyone feels heard, and the starting point is common ground. The third skill is following a process to create clarity about roles and responsibilities for direct support staff. Using a structured process, those who plan and manage look at what is expected of those who provide support and sort the expectations into 1) what should be done without error, 2) when the expectation is to use judgment and creativity, and 3) what should not be seen as the responsibility of those who are paid. Each of these skills can be practiced at increasing levels of sophistication. For example, the author conducts an initial 3- to 4-day training to teach paid staff to write plans that detail what is important to and for the individual as well as what needs to change and what needs to stay the same. This training is followed by mentoring and coaching with structured practice and feedback. This chapter offers ways to introduce the skills and give participants a framework for looking at the supports and services that they provide. Although the entire training is not described here, the following text serves as a good introduction.

TRAINING STAFF TO HELP PEOPLE BE SAFE AND HAPPY

Much of the difficulty that staff face in learning this approach comes from patterns of thinking and behavior embedded in typical practice and organizational culture. Maurice's story illustrates how these patterns can be traps.

Maurice is a soft-spoken man who is quite determined to get what is important to him. I was asked to look at his circumstances because staff were restraining him to keep him safe. Maurice lives in a group home in a climate where winter is very cold and the temperature is often well below 0° F. From time to time, Maurice insisted on leaving his home to walk to the store and would not wait for staff to drive him. Even wearing his warm winter coat, he was at risk of serious frostbite. Staff had a protocol that began with their asking him to wait until they could drive him, but that usually did not work. In order to stop him from leaving, they often had to resort to physical restraint. This was the description that was initially provided, and if it was all of the information that was available, then it would seem that staff were justified in physically stopping Maurice in order to keep him safe. However, when I looked with a small group of people at what is important to Maurice, we found that a critical part of his morning routine was to have toast and jam for breakfast. To Maurice, there was no acceptable substitute for toast and jam, and the group home regularly ran out of jam. When Maurice got up in the morning and found there was no jam, he would put on his coat and head for the door. Staff rationalized their approach by saying that it was important for Maurice to learn patience, but Maurice was expressing with his behavior that it was important to him to have the breakfast that he wanted.

Ignoring what was important to Maurice led to a power struggle rather than simple problem solving. Once those supporting Maurice took a step back, they could see that buying two jars of jam would meet Maurice's needs. The situation went from a lose-lose situation to a win-win situation because Maurice had something that was important to him, and staff no longer needed to try to stop him from leaving the house. From the perspective of the agency, the investment in another jar of jam meant that Maurice was no longer at risk of injury from the cold or from being restrained, and staff were happier because they no longer had to enforce a rule that made no sense.

In this situation and dozens of others with which the author has been asked to help over the years, obvious answers emerged when the situation was examined through the lenses of both what is important to and what is important for, and yet those answers had eluded direct support staff, their managers, and their consultants. It seems that everyone has been so immersed in a culture of control that only focuses on what is important *for* the person that they never take a step back and look at the situations in a manner that also accounts for what is important *to* the person. In fact, this singular focus had an odd effect. When staff hear that they are to also focus on what is important *to* the person, they often stop paying attention to what is important *for* the person. Part of this is caused by an aspect of the organizational culture, which expects problem solving to be done by managers and professional staff and does not meaningfully engage direct support staff. The combination of staff skill deficits and organizational culture creates the mythology that person-centered planning puts people who use services at risk of being hurt. If those people who use services are to be happy and safe, then both the skill deficits and the issues in organizational culture have to be addressed.

An outline follows for training that will help staff—those who are paid to provide, manage, and plan for services—acquire the skills and knowledge needed to move from a single focus to the ability to perceive a reasonable balance of both perspectives. The exercises begin to chip away at issues of organizational culture by changing the role of the direct support staff. The exercises and material that follow do not provide training in person-centered planning— they provide training in person-centered thinking. Practice in changing how staff think about these issues is the key to changing the practices in how staff work. Those who wish to use the material are welcome to do so, with two cautions: 1) those who teach need a deeper understanding of the material than those who apply it in everyday life and 2) they need to practice the exercises in front of a small, friendly, but critical audience before using them with large groups. (See specific use limitations for each exercise on the copyright page of this volume.)

INTRODUCING THE CONCEPTS

The following three figures introduce the concepts. Figure 7.1 illustrates where the field has been. In the past, the service system has typically grouped people according to disability issues. People who have similar issues live to-

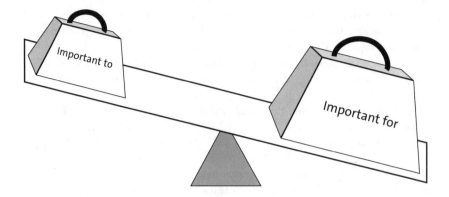

Health and safety dictate lifestyle.

This is where we were. "Important for" includes not only issues of health and safety but also what others see as being important for the person. These may range from how someone dresses to how he or she spends his or her days.

Figure 7.1.   The field's customary priorities. (Smull & Allen, 2002; Copyright © 2002 Smull & Allen; reprinted with permission.)

gether and spend time during the day together. Those things that are important for the person, as part of the group of "similar" people, are given much more weight than those things that are important to the person. Within this context, what is important to a person refers to those things that the individual is paying attention to, those things that he or she is expressing with words or behaviors. It does not include those things that professionals think should be important to the person.

Issues of health or safety compose most of what is important for the person, but what is important for him or her also includes things that help the person be a valued member of his or her community, even when the person is not paying attention to them. An example would be someone who dresses for the weather but not for the occasion. If staff were helping that person go on a job interview, it might be important to help him or her select attire that goes with the job.

Figure 7.2 illustrates the point that, although the system needs to move away from having issues of health and safety dictate lifestyle, it also must avoid having people hurt in the name of choice. Examples can illustrate how this is true for everyone. The trainer should think of simple examples from his or her own life, then ask the trainees to think of examples from their lives and the lives of those that they support. It is important to keep in mind that these simple figures represent complex concepts; understanding the basic ideas is an essential step before moving into complex examples, such as the interactions

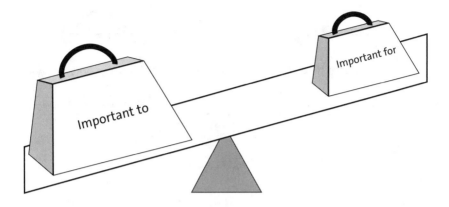

All choice, no responsibility, dictates lifestyle.

This is what we need to avoid. One mistaken assumption about person-centered planning is that we only listen to what is important to the person and ignore what is important for him or her.

Figure 7.2.   What the field should avoid. (Smull & Allen, 2002; Copyright © 2002 Smull & Allen; reprinted with permission.)

among competence, informed choice, and what might be described as the right to go to hell in your own hand basket.

Figure 7.3 represents the goal for all individuals, whether they have disabilities or not—this is about supporting humans, not just about supporting people with disabilities. If time and circumstances permit, trainees should discuss the idea of balance and how it works within their own lives. How to achieve this balance is the focus of the rest of the training.

HOW NOT HAVING WHAT IS IMPORTANT AFFECTS HEALTH AND SAFETY

Those who plan for and those who provide services need to understand that not having what is important to one in everyday life often has a negative impact on health or safety. This applies to all individuals, not just to people with disabilities. As Figure 7.4 suggests, all people are supported, and all people contribute to their communities. Work is only one way to contribute; another way is through relationships. Trainees should take time to briefly discuss the varied ways that people give and receive support and how they make their contributions. It is important to help people see that the support that they give to others is part of what they contribute, and the support that they receive is part of what others contribute to them.

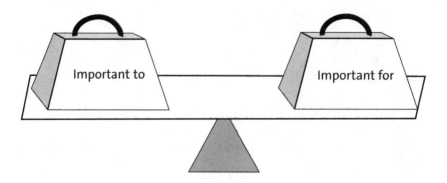

Balance should dictate lifestyle.

What we are seeking for each person is balance. This is what we seek in our own lives. When our lives feel out of balance, we look to see what we can change to get a better balance. We are trying to do for others what we do for ourselves. It requires that we know both what is important to the person and what is important for him or her and that we recognize that this is an ever shifting balance.

Figure 7.3.   The goal for all individuals. (Smull & Allen, 2002; Copyright © 2002 Smull & Allen; reprinted with permission.)

Figure 7.4 illustrates that the hierarchy within the triangle rests on feeling healthy and safe on one's own terms—nearly everyone engages in behaviors that others say are either not healthy or not safe. The trainer should pose a series of questions such as

- How many people feel that they would benefit from losing weight?

- How many are planning to do it at some nebulous future date?

- How many are doing it right now?

- How many people, when they have had a bad day, go home and eat or drink something fattening?

- What would happen if it was not just a bad day but a bad year?

- If the trainer arrived in the middle of that bad year and said to those who were gaining weight, "Time for a 1,200 calorie diet!", would that improve the bad year?

To help trainees to further see the relationship between what is important to people and what is important for people, the trainer should lead them in an exercise known as "driving each other crazy."

Each of us wants to live lives in which we:

(with apologies to Abraham Maslow)

It is about people, not about "disability." It is true for all of us.

- We all need and receive support.
- We all contribute—not just through our jobs but also through our relationships and how we spend time.
- Do the people who use services get the support that they need to have opportunities to contribute?

The triangle:

- Walk through from top to bottom.
- Note how "dreams" change as things are missing (e.g., my dream is to live somewhere I feel safe).
- Emphasize how having what is important relates to being healthy and safe. When things that are important to a person are missing, he or she often acts in ways that are contrary to what is important for him or her.

Ask: How many of you eat or drink something fattening as a way to comfort yourself after a bad day? What would happen if you had a bad year or a bad decade? Use this relationship between what is important and health and safety as the transition to driving each other crazy (Exercise 1).

Figure 7.4.   Ways in which all people are supported by and contribute to their communities. (Smull & Allen, 2002; Copyright © 2002 Smull & Allen; reprinted with permission.)

EXERCISE 1

Driving Each Other Crazy

The goals of this exercise are to help participants

- Understand how a person-centered plan is a promise and that plans that are developed but not implemented represent a betrayal of trust

- See what the effects of being powerless and not listened to would be on their own lives (and see the effects on other people who are also not labeled)

- Understand that an entire constellation of behaviors and "symptoms" (e.g., hitting other people, breaking things, withdrawal, being desperate to please) may be a response to years of not being listened to and feeling powerless

Cautionary Note

Done well, this is a powerful exercise that causes people to understand what it is like to be powerless and ignored. It then puts them in touch with their responses, which can range from outwardly expressed rage, to inwardly directed self-destruction, to desperate attempts to "get along." It ends with asking what would need to happen after they had been betrayed by a facilitator of plans who they had trusted. This exercise is too depressing to do last, whether it is the last in a series of activities or at the end of the day. It should be done early, and toward the end of the training, the trainer should remind people how they felt. This exercise should only be done as a stand-alone activity if there is enough time to help people process what they would do to make sure the situation does not occur with the people who they support. This exercise is designed to make people who have power and control feel temporarily helpless. It is not designed to remind self-advocates of how disempowered they were (and occasionally still are). This exercise will not work in situations in which people are afraid of self-disclosure.

Logistics

The exercise can be done with small groups or with large groups. It requires a minimum of 20 minutes but can take an hour, offering more opportunities for discussion. The facilitator needs markers and either flip chart paper, "wall paper," or

From Michael Smull and William Allen. (1998). *Essential Lifestyle Planning: A Trainer's Guide for Facilitator Training* (pp. 48–50). Napa, CA: Authors. Adapted by permission. Copyright © 1998 by Michael Smull and William Allen.

blank transparencies. It works best with six or seven sheets of flip chart paper posted in advance, with one person recording while someone else leads the exercise.

The Exercise in Detail

Start by asking people

- What behaviors or habits irritate you?

- What are the things that other people do that are like fingernails on a black-board or that make you swear?

- What are the things that drive you crazy whether at work, at home, or while out?

As people share their answers, write them down. Fill up the page. Encourage people to share until the group begins to run out of contributions. Then tell people

> *Imagine you are now living in a place where all of these things happen. [Read out some of the items strung together as a description of what happens there.] For example, you are living some place where the people who are in charge are always whining. They never listen to you and are rude and condescending while they lie to you. You are surrounded by people who eat with their mouths open and pop their chewing gum while they click their pens, and so forth. All of these behaviors are present, and other behaviors that you thought about but did not share are also present. However, you cannot leave this place. You have to stay. How do you feel, and how do you show other people how you feel? Remember, the question is how do you feel, and not how would another person feel.*

Write down the responses and then review them, letting the participants know how the system that runs this imagined place would respond to their behaviors. The general rules for the system responses are as follows:

- People who are aggressive are allowed to move but to someplace where what makes them crazy happens more, where they get some medication (e.g., Mellaril), and where the place is locked.

- People who run away are caught and moved to the same place that the aggressive people have moved to, a place that is locked.

From Michael Smull and William Allen. (1998). *Essential Lifestyle Planning: A Trainer's Guide for Facilitator Training* (pp. 48–50). Napa, CA: Authors. Adapted by permission. Copyright © 1998 by Michael Smull and William Allen.

- People who scream, are "noncompliant," or exhibit other similar behaviors are subjected to a behavior program in which something that is important to them is taken away. They have to earn its return by not screaming, but there is no change in their setting.

- People who are passive get ignored.

- People who withdraw get a socialization program run by a staff person who is particularly irritating.

- People who try to please are praised but still see no change in the behaviors they have to tolerate.

Then tell the participants

> It is now a year later, and nothing has changed. The behaviors that drive you crazy are still present. No one has acted on your distress except as was just described. How do you feel and how do you behave? What are you doing? Again, remember the question is how do you feel, and not how another person would feel.

Write down the responses and go over them, applying the same kind of rules. Severe depression will get medication; self-injury, a restrictive program; physical illness will get medical treatment. The general rule is that this system will respond to symptoms but not causes. Then tell the participants

> It is now 5 years later. The behaviors that make you crazy are still going on. But now someone comes and does a person-centered plan with you. This person is truly gifted at listening and hears what you are saying with words and behaviors. The planner hears your distress and captures it on paper. The plan is reviewed with you and you discover that it not only says just what makes you crazy but also says what needs to change so that these behaviors will no longer be part of your life. After this remarkable experience, the planner leaves, giving the plan to the facility manager on the way out. The facility manager says, "Just what I needed for the people from licensing who are coming next week." The plan goes into your file folder, but nothing really changes, and everything goes back to the way it was. Now, how do you feel and how do you behave?

Write down the responses and read them back to the participants. Emphasize the themes in how people feel. Then tell the participants

From Michael Smull and William Allen. (1998). *Essential Lifestyle Planning: A Trainer's Guide for Facilitator Training* (pp. 48–50). Napa, CA: Authors. Adapted by permission. Copyright © 1998 by Michael Smull and William Allen.

This is a place like those found in the soap operas. The first planner was actually the evil twin of the real planner. The manager was told by licensing to implement the plans or look for other work and says, "Finally, now I have permission to do what I always wanted to do." The planner is eager to make good plans, and the manager is ready to implement them—what will it take for you to trust them?

Write down what the participants share.

Alternative Endings

If time allows, facilitate a discussion. Ask the group what they learned and write their answers down. Point out that doing a good person-centered plan is making a kind of promise and that it is better to not make any plan than to make a plan without commitment to implement what has been learned. Be sure to point out that much of the challenging behavior that people exhibit is explained by this exercise. Emphasize how the group demonstrated that the absence of what was important to them caused most of them to behave in ways that made them less healthy or safe. Note that what they shared at the end of the exercise are the strategies that need to be used when planning with people who have had plans that were not implemented. If time has run out, just review what people shared at the end but do it from the perspective of the people that receive support. Cover the same points as previously noted by helping the group to articulate them.

From Michael Smull and William Allen. (1998). *Essential Lifestyle Planning: A Trainer's Guide for Facilitator Training* (pp. 48–50). Napa, CA: Authors. Adapted by permission. Copyright © 1998 by Michael Smull and William Allen.

Developing Skills

Once people have been sensitized to the issues, they need to begin to develop skills to address them. What follows are ways to introduce the skills and give participants a framework for looking at the supports and services that they provide. The training uses vignettes, brief descriptions of a person and his or her circumstances, as the core of each exercise. Those who wish to do this training are welcome to use the vignettes that follow or develop their own. Stories that the trainer personally knows are more powerful, but each story needs to be tested to make sure it works as intended. Nearly all of the exercises use the same framework.

- The relevant material to do the exercise is embedded in the story.

- After telling the story, the conceptual framework is presented.

- Training participants are guided in using the information from the story within the conceptual framework.

- The group discusses the process, outcome, and applicability of the exercise.

Trainers who are using their own stories should test them in front of a small, friendly audience to make sure that they have the information needed and that the stories do not unintentionally support antithetical outcomes and are not confusing. The exercises and activities are not all of the training that is needed but serve as a good introduction.

Introducing Skills Using Julie's Story   Julie's story, in Exercise 2, helps introduce the first two skills. People can see how presenting information in the frame of what does and does not make sense leads to problem solving and begins to build skills in sorting out what is important to and what is important for a person.

EXERCISE 2

Julie is a woman in love for the first time. She has spent most of her life in an institution in which she had no close relationships. Efforts to help Julie develop relationships have been unsuccessful. Her medical issues have occupied much of the attention of those who support her and have limited what she has been able to do. About 2 years ago, she moved from the institution to a group home, where she met Teddy the Yorkshire terrier. Teddy was the group home manager's dog, but when the manager moved, Teddy stayed. Figure 7.5 summarizes how life was going for Julie at one point in time.

Let people read this on their own and then point out to people that life for Julie is going as well as it ever has. Help people see that the left side (what makes sense) of the framework in Figure 7.5 gives the people who are paid to support Julie credit for their accomplishments. Although Julie's life is going better than it ever has before, there is room for improvement. The issue that participants should address is that of Teddy being shut in another room during meals. Walk through what is noted about Julie and Teddy. The severity of Julie's diabetes requires that her food be weighed so that staff know how much insulin to give her. When Julie feeds Teddy off of her plate, it thwarts the purpose of weighing her food. In response, staff put Teddy in another room while Julie eats. This makes Julie unhappy (which adversely affects her blood sugar). Some of the other people who live in the house frequently let Teddy out during the meal, and he runs to sit beside Julie, who then feeds him from her plate, so again staff do not know the correct amount of insulin.

Ask the people in training what they would do if they were managing that house. Someone should quickly offer the suggestion that the staff create a "Teddy" plate from which Julie could feed Teddy. Point out that he or she just suggested a solution that began with what was important to Julie and accounted for what is important for Julie. Set up flip chart paper so that it looks like Figure 7.6. Ask people to tell you what is important to Julie, what is important for Julie, and what else they would need to learn or know. As people make suggestions, record them where they make sense. If people suggest something as being important *to* Julie that is important *for* her, have a discussion. Remind people that things that are important to her are those things that she is paying attention to. It is limited to those things she is saying with her words or behavior. When the information is not present, then it is something that is recorded under "What else do you need to learn or know?" As people run out of things to add, point out that the things that people need to learn are largely known by those who spend the most time with Julie.

"Helping People Be Happy and Safe: Accounting for Health and Safety in How People Want to Live" by Michael Smull. In **Quality Enhancement in Developmental Disabilities: Challenges and Opportunities in a Changing World** edited by Valerie J. Bradley and Madeleine Kimmich. Baltimore: Paul H. Brookes Publishing Co. Exercise copyright © 2003 by Michael Smull.

	What makes sense? What works? What needs to be maintained? (*The upside right now*)	What doesn't make sense? What doesn't work? What needs to change? (*The downside right now*)
From Julie's perspective	Shopping as often as possible, daily even, for favorite things Having lots of jewelry and watches to choose from and no one getting into them until I say it's okay Having my sister, Joanne, who lives in Seattle, in my life Lots of clothes in my favorite colors: blue, red, and black Getting my nails polished in many colors and layers Living with my new friend, Teddy the Yorkshire • Sleeping on my bed at night • Eating snacks from my plate • Laying in my lap	Staff not letting me drink whatever I want Teddy having to go in the other room during mealtimes Whenever there is no work to do at the workshop When I go shopping, staff not letting me buy some things I want
From staff perspective	Doing activities with her favorite people, especially John Dandy Keeping Julie from falling, and reminding her to use her walker Keeping her blood sugar level stable. Staff know Julie's signs of high and low blood sugar Maintaining Joanne as an active person in Julie's life Planning before Julie goes shopping what she is going to buy	Julie is less steady on her feet and falling more than she used to. If staff don't make a plan with Julie, she will want to buy more than she has money for. Julie may get very upset, which can alter her blood sugar level. Julie gives Teddy food off her plate, which means that staff cannot accurately track her nutrition.

Figure 7.5. What is and is not working for Julie, from her own perspective and from the staff's perspective. (Smull & Allen, 2002; Copyright © 2002 Smull & Allen; reprinted with permission.)

What is important to Julie?	What is important for Julie?

What else do you need to learn/know?

Create a flip chart version of this figure and ask the audience to answer these questions. Record their answers.

Then, go to Figure 7.7 and lead a discussion around what are the core responsibilities, where are judgment and creativity used, and what is not our paid responsibility.

Figure 7.6.   Discussion chart for Julie's story in Exercise 2. (Smull & Allen, 2002; Copyright © 2002 Smull & Allen; reprinted with permission.)

The Doughnut Principle

As noted previously, one of the common challenges in helping staff find a balance in supporting people who use services is keeping them from getting stuck in looking at just what is important to or just what is important for a person being supported. When they only look at what is important to a person who is being supported, they often use choice as an excuse. What is important for the person is ignored, and people who use services are put at unnecessary risk and perhaps injured. At the same time, because a balance is needed between what is important to and what is important for a person, it is also crucial that those who are paid be creative in helping people become better connected to their communities. All of these expectations together create an acute need for clarity regarding the expectations of performance and behavior for those who provide the support. The exercise that follows is designed to help participants understand how to get such clarity. It is derived from Charles Handy's doughnut principle (Handy, 1995) and has been adapted by Smull and Allen (2002).

EXERCISE 3

The exercise can be done with a group of almost any size. It requires that the "doughnut principle" be displayed (see Figure 7.7). The facilitator explains what is meant by each of the labels.

- Core responsibilities: Those things that staff are expected to always do. Failure to do them will result in discipline and/or dismissal. (Be careful to point out that staff should not be punished for things that they did or did not do only because it was determined to be a core responsibility after the event.)

- Judgment and creativity: Areas in which staff are expected to make decisions about both whether to do something and how to do it, using their own judgment and creativity. If they get it wrong, the expectation is that managers will see what can be learned from the experience, rather than punishing the staff.

- Not our paid responsibility: Just what it says. Areas in which staff have no paid responsibility for what happens. (This is the domain of friends, those whose power lies only in the relationship.)

Introduce the concepts by telling Janice's story and then displaying the doughnut that illustrates how the issues were sorted.

> *Janice is a self-advocate who has been described as a busy woman who would like to be busier. She is fiercely independent but is always ready to help others. She had wanted to move from her mother's house for some time, and, when she was 24, she got an opportunity to do so. A local agency was willing to help Janice live in her own apartment with a paid roommate. Janice was very excited by the prospect and her mother was supportive but also concerned. Janice has a form of cerebral palsy referred to as "rag doll syndrome" and needs assistance in all areas of daily living. She is quite skilled in driving her power chair and communicates very clearly as long as she has her Delta Talker.*

Janice's doughnut shows that part of staff's core responsibility is caring for the G-tube that Janice uses to eat (see Figure 7.8). Point out that, in 24 years, there has been no skin breakdown around the G-tube, and, if there were, the staff person would have been dismissed. Also note that, although the graphic is an excellent way to present the concepts, it is not the best way to list the responsibilities. For example, among the core responsibilities that are not listed is making sure that Janice gets 1,500 cubic centimeters of fluid per day through the G-tube. Janice cannot take in anything by mouth and does not feel thirsty. It is the staff's responsibility to keep track of fluid intake. Also point out that learning how Janice

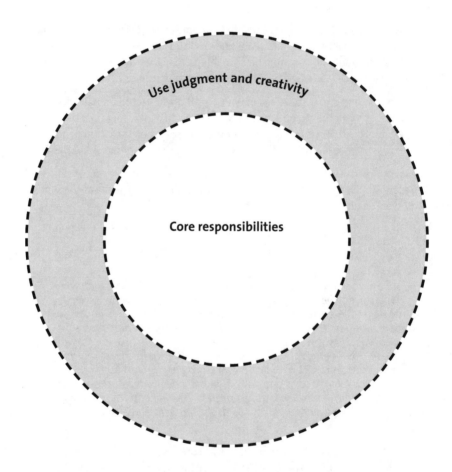

**Not our "paid" responsibility
(Domain of friends)**

Use judgment and creativity

Core responsibilities

This is used to introduce the doughnut principle. Do the doughnut exercise using stories that will work for your audience.

Figure 7.7.   The doughnut principle. (Handy, 1995; Smull & Allen, 2002; Copyright © 2002 Smull & Allen; reprinted with permission.)

**Not our "paid" responsibility
(Domain of friends)**

- Don't interfere with the private time I spend with my friends. I don't need an interpreter. They are my friends and we communicate.
- Don't interfere with how I choose to handle the love interests in my life. I will ask for any advice I want and from whom I want it.

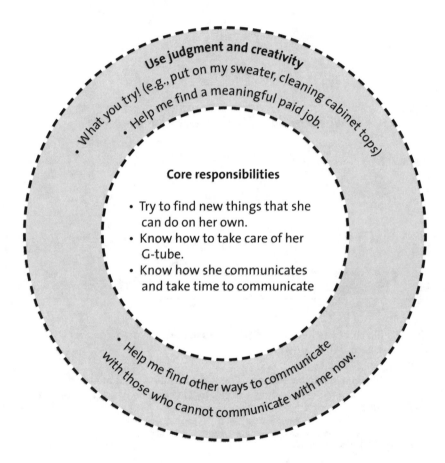

Use judgment and creativity

- What you try! (e.g., put on my sweater, cleaning cabinet tops)
- Help me find a meaningful paid job.

Core responsibilities

- Try to find new things that she can do on her own.
- Know how to take care of her G-tube.
- Know how she communicates and take time to communicate

- Help me find other ways to communicate with those who cannot communicate with me now.

This is used to introduce the doughnut principle. Do the doughnut exercise using stories that will work for your audience.

Figure 7.8.   Janice's doughnut. (Smull & Allen, 2002; Copyright © 2002 Smull & Allen; reprinted with permission.)

What is important to Janice?	What is important for Janice?

What else do you need to learn/know?

Create a flip chart version of this figure and ask the audience to answer these questions. Record their answers.

Then, go to Figure 7.7 again and lead a discussion around what are the core responsibilities, where are judgment and creativity used, and what is not our paid responsibility.

Figure 7.9. Discussion chart for Janice's story in Exercise 3. (Smull & Allen, 2002; Copyright © 2002 Smull & Allen; reprinted with permission.)

communicates and taking the time to communicate with her is a core responsibility, but helping her find new ways to communicate is part of judgment and creativity. Similarly, helping her find new things that she can do on her own is a core responsibility, but figuring out what to try is a part of judgment and creativity. Although Janice needs a lot of assistance in accomplishing physical tasks, she does not want staff to interfere with her social life. How she spends time with her friends and who she dates (or talks to about dating) is not part of the responsibility of those who are paid.

After you have reviewed this with the training participants, give them a handout that looks like Figure 7.9. Have your own version completed and after the participants have had a few moments to work on theirs, share yours with them.

What is important to Janice?	What is important for Janice?
To be independent—to do everything she can on her own To be understood and have people take the time to understand her To have a typical life for someone her age	To stay healthy by having paid people help her To be helped with all activities of daily living To ensure that there is no skin breakdown To ensure that she gets 1,500 cubic centimeters of fluid per day
What else do you need to learn/know?	

Figure 7.10.   A partial list of what is important to Janice, what is important for Janice, and what other information is needed. (Smull & Allen, 2002; Copyright © 2002 Smull & Allen; reprinted with permission.)

"Helping People Be Happy and Safe: Accounting for Health and Safety in How People Want to Live" by Michael Smull. In **Quality Enhancement in Developmental Disabilities: Challenges and Opportunities in a Changing World** edited by Valerie J. Bradley and Madeleine Kimmich. Baltimore: Paul H. Brookes Publishing Co. Exercise copyright © 2003 by Michael Smull.

Ask them how they did. A partial list for Janice is shown as Figure 7.10. Now ask people to listen to Bob's story. Tell them to imagine that they are Bob's support coordinator, and they are going to figure out what their responsibilities are in Bob's situation.

> *You are a support coordinator who has just been asked to work with Bob. Bob is an articulate man in his mid-twenties who has a mild cognitive impairment. Very early on in your conversations, you learn that Bob has bipolar disorder, which is largely (but not completely) controlled by medication. As you talk with Bob, you find that it is very important to him to have a typical life that includes going out to a neighborhood bar on the weekends. Bob's descriptions of an evening at the bar are filled with talk about playing pool and spending time with friends. It is clear that this is how he stays connected with some of his friends. As you continue to listen, you find that talking about drinking is more important to Bob than actually drinking, but that Bob often has a couple of beers on a weekend night. On at least one occasion, he has had four or five beers. Bob also tells you that he stops taking his medication on Friday mornings (he starts again on Sundays), because he knows that he is not supposed to drink when taking these medications. Bob has been hospitalized because of his bipolar disorder, and there is some indication in the records that these hospitalizations happened after Bob stopped taking his medications. Bob recently moved out of the family house and lives with his girlfriend. He is his own guardian and does not have a good relationship with his parents. His girlfriend can tell you the indications of Bob becoming manic (the beginning of a cycle for him) and the signs of depression. She can also tell you what she does when that happens.*

Set up flip chart paper so that it looks like Figure 7.11 and facilitate completion of it. Help people work through the placement of items if their suggestion is different from your sense of the proper location. Keep in mind that participants may make suggestions that you have not thought of. If you are not sure if what is being suggested is correct, ask the participants what they think and listen carefully. When this part is completed, point out to the participants that more items are listed under "What else do you need to learn/know?" than in the other areas. Help people see that answers that work for people with complex issues typically require more information than is available at the beginning. A partially completed list is shown in Figure 7.12.

Now ask people to complete a doughnut on the responsibilities that they would have as the case manager. Use the doughnut from Figure 7.7 to remind the participants of the concepts but put up three sheets of flip chart paper as shown in Figure 7.13 to actually record the responsibilities. This works best if someone other than the trainer records what is to be written, while the trainer facilitates

"Helping People Be Happy and Safe: Accounting for Health and Safety in How People Want to Live" by Michael Smull. In **Quality Enhancement in Developmental Disabilities: Challenges and Opportunities in a Changing World** edited by Valerie J. Bradley and Madeleine Kimmich. Baltimore: Paul H. Brookes Publishing Co. Exercise copyright © 2003 by Michael Smull.

What is important to Bob?	What is important for Bob?

What else do you need to learn/know?

Create a flip chart version of this figure and ask the audience to answer these questions. Record their answers.

Then, go to Figure 7.7 again and lead a discussion around what are the core responsibilities, where are judgment and creativity used, and what is not our paid responsibility.

Figure 7.11.   Discussion chart for Bob's story in Exercise 3. (Smull & Allen, 2002; Copyright © 2002 Smull & Allen; reprinted with permission.)

What is important to Bob?	What is important for Bob?
To be one of the guys To keep his friends To be in charge of his own life To have a typical life To stay healthy	To take his medications as prescribed To stay out of the hospital and not cycle To be connected to his community

What else do you need to learn/know?

How dangerous is it for Bob to go off his medications and have a few beers?

Would it be okay for him to drink 1 or 2 beers and be on his medication? Is there another medication that would allow him to have 1 or 2 beers?

How well does Bob understand the risks he is taking?

Would he be willing to drink nonalcoholic beer?

Figure 7.12.   A partial list of what is important to Bob, what is important for Bob, and what other information is needed. (Smull & Allen, 2002; Copyright © 2002 Smull & Allen; reprinted with permission.)

the discussion. As people propose items for each category, the trainer should ask them to test the items against the definitions. For example, for some of the items proposed as core responsibilities, the trainer should ask, "Is this something for which, if it is not done, the support coordinator should be in trouble?" As in the previous exercises, the trainer should have in mind what would go under these headings. A partial list is offered as Figure 7.14.

 "Helping People Be Happy and Safe: Accounting for Health and Safety in How People Want to Live" by Michael Smull. In **Quality Enhancement in Developmental Disabilities: Challenges and Opportunities in a Changing World** edited by Valerie J. Bradley and Madeleine Kimmich. Baltimore: Paul H. Brookes Publishing Co. Exercise copyright © 2003 by Michael Smull.

Core responsibilities	Use judgment and creativity	Not our "paid" responsibility

Figure 7.13. Discussion chart for areas of staff core responsibilities, judgment and creativity, and what are not paid responsibilities. (Smull & Allen, 2002; Copyright © 2002 Smull & Allen; reprinted with permission.)

Core responsibilities	Use judgment and creativity	Not our "paid" responsibility
Helping Bob make an informed choice	Informing Bob of the risks	Deciding whether or not Bob drinks
Informing Bob of the risks of his behavior	Educating yourself	Defining what Bob's psychiatrist does in response to the information
Informing yourself of the actual risks and alternatives	Exploring alternatives	
Working with Bob to ensure that his psychiatrist knows about Bob's drinking	If part of the issue is the response of the psychiatrist, helping Bob find another psychiatrist	
Making an effort to explore with Bob alternative ways to get what is important to him and important for him		

Figure 7.14. A partial exploration of staff core responsibilities, judgment and creativity, and what are not paid responsibilities for Bob in Exercise 3. (Smull & Allen, 2002; Copyright © 2002 Smull & Allen; reprinted with permission.)

Problem Solving and Goal Planning:
What Does and Does Not Make Sense

Those who manage, plan, and provide services are often trapped by

- Being too close to the issues and having no way to step back

- Having a culture of looking at issues as either black or white and thereby missing both what is working and what can change within the current structures

- Feeling powerless to help people make significant changes and coping with that feeling by denying that change needs to happen

- Having been trained to write goals that are compliance-driven (i.e., meeting the perceived requirements of those who inspect programs rather than those of the person receiving services) and thus are unrelated to helping the person to have a life he or she enjoys

The "what makes sense and doesn't make sense" (WMS/DMS) framework directly addresses all but the last of these issues and sets up a mechanism for writing goals that help the person using services get more of what is important to him or her, while nonetheless attending to what is important for him or her. Embedded in the framework are two core principles of negotiation: everyone feels heard and the starting point is common ground (Fisher, Ury, & Patton, 1991). Using this framework requires the learner to become skilled in

- Taking issues and teasing them apart so that what is and is not working within a given setting or situation is explicitly identified

- Being able to do this analysis from multiple perspectives

- Using the information to create goals that assist people in moving toward lives that have a better balance between what is important to them and what is important for them

In the following exercise, the skills are introduced and practiced sequentially. It is important to note, however, that the concepts were introduced earlier with Julie's story. If this training is done in isolation from the other exercises, the trainer should begin by presenting a story with an example of a completed WMS/DMS framework. It is crucial that the discussion that follows uses the framework to produce clarity in a situation and leads to problem solving that gives the person better balance between what is important to and what is important for him or her. Julie's story may be used even if trainers have already seen it, using a shorter version to remind people of the concepts.

EXERCISE 4

Analyzing an Issue, Teasing the Issue Apart, and Creating Balance

Show Figure 7.15 and point out to the participants that we all make decisions in our own lives by weighing what is working and what is not working in a situation. Ask people to reflect on their own relationships. Ask them how many have had more than one job in their lives. How many have had jobs that they quit and moved on? Do they remember that when the job started, what was working far outweighed what was not working? Then, shortly before the job ended, what did not make sense and was not working far outweighed what did work. Weighing what works and makes sense against what does not work or does not make sense is what we all do when making decisions about whether to stay in a situation or

	What makes sense? What works? What needs to be maintained? (*The upside right now*)	What doesn't make sense? What doesn't work? What needs to change? (*The downside right now*)
From the perspective of:		

Figure 7.15. Discussion chart for exploring the "what makes sense and doesn't make sense" (WMS/DMS) framework in Exercise 4. (Smull & Allen, 2002; Copyright © 2002 Smull & Allen; reprinted by permission.)

 "Helping People Be Happy and Safe: Accounting for Health and Safety in How People Want to Live" by Michael Smull. In **Quality Enhancement in Developmental Disabilities: Challenges and Opportunities in a Changing World** edited by Valerie J. Bradley and Madeleine Kimmich. Baltimore: Paul H. Brookes Publishing Co. Exercise copyright © 2003 by Michael Smull.

to leave. This is true throughout people's lives. The participants will be learning how to take a largely unstructured, mostly unconscious process and make it conscious and structured.

To begin to see how it works, take a blank version of Figure 7.16 and ask how many of the participants have ever had a new puppy at home. (If few have had a new puppy, you can also use a new baby as an example.) On the left-hand side of the blank chart, write "From the puppy owner's perspective." Ask the participants to tell you what did and did not make sense about having the new puppy. Using their remarks and spending no more than 5 minutes, generate a list with content similar to that of Figure 7.16. Point out that what does not make sense in the short run causes some people to return the puppy, while others feel that what does make sense outweighs the downside. Note that the reasoning that people use to make all their decisions only becomes clear once they have articulated all sides in enough detail.

Next, illustrate how it is important to look at situations through multiple perspectives. Look for a situation that most of the participants have experienced. The one used here is Bill, who is about to leave a day service. Put a sheet of paper (or two) with the headings as shown in Figure 7.17 but without the content. Ask the participants to think of all of the people that they have helped leave day services for community jobs and create a "composite" person. Point out that the moment in time that this is occurring is just before the person leaves. Ask them why Bill would want to leave, and record the answers under what does not make sense to Bill. Ask them what the family liked about the setting and why they might be concerned about Bill leaving the day service. Record the responses under what makes sense to the family. Note that this is where typical planning stops, and it often results in people like Bill having to stay in a place where they are unhappy.

	What makes sense? What works? What needs to be maintained? (*The upside right now*)	What doesn't make sense? What doesn't work? What needs to change? (*The downside right now*)
New puppy owner's perspective	Unconditional love Terminal cuteness Endless entertainment Knowing that the downside is only temporary	"Accidents," mess Need for care Nighttime crying Chewed shoes, furniture

Figure 7.16. Discussion chart for exploring the "what makes sense and doesn't make sense" (WMS/DMS) framework in Exercise 4 from the perspective of a puppy owner. (Smull & Allen, 2002; Copyright © 2002 Smull & Allen; reprinted by permission.)

"Helping People Be Happy and Safe: Accounting for Health and Safety in How People Want to Live" by Michael Smull. In **Quality Enhancement in Developmental Disabilities: Challenges and Opportunities in a Changing World** edited by Valerie J. Bradley and Madeleine Kimmich. Baltimore: Paul H. Brookes Publishing Co. Exercise copyright © 2003 by Michael Smull.

	What makes sense? What works? What needs to be maintained? (*The upside right now*)	What doesn't make sense? What doesn't work? What needs to change? (*The downside right now*)
Bill's perspective	All my friends are there. I have a place to go. I know the neighborhood.	I get bored when there is no work. I don't like working on the base contract. I have to put up with co-workers who I don't like.
His family's perspective	He is out of the house from 9 to 3 everyday. He is safe. He can't get fired, which gives the family a sense of security.	Bad days at the service lead to bad evenings at home. He is picked on by a bully there. Whenever the day service is closed, the family has to get someone to help with Bill or Mom has to take time off from work.

Figure 7.17. Discussion chart for exploring the "what makes sense and doesn't make sense" (WMS/DMS) framework in Exercise 4 from the perspectives of Bill, who is about to leave his day service, and his family. (Smull & Allen, 2002; Copyright © 2002 Smull & Allen; reprinted by permission.)

Now ask them what makes sense to Bill at the day service and what does not make sense to the family about the day service. Record their responses in the appropriate quadrant. (Throughout, the trainer needs to make sure that what is being proposed actually goes in the section being discussed. If the item proposed does not go where it is suggested, gently lead a discussion about where it should go and record it there.) When the participants are indicating by their suggestions that they understand where things are placed, stop. The trainer should now have items that are similar to those in Figure 7.17. Begin with showing how you have already addressed one of the core principles of negotiation: that everyone feels heard (Taylor, Ury, & Patton, 1991). If you have captured the perspectives of the key stakeholders, then they feel heard.

The second principle of negotiation is to start with common ground (Taylor, Ury, & Patton, 1991). Tell the participants that when they are using this process, where there is strong disagreement, they should start any discussion with those items that reflect agreement across perspectives. Point out that, on the right side of the chart, there are some things that should be addressed before Bill leaves. All of Bill's friends are at the day service. How can he maintain those friendships if he leaves? What might happen if he loses all of his friends? The family feels that Bill

 "Helping People Be Happy and Safe: Accounting for Health and Safety in How People Want to Live" by Michael Smull. In **Quality Enhancement in Developmental Disabilities: Challenges and Opportunities in a Changing World** edited by Valerie J. Bradley and Madeleine Kimmich. Baltimore: Paul H. Brookes Publishing Co. Exercise copyright © 2003 by Michael Smull.

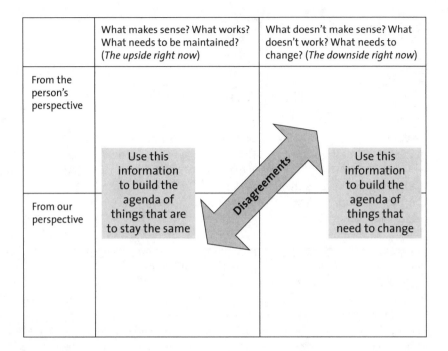

	What makes sense? What works? What needs to be maintained? (*The upside right now*)	What doesn't make sense? What doesn't work? What needs to change? (*The downside right now*)
From the person's perspective		
From our perspective	Use this information to build the agenda of things that are to stay the same	Use this information to build the agenda of things that need to change

Illustrate how this can be used to develop action plans that help people move toward the lives that they want. From the left-hand column, items are selected that you wish to maintain or enhance. From the right-hand column, choose things that need to change. Point out that disagreements often turn up on one of the diagonals.

Figure 7.18. How to use the "what makes sense and doesn't make sense" (WMS/DMS) framework to make decisions and create action plans. (Smull & Allen, 2002; Copyright © 2002 Smull & Allen; reprinted by permission.)

is safe now. Wherever he goes, they will need to continue to feel that he is safe. What does *safe* mean to them, and what are they worried about? How might those issues be addressed in a job setting? Point out that if this is done well, it provides a framework for discussion that leads to good action planning. Use Figure 7.18 to illustrate this. Note that most disagreements will appear on the diagonals (only one is shown).

"Helping People Be Happy and Safe: Accounting for Health and Safety in How People Want to Live" by Michael Smull. In **Quality Enhancement in Developmental Disabilities: Challenges and Opportunities in a Changing World** edited by Valerie J. Bradley and Madeleine Kimmich. Baltimore: Paul H. Brookes Publishing Co. Exercise copyright © 2003 by Michael Smull.

EXERCISE 5

Using Your Own Job

Part of the challenge in doing training is to have examples that resonate for the participants. One way to accomplish this is to have the participants apply the activity to their own lives. With this in mind, the next part of the training is to have the participants develop their own WMS/DMS framework focused on work.

Each participant should have a blank chart, as shown in Figure 7.19. Begin by reassuring them that they will not be asked to share what they write, and that they can take whatever they write with them when they leave. (This works best when people see an example, so the trainer needs to have already developed his or her own framework and be comfortable in sharing it.)

Ask the participants to think about their current job, or, if they have concerns with talking about current issues, think about a previous job. If people who use disability services are in the group and they have not had a job, ask them to think about a day service or school. Ask them to write their names on the top row and then fill out just that row (in their perspective only). Point out that it says "right now" on both sides. If they are doing this about a past job, they should change that to "as of" with a month and year. Point out that if this exercise is going to help with action planning, it has to represent a snapshot in time and not a mix of what is and what should be. Ask them to think about the little things as well as the big things, about what they do as well as the environment (e.g., the people they work with, the commute, food).

Then ask them to think of someone in their life with whom they talk about work. It can be their partner, a family member, a close friend, a colleague, or their boss. Write the name of that person in the space provided in the second row. Ask them to think about it from that person's perspective, and to write down their guesses about what that person would say.

Now ask them to look at the columns to find where there is agreement between themselves and the other person. Ask them to circle some of the items that agree. Remind them that the discussion should always begin where there is agreement. Refer the participants back to Figure 7.18, and note the importance of identifying things to maintain or enhance as well as things to change. Ask if some of what they would want to maintain has more to do with the environment than with the job duties.

Ask them to look at what does not make sense. They should readily see those things that "just go with the territory," things that cannot be changed without changing jobs. Ask them to look for at least one thing that could be changed

"Helping People Be Happy and Safe: Accounting for Health and Safety in How People Want to Live" by Michael Smull. In **Quality Enhancement in Developmental Disabilities: Challenges and Opportunities in a Changing World** edited by Valerie J. Bradley and Madeleine Kimmich. Baltimore: Paul H. Brookes Publishing Co. Exercise copyright © 2003 by Michael Smull.

At work

	What makes sense? What works? What needs to be maintained? (*The upside right now*)	What doesn't make sense? What doesn't work? What needs to change? (*The downside right now*)
Your perspective		
Perspective of your friend or parents		

Figure 7.19. Blank chart for Exercise 5. (Smull & Allen, 2002; Copyright © 2002 Smull & Allen; reprinted by permission.)

within their current job. See how many people can find at least one thing that does not make sense that they have control over and could change if they wanted to and made the effort. For many people, this will have been something from the list of what does not make sense from the perspective that is not theirs. It is an area of disagreement. Have the trainees imagine that someone else was helping to plan with them: Ask them how they would want that person to deal with it.

For each of the questions posed, the trainer should have an example to illustrate the points. The examples can be from a volunteer (or volunteers) from among the participants, or it can be from the trainer's example. As you look for examples, note that the more detailed the analysis that goes into the framework, the better it works. Point this out to the participants. Note that where the framework is not working, it is usually the absence of detail that is the problem. Make sure to use real examples, regardless of where they are from; examples will make the training much more powerful.

"Helping People Be Happy and Safe: Accounting for Health and Safety in How People Want to Live" by Michael Smull. In **Quality Enhancement in Developmental Disabilities: Challenges and Opportunities in a Changing World** edited by Valerie J. Bradley and Madeleine Kimmich. Baltimore: Paul H. Brookes Publishing Co. Exercise copyright © 2003 by Michael Smull.

EXERCISE 6

Using the Framework
to Build Action Plans: Eric's Story

The WMS/DMS framework is most often used to build action plans that describe what is going to be done to help the person move toward a life that makes sense for him or her. When this framework is done well, what needs to be done and the goals and steps to accomplish the goal become clear. However, creating that clarity often requires that those involved create the framework twice. How this works is illustrated by Eric's WMS/DMS framework.

> Eric had recently moved to a group home from an institution where he had spent most of his life. The first framework (Figure 7.20) was done after a person-centered plan had been developed. Those who developed this framework used it to decide where they would focus their efforts. They then did the framework again focusing on communication and being comfortable (see Figure 7.21).

Give people time to read the first chart, pointing out a few items. Ask them where they would focus their efforts. Do they have enough information to develop an action plan? Tell the participants that the people who were supporting Eric felt that they should focus on Eric's communication and physical comfort, so they developed the framework again (see Figure 7.21). Compare the detail in the two charts, and ask the participants if this makes it easier to develop an action plan. (The answer should be affirmative.)

Now ask them to develop an action plan about either communication or comfort, using the format shown in Figure 7.22. They should pretend that Eric is being supported by their agency (or an agency that they know). Walk them through the format, noting that the reason it calls for discussion and justification is to make sure that action plans actually reflect trying to help the person have a better balance between what is important to him or her and what is important for him or her, and not just goals to satisfy those who inspect.

Give the participants a few minutes to work on an action plan. Then, share an example from the group (or one that the trainer has prepared) and facilitate a dis-

 "Helping People Be Happy and Safe: Accounting for Health and Safety in How People Want to Live" by Michael Smull. In **Quality Enhancement in Developmental Disabilities: Challenges and Opportunities in a Changing World** edited by Valerie J. Bradley and Madeleine Kimmich. Baltimore: Paul H. Brookes Publishing Co. Exercise copyright © 2003 by Michael Smull.

	What makes sense? What works? What needs to be maintained? (*The upside right now*)	What doesn't make sense? What doesn't work? What needs to change? (*The downside right now*)
What we think is Eric's perspective	People who support him listen. He gets to send and receive e-mail. People who support him like to have fun and are willing to be silly. He gets to visit with his dad. He likes when Ruth and Diana and others get the computer to work for him. He likes going lots of places.	He doesn't have an electric chair (to move). He has to wear hand splints. He has to spend time out of his chair. He stays at home when others go out. He wants a job but doesn't have one. Having tube feedings on a set schedule means that he has to stay home. He doesn't get to use the computer whenever he wants. The computer needs a sound card, speakers, and a joystick. He has to stay on a positioning schedule even when he wants to do other things.
Eric's staff's perspective	Staff help him be in contact with his family and friends. People include him in what's going on. Staff are assigned to Eric during the day to support community inclusion. Ruth and the other staff are fitting in and figuring out how to make the computer work for Eric "when they can." Eric is in enhanced residential services, but he wants to have a paid job. People do *try* to understand what Eric is saying.	Eric's schedule is restricted by his feeding schedule. Staff don't know how to do things differently in regard to his access to the computer now. Why has it taken so long to get him one of his own? There is a lack of guys for him to do "guy things" with. Eric has a lot to say and no really clear, fast way to say it (in a way that lots of people can understand). Eric has staff who work with him who don't understand him, and it takes a long time to learn what Eric is saying. Eric hates his hand splints so much that he'll hurt himself so that he doesn't have to wear them.

Figure 7.20.   Eric's first framework in Exercise 6. (Smull & Allen, 2002; Copyright © 2002 Smull & Allen; reprinted with permission.)

	What makes sense? What works? What needs to be maintained? (*The upside right now*)	What doesn't make sense? What doesn't work? What needs to change? (*The downside right now*)
What we think is Eric's perspective	*Communication* People who support him listen. He gets to send and receive e-mail.	*Communication* Staff can't quickly know what he's saying. Eric is limited to "yes" and "no" when he has so much more to say. It takes a very long time for Eric to communicate.
	Being Comfortable People try to make Eric think of something else when he is not comfortable with his position. It's quiet where he lives, with few sudden or loud noises that surprise him.	*Being Comfortable* Eric has to wear hand splints that he hates and that hurt him. He has to spend time out of his chair. His positioning schedule limits his activities. He has to be in that crawligator.
Eric's staff's perspective	*Communication* Eric continues to be patient as staff try to figure out better ways to understand him. Eric loves computers and maybe that will be a way he can tell staff more clearly what he wants to say. Staff help him stay in contact with his family and friends. Ruth and the other staff are figuring out how to make the computer work for Eric "when they can."	*Communication* Eric's got a lot to say and no really clear, fast way to say it (in a way that a lot of people can understand). Eric hates and won't use the communication system chosen for him. There are communication systems out there that Eric would love to learn to use, and staff don't know how to get one.
	Being Comfortable Staff spend time with Eric when he's in his crawligator, which helps keep his mind off of it. Most of the time, Eric is comfortable. Staff is trying to get someone to look at his hand splints.	*Being Comfortable* Eric will scratch his wrists and hands so that he won't have to wear his hand splints. He yells and cries when he's in the crawligator, and staff have to tell him he must use it. Staff have to do things to Eric that they know make him uncomfortable or that hurt.

Figure 7.21.   Eric's second framework in Exercise 6. (Smull & Allen, 2002; Copyright © 2002 Smull & Allen; reprinted with permission.)

Action Plan/Goals

Desired outcome: _____

Discussion/
justification: _____

_____

_____

What needs to be done?	Who is responsible?	By when?

Figure 7.22.   A sample action plan. (Smull & Allen, 2002; Copyright © 2002 Smull & Allen; reprinted with permission.)

cussion. Help them see that the action plan "writes itself" when the framework is done well. Trainees are typically concerned about not having enough time to follow such a detailed process. One way to alleviate this concern is for the staff person facilitating the meeting to give everyone markers and have them all get up and write. This is not only faster than having just one person write, but it also keeps one or two people from dominating the conversation and the analysis.

"Helping People Be Happy and Safe: Accounting for Health and Safety in How People Want to Live" by Michael Smull. In **Quality Enhancement in Developmental Disabilities: Challenges and Opportunities in a Changing World** edited by Valerie J. Bradley and Madeleine Kimmich. Baltimore: Paul H. Brookes Publishing Co. Exercise copyright © 2003 by Michael Smull.

EXERCISE 7

Using WMS/DMS
to Evaluate Services: Gerald's Story

The other common use of the WMS/DMS framework is to evaluate the quality of services. Done well, it tells those who are checking for quality what is happening within a residential or day setting. Gerald's WMS/DMS framework illustrates the point (see Figure 7.23). Share Figure 7.23 with the participants. Ask them to take a moment to read it and then ask them if they see anything in the framework that would cause them to be concerned. Record their responses; if they have not raised the issue of eating food wrappers, bring it to their attention. Note that this is a serious issue of health and safety: he could choke, get an intestinal obstruction or perforation, or even be poisoned by some of the inks on some of the packaging. This framework not only raises this issue but gives it a context.

Ask the participants what their guesses would be about the problems in that group home. What would they do if they were in senior management? After they discuss the issues, let them know that what did happen was that the manager was relieved of her duties and Gerald moved. He now lives in a place where he really gets enough healthy food to eat and is neither eating food wrappers nor becoming obese. When the people who support him paid attention to the issue of shaving, they first discovered that not shaving made his face itchy. Then they found that it was the sound of the electric razor that disturbed him and that it works for him to have a shave every other day (or so) with a safety razor.

 "Helping People Be Happy and Safe: Accounting for Health and Safety in How People Want to Live" by Michael Smull. In **Quality Enhancement in Developmental Disabilities: Challenges and Opportunities in a Changing World** edited by Valerie J. Bradley and Madeleine Kimmich. Baltimore: Paul H. Brookes Publishing Co. Exercise copyright © 2003 by Michael Smull.

	What makes sense? What works? What needs to be maintained? (*The upside right now*)	What doesn't make sense? What doesn't work? What needs to change? (*The downside right now*)
Guesses about Gerald's perspective	Gerald is comfortable in his house. He has the same routine most days. New staff have stayed around, and he is getting used to them. He sees his grandfather every week. Gerald has privacy in his room. He is getting to do more of what he wants: going outside and having staff pay attention to him. He has a room to himself (no roommate).	He doesn't go riding around as much as he wants. He doesn't get to eat as much as he wants. Lately, at home, things have been changing daily, and staff don't have as much time to spend with Gerald. He doesn't get to see his grandfather as much as he wants. He has to shave. He doesn't get to do the things he wants to do or go the places he wants to go as much as he would like.
Perspective of Gerald's service coordinator	Gerald is safe. He is eating enough but not too much. He has privacy in his room, and others respect his privacy. Staff are working well together and trying to figure out how to best support Gerald. Staff are getting some training on how to support Gerald regarding his autism. Staff try to make sure that Gerald's room is a refuge for him. He does not share his room with anyone.	Gerald spends a lot of time sitting at the kitchen table. He is not able to leave the house whenever he wants. He eats things that are harmful to him (e.g., food wrappers, packaging), and staff don't know why. Staff who support Gerald don't understand why he gets upset. Staff who support Gerald don't know what interests him and what they do know, they don't get to do as often as they think he would like. Gerald's home can be stressful for him when people are in the hospital or staff are busy with crises. Staff have to hold Gerald to shave him.

Figure 7.23. A framework for Gerald. (Smull & Allen, 2002; Copyright © 2002 Smull & Allen; reprinted with permission.)

CONCLUSION

This chapter has presented concepts and skills that support a process whereby people who use services can be both happy and safe. The reader should keep in mind that the concepts are simple in structure but complex in application. At its core, the message is that those who support people who use disability services should examine issues of health and safety in much the same way as these issues are examined by people who do not use disability services. This construct does not devalue clinical information nor does it ignore professionals. What is expected is that the professional should take a proactive role in helping those who provide support to look at how the person can have what is important to him or her, while addressing issues of health or safety. Where significant issues of health or safety create boundaries in what the person can do, the problem solving is focused on how to help the person have as much of what is important to them as is possible. Conceptually, this is not different from the amateur runner or basketball player who is injured and goes to the doctor to learn how she or he can stay fit during the healing process and how to return to the activity as quickly as possible. The physician lets the person know what the boundaries are (e.g., no significant weight bearing on the injured ankle for 6 weeks) and then helps problem solve with the person (e.g., "running" in a swimming pool). Doing this with people who may not be able to participate in setting boundaries or in problem solving in traditional ways increases the responsibilities of those who are paid to provide support.

Part of the challenge of doing this work lies in the fact that the present service system is comfortable with having all of the control reside with the team and having the team only pay nominal attention to the wishes of the individual. The concepts and skills presented here can facilitate a rational shift from keeping control to sharing control. In sharing control, staff and those being served look together for the balance between what is important to and what is important for each individual.

REFERENCES

Handy, C.B. (1995). *The age of paradox.* Boston: Harvard Business School Publishing.
Smull, M., & Allen, W. (2002). *Helping people be happy and safe: Accounting for health and safety in context of how people want to live.* Workshop and slide show.

SECTION III

Outcomes
for People

An important and positive development in the assessment of performance in public developmental disabilities (DD) systems is the inclusion of people with disabilities in formal oversight as well as the design and development of monitoring tools. The participation of self-advocates in quality enhancement is a reflection of the increased prominence of individual choice and empowerment in the calculus surrounding resource allocation and planning. As self-advocates become more powerful in decisions regarding the supports they will receive, so they also become valuable informants regarding what constitutes quality.

The participation of people with disabilities in quality enhancement activities also reflects a recognition that the primary window through which to view the quality of a service or a provider is through the eyes and experiences of the individual receiving supports. This suggests that people with disabilities should not only be informants, but they should also set the criteria by which quality is determined. The two chapters in this section provide powerful evidence that the inclusion of individuals with disabilities in quality monitoring enlivens and helps to facilitate the survey process, improve response rates, and build relationships.

Chapter 8 describes the development, application, and results of the Ask Me! Project in Maryland. The Ask Me! Project, initially conceived in 1996, uses one of the first surveys in which people with disabilities played a substantial role in the design and in which their perceptions of quality formed the basic domains. The survey, which is facilitated by people with disabilities, has been given to approximately 2,500 people. The process is voluntary and includes providers who are willing to have the results made public. The survey process has been validated, and in fact, the results indicate that the involvement of people with disabilities as interviewers increases the response rate.

Chapter 9 describes a statewide independent monitoring process in Pennsylvania. This process also involves people with disabilities using surveys, and

161

it is tied into both a systems-level quality enhancement process as well as an individual quality enhancement outcome. The survey is a version of the Core Indicators Project (see Chapter 13), and the results can be compared to a national baseline. To date, the surveys have generated important findings including the need for better complaint and grievance mechanisms, access to keys for individual residences, access to individual communication devices, and increased emphasis on building friendships and relationships.

CHAPTER 8

Ask Me!^{SM}

A SURVEY OF QUALITY OF LIFE
DESIGNED BY AND FOR PEOPLE
WITH DEVELOPMENTAL DISABILITIES

SARAH BASEHART, CRISTINE MARCHAND, AND GORDON SCOTT BONHAM

The state of Maryland is home to a unique and valuable approach to quality enhancement for services for people with developmental disabilities. Known as the Ask Me!^{SM} Project, this effort consists of face-to-face interviews conducted by individuals who themselves have developmental disabilities. These interviews assess the quality of life of consumers who receive publicly provided services and supports. The project serves multiple purposes, enhancing both system functioning and individual empowerment. This chapter describes the interview process and presents summary findings on consumers' quality of life.

THE NEED FOR A QUALITY-OF-LIFE SURVEY

People with developmental disabilities want greater choice and control over the services and supports they receive. They want opportunities to express their views about the services they receive and to be part of efforts to improve them. Yet, consumer satisfaction surveys have often been developed and administered by professionals and authority figures.

Two agencies in Maryland sought to change that. People on the Go of Maryland is the statewide self-advocacy group for people with developmental disabilities. The Arc of Maryland is a statewide advocacy organization dedicated to improving the quality of life of people with mental retardation and related developmental disabilities and empowering self-advocates. Together, they proposed a consumer-directed approach to assessing consumer satisfaction and quality of life through the Ask Me!^{SM} Project. Ask Me!^{SM} uses a survey developed by and with people with developmental disabilities. People with

---

Ask Me!^{SM} is a registered service mark of People on the Go of Maryland and The Arc of Maryland.

developmental disabilities administer it by interviewing people who receive services that are funded through Maryland's Developmental Disabilities Administration (DDA). Experience has shown that when individuals with developmental disabilities are interviewed by interviewers with disabilities—using survey questions developed by people with developmental disabilities—the survey results are more valid and meaningful. The interviewer is more likely to understand and be understood by the interviewee, as they typically share more common experiences than those who do not receive services themselves. Data from the first 3 years of the project showed that when people with disabilities facilitated the interview, the response rate was 80%.

In 2001, 44 trained interviewers, all of whom have developmental disabilities, surveyed more than 1,000 people from 35 different service agencies statewide. Ask Me!^{SM} staff provided technical assistance to agencies to assist them in incorporating the results throughout their organizations, toward the goal of strengthening their quality enhancement efforts and program quality.

Ask Me!^{SM} is based on the following premises:

- People with developmental disabilities are in a better position to elicit more meaningful responses from other individuals receiving services than are interviewers who do not have developmental disabilities.

- By directly asking people how they view their lives, the project has the potential to increase the empowerment of people with developmental disabilities who are receiving services.

- Because the interviewers themselves have disabilities, the experience they gain in working as interviewers may open professional paths for them as the project expands statewide.

- Agencies are keenly interested in the views of the individuals they support and how to address those views.

- State public policy and funding priorities can be derived from better understanding the views of people who receive services.

The most effective quality enhancement mechanism is an informed constituency. Individuals who understand their rights, have the opportunity to express their views, and are encouraged to speak out can enhance the quality of their own individual services and supports, as well as the entire professional array of services. Consumer satisfaction surveys are integral to Maryland's quality enhancement system, although they alone are not sufficient to ensure quality. Critical also to a comprehensive quality enhancement system are state and local licensing authorities, state regulations governing health and safety and quality supports, consumer appeal rights, self-advocacy, and effective enforcement mechanisms. However, as one of the most direct methods to elicit personal responses from consumers, the Ask Me!^{SM} survey is an important, integral part of the quality enhancement system in Maryland.

The Ask Me!^{SM} Project is unique to the state of Maryland. It provides the opportunity for individuals with developmental disabilities to express their satisfaction with their lives through face-to-face interviews conducted by individuals who also have developmental disabilities. Through the survey, people can have a voice in the evaluation of the services they receive and, ultimately, can make a real difference in the service delivery system in Maryland, while also improving their own quality of life. The Ask Me!^{SM} Project findings are being used statewide to move policy and services toward greater self-determination by people with developmental disabilities.

ASK ME!^{SM} SURVEY DEVELOPMENT

The concept for the Ask Me!^{SM} Project began in 1996 with a broad-based consortium of key stakeholders in Maryland, ranging from statewide advocacy and self-advocacy organizations to provider organizations and the state's public governmental agency with statutory responsibility to administer policy and programs for people with developmental disabilities. (Key stakeholders include the DDA, Maryland Disability Law Center, Maryland Developmental Disabilities Council, People on the Go of Maryland, The Arc of Maryland, and the Maryland Association of Community Service for Persons with Developmental Disabilities.) The Maryland Disability Law Center provided the impetus for the survey through litigation regarding quality-of-community programs. In the subsequent consent decree, the Maryland Developmental Disabilities Administration agreed to conduct a consumer satisfaction survey.

Initial development of the Ask Me!^{SM} survey relied heavily on the involvement of people with developmental disabilities. The first 3 years of the project measured consumers' perceived quality of life using a questionnaire based on an adaptation of Schalock and Keith's (1993) *Quality of Life Questionnaire*. A team of self-advocates from People on the Go of Maryland worked with Dr. Robert Schalock, Dr. Gordon Scott Bonham, and The Arc of Maryland to make the questions and responses more direct and easy to understand and administer. The name of the survey and project (Ask Me!^{SM}) came from People on the Go's *Signs of Quality* question "Did you ask me?" The *Signs of Quality* lays out a litmus test of questions identified by self-advocates as important for quality of life and services. A number of these questions did not appear in the Schalock and Keith questionnaire, and the initial Ask Me!^{SM} questionnaire included a new section about dignity.

Dr. Bonham served the project as primary survey researcher, working closely with self-advocates to continually examine the questions, update the survey questionnaire, and explain survey results. Dr. Schalock, nationally recognized for research in the area of quality of life, assisted the project in developing the survey dimensions and continues to provide annual consultation on survey design issues.

People with developmental disabilities continue to play a central role in modifications to the survey. Since the 1993 *Quality of Life Questionnaire,* the understanding of core domains for quality of life has expanded to involve physical well-being, emotional well-being, material well-being, interpersonal relationships, personal development, social inclusion, individuals' rights, and self-determination (Schalock & Verdugo, 2002). Members of People On the Go conducted a series of reviews and pre-tested a new Ask Me![SM] survey instrument based on these internationally recognized core domains. The new survey first used in fiscal year (FY) 2001 also incorporates findings and recommendations by people with developmental disabilities, reflects changing state regulations of the DDA, and incorporates ever-evolving understanding of the principles of self-determination.

Illustrative of the role that people with developmental disabilities have in the ongoing refinement of the survey is the section on transportation. The people developing the initial survey, recognizing the importance of transportation, added one question. This one question proved so important to the quality of life of people who receive services that interviewers developed four new questions on additional dimensions of transportation for the second and subsequent years of the survey.

IMPLEMENTATION OF THE ASK ME![SM] SURVEY

With funding and policy commitment from the Maryland DDA and Maryland Developmental Disabilities Council, the Ask Me![SM] Project began in FY 1998 as a pilot project, with 10 participating provider agencies and interviews with 237 people. Since then, the volume of interviews has increased each year, bringing the number of interviews to 1,000 in FY 2001. In FY 2002, the project will move from its 4-year pilot state to a long-term quality assurance program, funded by DDA.

The project requires standardized protocols for conducting interviews, selection of random samples of people to be interviewed, agency protocols and orientation, reporting suspected abuse or neglect, termination of an interview, confidentiality procedures, and proxy interviews for individuals who cannot understand the survey. In the event that a proxy is needed (i.e., the person selected to be interviewed cannot understand or complete the survey), two individuals are interviewed according to a hierarchy of most desired proxies, with family members being first priority.

Interviewer Tasks and Skills

It is the Ask Me!^{SM} interviewers who bring the project to life. They carry out the project work on site, increase observers' awareness of the competence of people with developmental disabilities in their role as interviewers, and effectively present the importance of quality-of-life issues. In FY 2001, 46 individuals with developmental disabilities were employed by the project in a variety of positions: 1) 44 individuals served as interviewers; 2) two of the interviewers were primarily employed in staff support positions, assisting with on-site logistics and supporting the other interviewers; 3) one interviewer also worked with the project researcher, Gordon Bonham, entering data from survey forms and background information; 4) two former interviewers served as quality assurance consultants to observe the interview sessions and rate the interviewers on their skills, suggest areas for improvement, and ensure interview protocols are followed; and 5) several self-advocates are regularly involved in training and conference presentations about the project.

During the past 4 years, the Ask Me!^{SM} Project has employed 104 individuals with developmental disabilities as interviewers. They primarily work in teams of two, with a lead interviewer reading the questions and the other team member pointing to the response categories on the flash card and helping with any problems. Either of the interviewers can record the answers. The team approach allows flexibility in adjusting to any difficulties that one of the team members might have; for example, a team member who cannot read could perform the tasks that do not require reading, such as pointing to the flash card. In addition, most interviews with proxy respondents are completed by a single interviewer. Neither the number of interviewers nor the gender composition of the interviewing team affects the outcome of the interviews, as measured by the number of questions completed, the percentage of questions receiving the most positive response, and the quality-of-life scale scores.

Necessary qualities for interviewers include listening skills, understanding of the project's goals and expectations, ability to conduct objective interviews and follow protocols, interest in traveling, sensitivity, self-motivation, dependability, and self-advocacy skills. Accommodations are made for interviewers who require augmentative or alternative communication strategies and technology.

Interviewers vary in the number of interviews they conduct in a year; on average, each interviewer participated in 32 interviews. Eight interviewers completed 50 or more interviews, and seven completed fewer than 10. Some data suggest that more experienced interviewers receive slightly less positive answers on transportation and in several quality-of-life domains. Interviewing teams are based on the four geographic areas of Maryland. The Arc of Maryland conducts annual recruitment for interview positions. Recruitment is through local self-advocacy groups, service coordination, vocational rehabilitation, provider agencies, local chapters of The Arc, and People on the Go members.

Interviewer Training

Annual statewide training for new and experienced interviewers includes

- Information on the prior year's survey results and recommendations
- Qualities of good interviewers
- The Ask Me![SM] Project's goals
- The role and responsibilities of interviewers
- Interview protocols to ensure reliability and validity
- Confidentiality requirements
- Problem-solving techniques to deal with potential on-site challenges
- Protocol for reporting abuse and neglect
- Protocol for terminating an interview
- Opportunities to practice team interviewing techniques
- Opportunities to build teamwork

Following the statewide training, interviewers meet regionally to practice interviewing again prior to their first actual on-site interview session.

CONTINUOUS QUALITY IMPROVEMENT

How does the project ensure that interviews are conducted according to the project protocols, to preserve the integrity—reliability and validity—of the survey? All interviewers participate in monthly regional training sessions designed for continuous quality enhancement. Another quality enhancement measure involves videotaping an actual interview. Interviewers and project staff together view the videotape, enabling the interviewers to see themselves in an actual interview. Interviewers are supported in drawing their own conclusions about improving their skills. Those involved with the project share a strong belief that the protocols, which are strictly followed, and the continuous interviewer training design contribute to the high validity and reliability of the results.

Internal Consistency and Respondent Bias

The survey includes three pairs of questions to check the internal validity of responses: two questions worded exactly the same way and placed several questions apart; questions with only slight differences in wording; and questions addressing the same concept but using different words. Figure 8.1 presents the results of this internal consistency check for FY 2001. As the figure indicates, using different words for the same concept does affect the consistency of self-respondents and proxy respondents. The figure also shows that self-respondents do not differ from proxy respondents in the consistency of their answers.

Among these complete interviews, 80% of the respondents responded for themselves, including 67% of those diagnosed as having profound mental retardation (see Figure 8.2). Although survey procedures counted a person answering five questions as a self-respondent, most self-respondents answered all the questions in the survey (see Figure 8.3). Self-respondents are even less likely than proxies to skip a question.

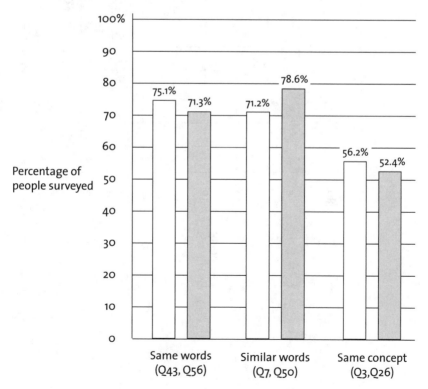

Figure 8.1.   Internal agreement among questions in the Ask Me!ᔆᴹ survey.
(*Key:* ☐ self response; ▨ proxy response)

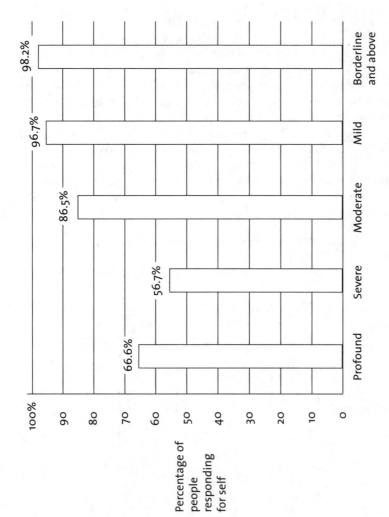

Figure 8.2. Percentage of self-respondents, by degree of mental retardation (MR), who participated in the Ask Me!SM survey.

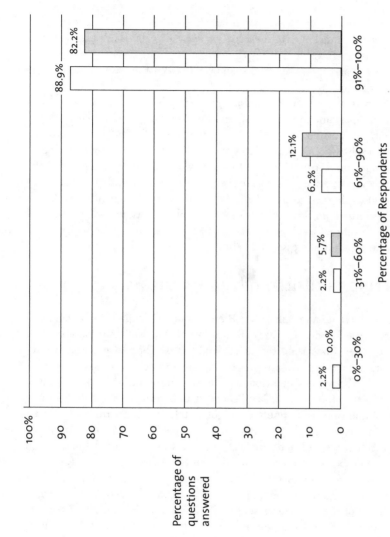

Figure 8.3. Percentage of questions answered by self-respondents and answered by proxies in the Ask Me![SM] survey.
(*Key:* ☐ self response; ▨ proxy response)

The literature on interviewing individuals with mental retardation (e.g., Matikka & Vesala, 1997) notes a tendency toward acquiescent responses. Ask Me!^{SM} interviews show little evidence of acquiescence (or first response) bias or nay-saying (or last response) bias. During the 4 pilot years of the survey, 8% or fewer of the respondents gave the positive answer to almost all (at least 91%) of the questions, and 1% gave the negative answer to almost all the questions (91% or more). However, self-respondents average more positive responses than do proxies and are more likely than proxies to answer 91% or more of the questions with the positive response.

Proxy bias consistently appears as a greater problem in the Ask Me!^{SM} survey than any bias among people responding for themselves. When the same respondent participated in both the first and second years (as a proxy both years or as a self-advocate both years), the quality-of-life measure appeared to be stable from one year to the next. However, when proxy respondents gave the answers one year and the people gave their own answers the other year, proxies indicated much higher quality of life than did the people themselves. Other analyses performed on these data also point to proxy bias, leading to the conclusion that every effort should be made to ask consumers themselves about their lives in order to increase data validity.

INCREASING THE UTILITY OF THE ASK ME!^{SM} SURVEY

The Arc of Maryland and Ask Me!^{SM} Project staff have engaged in several important activities to increase the usefulness of the Ask Me!^{SM} survey. One such activity has been translating the survey and process for deaf people with developmental disabilities. An attempt during the second year to have a deaf interviewer use the regular questionnaire proved unsuccessful because it often required fingerspelling of words and concepts unfamiliar to many deaf people. A subset of questions was pretested by a deaf staff person the third year, and a deaf focus group reviewed the results and examined the remaining questions for applicability to people who are deaf. The goals were to modify questions so that they could be asked and responded to in American Sign Language (ASL) and to identify areas not covered in the survey that are important to the Deaf community. Communication emerged as a major area of concern for deaf people in all aspects of life, including shopping, visiting with family and friends, going to doctor or dentist appointments, and having access to an interpreter. During FY 2001, the ASL version of the survey obtained information from 56 deaf people, which will be useful in improving services and the lives of deaf people.

A number of activities have occurred to make the Ask Me!^{SM} survey more useful to provider agencies. The number of provider agencies participating in the Ask Me!^{SM} process on a voluntary basis increased from 10 in FY 1998 to

35 in FY 2001. These agencies represent rural, suburban, and urban areas of the state and provide services to people with varying disabilities and levels of disability. Only one agency has declined to participate a second time. This has given agencies multiple years of results, depending on their starting date. To help these agencies make best use of their Ask Me!^{SM} experience, the project has provided statewide and regional trainings on the following topics:

- Statewide findings from the survey

- How to integrate the Ask Me!^{SM} survey into agencies' quality enhancement plans, including examples of how other agencies have applied their data

- How to make your Ask Me!^{SM} results easily understood by the board of directors, agency staff, and self-advocates

- How to read the Ask Me!^{SM} data for individual agencies and suggestions on using the data, including its combination with other satisfaction data

- How agency staff can support self-advocates to get what they want in life

- The importance of agency commitment to enhancing the quality of lives of their consumers by focusing on the internationally recognized domain areas rather than on specific indicator questions

The training and technical assistance to agencies have been effective. Agencies have applied the survey results to make proactive, positive changes within their organizations. For example, several agencies have conducted development and training for their boards of directors, staff training, agency and staff reorganization, staff recruitment and orientation, self-advocacy leadership development and support, program restructuring, strategic planning, and budget allocation.

KEY SURVEY RESULTS

Through a grant with the Maryland Developmental Disabilities Council, Ask Me!^{SM} conducted an evaluation of Maryland's Robert Wood Johnson Self Determination Initiative by interviewing individuals at the point they were selected for the initiative and 18 months later in order to determine changes in quality of life (Bonham & Basehart, 2000). Change occurred over time in ways predicted by findings from the pilot years about the interrelationships of quality-of-life domains and their relationship with transportation availability. The evaluation showed that high-quality service coordination can increase quality of life.

Ask Me!^{SM} focuses on people's long-term quality of life rather than short-term service outcomes, such as satisfaction with discrete services. Asking about the presence or absence of a specific service seldom provides much insight into an individual's quality of life. The Ask Me!^{SM} survey does measure one short-term service outcome, transportation, because research has revealed a strong relationship between the perceived availability of transportation and long-term quality of life. Transportation availability directly affects six of the eight quality-of-life domains and indirectly affects the remaining quality-of-life domains.

Specific findings from each year of the survey are presented by Bonham and colleagues (1998, 1999, 2000, 2001). Several key findings emerged from analysis of all 4 years of Ask Me!^{SM} surveys:

- Transportation consistently affects all aspects of people's quality of life.

- A person's quality of life is not dictated by his or her physical characteristics or disabilities. Sex, age, sight, hearing, speech, behavior, seizures, wheelchair use, and medical fragility had minor effects, if any, on only one or two quality-of-life measures.

- Cognitive ability does not affect a person's perceived quality of life in most domains. When cognitive ability does show a relationship with quality of life, it is smaller than the effect of transportation availability.

- Most people with developmental disabilities can respond for themselves. Four fifths of the people interviewed could respond for themselves, including two thirds of those with profound mental retardation (see Figure 8.2).

- Self-respondents are better than proxy respondents. Self-respondents answered more questions than did proxies. Proxies tended to under-report the quality of life in some domains but over-report the availability of transportation and the quality of life in other domains.

- People respond to the same questions in approximately the same way, whether the question is asked twice in the same survey or asked in 2 different years.

- The quality of life expressed by individuals served by one agency may significantly differ from that expressed by people served by another agency (see Figure 8.4). These differences are generally consistent over time in the absence of explicit agency change. This suggests that the way a service is provided and the ways agencies support individuals are important.

FUTURE ACTIVITIES TO EXPAND USE OF SURVEY AND SURVEY RESULTS

Plans have been made to expand use of the Ask Me!^{SM} survey in Maryland and to expand public access to Ask Me!^{SM} materials and results. Beginning in FY

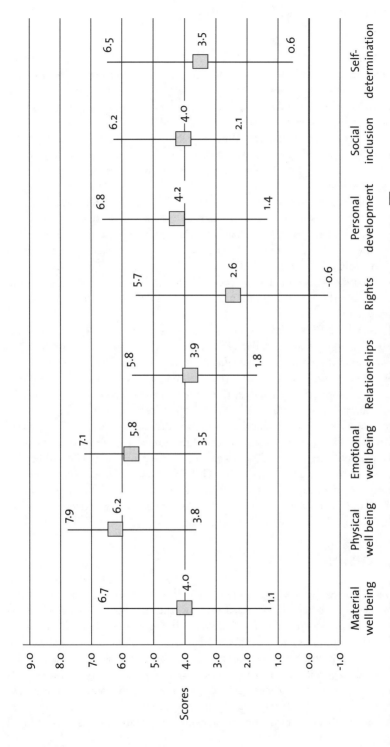

Figure 8.4. Ranges (vertical lines) and averages of agencies' quality-of-life scores in the Ask Me!SM survey: Fiscal year 2001. (Key: ▢ average)

2002, Maryland DDA has made the Ask Me!^{SM} survey mandatory for all provider agencies receiving state funds. A 4-year interview cycle has been designed to allow the project to reach people served by most agencies within that period, while providing a representative state sample every year: 1) large agencies, providing services to 300 or more individuals, will be interviewing sites every year; 2) agencies providing services to 130–299 people will be sites every other year; 3) agencies who serve 55–129 people will be sites every fourth year; and 4) a sample of small agencies serving fewer than 55 people will be included also.

As people with disabilities and their families look for services, they may be able to use the survey results in making decisions about support providers. The DDA-funded service coordination offices publish a guide to services. In the future, it is anticipated that the Ask Me!^{SM} survey results will be published in this guide. In addition, the Maryland section of *The ArcLink* (www.TheArcLink.org), an interactive web site for individuals and families, will offer agencies the opportunity to include their Ask Me!^{SM} results on line for informational purposes.

As Ask Me!^{SM} becomes more widely recognized, other states may be interested in undertaking similar efforts. The Arc of Maryland currently has available a training manual for organizations interested in replicating the project in other states. The *Ask Me!^{SM}* training manual provides all necessary materials and information to conduct the survey. The training manual is available at cost to state agencies, self-advocacy groups, or providers; it includes the survey, interview protocol, and interviewer training information. These copyrighted materials are only available through purchasing the training manual. (All documents are also on disks to ease use for organizations.) To protect the integrity of the Ask Me!^{SM} materials, The Arc of Maryland has developed a licensing agreement. If an organization or state wishes to use the survey outside of Maryland, it must become certified to use the survey. The licensing agreement outlines the certification requirements.

CONCLUSION

Over a 4-year period, nearly 2,500 individuals with developmental disabilities in Maryland have been interviewed through the Ask Me!^{SM} Project. This experience has demonstrated that people with developmental disabilities *want* to express their opinions and *can* express their opinions when interviewed face-to-face by interviewers with developmental disabilities. Ask Me!^{SM} is demonstrating that agencies that provide services wish to be responsive to individuals they support and that these agencies can make significant organizational changes when presented with valuable information and technical assistance. Consumer quality-of-life surveys can also influence statewide systems and lead to public policy improvements. Clearly, Ask Me!^{SM} and other similar quality-of-life measures are key components of quality enhancement systems, as states, people with disabilities, advocates, and professionals seek to improve the quality of life of people with developmental disabilities.

REFERENCES

Bonham, G.S., & Basehart, S. (2000, August). *Quality of life of Marylanders with developmental disabilities participating in the Robert Wood Johnson Self-Determination Initiative: Final report.* Annapolis: The Arc of Maryland.

Bonham, G.S., Basehart, S., & Marchand, C.B. (2000, December). *Ask Me! FY 2000: The quality of life of Marylanders with developmental disabilities receiving DDA-funded supports.* Annapolis: The Arc of Maryland.

Bonham, G.S., Basehart, S., & Marchand, C.B. (2001, November). *Ask Me! FY 2001: The quality of life of Marylanders with developmental disabilities receiving DDA-funded supports.* Annapolis: The Arc of Maryland.

Bonham, G.S., Pisa, L.M., Basehart, S., Marchand, C.B., Harris, C., Heim, S., & Ingram, A. (1999, November). *Ask Me! Year 2: The quality of life of Marylanders with developmental disabilities receiving DDA-funded supports.* Annapolis: The Arc of Maryland.

Bonham, G.S., Pisa, L.M., Marchand, C.B., Harris, C., White, D., & Schalock, R.L. (1998, February). *Ask Me! The quality of life of Marylanders with developmental disabilities receiving DDA-funded supports.* Annapolis: The Arc of Maryland.

Schalock, R.L., & Verdugo. (2002, August). *Quality of life handbook for human service practitioners.* Washington, DC: American Association on Mental Retardation (AAMR).

CHAPTER 9

Independent
Monitoring for Quality

THE PENNSYLVANIA EXPERIENCE

CELIA S. FEINSTEIN AND GUY CARUSO

Historically, the assessment of quality in community programs for people with mental retardation relied on compliance measures that judged quality on the basis of adherence to various government regulations, primarily in the areas of health and safety (Feinstein et al., 2000; Lakin, 2000). One problem with such a compliance approach is that, at its most basic level, it does not measure quality but rather threshold capacity. This is underscored by the number of court cases involving substandard conditions in facilities that were certified as meeting the standards associated with intermediate care facilities for people with mental retardation (ICFs/MR) (Lakin, 2000). The concentration on health and safety often ignored dimensions such as satisfaction, choice, dignity, and respect.

In addition, this type of monitoring was most often performed by professionals and based on staff responses, rather than the responses of those people most directly affected by the services and supports delivered. According to Mochan and colleagues,

> State licensure and county monitoring required no actual service recipients to be present or consulted during inspections. Often service providers received advanced notification of monitoring visits. Quite naturally, they sought to create problem-free environments and documents showing full compliance with all rules. (1996, II-1)

The compliance approach relied on the creation of standards and the monitoring of compliance with these standards by professionals with little or no input from consumers (Feinstein et al., 2000).

The authors would like to thank Robin Levine, Christopher DeRosa, James Lemanowicz, and Allison Carey of Temple University, and the Pennsylvania Office of Mental Retardation for their work on the development and implementation of this chapter.

A shift has become apparent, from standards-based compliance measures to an assessment of individual outcome measures including satisfaction, interdependence, productivity, and inclusion. The current approach is one that views quality in terms of the extent to which the services and supports delivered to people with mental retardation and other developmental disabilities help to attain their "desired conditions of living related to home and community living, employment, and health functioning" (Schalock, 1994, p. 121). Therefore, what is defined as *quality* in part depends on the needs, desires, and perceptions of individuals receiving services and supports (Sundram, 1994). Within this model, measures of quality take into account, for example, consumer satisfaction, consumer choice, and the degree to which consumers are treated with respect and dignity (Oregon Developmental Disabilities Council, 1997).

Another concern arose in the shift toward consumer outcomes about who was collecting the information from individuals with disabilities. A shift from a professional surveyor model to one in which consumers and other lay people were the key data collectors emerged. How better to make individuals feel comfortable in giving their opinions about the most critical aspects of their lives than to have other nonprofessionals, including people with disabilities, family members, and other interested people, collecting the information.

Citizen monitoring (of which Pennsylvania's independent monitoring is one variation) "is a process for citizens who are not service providers, program staff, or human service bureaucrats to gather the experiences, outcomes, and candid opinions of citizens who are service recipients of the mental retardation (or developmental disabilities) service system" (Mochan, 1996, p. II-2). In the citizen monitoring model, professionals working in the field are excluded as monitors. Consumers play a central role in instrument development, data collection, and data analysis, and they are also the primary respondents to the multiplicity of questions.

Oregon and Oklahoma developed similar citizen monitoring projects, referred to as Advocates Involved in Monitoring (AIM). (Oklahoma's project was modeled after Oregon's project.) Interviewers were volunteers who were individuals with disabilities, family members of people with disabilities, friends, and advocates. No service professionals working for monitored systems could serve as interviewers. Two concepts central to these monitoring systems were customer satisfaction and customer choice: "Customer satisfaction is the key to high quality services and customer choice encourages competition and quality" (Oregon Developmental Disabilities Council, 1997, p. 1).

In Maryland, the Ask Me! Project is unique for its commitment to hiring people with developmental disabilities as interviewers (see Chapter 8). The Ask Me! Project hired people with developmental disabilities, most of whom received state-funded services, to conduct quality-of-life interviews with consumers. Concerning the involvement of people with disabilities in the Ask Me!

Project, Bonham and colleagues stated, "The project believes that people with developmental disabilities elicit and provide data on quality of life that is at least as valid and reliable as data collected from or by others, if not more valid and reliable" (1999, p. 1).

As Lakin (2000) found, the inclusion of people with disabilities in the monitoring process has increased over the past few years but is still the exception rather than the rule. People with disabilities are being consulted to help define *quality* and to help in the development of efforts to measure quality. As consumer-directed monitoring programs grow, Lakin also suggested several limitations of monitoring projects: 1) the findings of monitoring projects had little impact on licensing, certification, funding, or program requirements or decisions; 2) the "add-on" status of monitoring projects reduced their ability to create change and gain access to programs and increased the perception of monitoring as an extra burden; 3) projects were often limited by funding and reliance on volunteers; and 4) teams often lacked a clear purpose, agreed-on outcomes, and well-defined reporting procedures, which caused them to struggle to define the purpose and benefits of their project. The Pennsylvania Independent Monitoring for Quality Project (now IM4Q) has addressed each of the limitations stated by Lakin in the development of its program guidelines.

HISTORY OF INDEPENDENT MONITORING IN PENNSYLVANIA

In 1997, Pennsylvania's Office of Mental Retardation (OMR) began to disseminate its "Multi-Year Plan," which represented a significant attempt to disseminate OMR's vision, values, and goals for the ensuing years. The plan, developed by OMR's Planning Advisory Committee (PAC), included several recommendations, one of which stated that the capacity for independent monitoring should be developed in Pennsylvania.

Through the PAC, a subcommittee was formed to address the aforementioned recommendation. The PAC subcommittee included consumers, families, providers, advocates, county representatives, direct support staff, and OMR staff. The charge to the subcommittee was to develop a process for the conduct of independent monitoring. The Developmental Disabilities Council, in collaboration with OMR, committed to fund the initial development and training work required to establish independent monitoring. Technical advisors were contracted to assist in the subcommittee's deliberations.

The PAC subcommittee produced a document describing independent monitoring; the subcommittee recommended that the process include the collection of a minimal set of data by all counties in Pennsylvania. The document was accepted by the PAC and reviewed and revised by OMR. The stated purposes of independent monitoring include the following:

1. Monitoring on an annual basis one third of the individuals in each county who are living in licensed residential settings including private ICFs/MR. The sample was meant to include both children and adults.

2. Providing information about life outcomes including the satisfaction of people receiving supports through Pennsylvania's OMR

3. Through the focus on consumer outcomes, providing families and consumers with information to assist in making informed choices about where and from whom services and supports are received

4. Identifying best practices across Pennsylvania

5. Eventually issuing performance profiles of providers, reporting strengths and areas for improvement

6. Continuously improving the quality of services and supports provided to people with mental retardation and their families in Pennsylvania by focusing on a model of continuous quality improvement and enhancement

7. Creating a process to ensure necessary change at the state, county, and provider levels

8. Providing information through an entity that is independent of "hard" service delivery (e.g., residential services and supports, day services and supports, early intervention)

Instrument Development

When the PAC Subcommittee on Independent Monitoring first began to meet, it was decided that in addition to the development of a process for independent monitoring, a core set of questions would be asked of each individual surveyed. Programs could customize the survey instrument to meet their needs, but in order to create a statewide snapshot, it was necessary to ask the same core set of questions of all individuals monitored.

One of the technical advisors to the program began the task of amassing the various instruments that had been developed around the country for similar efforts. It was decided by the subcommittee that Pennsylvania would develop its own instrument, rather than use any of the existing surveys in total. The instruments reviewed included the National Core Indicators Project (NCIP) Consumer Survey, Ask Me! Project, Advocates Involved in Monitoring (AIM), 1990 National Consumer Survey, the Consumer Survey from the National Home of Your Own Project, Vermont's Consumer Satisfaction Survey, and the Citizen Monitoring Instrument from ARC Allegheny. Other instruments were reviewed as well, but it was believed that the aforementioned instruments provided more than an adequate basis from which to develop a Pennsylvania-specific instrument. An instrument was developed and revised several times to reflect the input of the PAC subcommittee. The resulting instrument, "Essential Data Elements," is composed of the following sections:

- Presurvey Form: This form is completed prior to the scheduling of the interview with the individual. It provides information about where the person lives, the name of the person to contact to schedule the appointment, whether the home is accessible, the case manager's name and telephone number, and whether the individual has a communication style or language (e.g., American Sign Language, Spanish) that might require the use of an interpreter.

- Demographics: This section includes questions about type of residential setting, Social Security number, and so forth.

- Satisfaction: This section can only be completed by the individual receiving services and supports; the person answers questions about satisfaction with where he or she works and lives and satisfaction with staff who support him or her.

- Dignity, Respect, and Rights: This section can also only be completed by the individual receiving services and supports; questions are asked about whether roommates and staff treat the person with respect, whether the person is afforded his or her rights, and whether he or she has fears at home, at work, or in the community.

- Choice and Control: This section may be answered by the individual or by a family member, friend, or staff person; questions are asked about the extent to which the individual exerts choice and control over various aspects of his or her life.

- Relationships: This section may be answered by the individual or by a family member, friend, or staff person; questions are asked about friends, family, and neighbors and the individual's opportunities to visit and see them.

- Inclusion: This section may be answered by the individual or by a family member, friend, or staff person; questions are asked about opportunities for community inclusion. A section of the Harris poll is included for comparative purposes.

- Monitor Impressions: This section of the instrument is completed by the Independent Monitoring Team, after they have completed their visit; questions are asked in the areas of physical setting, staff support, and opportunities for growth and development.

- Major Concerns: This form is to be completed whenever there is a possibility of physical danger, significant sanitation problems, or physical or psychological abuse or neglect. Each program is required to develop a mechanism for communicating this information; in the event of imminent danger, teams are instructed not to leave the home until resolution of some kind is achieved.

- Family/Friend/Guardian Survey: A telephone survey is conducted with each family once the individual gives his or her approval; questions relate to family members' satisfaction with the relative's living situation and their relative's perceived satisfaction.

MERGER OF THE INDEPENDENT MONITORING FOR QUALITY (IM4Q) PROGRAM AND THE NATIONAL CORE INDICATORS PROJECT (NCIP)

In 1999, Pennsylvania joined several other states as a participant in the NCIP, sponsored by the National Association of State Directors of Developmental Disabilities Services (NASDDDS) and the Human Services Research Institute (HSRI). (See Chapter 13 for a complete discussion.) This project involves an effort to establish performance measures for states to judge their developmental disabilities service systems. The NCIP includes several levels of surveys including consumer surveys, family surveys, provider surveys, and so on. Many of the questions developed for use in the consumer survey portion of the NCIP also appear in the Essential Data Elements Survey, the instrument used for the Independent Monitoring Program.

A major issue emerged as the two projects proceeded on parallel tracks. The result was that individuals could be surveyed by two separate entities in a relatively short period of time, and many of the questions in the two surveys were duplicative. The statewide independent monitoring steering committee and the OMR discussed the issues and decided to marry the two efforts, albeit on a faster track than most people would have liked. As a result, on July 1, 2000, the two efforts were combined into one project called Independent Monitoring for Quality (IM4Q).

The Relationship Between Local IM4Q Programs and Other OMR Monitoring

The IM4Q program is one part of a much larger effort by the Office of Mental Retardation to provide continuous quality improvement and enhancement in Pennsylvania. IM4Q is not meant to replace processes that now exist through OMR (e.g., licensing). IM4Q is unique in that people with disabilities, family members, and interested others—all of whom are without conflicts of interest from the mental retardation services and support system—are the people interviewing people receiving services and support. This process provides an independent and external source of information that is not gathered by OMR, the county program, or provider systems.

Technical Advisors

From the inception of the idea for independent monitoring, OMR provided technical assistance to the program through independent technical advisors. These advisors worked closely with the statewide steering committee, local programs, and regional OMR offices. In addition, the technical advisors held quarterly regional meetings of the local IM4Q programs to learn what was working and what needed improvement. The advisors provided assistance in the development of each local program, developed and provided training on the interviewing instrument (Essential Data Elements), analyzed the data collected by the local programs, and worked closely with OMR in embedding IM4Q within its continuous quality enhancement system. Technical assistance was provided by staff from the Institute on Disabilities, Pennsylvania's University Center for Excellence in Developmental Disabilities at Temple University.

The IM4Q Statewide Steering Committee

The OMR has created an IM4Q statewide steering committee to ensure that the purpose and principles of IM4Q are upheld and followed by providing advice to OMR on IM4Q, as well as to the local programs. The committee reports directly to OMR and has no operational role/responsibility to county government or to providers of services. The committee is composed of 18 members, 10 voting and 8 nonvoting. The committee's roles and responsibilities are to

- Participate with the regional OMR in the final selection of local programs

- Provide oversight for the development and revision of the interview instrument

- Review the analysis of the data collected from the local programs across the state and issue a statewide report

- Issue recommendations to OMR from the analysis of the statewide report

- Resolve conflict-of-interest questions for local programs

- Review and analyze the external evaluations of local programs

- Arrange for an external evaluation of the statewide IM4Q program

- Advise the OMR on the development of policies and procedures for independent monitoring

- Ensure that technical assistance is provided to the local programs

- Develop relationships with the local programs

- Hold necessary meetings to conduct the business of the committee

- Arrange for a yearly retreat/conference to be held for all the local programs

The County Mental Health/Mental Retardation Office

Pennsylvania has 67 counties, some of which join together to provide mental health and mental retardation (MH/MR) services. Forty-six county MH/MR programs receive money from OMR to provide mental retardation services either directly or by contract. Each county, with the input of the statewide steering committee and the regional OMR, selects a not-for-profit (501[c][3]) agency as the local IM4Q program. The county program develops a contract with the local program that complies with OMR fiscal regulations. The contract is meant to be a formal agreement between two parties that defines in advance the payment, services, and rules of the relationship. Therefore, the local program needs to be actively involved in the development of such a contract with the county program. The county program needs to separate itself from the local monitoring program, so that the local program is operated as a separate entity. The county program provides names of individuals to be monitored and any other OMR required information within OMR time lines.

The Local IM4Q Program Governing Board

It is the local program's responsibility to conduct the agreed-on number of interviews for the county program as identified by the OMR and through the contract with the county program. Each local monitoring program has an official governing board. A governing board can take two primary forms: a board solely for the independent monitoring program or a committee that is part of an already established board. The governing board must meet specific requirements: 1) establish independence and be as conflict-free as possible and 2) attain nonprofit status or merge with an existing conflict-free nonprofit entity. The requirements for the composition of the governing board are

- 51% must be people with disabilities and family members of people with disabilities.

- Of the 51%, at least 33% must be people with developmental disabilities and at least 33% must be family members of people who have disabilities and who are unable to verbally speak for themselves.

- Remaining governing board members should be interested others who have no conflicting responsibilities.

The local IM4Q program governing board will carry out or assign the following tasks:

- Establish and sign all contracts with the county MH/MR program

- Develop procedures and policies for the operation of the local program

- Develop a direct relationship with the county MH/MR advisory board, which has a statutory obligation to review and evaluate services

- Arrange for a yearly external evaluation of the local program's work

- Hire, supervise, and evaluate the local program's coordinator

- Collaborate with the Statewide Steering Committee

- Find facility or office space, if necessary

- Recruit and establish orientation and training of monitors

- Develop and maintain a database program for the local program to coordinate the monitoring visits

- Ensure that monitoring interviews with people identified in their sample occur

- Develop methods to report findings back to the county and for the county to communicate with the provider agency and the MH/MR advisory board

- Follow-up with the county after monitoring to ensure that issue resolution has occurred

- Ensure that local program data-entry staff are properly trained for data entry, all collected data are entered meeting IM4Q time lines, and program information is kept secure and confidential in compliance with federal, state, and local standards

- Make needed changes to ensure a successful local program and fulfill any obligations to the statewide IM4Q program

Local IM4Q Program Team Members (Monitors)

The local program must have monitors who are people with disabilities, family members of people with disabilities, and other interested people who are not human services workers. Monitoring teams, with no fewer then two people, should be composed of members from each listed group in such a way that maximizes their skills and abilities. Local programs are directed to strive to have at least one individual with disabilities on each of their monitoring teams.

No person is to conduct any interviewing until all applicable laws have been complied with, such as that required by the Pennsylvania Child Protective Services Act. If a team member is scheduled to interview a child, it is also necessary in Pennsylvania to obtain an Act 33 Child Abuse Clearance. Team members must be as conflict-free as possible, and each team member must sign and abide by statements of confidentiality. Team members receive specific orientation and training appropriate to their role as monitors prior to monitoring. Possible topics for team member orientation include:

- Values orientation, including issues such as self-determination

- What is independent monitoring on the local level? On the state level?

- What is your role as an independent monitor?

- What is expected of you as an independent monitor?

- What is the monitoring instrument being used, and how do you use it?

- What is the best way to interview? What are the techniques and skills needed?

- What are proper protocol, manners, decorum, and relationships to have when visiting with a person to be interviewed?

- How would you address unusual or serious situations while on site, and what should you do in these situations?

- What are possible confidentiality issues?

- How do you properly report after an interview?

Formation of an IM4Q Monitoring Team

The local program develops guidelines on forming an effective team. Some criteria that are considered include

- The number of individuals on a team (must be more than one)

- The balancing/pairing of team members' abilities in creating a competent team

- Consideration of any potential conflicts of interest

- Match of team members to the person being interviewed (e.g., cultural awareness, physical access issues, communication needs)

- Experience of a particular team with the setting in which a person being interviewed lives and works

The IM4Q Process

Once a team is formed, it is assigned a person to interview. Either the team leader or a local program coordinator arranges the interview by calling the individual to be interviewed or communicating with his or her staff or family that an interview is to be arranged at a time and place convenient for the person. Interviews may take place at the person's home or at some other place of his or her preference.

In terms of recruitment of team members, programs have employed a variety of methods. Local advocacy groups, local colleges and universities, and local newspapers have all proven to be excellent referral sources. Each program handles payment of team members in a slightly different way. Some projects pay team members as consultants, others consider team members as part-time employees, and still others consider team members as volunteers and either provide a stipend or reimbursement for travel. In any case, this work is considered episodic in nature, and cannot be seen as full-time employment for anyone. However, the work is generally flexible and ongoing and seems to fit well in many peoples' schedules. The flexible work schedule and payment scheme seems to work well and as a result, the retention of team members has not been a significant issue. In some counties where there have been few efforts to develop self-advocacy, the recruitment of people with mental retardation has proven to present a greater challenge. Programs have shared recruitment strategies with one another, which has helped to some extent. Pennsylvania has a strong self-advocacy network that has also been an effective referral source.

Follow-Up Activities: "Closing the Loop"   At the time of an interview, the person interviewed is asked for permission to share the information he or she offers with the county program, the provider, and the state. If the person agrees, the team may develop specific considerations to offer the county program regarding what the person desires. The team also offers the county program other considerations that might further improve the life of the person interviewed. The term *consideration* is offered instead of the term *recommendation* because the team is presenting information intended to generate discussion among the county, the provider, the person being served, and the person's family, friends, or guardian. Some considerations may be beyond the scope of an individual and may instead reflect county-level issues or concerns. Therefore, the local program establishes a process with the county program, with reasonable time lines specified, by which individual and system considerations can formally be reported. The county must inform the local program in writing regarding action taken on specific considerations and the outcomes. As part of this process, which has come to be known as "closing the loop," local programs also report their considerations to the county MH/MR Advisory Board.

If there is no response to the considerations in the agreed-on local program and county program process, a system for taking the information further is developed. If such actions fail, the local program can do several things to prompt a response. The local program can formally share concerns with the county commissioners, Pennsylvania Protection and Advocacy (P&A), other advocacy groups, the local authorities—including the police—and any additional entity that it deems appropriate if it feels that the county program or the OMR has not been sufficiently responsive.

Local IM4Q programs cannot become the implementers of change in a person's life or advocate beyond a person's satisfaction with any changes. The local program's power is its ability to report accurately what a person wants to the county and to conduct follow-up activities to determine whether the county addressed what a person wants in a meaningful manner with the provider of services, the person served, and his or her family. Such a "checks and balances" process benefits everyone.

Safeguards to Ensure the Independence of IM4Q

The following five elements—the statewide steering committee, written roles and responsibilities for all parties, monitoring team structure, dissemination of reports and lessons, and external evaluations—have been consciously created as part of IM4Q to safeguard its independence.

IM4Q Statewide Steering Committee   The Statewide Steering Committee advises the OMR on IM4Q, and its voting members are primarily people with disabilities and family members. The committee receives reports of the independently analyzed data and makes independent system recommendations to the OMR to promote continuous quality improvement and enhancement.

Written Roles and Responsibilities for All Parties Involved in IM4Q   The approved guidelines for IM4Q specify its purpose, principles, and the roles and responsibilities of all parties involved (Caruso, 2000). Local programs are selected through a process involving the Statewide Steering Committee, the regional OMR Office, and county programs, based on specific criteria that stress the independence of the local program from service delivery.

Monitoring Team Structure   Teams, which must include at least two people, are composed of individuals with disabilities, family members, and interested others (not human services professionals). Team members must be free of conflict of interest and must have no direct relationship with the individual being interviewed. The team interviews people receiving services and supports and develops an independent team report. Teams must immediately report major concerns regarding health and safety of people interviewed to the local program coordinator who in turn reports such concerns to the appropriate county contacts and to the local program governing board.

Dissemination of Reports and Lessons Learned   Local programs receive a statewide report of the analyses of all the yearly data collected and individual county reports. Local programs can use these reports to promote continuous quality improvement and enhancement within their county and may share these reports. The regional OMR office hosts and facilitates regional local program meetings for the local programs to share concerns and information they have learned. Local programs also meet separately from the regional meetings to foster their own learning. A statewide retreat is convened annually by the steering committee to share with local programs any changes or lessons learned by the IM4Q program and to learn together.

External Evaluations   Each local program is expected to arrange for an annual external evaluation based on guidelines offered by OMR. These external evaluations are shared with the steering committee and are another way for the local program to safeguard its independent functioning.

Results

During 1999–2000, the first year of program implementation, 2,796 face-to-face interviews were conducted by 19 county MH/MR programs. In the second year of the program, 2000–2001, more than 5,000 interviews were conducted through 41 IM4Q programs contracting with 46 MH/MR programs. The following highlights and recommendations are offered as a summary of the 1999–2000 monitoring efforts.

Satisfaction   Most people receiving services in Pennsylvania are satisfied with major areas of their lives. Seventy-nine percent say they want to stay where they currently live. Eighty-five percent like their jobs, and 89% say they usually like what they do in their free time.

Quality of Physical Settings   We asked the independent monitoring teams to evaluate different aspects of the physical settings around where people live, including the safety of the neighborhood, the exterior and interior of the structure, the personalization of each resident's space, and the home's accessibility. The responses were overwhelmingly positive—team members gave most of the settings top marks.

Considerate Interactions   Most people say their staff and their roommates treat them well. Seventy-eight percent say their roommates are "nice" or "very nice" to them, 90% say the staff at work are nice or very nice, and 91% of the staff at home are nice or very nice.

Quality of Staffing   Members of the independent monitoring teams formed many favorable impressions of the staff they observed. In general, teams perceived staffing to be adequate in terms of the number of people on site (92%), respectful of the people with whom they work (87% say "always" respectful), and supportive of control (87% say "always" supportive). Teams characterized 78% of staff as having "all" the skills necessary to support the individual about whom questions were being asked.

Reliable Transportation   Whether they are getting to work, going to a medical or business appointment, or traveling for leisure, the vast majority of respondents rate their transportation either "reliable" or "extremely reliable." Only 3%–6% characterize their transportation to any type of destination as less than reliable. Most people receiving services in Pennsylvania rely on transportation provided by the agency.

Respect for Privacy   Most people receiving services in Pennsylvania say they have privacy whenever they want it or at least most of the time they want it (90%). In contrast, only 4% say they rarely or never have the privacy they desire. Most respondents say that other people respect their privacy by knocking on the door of their home (85%) or the door of their bedroom (80%) before entering.

Support of Friendships   A high percentage, 93%, of the individuals surveyed say they have friends, and 84% say that they have someone in their lives to whom they feel "extra close." Although more could be done to create socializing opportunities with friends, the fact that 77% of the respondents say that staff "always" support them in making and keeping friends is a positive sign.

General Recommendations and Considerations   The data from 1999–2000 offer several recommendations and considerations:

People should have a greater say over where they live and what they do during the day. Providers dominate the choice of where to live, either by choosing the person's residence outright (34%) or by helping them to choose (20%). Providers also have the largest role in choosing a person's day activity (they choose for 34% of respondents and help with the choice for 39%). Even for those individuals who have input in the decision, stronger emphasis should be placed on seeing a variety of options in order to make a more informed choice. Only 39% saw more than one option for a place to live before deciding, and only 36% saw more than one day activity option.

People should have a more meaningful role in screening their potential roommates. Only 17% of the respondents chose all the housemates who live with them. Worse, of the 47% of the people in the sample who share a bedroom, 71% did not choose with whom they share it. Ideally, people should be able to live with whom they want, and minimally, they should have the "right of refusal" concerning potential roommates that any adult would demand. Underscoring the importance of this issue, respondents are more likely to be afraid at home than at work, and the category of "other residents" ranks highest on the list of things that cause the respondents fear at home.

A greater effort should be made to establish and use formal communications systems. Of 987 people in the sample who do not communicate verbally, only 176 (18%) have a formal communication system in place. Furthermore, when a system is in place, it is only being used in half of the cases. The independent monitoring teams described only 78% of the staff they met as having all the skills necessary to support the people in the sample, and the use of formal communications systems is one area in which it appears staff might benefit from more specific training.

Mail should not be read without permission. For 36% of the respondents, staff reads their mail without permission at least sometimes. For 19%, staff read the mail without permission always. Although staff assistance is required in some cases, respect for people's privacy and legal rights dictates that staff should still always secure permission before handling people's mail.

Friendships and family relationships should be supported with more opportunities to socialize. People in the state sample are less likely to socialize at least weekly with friends, neighbors, and relatives (49%) than people without disabilities in a nationwide sample (85%). Pennsylvanians also trail the national sample in the frequency of going food shopping, going out to eat, and going to places of worship, but the lack of socializing is most striking. Pennsylvanians are also much less likely to socialize (70%) than those in a nationwide sample of people with disabilities. It is difficult to foster the spontaneous, nonstereotypical socializing that is indicative of true inclusion, but more could be done to support people's relationships. For example, 22% say they never get to see old friends when they want.

Complaint procedures should be as explicit as possible. When asked whether they always know what to do if they have a complaint, only 75% of the respondents said they did. Although this percentage seems high, there is room for improvement. Knowing that one has an avenue to redress wrongs is essential, both for safety and for quality of life.

Individuals should have their own set of keys. In the sample, only 28% of the people had keys to their residence. For the majority, freedom of movement may be curtailed because they depend on staff to let them in and out of their own homes. These data have been presented by the steering committee to the state for its consideration. Activity has already commenced in several of the aforementioned areas in which policy initiatives are required.

WHAT HAS BEEN LEARNED FROM IM4Q

Many benefits have resulted from the IM4Q program. IM4Q has acted as a catalyst in actively engaging county MH/MR programs, providers, the Pennsylvania OMR, and community people in a continuous quality improvement and enhancement effort. IM4Q has increased the involvement of people with disabilities and their family members in shaping the service system by requiring a specific percentage (51%) to be on the governing boards of the local IM4Q programs. Many people have become monitors, including people who have disabilities, family members, and interested community people.

For a number of local IM4Q programs, college students have become monitors. This opportunity has provided them with a chance to really learn from people being served and supported. In addition, being on a team with people with disabilities and their family members has provided opportunities for them to work together and learn about one another. These interviewing and team experiences can have a significant positive impact on students' perceptions and attitudes about people with disabilities and their families.

Another important benefit of IM4Q is that for some people who are interviewed, their lives can change positively because team members heard what changes they wanted in their lives. The local IM4Q program shared these changes with the county, which in turn shared them with providers. A change process was thus created. People receiving supports have moved into the types of places they have asked for, had different work opportunities, changed roommates, and overall have increased the choices within their lives. Such a change process can only improve over time as long as independent people on local IM4Q program teams listen to what people receiving services have to say and pass that information on to those who can effectuate change.

In addition to the lessons learned, there are still several areas that OMR, in collaboration with the technical advisors and stakeholders, continues to work through:

- Interviewing individuals who do not communicate using words

- Establishing reliability and validity of the instrument

- Keeping the instrument at a length that meets the need of the system to obtain information but does not overly burden the individuals being surveyed

- Considering the idea of reimbursing consumer respondents for their time

- Recruiting individuals with cognitive disabilities to serve on teams

- Ensuring that local programs, in collaboration with the counties, have developed a system for "closing the loop"

CONCLUSION

The independent monitoring effort in Pennsylvania represents a significant shift in how a state government monitors the quality of community services and supports. This shift has involved significant changes in who does the monitoring, who responds to the questions asked by monitors, what questions are asked, and what is done with the information that is collected. This basic system transformation has had a significant impact on the people receiving supports, families, providers, counties, and the state. It is the hope and dream of many that once some of the major issues are resolved, such as those concerning reliability and validity of the instrument, these data will be summarized and used to provide data-based information to people with disabilities and their families on which they can make decisions about who will provide services and supports to them.

REFERENCES

Bonham, G.S., Pisa, L.M., Basehart, S., Marchand, C.B., Harris, C., Heim, S., & Ingram, A. (1999). *Ask Me! Year 2. The quality of life of Marylanders with developmental disabilities receiving DDA funded supports.* Annapolis: Maryland Developmental Disability Administration and Maryland Developmental Disabilities Council.

Caruso, G. (2000). *Pennsylvania's Independent Monitoring for Quality (IM4Q).* Philadelphia: Office of Mental Retardation and Developmental Disabilities Council.

Feinstein, C.S., Levine, R.M., Lemanowicz, J.A., & Carey, A.C. (2000). *Independent monitoring: A statewide summary 1999–2000.* Philadelphia: Temple University, Institute on Disabilities, University Center for Excellence.

Lakin, C.K. (2000). *Consumer roles in monitoring community services.* Unpublished manuscript. Institute for Community Integration, University of Minnesota, Minneapolis.

Mochan, R., Owens, M., & St. Peter, S. (1996). Introducing citizen monitoring. In S. St. Peter & M. Owens (Eds.), *Citizen monitoring: Learning from the views and voices of citizens who are not service providers* (pp. II 1–II1 7). Allegheny, PA: ARC of Allegheny.

Oregon Developmental Disabilities Council. (1997). *A foundation for quality assurance of community services for Oregonians with developmental disabilities.* Salem: Oregon Developmental Disabilities Council.

Schalock, R.L. (1994). Quality of life, quality enhancement, and quality assurance: Implications for program planning and evaluation in the field of mental retardation and developmental disabilities. *Evaluation and Program Planning, 17*(2), 121–131.

Sundram, C.J. (1994). Quality assurance in an era of consumer empowerment and choice. *Mental Retardation, 32*(5), 371–374.

SECTION IV

The Future of Public Oversight

This section offers three distinct perspectives on the public responsibility for ensuring quality in services to people with developmental disabilities. Chapter 10 discusses the evolution in quality enhancement at the federal level, especially at the Centers for Medicare & Medicaid Services (CMS), regarding the Medicaid-funded ICF/MR programs. Chapter 11 looks at where quality enhancement needs to go on a national level to enable people to achieve desired outcomes and enjoy high quality of life. Chapter 12 takes the reader to the international stage, examining comparable consumer-focused quality enhancement activities in Australia, Finland, and Norway.

It is clear from these chapters that much change is afoot in national approaches to ensuring positive outcomes for people receiving supports in the public sector. At CMS—in recognition that more and more people are living in their own homes, controlling their own lives, and truly being an inclusive part of their home communities—federal monitoring and oversight have broadened to include a focus on the desires of individuals served. CMS has made many significant changes in guidelines, ICF/MR survey processes, and training; is in the process of revising regulations and developing quality indicators; and has engaged the Council on Quality Leadership to assist with the monitoring and oversight of the ICF/MR survey process. Amid all of this change, one of the most challenging issues facing CMS is how to define its regulatory role to ensure that health and safety requirements are met, yet still allow for consumer choice.

In Chapter 11, Gettings speaks for those managing state public developmental disabilities systems by outlining the guiding principles and central components of the Comprehensive Quality Management Program for Public Developmental Disabilities Service Systems. Recognizing that such an endeavor is only one of a number of critical developments needed to ensure that people with developmental disabilities receive high-quality services and supports, Gettings emphasizes that establishing a quality management program requires "a strong, ongoing commitment" to learning from past mistakes and taking forthright steps to improve the appropriateness and quality of the services offered. This commitment to learning includes open communication, involvement of all stakeholders, and shared celebrations of success, complementing a shared responsibility for less satisfactory results.

Chapter 12 offers an international perspective on using consumer experiences to reflect on the quality of services and supports for people with developmental disabilities. Australia, Finland, and Norway each gather information on consumer outcomes to assess changes in system performance over time and use the outcome data to enhance and improve the quality of services. Australia's National Satisfaction Survey of Clients of Disability Services is a promising innovation. The early implementation issues are familiar to U.S. researchers, including provider cooperation and consumer engagement. In Finland, public authorities have created the Quality Network that uses the results of nationwide assessments of consumer outcomes and reviews of the performance of municipalities responsible for service provision in order to offer customers with disabilities and their family members, staff members of services, and municipalities continuous and intensive support to achieve their goals. Ultimately, they seek to have all citizens share responsibility for the quality of the system of public services.

Of the three international examples presented, Norway provides the longest experience in surveying consumers about their quality of life. Living condition surveys have been conducted in 1989, 1994, and 2001. These surveys are explicitly a policy tool, focused not so much on improving the services and supports received by each individual as on enhancing the situation for all people with intellectual disabilities. The purpose of the living condition surveys is "to uncover social problems, to compare social groups, and to describe progress over time" (Chapter 12).

CHAPTER 10

Federal Policy and Practice in Transition

A Look Ahead at the ICF/MR Program

CATHERINE HAYES, LINDA JOYCE, AND ELIZABETH COUCHOUD

Since the 1980s, an enormous shift has occurred in the philosophy and practice of providing services to people with developmental disabilities. As a result, the role of the federal government in funding and overseeing the delivery of services has changed dramatically. At the federal level, the Department of Health and Human Services (DHHS) provides funding and oversight through its Centers for Medicare & Medicaid Services (CMS). CMS (formerly known as the Health Care Financing Administration [HCFA]) funds services to people with mental retardation and other developmental disabilities through several mechanisms, including intermediate care facilities for people with mental retardation (ICFs/MR). This chapter reviews the ICF/MR program and some of the changes that CMS has already implemented for this program, and it discusses the transition that is occurring at the federal level as the system shifts from a provider orientation to a focus on the needs and outcomes of people who are served through Medicaid.

HISTORY

In 1971, Congress enacted into law the ICF/MR benefit as an optional Medicaid service through the passage of the Miller amendment to the Social Security Act (Title XIX). Congressional authorization for ICF/MR services as a state plan option under Medicaid allowed states to receive federal matching funds for institutional services that had been funded with state or local government money. However, it also required states to adopt and use federally established regulations and survey processes.

Three years later, in 1974, the first set of ICF/MR regulations were published in the *Federal Register.* At that time, more than 145,000 individuals with mental retardation were living in large public institutions. Thousands more were living in private facilities. The Social Security Act Amendments of 1965 (PL 89-97) had stated that "the primary purpose of such institutions (ICF/MR) is to provide health or rehabilitative services for the mentally retarded individuals (or persons with related conditions) and the institution meets such standards as prescribed by the Secretary" (Social Security Act, 1905[d][1]). The 1974 regulations further defined the ICF/MR benefit as

> An institution (or distinct part thereof) primarily for the diagnosis, treatment, or rehabilitation of the mentally retarded or persons with related conditions which provides, in a protected residential setting, individualized ongoing evaluation, planning, 24-hour supervision, coordination, and integration of health or rehabilitative services to help each individual reach his maximum of functional capabilities. ("Proposed Conditions," 1974)

An institution was defined as four or more people, therefore ICF/MR group homes were established with no fewer than four individuals.

The law also required that the facility, in order to qualify for the payment, provide clients with active treatment. The Secretary of Health and Human Services was given authority to define *active treatment* in regulations. The original definition of *active treatment* stated, "The overall objective of the plan is to assist the individual to attain or maintain the optimal physical, intellectual, social, or vocational functioning of which he is presently or potentially capable." The original intent of the program was to add federal funds to existing state funds and establish standards so that more than simple custodial care or "warehousing" would be provided.

WHAT HAS CHANGED?

As articulated throughout this book, the service delivery system for people with developmental disabilities has experienced a major shift since the 1980s. The system now emphasizes people living in their own homes, controlling their own lives, and truly being included in their communities. The concept of quality enhancement has broadened to include a focus on the desires of individuals served. Individuals, families, and the providers must be an integral part of planning.

The current ICF/MR regulations were developed in the mid-1980s and published in 1988. At that time, they reflected the developmental model, representing a step forward in the service delivery philosophy. Consumers, advocates, and providers welcomed the change. However, since that time, leading thinkers and advocates in the developmental disabilities arena have pushed forward to embrace a new individual support approach. As a result, some advocates, consumers, and providers have criticized the current ICF/MR regulations and oversight process as too prescriptive and out of step with the new philosophy. CMS officials have increasingly come to recognize the need for changes in the current federal approach, especially in light of changes in the composition of ICF/MR facilities: 1) homes have become fewer and smaller, and 2) residents increasingly are elderly and have multiple disabilities.

Facilities Are Fewer and Smaller

After years of steady growth, the ICF/MR program peaked in 1993, at which time 7,400 ICFs/MR existed; these served 144,000 people. Since that time, both the number of facilities and the number of people served by them have declined, and as of 2001, 114,177 people were served in 6,719 facilities, an overall loss of 681 facilities (see Figure 10.1).

Of particular interest is the change in the number of privately operated facilities, which the original ICF/MR benefit did not include. Privately operated homes have decreased in number from 6,439 in 1993 to 5,640 in 2001, an overall loss of 799 privately operated homes. This decline does not necessarily indicate that the homes ceased operation; it may reflect the movement of some providers away from the ICF/MR program and into the Home and Community-Based Services (HCBS) Waiver programs. However, despite the reduction in the number of private facilities, they still serve a significant portion of the ICF/MR population—slightly more than half (53%) of all people served by the ICF/MR program still reside in privately operated homes.

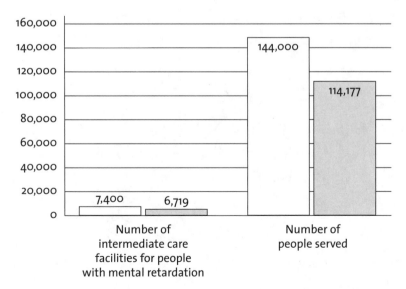

Figure 10.1.   Number of intermediate care facilities for people with mental retardation (ICFs/MR) and number of people served in 1993 and 2001. (*Key:* ☐ 1993; ▨ 2001)

As the total number of facilities has decreased, the smaller types of facilities have become more numerous. The number of large facilities (i.e., those with more than 50 beds) has declined to 380, just 6% of all facilities in 2001. In sharp contrast, the number of small homes (i.e., those with 16 or fewer beds) has increased to 5,982, constituting 89% of all ICF/MR homes (see Figure 10.2).

This increase in 16-bed facilities and the concurrent reduction in large facilities can be misleading. At one time, large institutions were very large— 500 to 1,000 beds—and were certified as one agency. During the 1990s, many institutions applied for and received separate provider numbers for each of their individual units. Each unit would be home to between 16 and 50 people. Although on paper there might now appear to be thirty 16-bed facilities in close proximity, in reality it may still be a large campus that serves 480 people. Although the vast majority of current ICFs/MR are small (with eight or fewer beds), the majority of ICF/MR beneficiaries (52%) are still served in homes with more than 50 people (see Figure 10.3). An additional 9% of the people are currently served in homes with 17–50 beds.

When the data for privately operated and publicly operated homes are separated, it becomes evident that privately operated homes (for profit and not-for-profit) are overwhelmingly small (93% have 16 or fewer beds), and they serve a significant portion of the ICF/MR population (63%) in these small homes (see Table 10.1). Nonetheless, 27% of the people served in private ICFs/MR are in facilities that accommodate 51 or more people. Thus, despite the clear trend towards smaller homes, the majority of people who are served

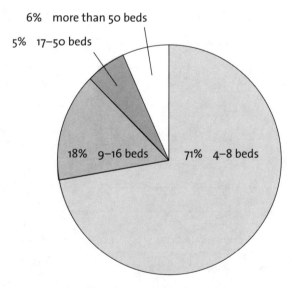

Figure 10.2. Percentage of intermediate care facilities for people with mental retardation of each size (N = 6,719).

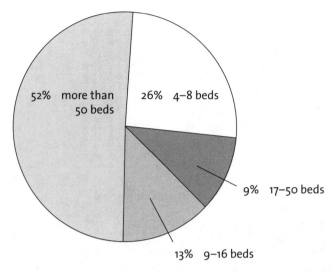

Figure 10.3. Proportion of clients in each size of intermediate care facilities for people with mental retardation in 2001 (N = 114,177).

by the ICF/MR program still live in large homes: 89% of those in publicly operated homes and 37% of those in private homes.

ICF/MR Residents Are Elderly and Have Multiple Disabilities

As one would expect, 99% of those in ICFs/MR have been diagnosed with mental retardation. The vast majority (70%) have been diagnosed with either severe or profound mental retardation. Data show that 51% are nonambulatory, 54% have speech impairments, 38% have visual impairments, and 40% have epilepsy (see Figure 10.4). Clearly, a large percentage of the people who

Table 10.1. Distribution of intermediate care facilities for people with mental retardation by size and type of operation and clients by size and type of facility

Facility size	Percentage of privately operated homes (n = 5,640)	Percentage of clients in privately operated homes	Percentage of publicly operated homes (n = 1,079)	Percentage of clients in publicly operated homes
4–8 beds	75%	42%	50%	6%
9–16 beds	18%	21%	16%	4%
17–50 beds	3%	10%	15%	9%
More than 50 beds	3%	27%	19%	80%

Source: The Online Survey Certification and Reporting System (OSCAR).

204

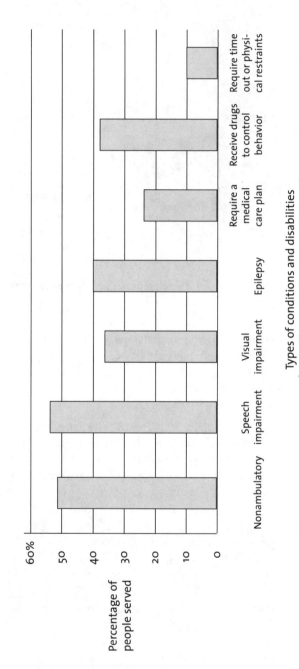

Figure 10.4. Characteristics of clients in intermediate care facilities for people with mental retardation (N = 114,177).

live in ICFs/MR have multiple disabilities. Nearly one quarter (23%) require nursing services 24 hours per day and a medical care plan. In addition, many may be medicated to control their behavior (37%) or may be placed either in time-out rooms or in physical restraints (10%).

The ICF/MR population is also aging, as evidenced by the growth in the segment of the population that is age 46 or older: 38%, up from 33% in 1996. The fact that this population is aging and has multiple disabilities emphasizes the need for CMS to continue to focus on health care needs because the ICF/MR benefit is still the only medical benefit for most people who reside in ICFs/MR.

IMPETUS FOR CHANGE

Recognizing that changes were occurring in the facilities and the population served by ICF/MR programs, in 1995, the White House began a series of partnership initiatives with CMS policy makers, regulators, providers, and consumers to discuss needed improvements in services for people with developmental disabilities. These discussions were designed to gather input to help guide CMS policy and practice. The primary question was "What do we need to do differently?" Such listening sessions were held throughout the country over the subsequent few years. At the same time, a growing number of comments from the field indicated a need for CMS to revise the ICF/MR survey process. Both providers and advocates voiced concerns that the survey process entailed too much focus on paper and record reviews and not enough on the outcomes that were occurring in people's lives. In addition, two federal reports issued at this time identified shortcomings in the operations of the ICF/MR program. These included a 1996 report by the General Accounting Office (GAO) and the 1993 Office of the Inspector General (OIG) report.

GAO Report: Federal Monitoring of Large Public Institutions Criticized

In 1996, the GAO issued a report, *Medicaid: The Level of Federal Oversight in Institutions for the Mentally Retarded Should Be Strengthened*. This report examined the reasons behind continued deficiencies found by the Department of Justice (DOJ) in the course of Civil Rights for Institutionalized Persons Act (CRIPA) of 1980 (PL 96-416) investigations in large public ICFs/MR. They found a potential for a conflict of interest on the part of states to influence the certification decisions regarding state-run ICFs/MR. The report criticized the reduction in the number of federal surveys of large public ICFs/MR, using as a baseline the number of federal surveys conducted in large public institutions as a result of the 1985 Wiekert initiative. Historically, CMS's primary oversight mechanism has been the federal monitoring survey that assesses state agency determinations of provider compliance (informally known as federal look-behind surveys). At one time in the program's history, as many as 52 federal and regional developmental disabilities specialists were assigned throughout the country to conduct look-behind surveys and to evaluate the quality of services delivered.

Office of the Inspector General Report

In 1993, the OIG issued a report, "Medicaid Payment to Institutions for People with Mental Retardation," that addressed the extent and variation among states in the reimbursement rates. The report encouraged CMS to take action to control ICF/MR reimbursement rates and to encourage states to adopt effective cost controls.

CMS'S RESPONSE

In response to the listening sessions and the GAO and OIG reports, CMS undertook two efforts: updating the ICF/MR guidelines and revising the survey process.

Updated Guidelines

In December 1995, the *State Operations Manual* (SOM) was updated and republished. This manual not only includes all the various interpretations and updates for the ICF/MR regulations that have been issued by CMS but also incorporates compliance principles and facility practice statements. The new guidance was designed to help surveyors make more consistent decisions and focus more on positive outcomes for individuals.

Facility practice statements were added for most standard requirements in order to clarify the specific requirement. In order to qualify for Medicaid reimbursement, ICFs/MR must be certified and comply with federal standards (referred to as *conditions of participation,* found in the *Code of Federal Regulations* at 42 CFR, Sections 483.400–483.480). There are eight conditions of participation: governing body, client protections, facility staffing, active treatment services, client behavior and facility practices, health care services, physical environment, and dietetic services. The conditions of participation are intended to protect the health and safety of individuals receiving services and to ensure that high-quality supports and services are provided to all individuals living in ICFs/MR. Compliance principles were written for each of the eight conditions of participation. These spell out what outcomes must be present for the condition to be met and what outcomes indicate the condition is not met. Each condition is composed of several standards or requirements. Facility practice statements were added for most standard requirements in order to further clarify that specific requirement.

Revised ICF/MR Survey Process

Also in 1995, HCFA (now the CMS) initiated a process to revise the current survey procedures for the ICF/MR program. The process was based on two major assumptions: that the 1988 regulations were still binding and that the survey process should be applicable in all settings, large and small. The revision sought to focus the survey on actual outcomes that occurred in the lives of the people who receive services. HCFA convened a work group of the various leaders in the developmental disabilities field, including state and regional office representatives along with representatives of leading consumer and provider groups. This work group developed five different drafts of the revised survey protocol before it was field-tested. The revised survey embraced three major changes: an expansion of data collection, introduction of a three-stage survey process, and addition of a new task.

1. Fifty-two requirements were designated as fundamental tags, and three additional requirements were later added. Tags are letters and numbers assigned to requirements for the Online Survey Certification and Reporting (OSCAR) system so that information about specific requirements is included in the data banks.

2. The work group designed a three-stage survey process: fundamental, extended, and full. The requirements examined on fundamental surveys are considered to be outcome requirements. When the desired outcomes are not present or undesirable outcomes are present and the surveyors find that a provider may not be meeting all the conditions of participation, they extend the survey to consider all of the requirements under the four fundamental conditions of participation—an extended survey. Frequently, this additional information assures surveyors that the condition is not out of compliance. Once a condition of participation is found to be out of compliance, the surveyors may survey for all requirements—a full survey. State agencies also have the freedom to determine in advance that they will conduct a full survey in any facility, as facilities are required to comply with all the ICF/MR requirements. HCFA encourages states to make that determination based on prior survey results, complaints, and other information, but states may make that determination for any reason.

3. HCFA also added a new survey task: review of facility systems to prevent abuse, neglect, and mistreatment and to resolve complaints. Although no additional requirements or standards were added to the regulations, this task was formalized as the second component, or Task 2 of 8, of the survey process. Task 2 focused surveyor attention on reviewing complaints and allegations of abuse, mistreatment, and neglect early in the survey.

The work group field-tested its proposed process through 13 pilot surveys. Five jurisdictions participated in the pilot: Indiana, South Carolina, Delaware, Connecticut, and Washington, D.C. The surveys occurred in April and May of 1995. The facilities involved were selected by the state agency and agreed to a dual survey, with the proposed process and the traditional process to be completed by two separate survey teams. The size of these facilities varied from 6 people served to 120 people. Five of the selected facilities had been cited for condition-level deficiencies the previous year.

The pilot test revealed several key differences between the proposed process and the traditional process. The pilot surveys appeared to reflect the negative outcomes that an individual experiences more accurately than the traditional process, which had focused more on process and structure citations. Most important, the revised process also focused surveyors on interviews, and observations with individuals served as the primary method of information gathering for the survey.

Implementation of the New Process

Late in 1995, HCFA circulated the revised process and guidelines for comment. Comments from consumer advocacy groups, providers, and state and regional offices, among others, were generally supportive of the changes and the new survey process. Overall, reviewers found that the revised process moved the focus from paper to outcomes. Among the specific suggestions incorporated into the final process were the need for training about such issues as:

1. How to conduct interviews with individuals with severe disability or communication issues

2. How to do observations without first doing a detailed review of the record

3. How to make compliance decisions with the new approach

4. How to use the record and comprehensive functional analysis in the new protocol

HCFA then published the revised survey process as part of the SOM (Transmittal 278). The final revision included a decrease in sample size and the addition of interviews with consumers as a required component of the process, and it formalized the three-stage survey process (focused, extended, and full). Overall, the protocol enabled surveyors to lessen the review burden on more competent providers and to ensure health and safety for individuals living in ICFs/MR.

Since the initiation of the revised survey process, fundamental surveys have become the norm. Close to 77% of all ICF/MR surveys are now fundamental. Approximately another 18% begin as fundamental surveys and are then extended to include all of the tags under the fundamental conditions (extended surveys). The remaining 5% are full surveys, with 1% beginning as fundamental, extending to include all tags under the fundamental conditions, and then extended further to include all tags under all conditions. The remaining 4% are determined in advance by the state agency as full surveys.

Training on the Revised Process   HCFA conducted a series of training sessions, including a train-the-trainers session. These sessions included provider and advocacy representatives. HCFA also developed and distributed a training package, "A Training Course for Surveyors on the Revised 1996 Survey Protocol." Regions and states were encouraged to hold joint training sessions and include providers. By October 1, 1996, more than 119 sessions were completed and 6,000 people participated.

Regional and State Joint Surveys   In order to provide direct federal oversight to a substantial percentage of those beneficiaries who reside in large public facilities, HCFA also established a survey process that was not as staff-intensive as the look-behind surveys. These were called joint or partnership surveys. HCFA regional offices were asked to monitor state agencies during state surveys. In fiscal year 1997, seventy partnership surveys were conducted. Analysis of the findings from these surveys revealed that partnership surveys exposed substantially more compliance issues than did state surveys: when not accompanied by a federal surveyor, state survey agencies found that 5% of public facilities did not comply with at least one condition of participation under the revised survey process. By contrast, when federal surveyors accompanied the team for a partnership survey of a public facility, the number of facilities that did not comply with conditions of participation or that were under immediate jeopardy increased significantly. *Immediate jeopardy* is defined as "a situation in which the providers' noncompliance with one or more requirements of participation has caused or is likely to cause serious injury, harm, impairment, or death to a resident" (42 CFR Part 489.3). Active treatment and client protections were the most frequently cited examples of noncompliance.

Updated Psychopharmacological Medications Resource   In 1997, HCFA developed and distributed *Psychopharmacological Medications—Safety Precautions for Persons with Developmental Disabilities: A Resource for Training and Education.* The manual was intended to assist both providers and surveyors in increasing the benefit from medications while minimizing the harm that they may sometimes cause. Regional offices, state agencies, and all administrators of the more than 7,000 ICFs/MR were mailed a complimentary copy of the manual. The 10 safety precautions are as follows:

- Rule out other causes.

- Collect baseline data.

- State a reasonable hypothesis.

- Intervene in the least restrictive and most positive way.

- Monitor for adverse drug reactions.

- Collect outcome data.

- Start low and go slow.

- Periodically consider gradual dose reduction.

- Maintain active treatment objectives.

- Maintain optimal functional status.

Contract with the Human Services Research Institute   During this time, HCFA also contracted with the Human Services Research Institute (HSRI) to conduct an extensive and nationwide review of the status of state quality enhancement activities. The study included a review of existing and potential quality indicators, a look at the current survey and certification process for ICF/MR providers, a review of the definition for *active treatment* in light of the current emphasis on services and supports, and a baseline survey on the use of psychoactive drugs in ICFs/MR. Completed in 1998, the study indicated that the field was ready for quality indicators. HSRI found that several states had begun work on their own indicators and recommended that HCFA move forward to develop a uniform set of quality indicators.

Additional Training   Over the next several years, HCFA developed a range of training sessions to address a wide array of issues related to the revised survey process. Topics included aging, person-centered planning, interviewing, abuse and neglect prevention, behavior interventions, and investigation skills. Several of these were broadcast as satellite training presentations and were made available to surveyors, providers, and advocates. The satellite training materials and the revised SOMs were made available to the public, through the National Technical Information Services of Springfield, Virginia.

CURRENT CHALLENGES

Two critical challenges still face CMS in providing high-quality services to people in ICFs/MR: review and reduction of the inappropriate use of restraint and seclusion and the promotion of systems to detect and prevent abuse and neglect.

Restraint and Seclusion

The media raised awareness about the dangers of restraint and seclusion beginning with a series of articles called "Deadly Restraint," published in October of 1998 by Connecticut's *Hartford Courant*. This was followed by additional media coverage on *Dateline* and *Foxfiles*, as well as coverage in other local and national newspapers. Concerns voiced as a result of these articles resulted in action by the 105th U.S. Congress. Three different legislative bills were introduced, two in the Senate and one in the House of Representatives. Senate Bill 736, "Individual's Right to Freedom from Restraint and Reporting of Sentinel Events," was introduced by Connecticut Senators Lieberman and Dodd. The same senators then introduced Senate Bill 750, also known as "Compassionate Care Act of 1999." Finally, Congresswoman Degette introduced House Bill 1313, "Patients Freedom from Restraint/Seclusion Act of 1999." These bills did not pass during this legislative session but instead became part of the law in the 106th Congress, as a part of the Children's Health Act of 2000 (PL 106-310).

Subsequently, in September 1999, the GAO published *Mental Health: Improper Use of Restraint and Seclusion Places Patients at Risk.* This study looked at various CMS regulated programs including hospitals, long-term care settings, home- and community-based services, psychiatric residential treatment facilities, and the ICF/MR program to see how CMS was regulating restraint and seclusion across government settings. The GAO report found that CMS regulations vary across programs and recommended that CMS ensure that safeguards are in place in order to guarantee that all beneficiaries are protected, no matter the setting. GAO further recommended that CMS require the reporting of all deaths and serious injuries caused by restraint and seclusion, that data be gathered on the use of restraints and seclusion, and that staff receive training to decrease the need for restraint and seclusion.

Recent CMS Activities Regarding Use of Restraint and Seclusion

The public, media, and Congress have grown increasingly concerned about the need to ensure basic protections for beneficiaries in all settings. Attention specifically has focused on the use of restraints and seclusion. To quickly respond to this issue, the conditions of participation describing patients' rights were separated from the larger package of hospital conditions of participation that were in process and published separately in the *Federal Register* as an interim final rule on July 2, 1999 ("Hospital condition," 1999). These provisions became effective on August 2, 1999.

In addition, on January 22, 2000, the regulations regarding psychiatric residential treatment facilities were published in the *Federal Register.* CMS published these as an interim final rule entitled, "Use of Restraints and Seclusion in Psychiatric Residential Treatment Facilities Providing Inpatient Psychiatric Services to Individuals Under Age 21" (2001). The rule also introduces a condition of participation that these facilities must meet to provide, or to continue to provide, the Medicaid inpatient psychiatric services benefit to individuals younger than 21 years old. Specifically, the provisions of this rule govern the use of restraint, seclusion, the reporting of deaths, serious injuries, and suicide attempts that result from restraint and seclusion.

Finally, Congress passed the Children's Health Act of 2000 (PL 106-310), governing restraint and seclusion in facilities with federally appropriated funds. The Secretary of Health and Human Services is to issue regulations to implement the new law, and CMS is forming a regulation team to address changes in law across all settings.

ICFs/MR and Restraint Regulations

Restrictive procedures, such as restraint and the use of time-out rooms, have been included in all three sets of the ICF/MR regulations. The most recent set of regulations included a new condition of participation called "Client Behaviors and Facility Practice" ("Conditions of Participation," 1988). These regulations permitted, as a professional accepted treatment modality, the use of restraints only as an integral part of an individual's program plan that is intended to lead to a less restrictive means of managing the behavior for which the restrictive procedure was used. In addition, a condition of participation called "Client Protections" was added that addressed the use of informed consent. The individuals served were to be advised of the risk of any proposed intervention or treatment. Individuals were also to be advised of the right to refuse treatment.

The ongoing process of creating and revising the ICF/MR regulations since the 1970s has highlighted the need for and importance of several vital regulatory requirements to address the use of restrictive techniques for behavior management. These include the need for

- A requirement for a functional assessment of need prior to use of restraint

- A description of the targeted or challenging behavior

- An understanding of the antecedent, or what is causing the behavior

- An understanding of what the behavior does for the person or the consequences of that behavior

- Requirements for an analysis of the risk of the behavior and the harm it will cause against the risk of using that restraint

- Careful monitoring of the implementation of the program

- Requirements that the restrictive procedure be removed as soon as possible

Abuse and Neglect—Who Is Safe?

President Clinton's initiative in 1998, aimed at eliminating abuse and neglect in nursing homes, and congressional interest in restraint and seclusion legislation heightened the public's awareness of the victimization of many of society's most vulnerable citizens. Policy makers responded in a variety of ways, from commissioning additional studies of the problem to marshalling government resources to directly address the issues.

Office of Inspector General Report: Review of Seven States' Approaches to Abuse and Neglect   In 2001, the OIG published a study summarizing its review of seven states to determine the extent of federal protections for people with disabilities and the procedures used by state agencies to identify, investigate, and resolve reports of abuse and neglect of people with disabilities. In "Reporting Abuses of Persons with Disabilities," the OIG found that CMS requirements for protecting people with disabilities from abuse and neglect are directed at facility providers, rather than state agencies. Although facilities receiving Medicare or Medicaid funding are subject to CMS's conditions of participation and state laws and regulations, the OIG estimated that up to 90% of people with disabilities resided in facilities that did not receive CMS funds. For the majority of individuals receiving services, therefore, the handling of incidents and inherent protections is left to non-standard laws and regulations that were developed by each state.

Understanding the Magnitude of the Abuse/Neglect Problem Most people with disabilities experience some form of violence or abuse in their lifetime. According to Sobsey (1994), people with disabilities experience a substantially greater risk for abuse than people without disabilities. Children and adults with disabilities are more likely to be abused, and the abuse is more likely to be chronic and severe (Sobsey, 1996).

Who Is Most at Risk? Sobsey (1994) reviewed many studies about abuse and neglect among people with disabilities. Although little research has been done on the physical assaults of adults with disabilities, Sobsey reported that offenses are fairly common. Firsten's study of women institutionalized with psychiatric problems found that "59.8% experienced severe physical assaults as adults, while 56.6% experienced severe physical assaults as children" (as cited in Sobsey, 1994, p. 46). A study by Stimpson and Best of women with a variety of disabilities found that "33.4% had been victims of physical assault" (as cited in Sobsey, 1994, p. 46). "Children and adults with disabilities are particularly at risk for becoming victims of sexual abuse or assault" (p. 67). Another study by Stimpson and Best "suggests that more than 70% of women with a wide variety of disabilities have been victims of violent sexual encounters during some time in their lives" (as cited in Sobsey, 1994, p. 69). Chamberlain, Ruah, Passer, McGrath, and Burkett found of 87 girls and women with mental retardation, ages 11–23, 25% had a known history of sexual assault (1984, p. 67). Senn predicted that "39%–68% of girls and 16%–30% of boys with developmental disabilities will be sexually abused before 18" (as cited in Sobsey, 1994, p. 68). Sobsey concluded, "Even when individuals have disabilities that are not caused by abuse, the risk of abuse appears substantially greater than the risk for individuals without disabilities" (p. 49).

Where Does Abuse Happen and Who Does It? Sobsey reported that abuse is "endemic to most, if not all, service environments" (1994, p. 248). National reports continue to reinforce that abuse and neglect occur in all settings: private and state-operated facilities, small ICFs/MR and HCBS Waiver group homes, and large institutional settings. One study of confirmed cases of abuse in large publicly operated residential facilities located in six states found that the most common types of abuse were neglect and physical abuse (McCartney & Campbell, 1998). Abuse occurred most frequently in residential settings in the afternoon and early evening, between the hours of 3:00 P.M. and 6:00 P.M. In-transit activities accounted for a particularly high incidence of abuse. Victims who were most at risk were those with maladaptive behaviors who had been abused in the past. Staff perpetrators were typically males assigned to the afternoon shift who were newer employees and were previous perpetrators. Other studies confirm that offenders vary widely in age, are more likely to be males than females, and most frequently are natural family members or paid service providers (Sobsey & Doe, 1991).

Factors Contributing to the Magnitude of the Problem   Limited research on abuse and neglect makes it difficult to identify and understand the magnitude of the problem. Definitions of abuse and neglect vary across local and state governments and by national provider and service groups. Within the federal government, various laws and regulations offer inconsistent definitions of abuse and neglect (e.g., Older Americans Act, and Developmental Disabilities Act). Furthermore, reporting requirements also vary significantly. These inconsistencies make comparative analysis of the incidence of abuse and neglect difficult, if not impossible. Complicating the issue is the fact that while reported abuse is all too frequent, *most* abuse goes unreported. Sobsey (1994) cited one study by Marchetti and McCartney that found that abuse reports tend "to be limited to serious instances of physical and sexual abuse," while verbal and psychological abuse goes unreported (p. 248). A study by Rindfleisch and Bean (cited in Sobsey, 1994) estimated that the actual percentage of abuse reported in the managed care of human beings is only 20% of reportable offenses, and this estimate may prove to be optimistic (p. 248).

CMS's Response to Preventing Abuse and Neglect   Recent federal efforts in both the ICF/MR program and the HCBS Waiver program have brought to light numerous incidents of abuse and neglect. The DOJ and CMS have both uncovered shocking levels of abuse and neglect. Media coverage, the GAO report, and the Pennsylvania Auditor General's report on deplorable living conditions in Pennsylvania's group home system have all underscored the critical nature of the problem. A growing concern that the needs of this vulnerable population could be better addressed have brought these issues into national focus. Of particular concern is the seeming lack of a systematic approach by state agencies and providers to identify and address the issues of abuse and neglect, in particular how to prevent and detect their occurrence. CMS has undertaken a number of efforts to address the issue of abuse and neglect of the most vulnerable populations of people, including those living in ICFs/MR.

Abuse and Neglect Prevention Forum   CMS created an Abuse and Neglect Prevention Forum in order to join forces to increase awareness of the problem, identify system issues, and explore the root causes of the breakdown in systems that prevent and detect abuse and neglect. Gathering representatives from the DOJ, state agencies, provider and advocacy groups, the Administration on Developmental Disabilities, and the Office of the Assistant Secretary for Planning and Evaluation (ASPE), CMS hosted four meetings to identify possible solutions to instances of abuse and neglect among beneficiaries. One purpose of the forum was to make recommendations to CMS on how to improve the identification and prevention of abuse and neglect among the most vulnerable of our citizens. These recommendations led to many of the changes described in the following subsections.

Standardized Definitions of Abuse and Neglect: Guidelines for Immediate Jeopardy   Realizing that change begins at home, CMS standardized its definitions of abuse and neglect to help ensure that all provider types were speaking the same language. CMS also revised the guidelines for identifying and investigating immediate jeopardy situations, with emphasis on clarifying expectations for providers and on increasing surveyors' awareness of possible abuse and neglect. CMS reinforced the importance of these changes by strengthening its training efforts with additional modules aimed at assisting surveyors in detecting possible abuse and neglect situations.

Key Components of a Provider's Approach to Abuse and Neglect Prevention and Detection   Underscoring a policy of zero tolerance, CMS requires providers to develop a systemwide approach to eliminating abuse and neglect encompassing seven key components:

1. *Prevent:* The entity has the capacity to prevent the occurrence of abuse and neglect and reviews specific incidents for lessons learned, which form a feedback loop for necessary policy changes.

2. *Screen:* The entity provides evidence and maintains efforts to determine if persons hired have records of abuse or neglect.

3. *Identify:* The entity creates and maintains a proactive approach to identify events and occurrences that may constitute or contribute to abuse and neglect.

4. *Train:* The entity, during its orientation program and through an ongoing training program, provides all employees with information regarding abuse and neglect and related reporting requirements, including prevention, intervention, and detection.

5. *Protect:* The entity must protect individuals from abuse and neglect during investigation of any allegations of abuse and neglect.

6. *Investigate:* The entity ensures, in a timely and thorough manner, objective investigation of all allegations of abuse, neglect, or mistreatment.

7. *Report/respond:* The entity must ensure that any incidents of substantiated abuse and neglect are reported and analyzed and that the appropriate corrective, remedial, or disciplinary action occurs in accordance with applicable local, state, or federal law.

In May 2001, CMS introduced state agencies and providers to the seven key components through a train-the-trainer curriculum and training session.

Reinstatement of Federal Monitoring and Oversight   The *Washington Post's* Pulitzer prize–winning articles on the deplorable conditions individuals experienced in the District of Columbia's group home system, coupled with the OIG and GAO reports, heralded the need for increased federal oversight to help ensure that individuals living in ICFs/MR and other group homes are receiving the supports and services to which they are entitled and for which providers receive federal dollars (Boo, 1999). For the first time in the history of ICFs/MR, CMS solicited bids from outside contractors to implement a new approach to federal monitoring and oversight. In September 2000, a 1-year, $3.5 million contract was awarded to The Council on Quality and Leadership in Supports for People with Disabilities (known as The Council) to implement a three-pronged approach to CMS's look-behind authority. This contract enabled CMS to deploy federal contract surveyors to conduct comparative surveys, direct complaint investigations, and handle crisis assignments. The contract sought to ensure the health and safety of individuals receiving services in ICFs/MR by using contract surveyors to 1) independently monitor the survey determinations made by state agencies, 2) observe and monitor ICF/MR services in both residential and day programs to eliminate abuse and neglect, and 3) be available for deployment in a timely manner in crisis situations that arise anywhere in the country that threaten the welfare of individuals served. The Council is assisting CMS to design criteria for site selection and to analyze findings to identify what, if any, discrepancies exist in interpretation of the regulations or survey process and procedures.

WHAT LIES AHEAD

CMS anticipates that attention in the coming years will focus on four key issues related to the federal ICF/MR program. These include eligibility for ICF/MR program services, CMS's oversight role, the tension between ensuring consumer safety and respecting consumer choice, and serving individuals who have engaged in dangerous criminal behavior.

Eligibility

CMS policy makers have been discussing how best to revise the regulatory definition of active treatment, to permit people with less severe functional deficits and conditions unrelated to mental retardation to be served in the ICF/MR program (and also in the HCBS Waiver program, due to its statutory link to the need for institutional services). To date, work groups have favored maintaining a strict eligibility requirement so that CMS does not expand eligibility, thereby greatly increasing costs to government, and continues to serve people with mental retardation who require intensive supports and services.

This position ensures that the program will continue to serve individuals with the most intense support requirements who are unable to advocate for themselves in addition to those with fewer intense needs, while retaining the high reimbursement rate designed for more people with more intensive needs. Resolution of the dilemma may require a statutory "delinking" of the ICF/MR and HCBS Waiver program to enable each program to target a specific population. If that occurs, the ICF/MR program could continue to serve those individuals most in need of intensive services, while the HCBS Waiver program could exercise more flexibility to define on a state-by-state basis who can be served.

Oversight

Along with dramatic changes in philosophy have come major conflicts between various groups on how services should be provided and which setting best meets the needs of individuals with developmental disabilities. Many consumer and advocate groups are opposed to institutional care and have a great fear of individuals being forced back into nursing home or custodial care settings. At the same time, parents and other advocate groups are concerned about oversight in community settings and are using as evidence an October 1996 paper published in the *American Journal on Mental Retardation* that reported "Risk-adjusted odds on mortality were estimated to be 72% higher in the community than in institutions" (Strauss & Kastner, 1996, p. 26). They have also expressed concern at the "epidemic proportions" of waiting lists for HCBS Waiver programs. The impact of the Americans with Disabilities Act of 1990 (PL 101-336) on this process is only in its embryonic stage and will require the test of time to realize its full potential. CMS, as a federal oversight and regulatory agency, is at a crossroad and needs to determine the role that it is going to play.

Safety versus Consumer Choice

One of the most challenging issues is how to define the regulatory role of CMS, ensure that health and safety requirements are met, and still allow for consumer choice. By setting standards, the government outlines minimum requirements that must be met for an agency to receive funding. Many parents and advocates fear that, without a national set of expectations and requirements, the field might slip back to the day when client abuse was even more widespread and when individuals received little more than custodial care. However, how can regulations be framed and implemented in such a way that they do not interfere with individual choice and self-determination? Where is the balance point between regulatory safety and individual choice? Whose choice takes precedence? What is the responsibility of the agency that receives federal funding to provide certain services? What is the role of the paid professional whose judgment differs from the individual's choice? What if the person makes a choice that is not in the norm or that may harm his or her health? Clearly, CMS needs to study best practices in this area. What works? When does safety or oversight go too far? How does CMS balance the critical need for oversight with freedom of choice? There is no doubt that choice and self-management play critical roles in the quality of one's life.

Individuals with Developmental Disabilities and Dangerous Criminal Behavior

As noted, determining who is in need of active treatment is an issue inherent to the ICF/MR program. Individuals with mental retardation and other developmental disabilities who are also guilty of dangerous criminal behaviors such as murder, rape, and assault pose special challenges. Recognizing that this population is at risk if admitted to the criminal justice system at large, CMS must develop strategies to determine how these individuals can best be served. Some states have addressed the problem by using the ICFs/MR to house court-ordered individuals together in locked down, fenced units, replicating a forensic or prison environment. Whether the ICF/MR benefit should be used to isolate people from their community, withhold their rights as citizens, and restrict their freedom of movement requires extensive analysis by CMS and subsequent input by stakeholders.

PLANNING FOR THE FUTURE, LEARNING FROM THE PAST

Learning from its experience in addressing these issues, CMS has recently initiated several important activities. These efforts are likely to carry the federal government well into the 21st century on a positive note of exploration and collaboration.

Updated ICF/MR Regulations

CMS is completely rewriting the ICF/MR conditions of participation in order to more significantly reflect changes in the field and new directions since the regulations were last promulgated in 1988. Prompted by requests from advocates and providers, the ICF/MR team initially began soliciting informal input from the field in 1996. Building on suggestions received, formal regulation team meetings were held throughout the spring, summer, and fall of 2000. Various divisions throughout CMS reviewed the initial draft of the revisions, and the regulation team is re-drafting the document to reflect recommendations received. Following a second internal CMS review, the proposed regulations will begin formal external review by the DHHS. CMS anticipates publication of the draft regulations in the *Federal Register* as a Notice of Proposed Rulemaking (NPRM), giving the public ample opportunity to comment on the revisions. The *Federal Register* is published daily and provides the public the opportunity to review and comment on proposed changes to rules and regulations set forth by the federal government. The public is given a set time frame to send comments regarding the draft regulations into the responsible agency. These must all be read, analyzed, and responded to in a later *Federal Register* before new regulations can be adopted.

Quality Indicators

Building on the quality assurance study completed for HCFA by HSRI in 1998, a second contract is in process to develop a set of quality indicators for use in ICFs/MR and other settings that serve individuals with mental retardation and other developmental disabilities. Quality indicators are being defined so that they can be used in data collection and analysis. A protocol will then be developed, and the indicators will be tested for usability, feasibility, and reliability.

Need for Collaboration

Given the magnitude and variety of issues facing CMS in its ICF/MR program, it is essential that collaborative bonds be formed across constituency groups and across service settings. Labor, management, providers, self-advocates, families, and other advocacy groups, professional organizations, regulatory bodies, and lawmakers must join forces to address the new challenges and future directions that affect the lives of people with disabilities.

Only by working together can the field creatively devise solutions that will improve the quality of life for the individuals being served and for those still needing services and supports. The common bond of service delivery to individuals with mental retardation and other developmental disabilities links the HCBS Waiver program and the ICF/MR benefits. Similar issues and challenges underscore the need for both programs to work across settings to resolve barriers to high-quality service delivery.

REFERENCES

Americans with Disabilities Act (ADA) of 1990, PL 101-366, 42 U.S.C. §§ 201 *et seq.*

Boo, K. (1999, December 5). Invisible deaths: The fatal neglect of D.C.'s retarded. *The Washington Post,* p. A01.

Chamberlain, A., Ruah, J., Passer, A., McGrath, M., & Burkett, R. (1984). Issues in fertility control for mentally retarded female adolescents: I. Sexual activity, sexual abuse, and contraception. *Pediatrics, 73,* 445–450.

Children's Health Act of 2000, PL 106-310, 42 U.S.C. §§ 288 *et seq.*

Civil Rights for Institutionalized Persons Act (CRIPA) of 1980, PL 96-416, 42 U.S.C. §§ 1997 *et seq.*

Conditions of participation for ICFs/MR, 53 Fed. Reg. 20496 (1988).

Firsten, T. (1990). *An exploration of the role of physical and sexual abuse in psychiatrically institutionalized women.* Toronto: The Ontario Women's Directorate.

Health Care Financing Administration (HCFA).(1997). *Psychopharmacological medications: Safety precautions for persons with developmental disabilities.* Washington, DC: HCFA and the Department of Health and Human Services (DHHS).

Hospital condition of participation patient rights. Interim final rule with comment, 64 Fed. Reg. 36070 (1999).

Marchetti, A.G., & McCartney, J.R. (1990). Abuse of persons with mental retardation: Characteristics of the abused, the abusers, and the informers. *Mental Retardation, 6,* 367–371.

McCartney, J.R., & Campbell, V.A. (1998). Confirmed abuse cases in public residential facilities for persons with mental retardation: A multi-state study. *Mental Retardation, 36,* 465–473.

Medicaid: The level of oversight of institutions for the mentally retarded should be strengthened. (1996). Washington, DC: U.S. General Accounting Office.

Pennsylvania Department of the Auditor General. (2000). *A performance audit of the commonwealth's oversight of group homes for the mentally retarded in western Pennsylvania.* Harrisburg, PA: Author.

Proposed conditions of participation for ICFs/MR, 39 Fed. Reg. 2226 (1974).

Rindfleisch, N., & Bean, G.J. (1988). Willingness to report abuse and neglect in residential facilities. *Child Abuse & Neglect, 12,* 509–520.

Senn, C.Y. (1988). *Vulnerable: Sexual abuse and people with an intellectual handicap.* Downsview, Ontario, Canada: G. Allan Roeher Institute.

Sobsey, D. (1988). Research on sexual abuse: Are we asking the right questions? *Newsletter of the American Association on Mental Retardation, 1,* 2, 8.

Sobsey, D. (1994). *Violence and abuse in the lives of people with disabilities: The end of silent acceptance?* Baltimore: Paul H. Brookes Publishing Co.

Sobsey, D., & Doe, T. (1991). Patterns of sexual abuse and assault. *Journal of Sexuality and Disability, 9,* 243–259.

Social Security Act Amendments of 1965, PL 89-97, 42 U.S.C. §§ 301 *et seq.*

Stimpson, L., & Best, M.C. (1991). *Courage above all: Sexual assault against women with disabilities.* Toronto: Disabled Women's Network Canada.

Strauss, D., & Kastner, T.A. (1996). Comparative mortality of people with developmental disabilities in institutions and the community. *American Journal on Mental Retardation, 100,* 26–40.

U.S. Office of Inspector General (OIG). (2001). *Reporting abuses of persons with disabilities* (No. A-01–00–02502). Washington, DC: OIG and Department of Health and Human Services.

Use of restraints and seclusion in residential treatment facilities providing inpatient psychiatric services to individuals under age 21, 14 Fed. Reg. 7147 (2001).

Weiss, E. (1998, October). A nationwide pattern of deaths. *Hartford Courant,* p. A01.

CHAPTER 11

Building a Comprehensive Quality Management Program

ORGANIZING PRINCIPLES
AND PRIMARY OPERATING COMPONENTS

ROBERT M. GETTINGS

In October 2000, a small, representative group of stakeholders from the field of developmental disabilities (DD) met at the Wingspread Conference Center in Racine, Wisconsin, to develop an action agenda aimed at reconciling the quest for health and safety with the promotion of individual choice and autonomy. This meeting was sponsored by The Council on Quality and Leadership in Supports for People with Disabilities (known as The Council), with grant assistance from the Federal Administration on Developmental Disabilities. The wide-ranging discussions that occurred during this 2½-day meeting illustrated the enormous variety of factors that influence the capability of service systems to deliver high-quality services and supports while addressing the varied needs and preferences of people with DD. The meeting also underscored the potential for forging a new consensus among all system stakeholders—self-advocates, parents, professionals, providers, and public officials—regarding the steps necessary to improve the quality and accessibility of long-term DD services (The Council, 2000).

Wingspread 2000 occurred during a period of tremendous change within the DD service sector. Since 1975, the focus of service delivery had shifted from large, state-run residential institutions to small, privately operated community programs. The total number of individuals living in small, publicly financed community residences had grown more than 700%, and the total number of residential sites had increased by more than tenfold. Meanwhile, individuals with DD and their family members were demanding a stronger voice in determining and managing the public supports they receive. This rapid expansion and diversification of community services, in turn, was exposing weaknesses in the state and local infrastructures for monitoring and improving the quality of the services and supports furnished to people with DD. By the time of the conference, it had become clear that the "inspect and punish" model, designed to ensure institutional compliance, was unworkable in the highly diversified and decentralized environment of the emerging community service system. Furthermore, it was clear that new quality management approaches, based on an entirely different set of operational premises, would have to be developed and instituted.

This chapter begins to flesh out one vital component of the Wingspread Conference agenda: defining the underlying aims, the philosophy, and the essential operating components of a comprehensive statewide quality management program. The conference participants recognized that building an effective quality management program will not guarantee the consistent availability of high-quality services and supports. Other factors that will have a profound impact on whether quality services and supports are made available to people with DD include the existence of a stable, well-qualified work force; skillful leadership at all levels of the service system; effective individual- and system-level advocacy; supportive communities; well-crafted public policies; and, of course, adequate public financing. These are just a few of the more obvious ingredients essential to producing high-quality services.

Some observers, no doubt, will contend that the shortcomings of existing DD service systems can be traced solely to the glaring inadequacies in public support for such services. Although additional public investments undoubtedly will be necessary in order to improve the quality of existing services and supports, it would be a serious mistake to assume that the answer to the present quality conundrum lies exclusively in greatly enhanced levels of public funding. If more money were the answer, a direct correlation would exist between the relative availability of public dollars and the quality of the services furnished to individuals with disabilities. On the contrary, the results of quality reviews generally indicate that, although adequate financial resources are a critical factor, they are by no means the only determinant of service quality.

As in any complex human enterprise, the search for answers should begin with the identification of 1) the principles that underlie the operation of a service system that fosters positive outcomes and 2) the essential components of such a system. In other words, if additional public dollars are to be invested wisely, agencies need a clear conception of how a state's quality management program should be designed to achieve the desired results. The initial steps toward articulating such organizing principles and essential design features began during Wingspread 2000.

More specifically, the agreements reached by one of the four small work groups that met during the conference served as the jumping off point for this chapter. The interchange among the participants sparked thoughts and concepts that probably would not have emerged from a more homogenous group of stakeholders; however, as almost always occurs in discussions of this type, some issues were left only partially explicated and others were completely overlooked due to time constraints. With due apologies in advance to the members of the work group for any misinterpretations, this chapter synthesizes and re-casts a number of redundant and overlapping points that emerged and fills various blank spots in the interest of propelling the discussion forward.

GUIDING PRINCIPLES

The term *quality management* is used throughout this chapter to denote a cluster of activities that encompass both quality assurance and quality enhancement functions. Too often, quality management is conceived of solely as a series of monitoring, oversight, and enforcement activities designed to ensure the safety, health, and well-being of vulnerable individuals who are receiving publicly funded services and supports. Although some states unquestionably need to expand their capacities and clarify their policies governing monitoring and oversight activities, that in no way minimizes the importance of having a quality management system that operates in a cyclical fashion, in which the pursuit of improved quality is never-ending and identified problems lead to prompt and effective corrective actions. In the management literature, this process has come to be known as *continuous quality improvement.* Regardless of the nomenclature used, no quality management program can achieve its objectives without a strong, ongoing commitment to learning from past mistakes and taking forthright steps to improve the appropriateness and quality of the services offered.

One of the guiding principles of a comprehensive quality management program, therefore, is that it must include explicit provisions for continually improving the quality of publicly funded services and supports at all levels of the service delivery system, whether the area in need of improvement is identified as the result of a formal quality assurance review or through formal and informal feedback from consumers, family members, and agency staff. Such quality enhancement activities must be backed up by explicit dollar and personnel commitments within agency budgets, again at all levels of the service system.

Moreover, the service system must make the results of its quality reviews available to the public on a regular basis, in a consumer-friendly format, and with a minimum of delay. The technology now exists to make the results of quality reviews available immediately, and this technology should be fully employed. The ArcLink, a web-based forum that empowers individuals to make sound service choices based on accurate information, is one example of the efforts now underway to assist individuals with disabilities and their family members to become more savvy consumers. The ArcLink is a joint venture of The Arc of the United States, the Arc of Indiana, and the Stone Belt Arc.

Consistent with the need to protect the privacy rights of affected parties, feedback on the results of all investigations also should be available for public review, along with a description of the follow-up actions that are being taken to prevent reoccurrences, where applicable. Public disclosure breeds confidence and avoids the appearance that problems are being swept under the rug.

In a publicly funded system of supports that is committed to the goal of offering consumers the maximum degree of choice and control consistent with their capabilities and desires, *quality* must be defined through individuals' lives and strategies for achieving it must be tailored to the needs, capabilities, and preferences of each person. Health and security must be common elements of any personal definition of quality, but the facets of everyday existence that make life worthwhile (e.g., maintaining relationships, learning and growing, working and playing) must be defined in individual terms. It is crucial, therefore, that the quality management program in every state avoid compromising the personal authority and autonomy of individuals who are receiving services and supports.

Quality outcomes are achieved when all key actors—people with disabilities, family members, friends, clinicians, direct support and managerial staff, state and local program and regulatory officials—are committed to a common set of service improvement goals and work collaboratively to reach these goals. In other words, quality must be viewed as everyone's business, not the exclusive province of one or another component of the service delivery system.

It follows, therefore, that a well-run, comprehensive quality management program must clearly delineate the roles and responsibilities of all system actors and define how each can contribute to achieving positive outcomes. Failure to identify shortcomings in support policies and service delivery practices frequently can be traced back to fuzzy lines of responsibility and accountability. Thus, as in any complex enterprise, it is important to draw clear lines of authority and make sure that all system actors are properly trained and supported, fully understand their duties and responsibilities, and are held accountable for their actions. Such training and assistance must include the preparation and ongoing support of people with disabilities, their family members, and friends to perform constructive quality management roles at all levels of the service delivery system.

Service systems must be operated in a manner that fosters a "culture of improvement," a commitment by all involved parties to join hands in building stronger support networks for program participants and their families. Creating and maintaining such a culture begins with the recognition that quality is a never-ending pursuit, demanding the best efforts of everyone within an organization. It also requires:

- An environment in which all participants, regardless of rank or status, are empowered to share their views, contribute to the service improvement process, and take initiatives without fear of retribution

- A willingness to make mistakes, re-group, and try alternative strategies

- Leaders who demonstrate in tangible ways their commitment to making positive outcomes the organization's top priority

- An acceptance of the individuality of each person and the flexibility to build a personal support network tailored to the particular needs and strengths of that individual

- A commitment to engaging in a continuous learning process

Service systems that are committed to achieving positive outcomes for the individuals and families they support establish and maintain an active learning environment in which all participants are afforded regular opportunities to share their experiences and learn about best practices. This implies a strong, ongoing commitment to competency-based training at all levels of the service system but also a willingness to create collaborative learning forums in which all participants are encouraged to share their views and engage in joint problem solving, without fear of negative consequences.

The quest for quality must reach beyond the confines of a state's formal quality management system (the principal focus of this chapter) and become embedded in the day-to-day operations of the service system at all levels. This means that every agency and organization that specializes in serving or advocating on behalf of people with DD must craft its own quality management program. It also means that these agencies and organizations must continue to pursue opportunities to collaborate with state and local job training and placement programs, housing agencies, religious groups, service and charitable organizations, universities and community colleges, and other generic community institutions in order to erect more resilient support networks for people with DD.

The achievement of positive outcomes must be recognized, rewarded, and celebrated. A comprehensive program of incentives and rewards, therefore, must be part of any quality-oriented service system. Depending on the nature of the achievement and the responsible party (individual or agency), such recognition could take many forms, including public awards, bonuses, career advancement, extended intervals between formal quality reviews, and so forth. The important point, however, is that a quality-oriented system must take every opportunity to celebrate outstanding performance and the individual and collective accomplishments of workers at all levels within the service delivery system.

In summary, then, the following guiding principles must be observed in designing and operating a comprehensive quality management program:

- Explicit provisions should be built in at every level of the service delivery system for pursuing continuous improvements in the quality of publicly funded services and supports.

- The results of all quality reviews and investigations should be made public, consistent with the need to safeguard the privacy rights of affected parties.

- Quality should be individually defined and pursued through personally tailored support and safety plans.

- A state's quality management policies and activities should not infringe on but rather should support and enhance the personal authority and autonomy of individuals receiving publicly funded services and supports.

- A commitment to positive outcomes must be evident at all levels of the service delivery system and recognized as a responsibility of all key participants, including everyone from the person with the disability through the highest administrative levels of state government. Quality is everyone's business.

- The quality management roles and responsibilities of all system actors should be clearly delineated.

- A culture of improvement should be fostered throughout the service delivery system.

- An active learning environment, in which all participants are afforded regular opportunities to share their experiences and learn about best practices, should be developed and nurtured within every component of the service delivery system.

- Public and private service agencies, along with state, regional, and local management entities, should seek opportunities continuously to collaborate with generic community resources.

- A comprehensive program of incentives and rewards should be part of any quality-oriented service system.

Using the above principles as a guide, the next logical question is how should one go about constructing a comprehensive statewide quality management program that operates in a manner consistent with these principles?

SYSTEM CAPABILITIES

The detailed operational features of a state's quality management system will be influenced by many factors. Geographic considerations, for example, come into play. Heavily populated, urbanized states may have to manage their quality programs differently than sparsely populated, rural states. Similarly, the fundamental features of the state's service delivery system will influence the organization of its quality management activities. The organization and execution of quality management functions might be somewhat different in a community services system directly administered by the state than in a system administered locally through a network of county or regional nonprofit, single-point-of-entry agencies. Finally, as states design their quality management systems, they must take into account the impact of federal Medicaid policies. The review protocol for state-run Home and Community-Based Services (HCBS) Waiver programs, which was promulgated by the Centers for Medicare & Medicaid Services (CMS) in the fall of 2000, holds far-reaching implications for the design and execution of a state's quality management system.

Although key quality management design features can be expected to vary from state to state, all comprehensive quality management systems must have certain common capabilities, regardless of how they are configured. These capabilities are summarized in the following sections.

Consumer Protections

Consumer protections is the capacity to effectively monitor the physical safety and security of individuals with disabilities who are enrolled in publicly funded programs. States have a fundamental obligation to ensure that the health, safety, and welfare of participants in publicly funded DD services are adequately protected. To provide such consumer protections, a state must be able to demonstrate that it has workable policies and procedures for ensuring the following:

- Program participants are free from physical and chemical restraints, except in instances in which the use of related interventions is therapeutically indicated, explicitly authorized by the responsible clinician, carried out in accordance with state policies, and the interventions are part of the individual's program plan.

- Program participants are protected from abuse, neglect, and exploitation, and procedures are in place to detect, report, and investigate related cases thoroughly and take prompt and effective remedial actions when appropriate.

- Serious (or sentinel) incidents are promptly and effectively reported and tracked, and appropriate follow-up actions are taken to rectify any individual malfeasance or systemic shortcomings that are uncovered as a result of such investigations.

- All deaths within publicly licensed or certified programs and facilities are thoroughly investigated and fully reported, and prompt steps are taken to rectify any underlying factors contributing to the death.

- An individually tailored personal safety/security plan is developed as part of each participant's individual program plan, and all staff members responsible for supporting a particular individual are fully conversant with the provisions of the plan and prepared to carry out their related responsibilities.

- Prompt actions are taken to protect the safety and health of program participants in the case of a natural disaster or when other unforeseen crises occur.

Service Planning

Service planning describes the capacity to develop comprehensive, individualized support plans and to ensure that all prescribed services and supports are delivered in a timely, effective manner in accordance with the terms of each individual's plan. The formulation of sound, well-conceived, person-centered plans is essential to building effective personal support networks. The capability to prepare and implement such plans, therefore, has to be recognized as an essential, frontline component of any comprehensive quality management system. Quality, in other words, needs to be built in at the front end of the service system. For this reason, local and area-wide service systems must have the capacity to 1) conduct complete, comprehensive assessments of the service and support needs of all participants, including the capability to perform or acquire any medical, psychological, or social evaluations that might shed light on an individual's service and support needs; and 2) assist individuals, with the help of family members and friends, to prepare person-centered plans that take into account their capabilities, interests, aspirations, and personal support needs. Local and area-wide service systems also must have in place systematic methods of reviewing the quality, appropriateness, and comprehensiveness of individual service plans and a process for initiating plan revisions on the basis of the results of such reviews.

Safeguarding Rights

Safeguarding rights requires agencies to protect the rights of all individuals who apply for or enroll in publicly funded DD programs and services. All components of the DD service system have a fundamental obligation to ensure that the individual rights of program participants are respected and observed. In carrying out its responsibilities in this area, the service system must

- Afford individuals and their loved ones clear channels for filing complaints and having their grievances fully, promptly, and respectfully considered by responsible officials at succeeding levels of the service system, with the aim of resolving the grievance in a manner satisfactory to all parties

- Ensure that the due process rights of individuals and families (including legal guardians) under federal, state, and local laws and regulations are fully observed

- Ensure that individuals are afforded the opportunity to choose freely among available community support options and among provider agencies and individuals that meet state-established credentials and qualifications

- Establish human rights functions within designated types of provider agencies and local and area-wide service authorities to oversee related activities and reconcile potential ethical or moral conflicts that sometimes arise in applying individual rights to particular service situations

The rights protection mechanisms employed within the service system (e.g., confidential telephone hot lines, an ombudsperson, impartial mediators) should be consumer-friendly.

Provider Oversight

Provider oversight is the capacity to ensure that all providers of community services and supports meet the qualifications, standards, and requirements established by the state. The vast majority of community DD services and supports are furnished through private agencies and organizations or individual practitioners operating under contractual agreements with the state (or, in some cases, sub-state entities acting on the state's behalf). State government, therefore, has an obligation to ensure that each of these service agencies and organizations or individuals operates in compliance with applicable state qualifications, standards, and requirements. Among the activities a state must have in place to ensure ongoing compliance with state-established requirements and standards are effective methods of

- Verifying the qualifications of services and support providers

- Ensuring that all pre-service and in-service training and continuing education requirements are met

- Conducting periodic and special licensing and certification reviews and analyzing and reporting the results

- Overseeing the implementation of correction plans and the imposition of penalties and disqualifications and engaging in other follow-up actions that result from provider oversight reviews

- Ensuring that provider organizations have adequate and appropriate internal quality assurance and enhancement policies and processes

- Arranging technical assistance to help provider agencies rectify deficiencies and formulate and carry out service enhancement plans

In addition, in jurisdictions in which performance contracting is used, a state must have the capacity to review and enforce other provisions contained in contractual agreements (e.g., achieving specified levels of consumer satisfaction, holding administrative costs below a certain percentage of total billable expenses).

On-Site Monitoring

On-site monitoring is the capacity to monitor the overall performance of the service delivery system. In addition to overseeing the compliance of provider agencies and individual practitioners with state-established qualifications, standards, and requirements, a state must have methods of independently verifying that enrolled individuals and families are being appropriately served. Instead of focusing on the prerequisites of effective services (i.e., inputs), as traditional licensing and certification surveys have, these reviews should concentrate on the benefits derived by consumers and families (i.e., outcomes). The types of monitoring activities that fit into this category include

- Assessments of the effectiveness of local and area-wide service coordination and case management systems in terms of the availability and quality of such services

- Assessments of the effectiveness with which case managers or service coordinators perform their various individual guidance or systemic advocacy and administrative support roles

- Consumer-centered quality reviews (i.e., on-site monitoring of program participants, usually applying a sampling methodology, in order to reach generalizations about agency- or system-wide performance)

- Independent, third party monitoring by peer review and stakeholder teams (i.e., parents, self-advocates, and neighbors) to assess the quality of life of program participants

Financial Integrity

Financial integrity requires the capacity to ensure that public funds are disbursed and managed in an accountable manner, fraudulent transactions are detected and investigated, and the responsible parties are punished. States have an obligation to ensure that tax dollars are used effectively, efficiently, and in accordance with the requirements of the law. This means that a state's quality management system must include methods of ensuring that 1) payment claims are verified for accuracy and completeness; 2) annual audits are conducted of the financial accounts of all service agencies and organizations in accordance with accepted auditing standards and practices, and any questionable transactions are identified and resolved; and 3) the personal accounts of individuals participating in publicly financed programs are secured and audited on a regular basis to prevent any fraudulent transactions.

In addition, a state must maintain an active program of fraud prevention and detection that includes the capacity to investigate alleged incidents of misappropriation of funds and the imposition of penalties to punish transgressors and prevent re-occurrences.

Health and Behavioral Health Surveillance

Health and behavioral health surveillance entails monitoring the health status of all individuals with DD who receive publicly funded, long-term community supports and ensuring that these individuals have access to appropriate, high-quality health and mental health prevention and treatment services. The incidence of chronic health and behavioral health conditions is much higher among recipients of DD long-term supports than it is among the general population. Yet, all too frequently people with DD—especially those with few, if any, active family connections—maintain only tenuous and incomplete ties to the health and mental health systems. To address this problem, states need to have methods in place to 1) assess the effectiveness of prescribed intervention strategies in the case of individuals with significant behavioral challenges and other mental health conditions; 2) monitor the health status of all people enrolled in community DD service programs to ensure that they are receiving the preventive health and medical treatment services they require, including any specialty services that may be needed to address underlying chronic health conditions; 3) establish mechanisms for determining when individuals are at risk of serious health consequences, the consequences of behavioral challenges (e.g., involvement with the criminal justice system), and the consequences of substance abuse; 4) track access to therapy (e.g., physical therapy, occupational therapy, speech therapy) and other professional services to ensure that individuals enrolled in community DD programs gain ready access to such services; and 5) monitor the therapeutic effectiveness of prescription medications (including, in particular, psychoactive and anticonvulsive medications) on the capacity of individuals with disabilities to live more complete and participatory lives within their homes and communities. Prescription medications should not be used to control or treat socially inappropriate behavior and should never be used in the absence of a specific psychiatric diagnosis and a properly designed treatment plan.

Consumer Satisfaction and Outcomes

Monitoring consumer satisfaction and outcomes requires the service system to collect structured feedback from individuals and families and comparative data on systemwide performance (both longitudinally and across jurisdictions) in areas deemed critical to achieving overriding systemic goals. State DD agencies have begun to use consumer and family satisfaction surveys and outcome assessment measures to obtain direct feedback regarding the degree to which state and local service systems are meeting the needs and expectations of individual service recipients and their families. The Core Indicators Project (CIP), a 5-year-old multistate collaboration sponsored by the National Association of State Directors of Developmental Disabilities Services, is one such effort to collect, analyze, and report comparative information and data on the performance of state MR/DD service systems. Twenty states now participate in the project. Several nonparticipating states have their own intrastate mechanisms for gathering consumer-based information on a regular, systematic basis.

Increasingly, these mechanisms are recognized as a critical component of a state's quality management system. Among the basic components of a consumer-oriented assessment system are 1) individual and family satisfaction measures, 2) indicators of comparative performance in key outcomes areas (e.g., employment, integrated community living), and 3) quality-of-life measures. Typically, data is gathered from a random sample of service recipients using statistically valid and reliable data collection instruments. Consumers and family members should be involved in the design and implementation of the assessment system and should have full access to the resulting information and data, consistent with privacy safeguards.

Quality Enhancement

Quality enhancement is the capacity to initiate a continuous cycle of activities designed to address weaknesses in the service delivery process and improve service outcomes, another critical feature of a comprehensive statewide quality management system. As noted previously, the pursuit of quality must be viewed as an overriding goal of every component of the service delivery system. If this goal is to become a reality, agencies and organizations at all levels of the service delivery system will have to establish programs and enunciate strategies to upgrade service quality and make these efforts an integral part of their operations. Quality enhancement initiatives can take many forms (e.g., a comprehensive training program to sharpen the skills and competencies of frontline workers as well as supervisory staff; the provisions of technical assistance and support; the organization of employee recognition and incentive programs). Regardless of the elements of an agency's quality enhancement program, however, it is critical that these efforts be linked to the state's overall quality assurance activities so that the results of quality reviews inform the development of the agency's quality enhancement activities. Increasingly, such activities need to be recognized as strategic investments in strengthening system-wide capabilities to support individuals with disabilities and their families.

This chapter represents an initial attempt to sketch out the principal elements of a comprehensive, statewide quality management program. Obviously, volumes could be (and, indeed, have been) written about each of the major topical areas identified here. So, it would be very easy to find areas in need of further elaboration. However, before developing a workable quality management program, first we need to identify the species of trees growing in this particular forest. Readers are challenged to identify missing elements in the proposed framework, rather than concentrating solely on how the presentation of the existing elements might be improved.

Finally, it is important to point out that the suggested framework is intended to form the basis for a quality management program that is not specific to any particular funding source or state organizational structure. Of most immediate concern to individuals and agencies that perform key roles within state MR/DD service systems, no doubt, is the fact that a number of requirements associated with financing specialized services and supports through the Medicaid HCBS authority were not taken into account in designing the proposed framework. As a result, the proposed framework is not fully aligned with the specifications published by the CMS. For example, under the existing policies of CMS, a state must be able to demonstrate that it has a methodology for determining level of care that establishes, to the satisfaction of the Secretary, that any individual found eligible for the HCBS Waiver programs otherwise "would require the level of care provided in a hospital or a nursing facility or intermediate care facility for the mentally retarded" (Social Security Act Amendments of 1965, as amended, Section 1915[c][1]). In a similar vein, CMS expects the single state Medicaid agency (SSMA) to exercise final decision-making authority over all Medicaid HCBS Waiver programs, irrespective of any interagency agreements the SSMA may have entered into with other state agencies; states, in turn, are expected to demonstrate that the SSMA is carrying out its responsibilities in this regard. Often states have their own idiosyncratic administrative and statutory requirements associated with the financing of various types of HCBS Waiver services, whether Medicaid dollars are part of the funding mix or not. It is not that these federal or state requirements are unimportant elements of a state's overall compliance obligations. Usually, there are sound statutory or regulatory grounds for instituting such policies. It is just that the subject policies are only tangentially related to maintaining and enhancing the quality of the services and supports furnished to program participants and, as such, do not fit within a quality management framework.

NEXT STEPS

In the summer of 2000, the Developmental Disabilities Quality Coalition (DDQC) was formed to serve as a collaborative forum for addressing the issues, challenges, and opportunities associated with building stronger, more inclusive community support networks for individuals with DD, nationwide. The founding member organizations of the DDQC include The Arc of the United

States, the National Alliance of Direct Support Professionals, the American Association on Mental Retardation, The Council on Quality and Leadership in Supports for People with Disabilities, the National Association of Protection and Advocacy Systems, the American Network of Community Options and Resources, the American Association of University Affiliated Programs for Persons with Developmental Disabilities (since renamed the Association of University Centers on Disability), the National Association of State Directors of Developmental Disabilities Services, the National Association of Developmental Disabilities Councils, and the Consortium of Developmental Disabilities Councils. At the conclusion of the October 2000 Wingspread conference, members of the DDQC were asked to assume responsibility for taking certain follow-up actions with respect to several key recommendations that emerged from the meeting. One of these follow-up actions was to prepare a paper fleshing out the components of a comprehensive state quality management system.

This chapter is intended to fulfill this requirement, thus advancing the cross-stakeholder dialogue that was initiated at Wingspread 2000. It is the hope of the author that this chapter will serve as a springboard for in-depth examinations of other critical dimensions of the quality management equation. For example, although this chapter focuses primarily on the basic architecture of a statewide quality management system, parallel analyses are needed that delineate the quality management roles and responsibilities of other key system actors, including community provider agencies, legal and lay advocates, university-based centers, and voluntary accreditation programs. In other words, if the chapter is to serve its intended purpose, other stakeholders will have to add their perspectives to the dialogue launched at Wingspread 2000 and carried forward in this chapter.

REFERENCES

The Council on Quality and Leadership in Supports for People with Disabilites. (2000). *Measure for measure: Person-centered quality assurance. The Proceedings of the Wingspread Conference, Racine, Wisconsin, October 19–21, 2000.* Towson, MD: Author. Available on line at http://www.ncor.org/wingspread.html.

Health Care Financing Administration (HCFA), U.S. Department of Health and Human Services (DHHS). (2000, October 10). *HCFA regional office protocol for conducting full reviews of state Medicaid Home and Community-Based Services Waiver programs.* Washington, DC: Author.

Prouty, R.W., Smith, G., & Lakin, K.C. (Eds.). (2001). *Residential services to persons with developmental disabilities: Status and trends through 2000.* Minneapolis: University of Minnesota, Research and Training Center on Community Living, Institute on Community Integration.

Social Security Act Amendments of 1994, PL 103-432, 42 U.S.C. §§ 101 *et seq.*

CHAPTER 12

International Innovations
in Monitoring Service Quality

GEOFFREY P. JONES, ROSEMARY LAWN, LEENA MATTIKA, AND JAN TØSSEBRO

The use of individual outcomes as a window to understanding the quality of services to people with developmental disabilities is certainly not limited to initiatives in the United States. This chapter describes three national efforts to capture the experiences of people receiving services and supports and to use these experiences as a means for assessing individuals' services and systems of services. The first discussion is based on the administration of consumer and family surveys in Australia. The second describes a comprehensive monitoring and quality enhancement process in Finland. The third provides an overview of national surveys conducted in Norway that link the experiences of people receiving services to those of the general population. All of the activities have in common the ability to benchmark aggregate outcomes over time and to use outcome data to enhance and improve the quality of services.

THE PUBLIC MONITORING OF
DISABILITY SERVICES IN AUSTRALIA

In 1998, researchers in Australia began the development of the first national Satisfaction Survey of Clients of Disability Services in Australia. This survey was done to compare the effectiveness of disability services across the different states and territories in Australia. The following section describes the Australian service context, reports on uses for the information collected, highlights issues for data collectors, and speculates about future developments in monitoring the quality of disability services in Australia.

Introduction to Services
in Australia: What Is Public Monitoring?

Public monitoring of government-funded disability services is the collection and publication of information about the performance of these services. *Perfor-*

235

mance is used here in a broad way to include inputs and outputs such as service outcomes, service quality, and the quality of life of people with disabilities. Part of public monitoring is the use of external quality assurance systems to strengthen confidence in the quality of services.

The Structure of Public Monitoring and Reporting of Disability Services   Australia has a national government (the Commonwealth) and state governments. Many services are provided by not-for-profit organizations through performance agreements with a Commonwealth- or state-funded agency. The Commonwealth is responsible for funding some types of disability services (mainly employment services), and the states for funding the others (e.g., accommodation support). Each tier of government has its own system of monitoring the disability services it funds. Each state and the Commonwealth require that funded services meet the national Disability Services Standards (DSS). The system adopted by each state to achieve this is different. Each state also uses unique performance indicators, often linked to its strategic plans, to report to the auditors-general in each state.

Nationally, there are two main reporting channels—through the Australian Institute of Health and Welfare (AIHW) by an annual return from all funded service outlets and through the Report on Government Services, produced by the Steering Committee for the Review of Commonwealth/State Service Provision. The work of both agencies is coordinated through the National Disability Administrators, a body that includes the most senior administrators of relevant Commonwealth and state agencies.

The Report on Government Services provides performance information for a range of services (e.g., education services, health services, community services) that permits comparison across jurisdictions in Australia. The report had not yet included quantitative information on the quality of disability services. The Steering Committee wished to start reporting such information starting in February 2000. The survey was the strategy adopted by the Steering Committee to achieve this end.

Background to the National Satisfaction Survey

The survey was part of an annual report about a range of government services across Australia. The survey objectives were:

1. To enable comparisons across Australia for selected service types for adult clients (i.e., accommodation support services, employment services, respite services, and case management) about the experiences of service users and their families. The most important comparisons to be made were among similar service types across states. Of lesser importance was the ability to make comparisons across service type within the same state.

2. To provide information for service improvement. Representatives from the various disability jurisdictions were hopeful that the survey would inform them regarding possible areas for service improvement.

Three entities collaborated to complete the survey:

- E-QUAL, disability consultants who consulted on survey instruments, interviewer training, and report writing

- Donovan Research, market research consultants who consulted on sample design, service provider contracts, mail-outs, and statistical analysis

- NCS Australia, a fieldwork agency that conducted face-to-face and telephone interviews. The fieldwork was carried out from July to November 1999.

Method

The stages of the survey method were:

1. Feasibility study/literature review (E-QUAL, 1998)

2. Development and refinement of survey instruments

3. Development of the sample

4. Data collection: Contact with service providers followed by mail-out of the family survey and client interviews

5. Data analysis and report writing

Survey Instruments   The starting points for the development of the survey instruments were the candidate indicators, presurvey form, consumer interview, and the family survey from the Core Indicators Project (CIP; Human Services Research Institute, 1998). These building blocks were consistent with the recommendations of a literature review (E-QUAL, 1998). The instruments were modified for the particular purposes of the survey, including services:

1. Expanding the indicators, consumer interview, and family survey to cover the four service types. The consumer interview focused on the experience of accommodation support and employment services. The family survey had sections for all four service types.

2. Ensuring that the consumer interview was suitable for all service users including those with physical, sensory, and other disabilities

Sampling   Sample sizes were derived for each survey and for each jurisdiction based on a specified desired level of accuracy. (The margin of error was set at +/- 6% for 95% confidence limits for any survey question for the four major service types in each jurisdiction.) Population sizes for each service type for each jurisdiction were available from the most recent national census data. There was no database of individual service users to work from. A sampling procedure in two stages was used:

1. Sample service providers from each service type within each jurisdiction

2. Sample clients from those service providers that agreed to participate. To meet confidentiality and consent requirements, service providers drew the sample.

Contact with Service Providers   As indicated, the survey relied heavily on the cooperation of service providers. Sampled service providers were contacted and sent a "provider pack." Participating service providers were required to sample clients as instructed, contact clients to gain their consent, and return a completed presurvey form on each client to be interviewed to the consultants. Service providers also had to provide details for the family mail-out survey (some opted to send out family surveys themselves).

Contact with Interviewees   The presurvey forms were sent to the fieldwork agency. The presurvey protocol directed interviewers to offer a face-to-face or telephone interview to a service user or to contact a family member if the person was determined to be unable to contribute to an interview. Interviewers made contact with subjects using the information given by service providers on the presurvey forms.

Issues for External Data Collectors

The survey raised issues for the consultants as external data collectors. These issues included enlisting the cooperation of service providers, coordinating with other surveys, capturing the views of people not able to contribute to interviews, interviewing efficiently, ensuring the validity of interviews with people with disabilities, calculating response rates, and gaining information for service improvement.

Enlisting Cooperation of Service Providers   The market research company initially contacted 649 service providers. The work required could take each service provider a day or more, and some chose not to participate. An additional 135 providers were contacted to replace providers who declined to participate, making a total of 748 provider contacts. The contacts with service providers were often frustrating for the staff involved, as the nominated contact people gave the survey a low priority or changed without passing on the relevant information. External data collectors need to understand the resources required and have strategies to enable this process to run smoothly.

Coordinating with Other Surveys or Quality Assurance Exercises   One of the most common reasons for declining to participate in the survey was that the service providers or their service users were involved in other surveys or quality assurance exercises. Appropriate notice from the jurisdictions could have avoided these service providers being sampled for contact, an assumption that was borne out in some jurisdictions in which such notice was given.

Capturing the Views of People Who Were Not Able to Contribute to Interviews The design phase of the survey created discussion about how to best capture the views of people who were not able to contribute directly to an interview. The two options considered were resampling to include another person from the same service or to use a proxy for the person (i.e., to approach his or her next of kin or a similar individual). It was decided to use the latter approach, on the grounds that resampling to find someone who was able to contribute to an interview ran the risk of excluding the experiences of those with the most severe communication difficulties altogether. The results show systematic differences in the responses of next of kin (22% of informants) and people with disabilities (78% of informants), suggesting that interviews with next of kin are not equivalent to interviews with people with disabilities. The results could be confounded by the type of services being used. For example, next of kin were more likely to be interviewed in place of users of large residential services (48%) than in place of users of other accommodation services (28%; E-QUAL and Donovan Research, 2000).

Interviewing Efficiently Telephone interviews, a departure from the CIP method, were offered as an alternative to face-to-face interviews in order to contain costs. Telephone interviews proved very practical for people with disabilities using dispersed community-based services (46% of all interviews with service users were by telephone). Most next of kin (89%) chose a telephone interview.

Ensuring the Validity of Interviews with People with Disabilities Procedures based on those used with the Com-QoL, a comprehensive approach to measuring quality of life for people with disabilities (Cummins, McCabe, Romeo, Reid, & Waters, 1997), were used during the pilot phase to try to establish the validity of responses for selected interviewees early on in an interview. This approach was discarded because it compromised rapport and provided little benefit. For the main survey, a version of the CIP approach to confirming validity was used. The issue of how to accurately exclude interviews made invalid by acquiescence or by questions being beyond the individual interviewee's comprehension remained unresolved.

Calculating Response Rates Service providers returned 2,819 usable presurvey forms, leading to 2,271 interviews. Only 239 (8%) of people declined to be interviewed once contacted—a high response rate for this stage of the sampling process; however, there is no data on how many clients did not give their consent to service providers or how many clients were taken out of the sample by service providers declining to participate in the survey. For these reasons, accurate response rates cannot be calculated and it is difficult to allay concerns about sample bias.

Gaining Information for Service Improvement   As indicated, the survey was developed in order to provide information on possible areas for service improvement for the jurisdictions. The jurisdictions decided to include open-ended questions in the consumer interview and family survey to meet this requirement. Fewer than 3% of consumer interviews included any response to the open-ended questions. The 2,437 completed family surveys generated more than 1,500 negative comments about access to services and about 500 negative comments about relationships with services and staff. The better information about service improvement came from the quantitative results of the consumer interviews and family surveys.

The Results and How They Have Been Used

The survey confirmed the ability of people with disabilities to speak for themselves about their life situations and about their experiences of disability services. The majority of interviews (62%) about accommodation and employment services were conducted with a person with a disability alone. Another 10% of interviews had the person with a disability as the main contributor, with support. For some service types (e.g., services placing people in open employment), the proportion of informants with disabilities rose to more than 90% (both alone and with support). The survey demonstrated that in all jurisdictions, apart from the two smallest jurisdictions (in which each had fewer than 40 service providers in total across all four service areas), the method resulted in survey results approaching the level of accuracy required for the target service types.

The survey enabled the Steering Committee to include quantitative information on the quality of disability services in the *Report on Government Services 2000* (Steering Committee for the Review of Commonwealth/State Service Provision, 2000). The survey resulted in a consultancy report that contained detailed comparisons across jurisdictions on many indicators of service quality and the quality of life of people with disabilities who use services (E-QUAL and Donovan Research, 2000). The numerical counts produced by the CIP question style led to results that are easy to interpret. For example, almost one in four (24%) people using accommodation services had some influence about with whom they lived; just over half (54%) had no say in this matter. Such results are easy to compare with accepted community standards. The survey will act as a model for other areas of government services on which the Steering Committee wishes to report.

The survey was also a success from the point of view of the National Disability Administrators. They were provided with information about the demand for services consistent with information from other sources and detailed information about how clients and their families experience different models of service delivery. As illustrated, the quantitative results give clear pointers for service improvement.

Specific uses for the survey method and results by different jurisdictions have included:

- Incorporating the results into a presentation used by the agency head to explain how the agency strategic plan and priorities were consistent with what consumers wanted

- Reporting results for that jurisdiction to meet state government reporting requirements, thus saving on the need for a separate survey

- Using the respite section of the family survey as the basis for a more comprehensive survey of respite services

The survey has also produced a wealth of data that may never be fully explored. Further work could:

- Identify items to which family respondents give responses similar to responses given by people with disabilities. This is important with respect to the issue of how to gain information about those clients unable to contribute to interviews.

- Make international comparisons (e.g., among those states participating with the CIP in the United States and in Australia)

- Inform the often-debated issue in Australia of whether nongovernment services and government services are of similar quality

The Future for Public Monitoring of the Quality of Disability Services in Australia

Public monitoring of the quality of disability services in Australia will continue to develop. Some current challenges are gaining relevance for large-scale monitoring; demonstrating that external quality assurance adds value; defining the roles for people with disabilities in external quality assurance; integrating indicators, standards, and monitoring events; understanding the value of consumer focus; and understanding the relationship between quality of life and quality of service.

Gaining Relevance for Large-Scale Monitoring Much of the large-scale monitoring of disability services in Australia has been prompted by accountability requirements of one arm of government on another. This may be called the "graphs in reports" approach, meaning the display of statistics and pie charts that may or may not relate to local circumstances, providers, or people with disabilities and their families. It typically means tight deadlines with little time for consultation with stakeholders to participate in survey design. The "graphs in reports" approach was a strong factor in the background to the present survey. As a consequence, it was and is a challenge to convince service providers, clients, and families that the exercise benefits them.

This point was illustrated during a conference presentation about the survey. A person with a disability forcefully discounted the results as containing only the views of people who were too frightened to speak out about the real state of disability services. He said that the results would be used as government propaganda. He clearly expressed alienation from the whole process.

Demonstrating that External Quality Assurance Adds Value
Related to the previous point is the need to establish that external quality assurance adds value. The Commonwealth has committed $17 million over the next 5 years to a new quality assurance system based around the national DSS. In other jurisdictions (all of which have adopted the DSS), the pressure of long waiting lists for services focuses funding priorities on the expansion of direct services. The new Commonwealth quality assurance system will have to demonstrate that it provides value for money.

Defining the Roles of People with Disabilities in External Quality Assurance   The new Commonwealth quality assurance system has also highlighted issues about the roles of people with disabilities in public monitoring. A group of people with disabilities is seeking to define for themselves a professional role of disability services auditor in the auditing teams. This role could be assigned specific tasks to ensure that people with disabilities have influence during audits. Ironically, the requirements to take up the professionalized role could tend to exclude the very people with disabilities who use the Commonwealth-funded services to be audited. The issues of safeguarding participation by service users in the auditing process are yet to be resolved.

Integrating Indicators and Standards and Monitoring Events
The numerous jurisdictions in Australia allow for diversity of approach to many issues. With regard to monitoring disability services, one consequence is that outcome indicators across jurisdictions are rarely directly comparable. This survey was an exception to this rule. The National Disability Administrators have acted on this issue. The report *Integrating Indicators: Theory and Practice in the Disability Service Field* (Australian Institute of Health and Welfare, 2000) recommended that participation data elements from the *National Community Services Data Dictionary* should be collected as part of the National Minimum Data Set for disability services.

A second opportunity for greater integration affects service providers and consumers. Currently, service providers that receive funding from several agencies may have to fulfill different external quality assurance requirements for each funding source. Likewise, people with disabilities and their families who use several disability services may be approached at different times each year for their feedback about the performance of each of the services and may also be asked to participate in one or more large-scale consumer feedback exercises. There is an opportunity to reduce the burden of overlapping quality assurance systems on service providers, consumers, and families alike.

Understanding the Value of Consumer Focus   Consumer (or customer) focus is listed as the first principle of quality management by the International Organization for Standardization (ISO) and has been adopted as such in Australia (*Standards Australia/Standards New Zealand*, 2000). The emphasis in the present survey on reporting the experiences of people with disabilities is consistent with this approach. However, the survey experience also points out some of the limitations of consumer focus with people with disabilities. The consumer focus approach assumes informed consumers who are freely able to specify their requirements and develop the services they require from a range of options. Many people with disabilities are not in this situation (E-QUAL, 2001). One danger is that positive consumer satisfaction information from people with disabilities may be used to justify services that do not measure up against objective measures of service quality. The challenge is to find the appropriate balance between objective and subjective indicators.

Understanding the Relationship Between Quality of Life and Quality of Service   The results for the survey were grouped into indicators about quality of service and quality of life. The grouping of the indicators in this way by the consultants was based on the assumptions that:

1. Quality-of-service indicators relate directly to the activities of a particular service. They include access to that service, opportunities to learn new things, staff turnover, and respectful treatment by staff from that service.

2. Quality-of-life indicators may not relate to the activities of a particular service (or any service used by that person). They include liking where you live and your job, having friends, using community services, and making important life choices.

The challenge for disability administrators is to be clear about whether they are interested in the measurement of quality of service, quality of life, or both, and the consequences of this decision. At present, service goals are often couched in terms of quality of life (Australian Institute of Health and Welfare, 2000), and quality assurance activities are directed toward quality of service (i.e., use of the DSS). If disability administrators wish to monitor quality of life, they will have to determine just how much influence disability services can be expected to have on the dimensions of measured quality of life (International Association for the Scientific Study of Intellectual Disabilities, 2000). The focus for quality assurance will have to shift from services to individuals, and the combined impact of services, often from numerous providers, on those individuals.

MONITORING SERVICE QUALITY IN FINLAND

Like the other Nordic countries, Finland has built health and social service systems for all citizens that are based on responsibility and control at the local municipal level. These services are almost totally financed by taxes gathered by the state and municipalities. A total of 448 municipalities provide these services either by organizing services themselves, buying them from joint authorities of municipalities, or buying them from private organizations. In order to provide specialized services for people with intellectual disabilities, the country has been divided into 16 special care districts (administered by joint authorities of municipalities), which encompass every municipality.

Changes from a centralized model of care to an inclusion model of service provision has meant that services organized by joint authorities have decreased and services organized by municipalities and private local organizations have increased. Of a population of 5.2 million, about 28,000 (0.5%) people are diagnosed as having mental retardation and are entitled to some form of income support. Of this number, about two thirds use specialized services, and the rest only use general welfare supports available to all people.

In Finland, the approach to monitoring the quality of services provided to people with intellectual disabilities has developed according to the paradigm shift from service- or program-centered ideology to individual- or consumer-centered approach. This paradigm shift touched the whole social and health care sector in the 1990s. The governmental strategy in quality assurance in Finland and the other Nordic countries was guided by information collection and supporting local voluntary development projects (Sosiaali-ja terveysministeriö, Stakes, & Suomen kuntaliitto, 1999; Stakes, 1995). The following section describes the steps taken by the Finnish Association on Mental Retardation (FAMR) in its pursuit of better services for people with intellectual disabilities through the creation of assessment methods and the provision of support to service providers. This section covers three phases: 1) the assessment of outcomes of services by subjective and objective quality-of-life indicators, living conditions of people in service units, and the working practices and cultural factors of service units; 2) the assessment of performance indicators and monitoring performance of municipalities responsible for service provision; and 3) the creation of an infrastructure for both of these activities to support the improvement of service quality from three viewpoints: customers with disabilities and their family members, staff members of service providers, and municipalities responsible for providing services for people with disabilities. In each of these areas, special instruments for the assessment and improvement of services have been created by the FAMR Research Unit.

Assi Model

The *Assi Model,* which takes its name from a common Finnish girl's name, is an assessment model developed by the FAMR Research Unit to help service providers to analyze their residential services. The model strengthens the interaction between recipients and providers. It gathers information from several viewpoints, especially from customers and personnel; produces an evaluation report and enables a discussion of the results with people involved in services; and helps in planning any further improvements needed in order to enhance the quality of life of people receiving services.

Assessment Scales   In evaluating service quality, three assessment scales are used: 1) the Subjective Well-being (SWB) Scale, 2) the Scale of Living Conditions (Elpa), and 3) the Scale of Organizational Culture (Kelpo). The SWB Scale (Matikka, Hintsala, & Vesala, 1998) was developed on the bases of FAMR's previous quality-of-life studies (Matikka, 1994, 1996, 2000, 2001). Information is gathered through interviews with individual recipients in eight areas of life: choices related to home, safety, activity, social relationships, happiness, health and stress, work, and mutual support.

The Scale of Living Conditions (Elpa) (Matikka & Toivonen, 2000) is intended to complement the information gathered by the SWB Scale. A direct support worker who knows the person receiving services well fills out this mail questionnaire. If the individual is not able to communicate, the mail questionnaire is the sole means of data collection. The Elpa scale contains six subscales: home, safety, activity, dignity, resources, and services used.

The Scale of Organizational Culture (Kelpo) (Matikka et al., 1999) measures organizational principles and practices. It is mainly based on the *Standard Rules on Equalization of Opportunities for Persons with Disabilities* (1994). Staff members complete the questionnaire during a group discussion. The scale contains five subscales: privacy, individual-centered support, professional qualification and organizational support, integrity, and security in case of emergency.

National Database   A national database compares the results of each unit with results drawn from the whole country. All data gathered is entered into the database maintained by the FAMR Research Unit. An evaluation report of any new unit contains comparison with this national data up to the present. Updating the national database with data from new units allows comparison criteria to be brought up to date. It also provides an opportunity to refine instruments based on the experience of each round of data collection and the comments on specific questionnaire items. The national database now contains data from more than 150 service units.

Assessment Process   The assessment process includes eight steps: 1) the service unit decides to assess quality by using the Assi Model, 2) methods are discussed and practical questions are raised, 3) the scales are reviewed to see how well they suit the unit, 4) data is gathered, 5) the FAMR Research Unit analyzes the data and compares the results with national norms, 6) reports are prepared, 7) feedback discussions with the unit are held, and 8) the unit makes decisions for further development work.

Asseri Model

The *Asseri Model,* which shares its name with many Finnish boys, is a working method developed by the FAMR Research Unit in order to evaluate the system of service provision for people with intellectual disabilities operated by municipalities. Analyses focus on coverage, quality, costs, benchmarking, and needs for modifying services. Evaluation data are gathered using the triangulation principle that examines services from the perspective of the different actors: people with disabilities, their family members, staff, and organizations. The methods include structured interviews of key people, questionnaires for units and personnel, and group discussions with consumers. Various statistical data, including the Statistics of Social and Health Care Database (Sotka), which is the national Finnish database maintained by Stakes, are used when comparing the structure of costs of disability services in different municipalities.

Thus far, five municipalities (with 7,000–80,000 inhabitants each) and one joint authority of municipalities (with a total population of 270,000) have been audited. Bringing consumers' opinions and needs to the evaluation discourse has created a positive process in which a multiplicity of views has replaced more narrow and cost-centered views on municipal services.

Quality Network

Evaluation of services both on a service unit and on a municipality level has been perceived as a good start for the improvement of services. The challenge, however, is to ensure that providers receive continuous and intensive support to achieve their goals and to change circumstances that were found to be in need of reform. To organize more intensive support, the FAMR Research Unit established the Quality Network for service providers in 2002. This network is based on the British model (British Institute of Learning Disabilities [BILD]) in which a local service provider becomes part of the Quality Network and receives support in self-assessment and service planning by paying an annual fee. The network stresses local teamwork and mutual support. The Finnish Quality Network will differ from the British model by offering tools like Assi and Asseri for quality assurance activities and emphasizing quality auditing and benchmarking. The Quality Network also will identify experts to further develop assessment tools and create new ones.

Future Challenges

The quality boom in Finnish public services in the 1990s brought consumer-centered evaluation to services provided for people with intellectual disabilities. This change became important early in the 1990s, given the radical reduction in centralized regulation and the onset of one of the worst recessions Finland had experienced. Since that time, the national quality strategy has emphasized consumer-centered planning, choices, and accessibility and has encouraged municipalities that are responsible for public welfare services to make these commitments to their consumers. In this regard, Finland followed other members of the European Union (Sosiaali-ja terveysministeriö et al., 1999).

It would be tempting to think that these developments have guaranteed high-quality services and supports for all individuals; however, insufficient resources have been allocated, especially to residential care for aging adults. Differences between rich and poor municipalities have increased nostalgia for when the state directed resources to public services by legislation. In 2001, the national government gave recommendations for organizing care for older adults and gave recommendations for people with disabilities in 2002. These moves suggest that the Finnish society no longer trusts the local authorities to deliver high-quality services on the basis of their goodwill alone. Future challenges will be combining quality assurance activities at various levels of society in a way that gives individuals power over their immediate environments and services and that makes all citizens responsible for the quality of the system of public services.

THE LIVING CONDITION SURVEYS IN NORWAY

This part of the chapter discusses the use of living condition surveys as a QA tool in services for people with intellectual disabilities in Norway. Such living condition surveys have been conducted as a quality assurance tool in services for people with intellectual disabilities in Norway three times: in 1989, 1994, and 2001. In order to understand the context for the application of this tool, however, a brief outline of the basics of the service system and the quality assurance system in Norway is provided.

Brief Outline of the Service System

As in many other countries, the system of services for people with intellectual disabilities has changed from being institution-based to being community-based. In Norway, however, the replacement of institutions took place in a relatively short time. In 1988, the Norwegian Parliament passed legislation that mandated the closure of all institutions. Implementation was based on a 5-year plan that began in 1991 and that was in large part completed by 1995. Today, there are no institutions in Norway.

The backbone of the new service system is the local authority, which is the municipality. Different parts of this political-administrative body are responsible for social services, activity/occupation centers, home services, nursing and care, housing, leisure activity support, and so forth. The main principle guiding the devolution of responsibility to the local level is the importance of administrative integration: Services for people with intellectual disabilities are supposed to be provided by the same authority and administration that provides similar services for other people. And during the last part of the 20th century, local authorities became the main service providers in all Scandinavian countries.

There are 436 municipalities and a total population of 4.48 million people in Norway. The mean population of the municipalities is 10,300 people, but the variation is enormous (225–458,000). There are 19 municipalities with fewer than 1,000 inhabitants, whereas 9 have more than 50,000 residents (Statistics Norway, 1999). Thus the population basis for services varies widely. In all municipalities, the local authorities run the services for people with intellectual disabilities themselves. Unlike the United States, private providers play an insignificant role.

Although there is a substantial variation, typically each adult using residential services has his or her own apartment of about 50 square meters with a bedroom, living room, kitchen, and bathroom. There are typically three or four similar apartments in the house, all rented from the municipality by a person with intellectual disabilities. There may or may not be staff rooms in the house. The houses are usually built for this purpose and are located on a residential street (Tøssebro, 1996). Most people with disabilities work at the municipal activity/occupation center, but different types of sheltered work are also common. Only about 5% work at typical workplaces (Document I-19/2000).

The Quality Assurance System

Regarding services for people with intellectual disabilities, one could argue that the quality assurance system operates at two levels: the individual level and the national or aggregate level. The living condition surveys are at the national level. The main quality assurance tool is, however, at the individual level. It is a system of rights and legal protection for all people who apply for public supports or services. The supports and services for each person are supposed to be based on an individual ruling, a formal decision by the administration on the amount and type of services the person is entitled to. This decision can be subject to appeals to the Fylkesmann, an appeal body representing the national government at the local level. One can also go to court. It is not at all uncommon for the Fylkesmann to overrule decisions of the municipal administration.

Appeals can be raised by the person him- or herself but also by their semi-guardians. A *semiguardian* is a spokesperson or legal representative, frequently a parent or a relative, who is appointed for people with intellectual disabilities in Norway.

The quality assurance system at the national level is a monitoring system aimed at determining whether services are developing according to the intentions or ideals. The focus is not on the services of each and every individual but on the situation of a group of people. Corrective action does not take place at the individual or local level but concerns potential changes in national policy. One component of this monitoring system is statistical reports from local authorities. For instance, the reports provide data on the number of people having their own apartment, the number of people living with their parents, the mean number of hours of home services and support, and the number of adults with no occupation or daytime activity.

The statistical reports give only a very superficial picture of how people with intellectual disabilities are living. The living condition surveys give a much more detailed picture. The employment of such surveys started as an evaluation of the deinstitutionalization reform. The first two surveys were conducted before and after people left the institutions (1989 and 1994), with the specific intention of studying changes in living conditions. The third study (2000–2001) was intended by the Department of Health and Social Affairs to provide a description of living conditions after the new structures had "settled," 10 years after the initial study. The next step will be to determine whether such surveys should be conducted regularly, thereby making them a regular part of the national monitoring system.

The Living Condition Approach

The tradition of living condition surveys was established in all Scandinavian countries during the 1970s. The approach grew partly out of the international social indicators movement (Duncan, 1969). This movement was a response to the dissatisfaction with the dominant position of economic welfare measures in the 1950s and 1960s. The criticisms were aimed both at the macro level (e.g., the gross national product as the measure of progress) and at the individual level: Those arguing for reform asserted that more than economic indicators were needed to get a balanced description of the well-being of citizens.

The first living condition studies were on groups at risk of experiencing social problems: a study of elderly people in Denmark and a study of people with low incomes in Sweden (Johansson, 1970). Both took place in the second part of the 1960s, and both included a wide range of social indicators, though the indicators mostly referred to conditions rather than experiences. The Swedish study introduced one more innovation—the inclusion of data on the population at large for purposes of comparison. This data provided a standard of comparison between the conditions of disadvantaged groups and other social groups. Thus, what started as studies of social problems and disadvantaged groups grew into studies of the population at large.

The purpose of living condition surveys today is to uncover social problems, to compare social groups, and to describe progress over time (e.g., whether the income gap between men and women is decreasing). In short, the surveys evaluate the results of the welfare state policy (Elstad, 1983). In Norway, the first living condition survey was conducted in 1973. It was subsequently repeated about every fourth year until it became annual after 1997.

The living conditions surveys typically include questions about the following life domains: income and earnings, economic wealth and possessions, housing or accommodation, health, education, social relations, work or occupation, working conditions, leisure and cultural activities, and participation in political and organizational life. The list of life domains has been pretty much the same since 1970 and is supposed to capture things and activities that people normally value (*Utjamningsmeldinga* [*White Paper on Equalization*], 1998/1999).

Living Condition Surveys and People with Intellectual Disabilities   Living condition surveys, social problems, and social policy are linked. Nevertheless, several groups at risk are excluded from the surveys, if not on purpose then in practice. People with intellectual disabilities are one of these excluded groups, but also excluded are deaf people, people without a permanent address, and immigrants, among others. People who live in institutions are excluded on purpose. Other groups are missing for practical reasons, including that they are difficult to get in touch with, cannot speak the dominant language, and so forth. Very small groups also tend to be poorly represented. The exclusion is puzzling given that many of these groups are of special interest to the welfare state policy.

Earlier, the exclusion of people with intellectual disabilities was hardly noticed because they were living in institutions and therefore were decoupled from the general way of thinking about living conditions. The status of individuals with intellectual disabilities became more of an issue after 1985 when a public committee was appointed to evaluate the institutions (Norwegian Public Reports, 1985). The committee report argued that because institutions were places where people with intellectual disabilities spend most of their adult life, they should be evaluated according to the concepts (if not the actual tools) that were used in descriptions of life circumstances for other people.

The public committee report argued that the living conditions were unacceptable and could not be made satisfactory within the institutional structures. They recommended closure and resettlement in the community (Norwegian Public Reports, 1985). As a result, "improved living conditions" became one of the core goals of the nascent reform in the Act on Dismantling of Institutions for People with Intellectual Disabilities (Bill 49). And with this foundation, it was logical that the living condition approach became an important construct for the evaluation of the reform, this time moving beyond the concepts to use of the actual tools (Tøssebro, 1988).

The Adaptation of Living Condition Surveys to the Study of People with Intellectual Disabilities

It is appealing to compare the life circumstances and living conditions of people with intellectual disabilities with the general population in the same way. It is definitely ideologically correct, but is it possible or meaningful? Is not the situation of people with intellectual disabilities too special, making a comparison a "normalization play"? And by using a questionnaire designed for the typical population, does one not run the risk of missing the issues that are most important in the lives of people with intellectual disabilities? In recognition of these concerns, the Norwegian studies include some adaptations to the general living condition surveys. The main principles, however, remained untouched, the adapted surveys include the same life domains, and some questions are identical. Modifications are described more fully elsewhere (Tøssebro, 1998). A summary follows.

The first problem concerns the respondents. A substantial proportion of the individuals with disabilities cannot speak, and for those individuals who are verbal, the questions on the typical living condition survey are too complicated. Furthermore, many people with intellectual disabilities are likely to employ coping strategies that are not consistent with being a reliable respondent (Heal & Sigelman, 1995). As a consequence, the Norwegian team chose to interview staff. Admittedly, such an approach has inherent problems. For one thing, it gives the very uncomfortable impression that the surveyors are going behind the backs of the people themselves. Furthermore, although the living condition surveys focus on conditions rather than experiences, some judgments tend to be included, such as "Are you bothered by traffic noise or other noise near your apartment or house?" Staff respondents should be able to distinguish between their own and the respondents' judgments, but such distinctions can inevitably become blurred. The consequence is that a survey of people with intellectual disabilities in which the respondents are staff has to be based on fully descriptive and nonevaluative questions. Where evaluative questions are required, it should be clear that judgments solicited are those of the staff.

The second problem concerns the theoretical underpinning of questions. Although the debate about which topics to include in the surveys usually refers to predominant societal values (Elstad, 1983), it is also common to use the resources perspective. Rather than looking at goods or choices that people value differently, this perspective focuses on the resources that people can use to realize their preferences (Sen, 1992). The most typical generalized resource is income, with education and employment next. The problem, however, is that all these resources change meaning when applied to people with intellectual disabilities. Of course, money matters, but their choices are restricted by a lot of other things more linked to the provision of services. For example, the affordability of a holiday trip is contingent on who pays for staff expenses, the service provider or the subject? Furthermore, the number of years of education says something about their rights but nothing about the resources they can exchange on the labor market. The conclusion is thus that the resource argument is less relevant, and consequently that predominant values become even more important as a theoretical underpinning. This means a change of balance between questions and life domains.

The third problem concerns what is usually taken for granted among the general population. In a living condition survey, one never bothers to ask whether the house is homelike, if one has colleagues who do not have disabilities, or if the individual had any choice as to where he or she is living. In the traditional living conditions survey, such issues are omitted because they are taken for granted. In the life of people who have recently moved out of an institution and who receive 12- or 24-hour supports, such things cannot be taken for granted. These types of questions should be included in a survey of people with intellectual disabilities. A related problem concerns situations that are irrelevant to typical people. One does not typically include response alternatives such as "local day center" when asking people about their jobs, but it must of course be included when describing the life of people with intellectual disabilities.

It may be difficult to get a good picture of what these modifications lead to and what such a questionnaire looks like. Within the confines of this chapter, there is not sufficient room for a full description of questions and data, but the housing domain provides some examples. One asks about the type of house, its size in square meters, number of rooms, if it is rented or owned, indicators of poor standards, noise—these are all examples of questions identical or nearly identical with questions in the general living condition surveys. For individuals with intellectual disabilities, one also asks about staff rooms, markers of private space, whether the house is built for this specific purpose, whether it is on a typical street, the number of apartments in the house, and if other residents have intellectual disabilities, and whether the house stands out in the neighborhood. Such questions are not included in other surveys.

Does a Living Condition Survey Make a Difference?

The study of the living conditions of people with intellectual disabilities is interesting as a research issue, but is it quality assurance? Do findings in such surveys have any impact on the lives and services of people with intellectual disabilities? There are no clear answers to these questions because the surveys are not intended to monitor specific services but rather to illuminate the system as a whole. Action is thus political action, and the impact can be difficult to trace, especially on the individual level. Furthermore, one rarely sees concrete action caused by one particular finding or study. Findings are instead fed into the political process and public debate along with a variety of other inputs. Therefore, what causes which changes is hard to predict beforehand and equally hard to trace afterwards.

The experience from the 1989 and 1994 surveys in Norway shows, however, that changes did make a difference. For example, one of the main findings was that a considerable improvement in housing conditions took place but other changes during the reform years were unexpectedly small. One even saw a reduction in leisure activities. The new houses tended to appear uniform and somewhat different from typical houses, which meant they were easily identified as houses for people with intellectual disabilities. Findings such as these led to a couple of policy changes. Money was allocated for "leisure assistance," more effort was put into supported employment, and there was an ideological push towards more individualized living arrangements. One should bear in mind, however, that the 1994 survey was a reform evaluation and was more likely to have an impact on policy than living condition surveys taking place in an everyday context.

Conclusion

In Norway, it is now possible to trace the development of living conditions for people with intellectual disabilities over a 13-year span, from 1989 to 2001. Furthermore, it is possible to relate a substantial amount of these data to the living conditions of other social groups. For the discourse on intellectual disabilities, this is definitely enlightening and useful.

During these years, the use of living conditions surveys has been expanded to other groups who are disadvantaged or at risk. As noted, such reviews make it possible to identify groups lagging behind and to provide documentation that can be used for political action. Specifically, a survey of people with disabilities (except people with intellectual disabilities) was conducted in 1995, and more recently, the general surveys are being revised in order to identify people with disabilities. Although this revision does not include people with intellectual disabilities (because of the methodological constraints noted), serious consideration is being paid to the possibility of conducting special living condition surveys of people with intellectual disabilities at regular intervals in the future.

One important design issue in living condition surveys is the ability to compare data across time and across social groups. There is also, however, the possibility of comparing across countries. So far we are aware of one such study comparing Norway and Sweden (Tideman & Tøssebro, 1996), but there is a potential to utilize this approach for international and cross-cultural comparisons. One should bear in mind that such international comparisons have been an inspiration for reform and a prod to improve the well-being of people with intellectual disabilities.

REFERENCES

Australian Institute of Health and Welfare. (2000). *Integrating indicators: Theory and practice in the disability services field.* Canberra, Australian Capital Territory: Author.

Cummins, R.A., McCabe, M.P., Romeo, Y., Reid, S., & Waters, L. (1997). An initial evaluation of the Comprehensive Quality of Life Scale–Intellectual Disability. *International Journal of Disability, Development and Education, 44,* 7–19.

Duncan, O.D. (1969). *Toward social reporting: Next steps.* New York: Russell Sage Foundation.

Elstad, J.I. (1983). *Sosial-indikator-bevegelsen. Oversikt og vurdering {The social indicators movement. A review and assessment}.* Oslo: INAS.

E-QUAL. (1998). *Review of approaches to satisfaction surveys of clients of disability services.* Retrieved from http://www.pc.gov.au/research/commres/disabsvc/index.html.

E-QUAL. (2001). *Sail your own ship: A discussion paper about quality systems in disability services.* Perth, WA: Author.

E-QUAL and Donovan Research. (2000). *National satisfaction survey of clients of disability services. A report for the Steering Committee for the Review of Commonwealth/State Service Provision and the National Disability Administrators.* Canberra, Australian Capital Territory: AusInfo.

Heal, L., & Sigelman, C. (1995). Response biases in interviews of people with limited mental ability. *Journal of Intellectual Disability Research, 39,* 331–340.

Human Services Research Institute. (1998). *Core indicators project: Progress report No. 2. Center on Managed Long Term Supports for People with Disabilities.* Cambridge, MA: Author.

International Association for the Scientific Study of Intellectual Disabilities. (2000). *Quality of life: Its conceptualization, measurement and application.* A consensus document. World Health Organisation–International Association for the Scientific Study of Intellectual Disabilities.

Johansson, S. (1970). *Om levnadsnivåundersökningen {On the level of living study}.* Stockholm: Almenne förlaget.

Lov om avvikling av institusjoner for psykisk utviklingshemmete [Norway's act on dismantling of institutions for people with intellectual disabilities]. Bill 49 (1987–1988).

Matikka, L.M. (1994). The quality of life of adults with intellectual disabilities in Finland. In D. Goode (Ed.), *Quality of life for persons with disabilities. International perspectives and issues* (pp. 22–38). Cambridge, MA: Brookline.

Matikka, L.M. (1996). Effects of psychological factors on the perceived quality of life of people with intellectual disabilities. *Journal of Applied Research in Intellectual Disabilities, 9,* 115–128.

Matikka, L.M. (2000). *Subjektiivisen hyvinvoinnin asteikon kehittäminen kehitysvammapalvelujen laadunarviointiin {Development of the Subjective Well-Being Scale for the assessment of services provided for the people with intellectual disabilities}.* Valtakunnallisen tutkimus-ja kokeiluyksikön julkaisuja (No. 79). Helsinki: Finnish Association on Mental Retardation.

Matikka, L.M. (2001). *Service-oriented assessment of quality of life of adults with intellectual disabilities. Academic dissertation. FAMR Research Publication No. 83.* Helsinki: Finnish Association on Mental Retardation Research Unit.

Matikka, L.M., Hintsala, S., & Toivonen, S. (1999). *KELPO: A Scale of Organizational Culture* (1st ed.). Helsinki: Finnish Association on Mental Retardation.

Matikka, L.M., & Toivonen, S. (2000). *ELPA: An Assessment Scale for Living Conditions and Services* (3rd version). Helsinki: Finnish Association on Mental Retardation.

Matikka, L.M., Hintsala, S., & Vesala, H. (1998, February). *Subjective well-being scale* (3rd ed.). Helsinki: Finnish Association on Mental Retardation.

Norwegian Public Reports. (1985). *Levekår for psykisk utviklingshemmete {The living conditions of people with intellectual disabilities}*. NOU, 34.

Sen, A. (1992). *Inequality reexamined*. Cambridge, MA: Harvard University Press.

Sosiaali-ja terveysministeriö, Stakes, & Suomen kuntaliitto. (1999). *Sosiaali- ja terveydenhuollon laadunhallinta 2000 - luvulle {The quality management of social welfare and health care to the 20th century}*. Jyväskylä: Gummerus.

Stakes. (1995). *Laadunhallinta sosiaali- ja terveydenhuollossa. Valtakunnallinen suositus sosiaali-ja terveydenhuollon laadunhallinnan järjestämisestä ja sisällöstä {Quality management in social and health care}*. Jyväskylä: Stakes, National Research and Development Centre for Welfare and Health.

Standards Australia/Standards New Zealand. (2000). *AS/NZS 9004:2000, Quality management systems: Guidelines for performance improvements*. Sydney, New South Wales: Authors.

Statistics Norway. (1999). *Statistisk årbok (Statistical Yearbook)*.

Status for tilbudet til mennesker med utviklingshemming {The state of the services for people with intellectual disabilities}. (Document I-1/2000). Oslo: Department of Health and Social Affairs.

Steering Committee for the Review of Commonwealth/State Service Provision. (2000). *Report on Government Services 2000* (Volume 3). Canberra, Australian Capital Territory: AusInfo.

Tøssebro, J. (1988). *Velferd for psykisk utviklingshemmete, hvordan studere det? {How to study the well-being of people with intellectual disabilities}*. Trondheim: Helsefagshøgskolen.

Tøssebro, J. (1996). *En bedre hverdag? Utviklingshemmetes levekår etter HVPU-reformen {Improved everyday life? Living conditions of intellectually disabled people after resettlement}*. Oslo: Kommuneforlaget.

Tøssebro, J. (1998). Researching the living conditions of people with intellectual disabilities. In Hjelmqvist & Kebbon (Eds.), *Methods for studying the living conditions of persons with disabilities* (pp. 24–35). Stockholm: Swedish Council for Social Research.

United Nations. (1994). *The standard rules on the equalization of opportunities for persons with disabilities*. New York: Author.

Utjamningsmeldinga {White paper on equalization}. (1998–1999). Number 50.

Supports for the New Quality Enhancement

Development of comprehensive and integrated quality enhancement and improvement systems will require upgrading the data collection infrastructure of both states and providers, creating streamlined indicators of performance, and renewing the emphasis on the value of a competent workforce committed to individual empowerment as well as individual health and safety.

Chapter 13 describes a national effort to generate commonly applied performance measures—measures that will allow the comparisons among the states in key domains, including choice, health and safety, work, and so forth. Taub, Smith, and Bradley describe a consensus-building process among the states to arrive at the measures and the ways in which individual states are using the results for systems improvement. The case study that follows the chapter discusses the path followed by the staff of one provider in Massachusetts to create internal mechanisms to highlight performance and provide the basis for change and improvement. It is an honest and illuminating look at the evolution of a responsive provider-based quality enhancement process that can serve as a model for other providers.

Chapter 14 describes a key building block in the development of internal provider-based, high-quality systems—a flexible and responsive management information system. Ashbaugh stresses that a good management information system supported by good software is not only important for the collection and analysis of data but can also lessen the burden of documentation faced by direct support staff. To be productive, the system must be functional, flexible, and configured in an efficient fashion. In addition, when providers have responsive systems, they are in a position to provide information to people with disabilities and families regarding outcomes and performance.

Chapter 15 highlights a critical aspect of any high-quality system—a competent and dedicated direct support staff. As pointed out by the authors, direct support professionals are the critical ingredient in person-centered supports. Their performance can directly affect the quality of life of individuals with disabilities perhaps more directly than anyone else in the formal service system. The authors describe what some providers have done to increase the longevity of staff as well as to improve staff skills. Finally, they describe a range of best practice and research-based strategies to address issues of direct support recruitment, retention, and training. Examples include creating apprenticeship programs and postsecondary education programs designed to result in career paths for people who enter direct support roles. They also involve agency-based interventions such as improved training, better articulation of job roles and responsibilities, collaborative efforts to find new employees, internal career paths for employees, and a clearer expectation of what the job entails for potential employees.

CHAPTER 13

The National
Core Indicators Project

MONITORING THE PERFORMANCE OF
STATE DEVELOPMENTAL DISABILITIES AGENCIES

SARAH L. TAUB, GARY A. SMITH, AND VALERIE J. BRADLEY

How well do public systems perform in carrying out their fundamental mission to support people with developmental disabilities and families? Is performance improving? What outcomes are individuals achieving? How does the performance of one state's system compare to performance elsewhere? What are our opportunities for improving performance? The aim of the Core Indicators Project (CIP) is to aid state developmental disabilities authorities (SDDAs) to answer these questions.

In January 1997, the National Association of State Directors of Developmental Disabilities Services (NASDDDS) and the Human Services Research Institute (HSRI) launched the CIP. The number of states actively participating in the project has climbed steadily, reaching 24 in January 2002 (see Figure 13.1). The decision to launch CIP grew out of the recognition by NASDDDS and its member agencies that the increasing complexity of developmental disabilities services required vastly improved capabilities to evaluate system performance. State officials also recognized that improved oversight would require them to create systems that were data-based and data-driven. In other words, public developmental disabilities leaders understood that quality enhancement hinges on the capacity to systematically and rigorously measure performance and outcomes.

CIP began and continues as a voluntary collaboration among participating NASDDDS member agencies and substate entities committed to developing a coherent and comprehensive approach to performance and outcome measurement. Through the project, participating states pool their resources and knowledge to create performance monitoring systems, identify common performance indicators, work out sound data collection strategies, and share results. This sustained, ongoing multistate collaborative effort to jointly assess and improve performance is unprecedented.

Figure 13.1.   States that participated in the National Core Indicators Project (CIP) as of January 2002.

CURRENT CONTEXT

In order to understand the nature of this effort, one must consider the current landscape of the DD field. The collaboration of states draws momentum from a variety of contextual factors. Broad trends such as tailoring supports to the individual and emphasizing outcome-based performance measures are fundamental to the progress of CIP. Changing management approaches have created demands for quantitative data and accountability, and related health care fields have adopted managed care strategies and performance indicator systems. Prior to CIP, both individual state and federal initiatives began to address the development of performance indicator systems.

Emphasis on Person-Centered Outcomes

The increasing emphasis on outcomes and performance assessment is more than merely a change in measurement approaches. It stems from a fundamental change in the assumptions about what quality is and reflects a larger shift in the field—specifically from program-oriented, formulaic models of care to individually tailored supports based on individual choices and preferences. As a result, the adoption of performance indicators as a quality enhancement method is both a consequence of the change in expectations as well as a method for focusing on person-centered outcomes. As supports become more individualized, relying on strict input and process measures has less utility in a world that emphasizes flexibility, creativity, and tailoring supports to each person's unique capabilities and preferences.

Emphasis on Quantitative Data

Furthermore, the adoption of approaches such as total quality management has placed a premium on the development of quantifiable indicators linked to observable performance. Measuring outcomes and performance is the starting point for the design and implementation of effective quality enhancement strategies.

Pressure for Accountability

Federal and state policy makers increasingly expect and demand reliable information concerning the results that state agencies are achieving in developmental disabilities and other human services. More and more, funders are basing their decisions on hard evidence furnished by SDDAs concerning how well they are carrying out their missions and their effectiveness in ensuring quality. CIP, therefore, is a logical outgrowth of an intensified commitment to ensure that services and supports are accountable to people with developmental disabilities, their families, and the taxpayers.

Growth of Managed Care

In the mid-1990s, managed care appeared to be emerging as an alternative to the conventional purchase-of-service approach for the delivery of behavioral health and, potentially, developmental disabilities services. There seemed to be a serious prospect that many states would radically restructure not only their health care but also other long-term services systems along managed care lines. The threat of managed care caused considerable consternation. At the same time, however, it also prompted state officials in many states to take a fresh look at how they were managing their systems, especially with regard to the potential applicability of certain managed care strategies, particularly the strong emphasis on data-based system management.

Growth in the Use of Performance Indicators

The progress that was being made in other fields in developing performance indicators also influenced the formation of CIP. Some of this work was associated with the emergence of managed health care (e.g., Health Plan Employer Data Information Set [HEDIS]). In mental health, several efforts were underway to develop and implement performance indicators, including in the public sector (e.g., Mental Health Statistics Improvement Program [MHSIP] and American Academy of Mental Health Administrators performance indicators). This work strongly suggested the potential for developing performance indicators for DD services.

Individual State Initiatives

Prior to the multistate collaboration that led to the CIP, a number of individual states began to explore the development of systemic performance indicators. New Hampshire initiated the Quality Outcomes Project, which included individual consumer and systemic indicators. Similarly, Vermont developed performance indicators to monitor the state's more consumer-driven funding mechanism. Michigan used specific outcome indicators to grade each of its local service entities.

Related Federal Initiatives

State performance in the provision of Medicaid services in general and home and community services in particular also is receiving heightened federal attention. During the 1990s, there was a massive expansion of Home and Community-Based Services (HCBS) Waiver programs for people with developmental disabilities. The number of individuals participating in such programs exploded from roughly 45,000 in 1990 to 291,000 in 2000 (Smith, 2000). This rapid growth has caused increased attention to the quality of Medicaid-funded services and state performance in operating and managing HCBS Waiver programs. In addition, the federal Health Care Financing Administration (now the Centers for Medicare & Medicaid Services [CMS]) launched several initiatives related to performance and outcome measurement, especially in the arena of managed health care services. In the mid-1990s, federal officials began to explore the feasibility of developing performance measures for HCBS Waiver programs.

It seemed clear that states would be expected to collect and report more robust information concerning the quality and effectiveness of home and community services. In part, CIP anticipated the need for such information, even though it was not clear exactly what information states would be expected to collect with respect to HCBS Waiver services. In 2000, CMS has revamped its HCBS Waiver program review protocol. The protocol clearly encourages states to collect systematic performance and outcome data along several dimensions, including satisfaction with services. In this vein, CMS has commissioned the development of a "consumer experience questionnaire" that states may employ. The CMS instrument parallels the CIP consumer survey/interview instrument.

OVERVIEW OF CIP DESIGN

Constructing a performance and outcome monitoring system requires answers to three questions: What are the major concerns regarding performance and outcomes? What needs to be tracked in order to gauge performance in each area of concern? What data are needed in order to yield reliable information about performance? The areas of concern that frame CIP reflect topics that the participating states regard as critical to their capacity to gauge performance. SDDAs are mission-driven and, therefore, highly concerned that services and supports they purchase yield positive outcomes for individuals served through the public system. They also are charged with promoting economy and efficiency in the use of tax dollars, improving system access and responsiveness, and ensuring the health and personal security of individuals who receive services and supports.

The CIP performance indicators do not address every possible element of systemwide performance. The indicators are intended to operate in tandem with other performance tracking and monitoring systems that SDDAs operate. One key criterion for the selection of CIP measures was and continues to be the extent to which the indicator makes benchmarking between and among states possible. Therefore, indicators need to yield comparable data. Comparability is accomplished through the use of common data collection protocols (e.g., consumer and family surveys) as well as through common definitions of the particular phenomenon and data source addressed by the indicator. Furthermore, participating states also need to agree that the indicators will yield results that are useful in assessing system performance within each state. Longitudinal performance measurement helps the state to understand whether performance is improving or deteriorating from one period to the next.

Project Chronology

The development of performance and outcome measures began in 1997 with the formation of a project steering committee comprised of seven state agencies that had agreed to be field test states (Arizona, Connecticut, Missouri, Nebraska, Pennsylvania, Vermont, and Virginia). An additional eight states (Alabama, Colorado, Florida, Michigan, New York, Oklahoma, Rhode Island, and South Carolina) volunteered to serve as advisors and to share their expertise. The committee's work involved three main steps:

1. To identify mission-critical areas of concern. In CIP, these areas are expressed as concerns and described as performance and outcome domains and subdomains.

2. To define more finely the performance and outcomes that will be tracked. These are the CIP performance and outcome indicators. They describe in concrete terms how performance will be measured and monitored.

3. To identify the data that must be compiled in order to measure performance for each indicator

After identifying mission-critical domains (e.g., community inclusion, choice, health and safety), the group winnowed down a list of more than 130 possible performance indicators into a smaller set of approximately 65 that captured performance in the selected domains. After on-site conversations with staff in the field test sites regarding the feasibility of data collection, the group convened again and narrowed the indicator set to 61. Project personnel then developed data collection specifications and prepared project work plans for the field test states. In addition, the consumer survey/interview instrument was designed (with the invaluable assistance of the CIP's Technical Advisory Subcommittee). Project personnel also prepared the family survey instrument. Figure 13.2 illustrates one domain, consumer outcomes, and one subdomain, work, indicators for the subdomain, and data sources.

There were two especially noteworthy aspects to the development of the indicator set. First, the steering committee came into surprisingly rapid agreement regarding mission-critical areas of concern, especially with respect to outcomes. This positive result revealed that there was considerable convergence among the states concerning their fundamental missions and the underlying premise that the mission was defined by person-centered principles. Second, the committee also decided that the people receiving services and families would be the primary sources of information about outcomes and feedback concerning system performance. About half of the indicators are linked to consumer interviews and family surveys as their principle data source.

Field test state data collection got underway in earnest at the beginning of 1998. The project staff compiled the data and conducted various analyses that September. To ensure comparability of findings across states, data from the consumer survey was "risk adjusted" based on key functional characteristics found to be predictive of scores on the survey (e.g., sensory disabilities, ambulation, behavior challenges). Results of this dry run were shared with the steering committee, and additional modifications were made to the indicator set as well as to data collection protocols.

CIP Phase II started in January 1999 and included a total of 12 states (Arizona, Connecticut, Kentucky, Massachusetts, Minnesota, Nebraska, North Carolina, Pennsylvania, Rhode Island, Virginia, Vermont, and Washington). The Version 2.0 indicator set consisted of 60 performance and outcome indicators. Since then, the project has expanded its scope to include services for children with developmental disabilities and their families, continued to develop and refine the indicators, and recruited additional states to participate in the project. The Phase II data is considered baseline project data. Phase III spanned 2000–2001 and included four additional states (Delaware, Iowa, Montana, and Utah). Seven states joined in 2001 (Alabama, Hawaii, Illinois, Indiana, Oklahoma, West Virginia, and Wyoming). Twenty-three states are also now actively participating along with the Orange County Regional Center in California. Phase II and Phase III technical reports and other selected documents are available online at www.hsri.org/cip/core.html.

Domain: Consumer outcomes

Overview: The project's consumer outcome indicators concern how well the public system aids adults with developmental disabilities to work, participate in their communities, have and sustain relationships, and exercise choice over their lives. Other indicators in this domain probe how satisfied individuals are with services and supports. The concerns on which these indicators are based are commonly found in the mission statements of state developmental disabilities administrations (SDDAs).

Subdomain	Concern	Indicators	Data source
Work	People are receiving supports to find and maintain employment in integrated settings and earn increased wages.	The average monthly wage of people who receive supports	System or consumer survey supplement
		The average number of hours worked per month during the previous year	System or consumer survey supplement
		The percentage of people earning at or above the state minimum wage	System or consumer survey supplement
		The percentage of people who are continuously employed in community-based settings during the previous year	System or consumer survey supplement
		The proportion of all individuals who receive daytime supports of any type who are engaged in community integrated employment	System

Figure 13.2. One domain (consumer outcomes), and one subdomain (work), indicators for the subdomain, and data sources in the Core Indicators Project (CIP): Phase II indicators (Version 2.0).

States have to manage a myriad of project activities, including arranging for and conducting the consumer survey/interview. Participation also means that a state is willing to run the risk that its results may reveal serious problems. The fact that nearly half of the states have elected to participate is compelling evidence of their serious commitment to systematic performance measurement. Roger Stortenbecker, administrator of the Developmental Disabilities System in Nebraska (one of the original field test states) and co-chair of the CIP Steering Committee, reflected on the evolving role of CIP:

> The type of services and the way the service is delivered is changing in response to consumer demand for more flexibility and selection. We need to find a way to monitor for quality while not overstepping our limit of control over the relationship between consumer and service provider. The CIP allows us to pick up important data elements without regard to where the service is provided. (Personal correspondence, December 18, 2001)

SELECTED FINDINGS

This section highlights selected comparisons between Phase II (1999) and Phase III (2000) consumer survey results for the total sample. Phase II includes data on 12 states, and Phase III includes data on 11 states.

Community Inclusion

Participation in community activities was high in 2000, ranging from 57% to 96%. On most items, scores were marginally higher than 1999 results. See Figure 13.3 for more details.

Choice and Decision Making

Results for choice and decision-making indicators were mixed. For day-to-day decisions (e.g. choosing a schedule, free-time activities), most respondents have input or make these choices independently. Although patterns of results in 2000 were similar to baseline findings (1999), two items are worth noting: 41% of respondents in 2000 reported choosing with whom they live, compared with 32% in 1999. The percent of respondents who chose their staff went down slightly in 2000, from 31% to 26% (choosing home staff) and from 29% to 22% (choosing job staff). See Figure 13.4 for more details.

Respect and Rights

As was reported in 1999, 88% of all respondents reported that they had enough privacy. In 2000, 33% of all respondents reported having attended a self-advocacy group meeting or event, compared with a baseline proportion of 26%. Reports of rights restrictions were down slightly in 2000 (see Figure 13.5).

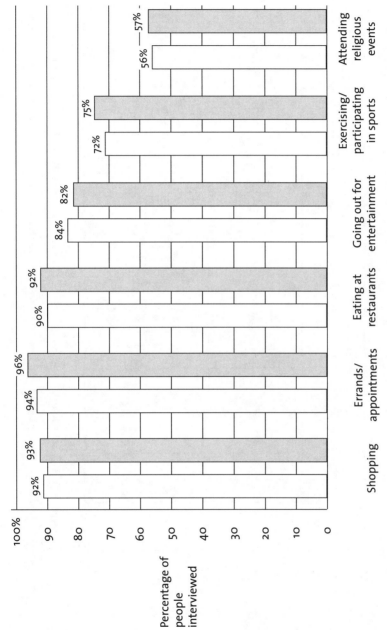

Figure 13.3. Selected indicators for the subdomain of community inclusion, as measured by the Core Indicators Project (CIP) consumer survey: 1999 and 2000. (Key: ☐ 1999, ▨ 2000)

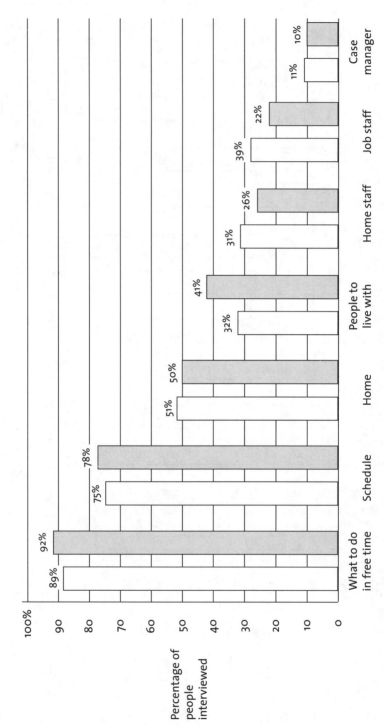

Figure 13.4. Selected indicators for the subdomain of choice and decision making, as measured by the Core Indicators Project (CIP) consumer survey: 1999 and 2000.
(*Key:* ☐ 1999, ▦ 2000)

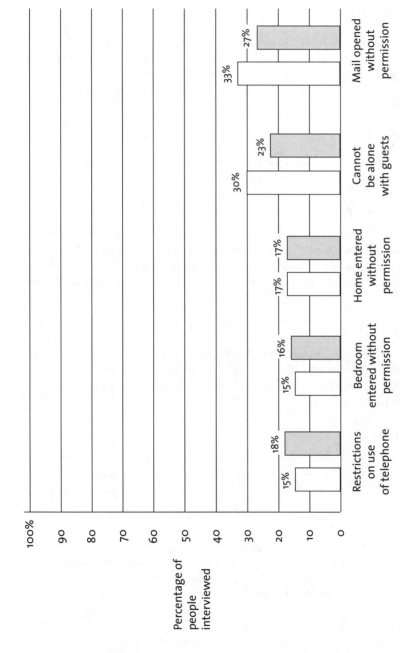

Figure 13.5. Selected indicators for the subdomain of respect and rights, as measured by the Core Indicators Project (CIP) consumer survey: 1999 and 2000. (Key: ☐ 1999, ▨ 2000)

Service Coordination

The majority of respondents report that they have access to their service co-ordinators. Eighty percent of all respondents report that they are able to talk to their service coordinators, compared with 76% in 1999; 90% of all respondents report that service coordinators get them what they need, compared with 79% in 1999.

Safety

Ninety-four percent of respondents report feeling safe in their neighborhoods. Ninety-six percent report feeling safe at home.

Relationships

Similar to 1999 results, the majority of respondents in 2000 report having friends (other than family and staff) and best friends, and they report being able to see their friends and family when they want (see Figure 13.6). However, a little more than half the respondents report "sometimes" or "always" feeling lonely.

Acceptability

Across the board, approximately 91% of respondents report that support staff (at home, in day program, and at jobs) treat them with respect. Place of residence is fairly stable across the sample—only 12% of respondents changed residences in the past year.

Health

Across the board, women's access to yearly gynecological exams is low (only 52% had an exam in the past year and 8% have never had one).

CIP AND STATE QUALITY IMPROVEMENT EFFORTS

These data indicate the richness of information available to participating states. The next challenge is to build this information into each state's quality enhancement systems and make the collection of the CIP data central to the state's quality management design. This will require changing CIP from a project to an established process. The *CIP Guidebook* made available to participating states includes the following recommended steps for using the CIP data in a continuous approach to system reform and enhancement:

- Secure buy-in from a range of stakeholders (e.g., consumers, family members, sister agencies) by helping them to understand the ways in which the data can be used to collectively improve state systems.

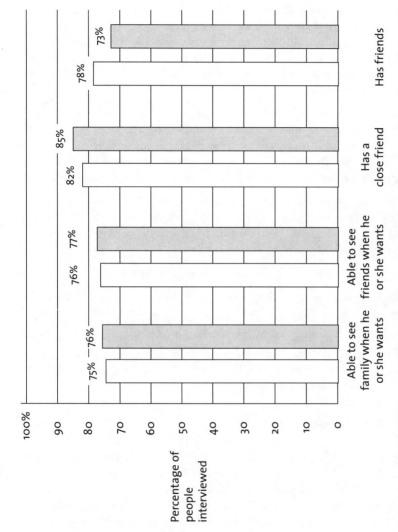

Figure 13.6. Selected indicators for the subdomain of relationships, as measured by the Core Indicators Project (CIP) consumer survey: 1999 and 2000. (*Key:* ☐ 1999, ▨ 2000)

- Create a permanent stakeholder group to review findings and to ensure that indicators continue to be valid.

- Develop benchmarks or standards for selected indicators (e.g., 90% of consumers choose with whom they live). In some instances, the benchmark may simply be maintaining the current level of performance (e.g., 100% of individuals receiving services have a personal physician). In other areas, the standard may be more aspirational (e.g., currently, 20% of individuals are in competitive employment; the standard for the next measurement period should be 25%).

- Identify priority areas or key issues that should be targeted for improvement over the next measurement period. Decisions about priorities should reflect strong consensus among those most affected (people with disabilities and their families), should be susceptible to change within the measurement period, and should reflect an adequate investment of resources.

- Develop change strategies to accomplish targeted improvement. For example, if consumer surveys indicate that individuals are not familiar with their rights, then collaboration with a self-advocacy agency may yield increased knowledge among system consumers.

- Create implementation teams to tackle each priority area.

- Measure progress to determine whether the priority objectives have been met.

- Begin the cycle again with the refinement of indicators, the revision of benchmarks, the determination of ensuing priorities, the exploration of improved change methodologies, the implementation of change strategies, and the measurement of results.

MAJOR ACCOMPLISHMENTS

The CIP has had both immediate and long-term influences on performance monitoring at all levels of the DD system. The core indicators, together with their respective data collection protocols, are widely used across the nation. The national database continues to grow, setting the stage for future trend analyses and benchmark development. Project reports are being generated and distributed on a more routine basis. Participating states are beginning to use the results for quality enhancement activities, and providers have found the project useful for making internal data system improvements.

At the National Level

The collaboration of SDDA representatives from around the country during the early stages of CIP resulted in a set of wide-ranging performance indicators. The indicators and corresponding measures have been fine-tuned but remain basically intact. It is expected that the indicator set will continue to evolve to reflect changes in systems of support and to improve the reliability and validity of the measures as more information is gleaned from the data.

CIP has also produced a companion set of valid and reliable data collection protocols. These tools include a direct interview protocol (i.e., consumer survey) for collecting information directly from individuals who receive services and supports, three distinct family surveys, and separate protocols for the collection of data concerning employment, staff turnover and stability, board representation, serious injuries, restraints, and deaths. CIP surveys are widely used, even beyond the participating states. The consumer survey has undergone psychometric testing to ensure its reliability and validity. Definitions and data specifications developed for cross-state compatibility of system data have been used by states to establish routine methods of collecting critical information from providers. As CIP moves from a development phase to a routine activity, the data reports will be produced and distributed with increasing regularity. With 2 years of data in hand and a third year of data collection underway, attention will turn to establishing benchmarks and more in-depth analysis of the results.

At the State Level

The CIP has already had both long-range and immediate influences on the ways in which states monitor performance and use performance data to influence system change. In Massachusetts, the CIP data are being used as the cornerstone for the state's strategic plan for the enhancement of services to people with mental retardation. It also will figure prominently in the state's proposed quality management initiative. In addition, both Massachusetts and Wyoming are using the CIP data as part of their HCBS Waiver reviews. In Pennsylvania, the CIP data requirements helped to shape the design of new and comprehensive management information system for the mental retardation services system. In Vermont, the results of the data collection have already resulted in an initiative to improve information to consumers and families regarding their rights (an indicator that previously fell below the state's expectations). Findings regarding the frequency of gynecological exams and the use of psychotropic medication have heightened state officials' awareness of crucial health issues. Several states used the data for additional purposes:

- Pennsylvania uses CIP information in conjunction with independent monitoring at the local level, and it is an integral part of Pennsylvania's overall quality management framework.

- Arizona also uses CIP for Medicaid requirements, advertises reports in its newsletter, sends reports to all families who participated, and shares its information with the state legislature and governor.

- Alabama will use the consumer survey as part of Wyatt settlement requirements.

- Rhode Island is in the process of putting together a statewide consortium of advocacy groups that will look at issues, trends, and best practices. This group will also review CIP data. In addition, they are working on creative ways to get the results out in accessible formats.

- Kentucky included CIP in its 10-year plan. Also, it is expanding its focus on team interviewing techniques to enhance consumer and family participation.

- Connecticut has presented the data around the state.

- Washington used the CIP data collection protocols to revise its incident reporting and mortality data system.

At the Provider Level

The value of the CIP project at the provider level is also worth noting. First, it reinforces the importance of using consumer-generated information as the foundation of any quality enhancement system. Second, it also helps providers— many of whom are in the process of revamping their internal management information systems—to anticipate the types of information that the state will require them to collect. Finally, especially in those states that have tried to close the loop by disseminating CIP data, it gives an indication of statewide norms and provides comparisons to the aggregate performance of providers in other states. The case study that follows this chapter provides some insight as to how one Massachusetts provider, Vinfen, met the challenge of developing internal performance monitoring mechanisms.

TECHNICAL CHALLENGES

There have been many technical challenges in conducting CIP. By far, the most challenging task is ensuring that measures are comparable across states. Creating standard measures general enough to meet a common definition but sufficiently specific to yield meaningful data was a major focus of Phase I and continues to be a challenge. Through much discussion, testing, and further refinement, feasible measures have been developed for most of the indicators. A few system indicators (e.g., indicators about injuries and the use of restraints) still pose measurement problems across states, primarily due to variations among states in defining terms and the scope of information captured at the state level. Finding a balance between cross-state comparability and robustness of measures is an ongoing process.

Another data collection challenge, which became evident early in the project, is the varying level of sophistication among states with respect to their information systems. Some states have mature, comprehensive, and automated management information systems. Others keep critical records by hand. As a result, the reliability, availability, and completeness of information varies across and sometimes within state systems. To account for these differences, CIP protocols request additional information from each SDDA about the sources of data. This information, along with basic profiles of state system configuration, provides a critical context for displaying and interpreting the data.

Participation in CIP requires patience and commitment. Participating SDDAs have both. A project of this nature necessarily has a long lead time before yielding useful results. Protocols had to be developed and baselines established for each state. The results of 1 or even 2 years' worth of data still leave many participants with the question, "What does it all mean?" Although information garnered has value in its own right for participating states, the goal remains to establish benchmarks that can provide a useful basis for judging state performance. With the wealth of CIP information now being collected on a regular basis in nearly half the states, this goal is within reach.

CORE INDICATORS PROJECT IN THE FUTURE

What does the future hold for CIP? The number of states participating in the project will increase but likely will stabilize at roughly 25. There are several states that, on their own, have developed sound approaches to collecting data about performance and outcomes. These states have less to gain by joining the project. There are other states in which the barriers to participation are difficult to overcome, including marshalling the resources necessary to participate.

The project has gone through an extended "ramping up" period. It now stands poised to give states more robust information concerning performance. The project's databases have grown quite large and increasingly reliable. There is every prospect that exploiting this data will result in improved understanding of where states individually and collectively stand in achieving person-centered outcomes. In other words, how far has the field actually come (and how long a journey is left)? Just as important is the role that this information can now serve to guide and inform discussions in the states about quality enhancement.

To be certain, the present indicators and data collection protocols will continue to change and evolve, especially as a result of the increased investments that states are making in revamping and improving their data systems. The indicators also will continue to evolve because the field itself refuses to stand still very long. When the project began, self-determination was a new concept. Today, it dominates discussions concerning future system directions. The present indicator set will change to include better measures to describe how effective state systems are in supporting individuals and families to direct and manage their own supports.

It also seems certain that the project will play an increasingly important role as a forum for states to exchange information and explore new methods of measuring performance and outcomes. One impact of the project has been an ever-expanding dialogue among states concerning performance measurement and how improved performance measures can be employed to effect positive change. It is anticipated that in the future, participating states will form communities of interest in order to pursue the development of increasingly sophisticated performance measurement approaches in a growing number of areas.

CONCLUSION

CIP's greatest significance has been and will continue to be the way it has changed the nature of the dialogue about public systems. It is no longer enough to espouse values or claim allegiance to a mission statement. Rightly, the dialogue now increasingly concerns the actual extent to which people are realizing valued outcomes. A connection has been made to individuals and families to include them in meaningful and systematic ways to provide direct feedback about the performance of the system from their perspective. The significance of CIP is that the dialogue about performance is becoming increasingly data-based and data-driven, and this lays an important foundation for quality improvement. It is to the credit of the states that helped launch CIP and the states that have joined the project since that they have willingly taken the very courageous step of measuring their own performance—good or bad—so that they could engage in meaningful quality enhancement.

REFERENCE

Smith, G. (2000). *Medicaid long-term services for people with developmental disabilities: 2000 status*. Alexandria, VA: National Association of State Directors of Developmental Disabilities Services.

Quality Assurance to Quality Enhancement

A PROVIDER PERSPECTIVE

BARRY SCHWARTZ AND MADELINE BECKER

In 1985, like many providers of services to people with disabilities that experience rapid growth, the senior management of Vinfen was concerned about consistency, quality, and conformance to regulations. Vinfen, a private, not-for-profit company based in eastern Massachusetts, was established in 1977 to provide a comprehensive array of community-based services to people with disabilities—primarily people with mental retardation and people with mental illness. By 1985, after 8 years of operation, Vinfen had a revenue base of $6 million, a level of growth that necessitated a mechanism to maintain the same level of quality standards in new program initiatives that family members, agency staff, people with disabilities, and funders had come to expect from the agency. To meet these expectations as programs expanded, the agency developed a quality assurance process that focused on compliance to the licensing standards set by funding agencies and general overall standards relating to quality of services. This case study describes the lessons learned as Vinfen implemented an internal quality assurance system and the ultimate creation of an outcome-focused, person-centered process.

QUALITY CONTROL AND DOCUMENTATION

In the initial stages, the effort concentrated on documentation. Each program or system was assessed on site by a four-member team of volunteer middle and senior managers to identify new training needs and to determine which areas needed management attention. The team reviewed documentation standards for consumer records, petty cash, and consumer funds. There was a list of physical site standards, human rights standards, and staff training documentation. Staff and consumer satisfaction surveys were added to the process the following year. A narrative report was written with recommendations for areas of improvement. Vinfen's commitment to staff was that they would not measure one program against another because each had a different level of funding and intensity of services. The goal was to have programs improve over time.

During this period, Vinfen was using the term *quality assurance* but increasingly terms such as *quality outcomes* and *quality improvement* slipped into the vocabulary. The teams developed program-specific tools to assess different program types and set corporation-wide averages or benchmarks. Although the quality enhancement process was successful in meeting initial objectives, Vinfen began striving for real quality, not just compliance. It was also very aware that the system was internal—Vinfen was assessing itself and concluding that it was doing a good job.

In 1987, Vinfen decided to have an external group assess the quality of its services. Accreditation by the Commission on Accreditation of Rehabilitation Facilities (now known as CARF . . . the Rehabilitation Accreditation Commission) was thought to be the best fit for Vinfen's range of services and provided legislators, stakeholders, and communities in general with a reliable and trustworthy seal of approval.

One of the CARF standards that Vinfen needed to address was a requirement for a program evaluation system that focused on efficiency and effectiveness outcomes in addition to consumer satisfaction data. Vinfen faced the need to choose outcomes that fit the spectrum of day, residential, educational, and clinical services that it provided, and it created a process that used information it was already collecting. The program evaluation data were not very evaluative but did represent a beginning point for collecting outcome data. This was also the period when managed care began influencing the behavioral health world and requirements for detailed documentation of outcomes and services provided were increasing. In response, Massachusetts quickly created performance-based contracting measures for human service providers. The challenge for Vinfen was to select outcome data that would be useful to its many different stakeholders: payors, accrediting agencies, individuals receiving support, their family members, and other stakeholders. Each of these groups requires or desires different information, in different formats, often requiring modifications to reports from one group to another and from one year to the next.

While focusing on outcomes, Vinfen was also making improvements to the quality enhancement process, including the development of a checklist rather than a narrative format, creation of a database for faster report generation and an easier way to compare results, and the development of program-specific tools and required submission of compliance plans to correct deficiencies. In 1992, after 7 years of an evolving quality enhancement system, the agency decided that integrating outcomes data with the quality enhancement data was the goal to pursue.

It became clear that despite all best intentions, the agency had adopted a traditional approach to quality assurance that was more focused on quality control and the identification and amelioration of errors than on quality enhancement. Each improvement effort made a difference from the management's perspective but had much less value from the perspective of the people providing the supports and the people receiving the supports. The benefits to the system were clear to senior managers—especially when new program managers were hired. Every manager now knew what the standards were and what needed to be in place. From the management's perspective, Vinfen had accomplished the initial goal of ensuring that it knew when a program was falling beneath the standard and that a plan was in place to address the areas needing improvement.

It was also easy to incorporate the CARF standards into Vinfen's existing system and use the quality enhancement process to prepare for upcoming accreditation survey visits. At the time, the agency was pleased with its quality enhancement process and began presenting at local and national conferences. Vinfen presenters included material from the quality improvement literature and quoted W. Edwards Deming and Joseph Juran. But as the team presented, it was learning that Vinfen's approach needed to evolve from quality assurance to quality improvement. After years of building on a foundation of quality control, Vinfen realized that simply renovating the system was not enough—it was time to build a new quality improvement system.

QUALITY IMPROVEMENT
AS AN OUTCOMES-RELATED PROCESS

The new quality improvement process, which began in 1999, concentrates efforts on increasing teamwork, improving the quality of documentation, raising safety awareness, and using outcome data to drive quality improvement plans. This shift in philosophy to an internally driven quality improvement process was enhanced through feedback from those involved at the program and supervisory levels. Vinfen learned that despite its best efforts at an inclusionary process, the previous reviews still tended to be compliance focused and were not consultative nor improvement driven. Management staff often felt the need to spruce up the program site and to expand the documentation—activities that required a lot of additional and sometimes unnecessary effort on the part of the program staff. The quality enhancement team would visit, review documentation, and leave. Direct care staff were often not involved in the actual review process. After the review, each program was provided with a scored report that included a tremendous amount of data, and management staff were expected to write improvement plans on *all* areas that were rated below a certain score. The result was the development of multiple plans for many of the programs. The management staff would often write these plans without input from direct care staff, and improvement plans were often not incorporated into daily operations of the program. It was a reactive process instead of a proactive process.

The most helpful part of the quality enhancement process was often the program preparation for the quality enhancement visits. Reviewing individual records, administrative documentation, and the physical site resulted in the identification of things that needed fixing. For direct support staff, this gave them an opportunity to learn the big picture. Based on this insight, Vinfen knew that the new and improved quality direction needed to involve staff at all levels throughout the process and the process needed to be ongoing—not just once a year.

The current quality direction engages all Vinfen staff in an improvement process that encourages the discussion and implementation of quality systems throughout the year. A program evaluation is conducted at each site annually. During the process, each Vinfen program completes a self-evaluation that focuses on improving the quality of services and adherence to program standards. All program staff participate in this annual program evaluation. The staff team assesses the program using tools that were designed to ensure compliance with licensing regulations, accreditation standards, federal and state regulations, and Vinfen standards. The tools assess documentation for the individual served, health and safety, program policies and procedures, medication administration performance, and discharge records. The program receives a "Quality Indicator Report," an outcomes report that provides staff with aggregated and specific program data on satisfaction (from the individual, family, service provider, staff, and consumer advocacy groups), program utilization (including hospitalization days and substance use treatment days), and critical incident data (including medication errors, court involvements, and illness and injury). Each program also reviews information received from external reviews (e.g., CARF, funding agency evaluations). The culmination of this process is a site visit by the most senior manager who supervises the program. The supervisor spends several hours facilitating a discussion about the strengths and needs of the program with all the staff. The program then develops a quality enhancement plan to address any identified need area based on a thorough review and discussion of the information. Staff take ownership of the plans because the staff are intimately involved in their development.

LESSONS LEARNED

Understand What You Want to Know and Why

Decision makers responsible for determining what information is to be collected must know what they want to know before collecting endless amounts of useless information. They should also anticipate information that may be needed in the future and either incorporate it into the current system or understand how they will add to the information collected at a later time. Organizations hope to use outcomes to improve the services provided, to satisfy various customers, to better manage operations, and to remain a viable business. The realization of these hopes is dependent on the usefulness and accuracy of information that is generated by the process. Outcomes are important because this information provides the data for outcome-driven decisions and provides evidence that the treatment, skills training, or rehabilitation provided makes a difference in the individual's life. Benchmarking data provide information about the variability between program types within an agency and allow for comparison between similar program types. In addition, there is increased interest in identifying and collecting standardized outcomes to be used as national benchmarks.

Vinfen provides aggregated data to all programs with the expectation that this information will ultimately lead to improved satisfaction and more effective program development. The agency's ultimate goal is to improve the quality of life for people receiving supports. Data is also collected to meet the specifications of performance-based contracting objectives, to fulfill responsibilities to accrediting agencies, and to substantiate documentation when writing grants and proposals.

Build Great Data Collection Systems

The creation of meaningful reports that reflect changing conditions over time requires a database. Management has to have access to information that assists in strategic planning, risk management, and quality enhancement. This is only possible if information is stored in a database that can be manipulated for specific purposes. Vinfen struggled for years with a commercial database. It was developed as a computerized client record that supposedly had the ability to collect information from remote sites and generate demographic and outcome reports. Although the system was on a different platform, Vinfen was assured that a Microsoft Windows version was only 6 months away. After 5 years of promises and mounting staff frustration with a cumbersome system that did not meet the agency's needs, Vinfen began searching for a software package that had all the elements of what it now realized it needed. Each package had its plusses and minuses, but no single product delivered even 60% of what Vinfen wanted. Ultimately, the agency chose to develop its own information database and contracted out the database development component.

The Outcomes and Records System (OARS) is made up of several domains such as demographics (including physical health, employment data, legal status, and so forth), medication information (including medication errors), functional skill level, assessments, incident reports, physical restraint reports, and individual support plans. OARS provides Vinfen's programs with an efficient and effective way of tracking and reporting information and outcomes for individuals served. It is a web-based program that allows for increased speed and availability to remote program sites. The data transfer with the main server updates instantly. OARS runs on common software titles for ease of use and database support. OARS contains built-in reports that show trends and analysis for use at program level remote sites. Customized reporting will also allow outcome data to be tracked and analyzed in any number of formats. Remember that entering data in a spreadsheet format may be easy to develop and use but cannot produce reports that compare data from various fields.

Budget Adequate Resources For Quality Improvement Systems

Senior management must be fully committed to quality enhancement and outcomes reporting. This is best demonstrated when required staffing and resources are allocated to the tasks of quality monitoring, management information systems, and training.

Focus on Improvement, Not Just Compliance

Although management will be tempted to first ensure that various standards and regulations are consistently being applied, a focus on continual quality enhancement will lead to more "buy-in" with staff and will ultimately have better results. Tracking real outcomes and not just data or numbers is a more powerful means of assessing quality, given that numbers are meaningless unless they are tied to desirable outcomes.

Keep the System Simple

Do not muddy the water with complex terminology or multiple variables. Make tools available to all users. Different program types may need tools that are specific to their areas if the information is to be useful. Ensure that all users have a common vocabulary.

Keep It Useful, Start Small, and Be Smart

Users will be encouraged in their focus on quality enhancement if they get reports that are concise, accurate, and useful. It may be wise to create a pilot on a small scale before trying full implementation. Mistakes are easier to rectify early on with a smaller database. Keep in mind that changing tools or rating scales from one year to the next means not being able to compare data from those years even when using a database. Even small changes may make comparisons problematic.

Train, Train, Train, and Reinforce Effort

Only through adequate training will programs receive reliable data. Be mindful of the adage "garbage in, garbage out." Data and information is only relevant if it is accurate. A common problem Vinfen experienced involved newly hired staff who did not fully understand what was being asked for. A second problem was keeping all information updated, especially when an individual was discharged from a program. Vinfen's senior managers focus on accomplishment during program reviews. Outstanding accomplishments receive acknowledgement by the division vice president and the chief operating officer. Program staff are given small gifts acknowledging program successes.

Share Information

The more people have access to the information, the more input agencies will receive in shaping and improving the process. Be wary of narrative reports, which may be nice to read and may reinforce the program staff but are difficult to use as a management tool. Measuring gains from year to year is difficult at best and does not provide data for decision making. To reduce defensiveness, Vinfen chose to compare a program with itself over time, instead of comparing one program with another. Different funding levels, intensity of supports required, and program goals all have an impact on how a program will be rated.

Renew the System

We are living in a rapidly changing environment that is both exciting and challenging. Processes and systems that were fine last year may no longer be functional today. The industry must continually push forward into new frontiers, and the time for quality enhancement as a goal has arrived. Do not settle for what used to be good enough. Challenge your organization to be all that it can be—a better place for employees, the people receiving support, and their families.

CONCLUSION

Vinfen's first quality direction came during a period of rapid growth. Management's need for a mechanism to ensure a consistent "product" led to the initial quality assurance effort. As the organization gained experience and expertise in the quality area, so too did it embrace the notion of continual quality improvement. The enhancements, which were built into each subsequent quality review, brought the organization to its current internally driven process. Although we are very happy with this "new and improved" quality direction, we fully expect that there will always be further improvements in our quest for quality.

CHAPTER 14

Selecting Application Software and Services to Improve and Ensure Service Quality

JOHN ASHBAUGH

Agencies serving people with developmental disabilities (DD) need to become more savvy in their use of information technology. Agencies are struggling to maintain and improve the quality of their services in the face of the ever-growing demand for services and supports, a shrinking labor pool, thinning resources, and the increased dispersion of consumers and supports in the community. Available information technology can help enormously. The electronic exchange of messages via e-mail, electronic sharing of client records, and electronic scheduling can contribute to more efficient coordination of services and supports by staff, contractors, consultants, volunteers, and others involved in the support of people with DD.

In addition to benefiting agencies, increased reliance on information technology can help direct services workers and consumers. Direct services workers must gain relief from the burgeoning paperwork now attending the delivery of services and supports. Workers spend significant amounts of time entering the same information on countless forms—time that would be better spent in service. Likewise, quality review teams spend precious time looking through case records, when such work could be done remotely through electronic desk audits, electronic queries allowing reviewers read-only access to client records. Through electronic means, consumers and families can also gain access to needed information on the appropriateness and quality of services and support offerings, enabling them to make more informed choices about service providers and to be more active participants in the service and supports process.

Demand for performance information is steadily growing at the national and state levels. A handful of efforts are already underway at the national level

285

to obtain indicators on the performance of mental retardation/developmental disabilities (MR/DD) systems: Quality Outcomes Project, Core Indicators Project (through the National Association of State Directors of Developmental Disabilities Services), and two MR/DD-related performance indicator projects in the Centers for Medicare & Medicaid Services (CMS, formerly the Health Care Financing Administration [HCFA]), with dozens more at the state level. Agencies must respond without intruding too much and without overburdening direct services workers. Workers can capture data electronically while they work using electronic input devices and electronic records systems. The time and cost involved in converting these data into useful forms (i.e., information for decision-makers) can be greatly reduced through the use of today's powerful relational database, spreadsheet, statistical, and report-generation software. The time and expense for decision-makers to gain access to this information can be greatly reduced through the world wide web.

An abundance of application software and services is now available commercially that meets these and other needs of end users. In this chapter, application software is variously referred to as *software packages* in the case of desktop and client/server software, *software services* in the case of web-based software, and *software, packages,* or *services* generally. The in-house development of software solutions (i.e., application software) makes little sense given the wealth of packaged software that can be configured or adapted to meet the needs of DD agencies. The difficulty is in deciding among the dizzying array of packages and services.

This chapter presents valuable information for every agency considering an investment in information technology for quality enhancement and administrative purposes. It speaks primarily to agencies delivering direct supports where the demand for information management is the greatest. Focusing on computer application software and services designed to improve the delivery of supports to people with DD, this chapter defines and discusses several important considerations in determining which application software will work best.

SOFTWARE SELECTION CONSIDERATIONS

Agencies must make several decisions when deciding which software to select. How functional is the software for the agency? Is it more important to have single-function software or enterprise applications? Is the software flexible enough to meet the peculiar and changing needs of the agency and work in combination with any existing agency software (legacy software) worth saving? Should the agency select desktop software or software that works on a client/server network? What are the system costs of each option? The following sections explore these questions and offer concrete suggestions for decision making.

Functionality

What functions does the software perform, how well does it perform its functions, and what is the value of these functions to the agency and its clients? Assuming that the vendor can demonstrate that the software indeed performs as expected, what is the practical value of the functions to the agency? Practical functions might include such things as mailing list management, scheduling, management of facility, vehicle maintenance, fund raising, individual planning or budgeting, billing, workflow management, reporting, and the automatic generation of form letters or reminders triggered by dates or events.

Agency decision-makers should be realistic. Which of the functions will the agency really use? Most software functionality goes unused and thus carries no value. Sometimes, agencies never intend to use these functions; they are known to be extra baggage at the time of purchase. At other times, agency users are unaware of the functions. Too often the agency expects to make use of more functions than it actually does, perhaps because the benefits that come from using the function are not worth the cost of setting it up and learning to use it. It is best to ignore functions that would simply be nice to have, recognizing that these are rarely ever used.

The quick way to decide among a variety of software packages in terms of function is to list the functions advertised and to scratch out those of little or no use immediately or in the foreseeable future. Which package has the most functions of real and immediate value to the agency? *First and foremost, choose software that offers the functions needed by the agency.*

Single-Function Versus Enterprise Applications

Application software typically applies to one basic activity, such as fund raising, billing, human resources, case management, payroll, or accounting. It consists of code written to perform data-based functions and a database structure to hold the data. Application software that is designed for accounting and most or all other functions involved in running an organization is commonly known as *enterprise software.* Enterprise software typically has a number of modules (i.e., basic functions), each of which corresponds to a single-function software package or service. However, in the case of enterprise software, the code and database are unified.

The single-function applications tend to have more user-friendly features (e.g., ease with which queries can be made) than the enterprise software packages; they have usually been around longer and thus are more highly evolved than their enterprise counterparts. Those favoring the use of a combination of single-function software packages, as opposed to one enterprise package, often use the term *best-of-breed software* to describe these packages, alluding to their functional superiority.

The advantage of enterprise packages is the integrated code and database. Users benefit in having to learn and use only one package and deal with only one vendor. Time is saved by 1) not having to enter the same piece of data multiple times into separate (nonintegrated) applications and 2) not having to enter data generated in one application into another to generate a report or bill. When databases are not integrated, it becomes fairly time-consuming to reenter data, which may force programs to pay an outside programmer to build electronic bridges to transmit data between applications; such costs are avoided by using enterprise applications.

Customers should be cautious: Not all individual packages compare favorably with enterprise packages in terms of functionality and user-friendliness, nor are all enterprise packages fully integrated. Repeated data entry and manual data transfers into different modules of the enterprise package are sometimes necessary, albeit to a lesser degree than would be required when using nonintegrated applications. If one enterprise software package offers the same functionality needed by an agency as a number of single-function packages and if these options are otherwise comparable, the enterprise package is the better choice.

Flexibility

Raw functionality is insufficient. The software must be flexible enough to meet the peculiar and changing needs of the agency and work in combination with any existing agency software (i.e., legacy software) worth saving. The flexibility of an application refers to the relative ease with which users are able to make changes to the application database, screens, queries, and reports. Applications range from highly inflexible to highly flexible. At one end of the spectrum are packages in which any changes to the computer screens, database, queries, and reports must be done by the vendor (or a trained programmer). At the other end are packages in which changes to the computer screens, database, queries, and most reports can be done by the user. Agencies will inevitably need to make changes to the computer screens, database, queries, and reports in order to meet their changing needs; more flexible application software will allow them to do this in less time and for less money.

The data fields, screens, and reports in less flexible packages are largely predefined. When agencies need data, screens, and reports beyond the standard, they must purchase programming time to have them customized. Customization can easily push the cost of systems beyond the reach of most agencies. Moreover, as it is the vendor's job to support users of their applications, they are reluctant to allow too much customization, given the difficulty of supporting the widely varying system set-ups that result.

The most flexible software is object-oriented. Object-oriented software is made up of objects. An *object* is a software module that contains a collection of related procedures and data. Each object has a basic purpose or function it performs (written as code). Unlike non–object-oriented software (in which code and data are separate), each object contains the data used in performing the function as well as the code. It is self-contained. Users make use of each object through a defined set of messages and can link the objects to one another to perform larger and broader functions.

The functionality, screens, and databases of object-oriented software are much easier to change than the functionality, screens, and databases of nonobject-oriented software. Object-oriented software is also less prone to crashing when substantial changes must be made to the code, and it is easier to integrate with other applications. The market is now insisting on object technology; all of the major vendors of the relational database management systems (RDBMS) prevalent today are working on object-oriented makeovers of their systems.

Some object-oriented software is designed to fit the needs of a variety of industries and agencies (e.g., Intersystems' Cache). Other software is tailored for particular industries (e.g., Danic Tools is designed specifically for health and human service agencies). When available, industry-specific software is better because it will be easier and less costly to configure and implement than the generic, cross-industry software. *Choose object-oriented software over conventional software of comparable functionality.*

Desktop Versus Client/Server Software

The next consideration in selecting information technology is whether the agency's individual computers need to be linked together to share data or programs (code). They might be networked using dedicated lines, or they might connect via modem over telephone lines or via an internet service provider (ISP) over the internet. (An ISP is a company that provides modem or network users with access to the Internet. Although some ISPs charge by the hour, most offer monthly or yearly flat rates. Agencies may be able to buy access from their local telephone company.) Desktop software is designed for use on a single computer, on which resides all software and data that the computer user needs. Client/server software is designed to work on a network of computers, where a dedicated computer (called a *file server*) handles some of the processing tasks, while multiple smaller computers (called *clients*) complete other processes by tapping into the server's central database and programs.

A rich array of desktop software is available off-the-shelf. The widest selling is Microsoft Office suite, which includes Word (for word processing), Excel (for spreadsheet analyses), Outlook (for e-mail and messaging), PowerPoint (for presentation graphics), and, in the Professional version, Access (for relational database management). Other popular Microsoft desktop software includes FrontPage (for web site building), Project (for project management), Visio (for diagramming), and Publisher (for desktop publishing).

In all cases, desktop software requires each desktop computer to install a licensed copy of the software. The software itself is not shared. Although files generated by desktop software might be stored on another computer and shared by multiple desktop computers across a network, the number of users who can efficiently make changes to it simultaneously are limited. This is because although the individual desktop computer can access a file, it is the desktop computer that must do the related computing, not the file server. The desktop computer basically borrows a copy of the file from the file server and after using it, sends (or saves) the changes back to the file server, overwriting the original file. For these types of applications, the file server simply acts as a central place to store files. It does not itself do any of the related computing. As databases increase in complexity and size and as the number of users increases, the amount of data that must be transmitted from server to desktop computer and back quickly becomes too much for the desktop computer or the network to manage. If the network is accessing the file across telephone lines or the internet, transmission times become unacceptably slow. This is not the case with client/server software.

Client/server software is designed to minimize the volume of information that must travel from computer to computer, be it over a network, telephone line, or across the Internet. Although the software is still housed on each user computer (or *client*), the database is housed centrally on the application server. Clients connected to the server all of the time (24 hours per day, 7 days per week) register changes to the database as they occur. Clients that connect to the server from time to time and use their own version of the database in the interim, synchronize their remote database with the central database by exchanging only the changes made to the central and client databases during the interim period. In either case, the transmission of entire databases from computer to computer is avoided. If a client/server database contains a mailing address that changes, only the changed address needs to be transmitted from the source computer to the other computers sharing the application, not the entire database as would be the case with desktop software. Likewise, processing tasks that would generate a high volume of network traffic if they were conducted on a central computer and distributed to other computers on the network can be programmed for execution on user desktops to lower network traffic. For example, client/server software might be configured so that the clients on the network are able to generate their own reports using data from the central database residing on the server, in order to avoid the much higher volume of network traffic that would come from the centralized generation and distribution of reports to the networked computers.

Other factors favor consideration of client/server software. Client/server databases are becoming increasingly sophisticated and easier to set up and maintain than desktop application databases. The most popular systems for very large organizations are Oracle and Informix; for mid-size and smaller organizations—the vast majority of DD agencies—Microsoft's SQL Server is most popular. Not long ago, setting up an Oracle or SQL database would take a significant amount of time because the system administrator would have to individually set and test more than 50 parameter settings, adjusting as necessary to optimize performance. Today, a client/server database can be set up in 1–2 days, with the system setting the optimal parameters automatically and dynamically. *If more than approximately 12 users will be sharing an application and database of any size and complexity, agencies should give serious consideration to client/server software as opposed to desktop applications in order to avoid deterioration of performance.*

Client/Server Versus Web-Based Software

Despite its advantages over desktop software, client/server software has inherent limitations, most notably, the challenges involved in keeping the software running on high numbers of widely dispersed computers. As agency systems grow, the work and expense involved in troubleshooting system and user problems, and installing software upgrades on clients can severely tax an agency's information technology (IT) staff or consultants. The job of system support becomes even more difficult when agencies find themselves with a range of unconnected, even incompatible, models of hardware and software.

Web-based software uses a standard "open" language, allowing computers of different platforms to connect with one another and to share text, graphics, images, sounds, and video information over the internet. Unlike client/server applications, both software and data reside and typically operate on a central server and can be accessed using internet browsers such as Netscape Navigator or Microsoft Internet Explorer—standard on personal computers.

Web-based applications are characteristically delivered and supported over the internet by application service providers (ASPs). ASP offerings typically include the installation, operation, upgrade, and support of application software; the software and data reside on ASP servers. User agencies make periodic payments to the ASP for services rendered over a multiyear contract period.

At this time, a number of well-established ASPs offer function-specific applications (e.g., billing, accounting, payroll) across a number of industries. Still others offer Microsoft and other widely used off-the-shelf applications to consumers (e.g., USInternetworking, Interliant, FutureLink); however, most ASPs provide applications on an industry-by-industry basis (e.g., insurance, advertising, financial services, health care). WebMD, formerly Healtheon, is the highest profile ASP in the health care field.

Web-based systems are the wave of the future. Their ability to connect disparate application and operating software and hardware will not only facilitate the development of agency-wide enterprise systems linking long-separate clinical and back-office applications but also will foster in the near future the development of extended multi-enterprise systems (i.e., systems linking service agencies, consumers, advocates, funders and others) in the DD community. These systems can run as a virtual private network (VPN) over the Internet with encryption and firewalls providing the necessary security. (A *firewall* is a security device situated between a private network and outside networks. The firewall screens user names and all information that attempts to enter or leave the private network, allowing or denying access or exchange based on preset access rules.) The user-interface with internet-based applications is simple and the training, simplified.

Because the web-based software and database can reside and execute on the server, agencies can avoid the headaches and costs associated with the installation, upgrading, and support of software resident on widely distributed clients. For the same reason, many personal computer malfunctions caused by erring users are avoided.

The ASP arrangements can yield significant benefit and savings for agencies. Agencies avoid the hassles and cost of recruiting and retaining technical staff to maintain and troubleshoot the system and to keep the system database, reports, and actions in tune with changing agency demands. They avoid the risk associated with maintaining and owning malfunctioning, obsolete hardware and software. The ASPs offer application-specific expertise and enough depth to mitigate the effects of staff turnover. Particularly important to most DD services providers, ASPs provide the means by which subscribing agencies can share many of the costs associated with operating information systems.

To date, most web-based services have not yet developed some of the functionality and user-friendly features of their more seasoned client/server counterparts. However, the functionality and features of web-based systems are growing rapidly. Out of necessity, client/server software developers are web-enabling their systems by building their own web-enabled user interfaces or by using *terminal emulation software,* which enables client/server applications to reside and execute wholly on a server with browser access (i.e., to operate as web-based software). Most terminal emulation software is licensed by vendors such as Microsoft, Lotus, Oracle, and other vendors to work with their own software. Citrix terminal emulation software is designed to work with the software of all different vendors, but users must pay a premium for its use. (A stand-alone Citrix server is required in addition to any servers required for the application software.)

The benefits of web-based services have yet to be fully realized. Whether the application software is web-based or web-enabled, the benefits derived from the ability of these systems to execute wholly on the server are limited by the narrow bandwidth (i.e., limited capacity) of the lines by which most agency users can connect to them (over the internet). As a rule, the more robust the application, the greater the volume of information that must be transmitted from server to client and the wider the bandwidth must be to accommodate.

Consequently, developers of more robust web-based and web-enabled systems are finding it necessary to house a portion of their software or adjunct software (e.g., report generation) on users' computers in order to avoid the transmission of large volumes of data from server to user and thereby maintain an acceptable level of performance over low-bandwidth lines. In so doing, they effectively compromise the most important advantage that web-based or web-enabled software holds over client/server software—centralized, nondistributed software.

The agency can fairly easily determine the effect of such a compromise. The vendor will require the agency to install the software or a portion thereof on users' computers. To assess whether the software will perform at an acceptable speed over the bandwidth available to the agency, the agency should actually test the software as it will be applied at the agency; if this cannot be done, the agency should check the software's performance with other agencies having similar requirements; and if this cannot be done, the agency should condition payment on the achievement of promised performance. *Choose web-based or web-enabled software if it has the functionality and flexibility desired, if the application has shown it will perform at an acceptable speed, and if the advantages of web-based over client/server and desktop packages are material to the agency.*

System Costs

Many costs are associated with the procurement, implementation, and operation of application software, some of which are immediate and obvious, others less so. It is important that all are considered: software costs, hardware costs, network costs, implementation costs, and support costs. The bottom-line question is what is the total cost associated with the ownership or use of an application?

Software Costs   The fundamental choice for agencies today is between client/server and web-based applications, the latter almost always provided by a vendor or other application service provider. Agency decision-makers need to understand the differences in the costs of these two principal modes of application procurement and deployment; they must be sure to recognize all of the costs associated with these two alternatives.

Software Costs Connected with Client/Server Applications Occasionally, upgrades of the application software will have to be purchased and installed. Software in addition to the application software is required. Client/server relational database software is required to manage the network connections and requests from multiple users. Software utilities are needed for the back-up of the system and to set up the firewalls necessary to prevent unauthorized access to the system.

Software Costs with Web-Based Applications   All software and upgrades required for the operation of the application would be provided by the ASP. The firewall can often be purchased and maintained by the ISP through which the agency connects to the internet. Although the ASP and ISP would pay the same amount to purchase the software as the agency does under a client/server arrangement, the ASP and ISP can spread these costs among the many agencies subscribing to their service, thereby reducing the cost to each agency.

Hardware Costs   Along with software costs, each option leads to hardware costs.

Hardware Costs with Client/Server Applications   A server dedicated to the particular application is required. Users' computers may have to be upgraded or new ones purchased to obtain the random access memory (RAM), processor speed, and the off-line storage needed by the application.

Hardware Costs with Web-Based Applications   Just as with the client/server application, an application server is required. Lower capacity, less powerful computers may be required by the agency, but this will not necessarily be the case; as indicated previously, the web-based software may be designed to run in part on users' computers.

Network Costs   Agencies should consider potential network costs that may be connected with the software option they choose.

Network Costs Connected with Client/Server Applications   Network bandwidth may have to be increased to manage the added workload - associated with the application. Additional or upgraded switches and routers may be needed to manage the added traffic on the network associated with the application. The operating system (e.g., Unix, Linux, Windows) may have to be changed to match the operating system on which the application is designed to run in order to avoid the extra time that would otherwise be required for middleware to crosswalk between the application and foreign operating system. Alternately, the bandwidth on the network lines could be increased to provide the extra speed necessary to compensate for the added translation requirements.

Network Costs Connected with Web-Based Applications   In addition to any costs for the build-up of the agency network, the agency must bear the cost of the internet connection and the costs of the primary and backup lines to the off-site application server run by the ASP.

Implementation Costs   Another category of cost that agencies should consider is implementation costs.

Implementation Costs Connected with Client/Server Applications   Implementation involves system configuration, data migration, bridge and report building, installation and testing, training, and support. Nearly every system needs to be configured to some extent to best meet the needs of the agency. System configuration may involve screen design, database structuring, the setting of rules to automatically trigger decisions and actions based on dates and events, and other tinkering necessary for the application to work within the agency infrastructure. The work involved in configuring the system may be limited in the case of relatively inflexible software but can be high in the case of highly flexible, configurable software. Software typically comes with an array of standard queries and reports. Other queries and reports must be custom built.

If the application is to accept data from or generate data for other applications, bridges may have to be built (i.e., code written) to transmit these data. The one-time transmission of data from existing databases to new ones may be managed using the import/export utilities in the software applications involved; however, where a significant amount of data must be transmitted from one application to another on a continual basis, a bridge is generally required.

Implementation Costs Connected with Web-Based Applications Although the same types of implementation tasks are entailed, the amount and cost of coding required in the configuration and customization tasks will generally be greater with the web-based systems. This is because the web-based systems lack the flexibility and functionality of their client/server counterparts and are thus likely to require more "work-arounds" to meet an agency's requirements, and because web-based coding is generally more expensive than the coding of nonweb-based software, given the higher power of the client/ server languages and higher compensation demanded by web-based coders.

Installation and Testing Costs Agencies should also consider the costs of installation and testing.

Installation and Testing Costs Connected with Client/Server Applications The software must be installed on the servers, computers, and other hardware and then tested. In addition to the initial testing by the vendor over a period of days, often a longer trial period of weeks or months is needed, during which the users test the system and their ability to manage it before the installation is considered final. Users must be trained. Although all vendors provide initial training, it is generally most cost effective for the agencies to provide their own subsequent training.

Installation and Testing Costs Connected with Web-Based Applications The software must be installed on the ASP server. Some software may also need to be installed on agency computers. The bulk of the installation and testing is done by and within the ASP. User training costs can be minimized through the use of remote training arrangements.

Support Costs Support needs are ongoing after the initial purchase, installation, and testing of a new software system, and the cumulative costs of support can be significant. Users invariably require vendor support; the amount required should decline over time. Support should include the cost of software updates (i.e., minor changes in code and functionality) and may include the cost of software upgrades (i.e., major changes in code and functionality). In the case of applications with databases of any size and complexity, an agency must dedicate a full- or part-time position to the implementation and subsequent support of the application. Responsibilities typically include 1) database modification and development, 2) data quality control, 3) system querying and reporting (beyond the standard queries and reports), 4) compilation and maintenance of a system policies and procedures manual governing system use, and 5) working with the network administrator (staff or consultant) to ensure a functioning agency network.

Support Costs with Web-Based Software   The amount of time required to manage the five support responsibilities is comparable for client/server and web-based systems. However, an inherent difference with web-based systems is the amount of time and related costs required to 1) install software updates, 2) train users, 3) troubleshoot the system, and 4) provide system security. Installing software updates and upgrades on agency computers is unnecessary if the web-based software resides wholly on the ASP server. The amount of time that must be spent in the training of users should be less to the extent that the web-based software comes with web-based training programs that can be used to facilitate or substitute for scheduled in-house agency training. The amount of user support should be reduced because the opportunity for user error and computer malfunction, the source of many problems, is minimal when web-based software and database reside on the central ASP server, not on users' computers.

The costs of providing system security should also be substantially lower with web-based systems delivered by ASPs. Most DD agency systems contain electronic records pertaining to the support of people funded by Medicaid, Medicare, or private insurance, and thus the security requirements associated with the Health Insurance Portability and Accountability Act (HIPAA) of 1996 (PL 104-191) apply. This act requires, among other things, organizations that receive Medicaid, Medicare, and private health insurance and that maintain or transmit client information electronically to implement security measures to guard the integrity and confidentiality of client information.

The HIPAA requirements are prohibitive. One of the most significant differences in an agency's costs of supporting client/server and ASP applications will be in complying with the HIPAA requirements. HIPAA guidelines strongly suggest that the responsibility for maintaining a secure environment for an agency's electronic data be assigned to a security officer or organization and that the agency appoint a privacy officer responsible for ensuring individuals' confidentiality. Even though, in smaller organizations, one person could fill both positions, the workload and expense implied is prohibitive for all but the largest agencies. The costs of site security will be far less for an ASP serving many agencies from a single site than for an individual agency with data residing on servers and computers across many sites.

Debate continues about whether the authentication (verification of the identity) of users can continue to be done using passwords over VPNs—common practice today—or whether the more sophisticated public key infrastructure (PKI) system (akin to the smart cards used by automated teller machines) should become the standard. The cost of implementing the PKI method is significantly higher. If it becomes the recognized standard, the cost to individual agencies will be prohibitive. This will create another economic advantage for ASPs, in which the cost can be shared among subscribing agencies.

Cost Sharing   Many of the costs associated with acquiring and deploying an application are about the same whether incurred by an ASP or individual agency. However, because the ASP is able to spread the costs among a number of agencies, the cost to subscribing agencies is a fraction of what the cost would be to an individual agency. The costs and risks associated with the acquisition, implementation, and operation of client/server application software are too much for smaller agencies to manage. *As a general rule, smaller agencies (those with less than $5 million in annual revenue) would be well-advised to look for ASPs offering the applications they need, rather than trying to acquire and maintain client/server software themselves.*

CONCLUSION

Application software can be used to considerable advantage by agencies serving people with DD, allowing them to better manage the delivery of services and supports and to ensure their quality. The time and expense involved in procuring, implementing, and maintaining these applications, however, is generally significant. Agencies should apply due diligence as they proceed: Look first for proven functionality of real value to the agency. Choose the fewest packages to get it. Make sure the software is flexible enough to meet the agency's particular and changing needs over time and to work with any existing applications worth saving. Consider carefully what combination of desktop, client/server, or web-based systems are the best fit for the agency, given the resources at hand.

Applications available to agencies serving people with DD continue to improve in functionality, flexibility, and affordability. Some agencies hesitate to make a substantial investment in application software or services today, for fear that better packages will appear tomorrow. Indeed, better packages will appear. The real question is whether the investment in the application being considered is justified today by the promised improvements in the agency's operation.

Some agencies continue to look to the state DD or Medicaid authorities to develop the systems needed. However, there is no reason to believe that the shortcomings of the state mainframe systems in years past will not be repeated with the client/server and web-based systems of the future. State systems will continue to be long on the functionality needed by the state and short on the functionality needed by the front-line agencies and workers. States will invariably run short of the funds and resources needed to properly maintain and support its systems.

Although this chapter has addressed some of the most important considerations in choosing software applications or services, it has not begun to address the full range of factors to be considered in selecting application software or services. Weighing many of these considerations demands an understanding of information technology that comes only through years of training and experience. If agency staff do not have the technical knowledge and experience required to judge the application's workability, ask board members, outside volunteers, or paid consultants. Judicious selection and use of application software can make a critical difference in DD agencies' ability to ensure and improve service quality.

REFERENCE

Health Insurance Portability and Accountability Act (HIPAA) of 1996, PL 104-191, 42 U.S.C. §§ 300 *et seq.*

CHAPTER 15

2001: A Direct Support Odyssey

MARIANNE TAYLOR, AMY HEWITT, AND JULIE F. SILVER

Stanley Kubrick's monumental film *2001: A Space Odyssey* was a magnificent tribute to the mystery, inevitability, and unpredictably of change. From its cinematic poetry of powerful apes hurling their first tools in a slow motion explosion of evolutionary thought to the complex grace of spacecrafts and stations spinning delicately to the measured strands of a 19th-century waltz, this film explored the power and mystery of growth and change in our lives. The film was also a testimony to the power and joy of learning as well as the fear that comes with pushing beyond the comfort zone of one's current reality.

Because the film offers insight into the dramatic tensions characterizing the human journey toward a deeper understanding of itself and toward discovering the mysteries of uncharted territory, it provides a metaphor for change and discovery as advocates for community support strive to learn and do everything possible to create high-quality supports for people with disabilities. As this book illustrates, there are many points on the journey toward high-quality services and indeed much unexplored territory. This chapter focuses on the role of the direct support practitioner in the quality matrix. It is intended to propel the developmental disabilities field toward the knowledge necessary to achieve better outcomes in human services by improving the quality of the direct service workforce. The goal of this chapter is to raise awareness of the challenges in finding, keeping, and sustaining direct support professionals and to offer strategies that are useful to employers and policy makers to address these challenges that arguably make the direct support workforce the weakest link in the quality enhancement chain. The chapter also highlights the steps necessary to reframe the developmental disability field's attitudes and actions regarding the direct support role, organizational approaches to employee development, and the field's approach to workforce development at the systems level. As we explore this terrain, we will share practical strategies and insights applicable to building and maintaining a quality direct support workforce including best practices currently underway in various parts of the country.

Achieving these goals first requires taking a look at how the evolution of views on community, support, and service participant empowerment affect direct support work and its practitioners and the implications for human service employment, given the economic conditions at the beginning of the 21st century. Although we spare you Kubrick's interesting convention of inserting black monoliths within the *2001* cinematic montage to focus your attention on key issues, we punctuate this story with our own monolithic discoveries: practical examples and models from our lives as advocates, former direct support professionals, and current mentors of direct support professionals. We also share observations gained from extensive research and consultation in the area of direct support workforce development.

The ideas, strategies, and interventions we draw on are part of an extensive and continually expanding toolkit that we have assembled on our collaborative odyssey throughout the 1990s searching for methods of attaining high-quality support for the people we care about: family members and friends who have relied on direct support professionals and all of the others who need help from direct support professionals from time to time.

EVOLUTION OF A PROFESSION

Through the cinematic imagery of *2001,* attention is directed toward the evolutionary origins of the human species. A dark rectangular monolith appears when the apes begin to use objects as tools, signifying the emergence of creativity, problem solving, and curiosity among apes as the "dawn" of humanity. The symbolism that forges the connection to the advanced civilization depicted in the film occurs when the alpha ape uses a bone as a tool and then hurls it skyward. At this point, the scene cuts to a pen floating in the weightless atmosphere of space as its owner dozes. Without the keen observation of science and the art that helps to interpret the science, it would be utterly impossible to accept that these ape-like creatures are humanity's ancestors. Indeed, some still do not accept this.

As a "community of practice," the developmental disabilities field has also evolved dramatically in the fundamental paradigms of its purpose and methods of support (Senge, 1999). The service landscape was so different in the mid-20th century that it is as startling and disturbing to consider it as the field's history, as it is to think about an ape as a distant ancestor! In those days, the mission was to keep people safe and comfortable (in custodial care) and apart from the rest of society. Many now recognize that this approach not only stripped people of their basic human rights, but it also failed to recognize that every human spirit yearns for love, family, and friendship. The presumption that people were unable to learn or direct the course of their own lives meant that direct support role expectations excluded teaching or supporting choice and empowerment. The emphasis was on health and safety, but despite this restricted focus, conditions in institutions were abysmal, and the locus of support shifted to the community. In contrast, the contemporary support philosophy is grounded in the facilitation of customer empowerment and choice and the recognition of the human entitlement to the friendship, resources, and ways of life open to all community members. These changes were accompanied by the widespread decentralization of service locations to permit more individualized and more typical living arrangements.

Of necessity, the direct support role has evolved in step with these changes in the field. Direct support practitioners are now expected to teach, counsel, coach, and empower others. They must work well independently or in teams as needed and proactively support the complex processes of self-determination, inclusion, and the achievement of meaningful life goals.

What has not evolved, however, is the perception, level of support, and validation of this role. In other words, the field asks a lot of direct support staff in contemporary service settings but has not provided the necessary status and support that accompanies complex work. As Lynn Seagle, the CEO of Hope House, said at an annual gathering of direct support professionals in New Hampshire, "Our voice does not match our touch."

When my son, John, was about 2 years old, my husband and I attended a family support meeting at a state institution. Our group was leery of meeting in this setting but reluctantly agreed. Child care was available, so we brought John. I cross-examined the babysitters about what room they would be in and what they would be doing to reassure myself that John was in safe hands. At the end of the 2-hour meeting, we went to pick him up but he was not where he was supposed to be. After a few panicky minutes, we located him in a completely different building. When we got there, he was lolling in his stroller, gazing at the television while staff also gazed at the TV. This provided my first personal and disturbing glimpse of custodial care. It was a stark contrast to the kind of direct support he received later in his integrated preschool setting from the assistant teacher, Deb.
—Marianne

Seagle's point can be seen in the turmoil caused in the field by the word *professional* used in conjunction with direct support. It can be seen in the miserable wages offered and in the exclusion of direct support staff from vital planning and organizational processes. It can also be seen in agencies' throwaway mentality about this workforce (i.e., there will always be someone to take the job) that has obscured the need to develop career paths and that has discouraged investment in relevant educational and training programs. It can be seen in the field's apathy about the workforce issues and the powerless feelings many administrators and directors have regarding their ability to do anything about these challenges.

The devaluation of the direct support role that has occurred within the field steals the thunder from bold rhetoric around inclusion, self-determination, and person-centered thinking. It sends the message that custodial care is okay because paltry staff wages create an unwritten contract for minimum wage, minimum commitment labor and because direct support staff are not provided with the training and support they need to fulfill the job.

Nathan really wanted to make some friends, meet new people, get a driver's license, and join a herpetology club (for snake and lizard enthusiasts). His provider agency had difficulty with getting staff to focus on these desired outcomes. Instead, they wanted to teach him budgets, help him with laundry, go grocery shopping, and clean his apartment. They remained focused on a custodial and developmental philosophy toward services. —*Amy*

There are two faces to crisis—danger and opportunity. It seems to apply to the direct support workforce situation. The presence of enormous difficulty with finding and keeping direct support staff has led the field to begin to revise prior mental models of direct support and begin to formulate a new vision and definition of the role: one that includes an understanding of the complex work that direct support professionals do and provides the tools and infrastructure to ensure that direct support workers can provide the best support to the people who need their assistance.

My friend, Beth Williams, was a survivor and protester of custodial care. She had very little control of her body but was able to operate an electric wheelchair with her right hand. When her father died, her mother could not manage her care, and Beth went into a state school as a young girl. When she reached the age of 50, the state school staff told her that she would be moving to the "community" and into a nursing home. She refused to go. Later, she was offered a real home and ended up living in an accessible apartment with her friend and housemate, Georgia. She chose to live in the town of Brookline because it had curb cuts and accessible transportation services. It also had a library where she used to meet regularly with Judith, a storyteller and former direct support professional. Judith taught Beth some things about telling stories. At Beth's funeral 2 years ago, her wide circle of friends laughed uproariously when one friend read the stories she wrote. Beth would have loved this. —*Marianne*

For 3 years, leaders in the field, direct support professionals, and other stakeholders throughout the country worked collaboratively to build the framework for a new profession comprising the skill and knowledge sets linked to effective direct support work, as well as the ethical code necessary to guide direct support practice. By 1996, they had accomplished the task of conducting an in-depth analysis of the occupation as it is best practiced in contemporary, community settings. This analysis was validated, and a new role definition was created along with specifications of the skill and knowledge sets that compose direct support as it is practiced in forward-looking environments (Taylor, Bradley, & Warren, 1996). Using similar approaches, supervisory competencies were also identified (Hewitt, O'Nell, Sauer, Sedlezky, & Larson, 1998).

Harris spent his childhood and most of his adult life in an institution. When he moved to a group home where I worked, I hooked him up with a local synagogue. Harris attended services regularly and made many friends there. It was at his friends' insistence and Harris's desire that he celebrate his bar mitzvah (something he was not able to at the traditional age of 13). All of the regulars at Saturday morning services took part in the service, helping Harris participate in the rituals and honoring his membership in the service. When the rabbi bestowed the blessing on Harris at the end of the service, he said, "Harris, you've been coming here every week for 2 years. We all look forward to seeing you here. This is YOUR temple, Harris. You belong." Harris nodded in agreement. Many of us wept at the profundity of Harris's understanding and the gifts he brought to his congregation. —Julie

These reform efforts were strengthened in 1996 with the inauguration of a special interest group (SIG) on direct support in the American Association on Mental Retardation (AAMR) and the creation of a new, less expensive, membership rate to increase the presence of direct support professionals in the organization. In the spring of 2001, AAMR members voted to elevate the SIG to a "division" status. Also, with the support from the late John Kennedy, Jr., a collection of issue papers on direct support was published in collaboration with the President's Committee on Mental Retardation in *Opportunities for Excellence* (Jaskulski & Ebenstein, 1997). The National Alliance for Direct Support Professionals (NADSP) was organized in 1997 to advocate for advancement of the direct support profession. The NADSP mission statement reads, "As a coalition we have committed ourselves to a concept of professionalism that is not about power and control, but is about knowledge, skill and ethical practice" (1997). Since that time, the NADSP has shepherded the development of a code of ethics (NADSP, 2001), thus completing the basic framework of a professional identity for direct support. The NADSP worked closely with the field and the U.S. Department of Labor to develop the content guidelines for classroom and field-based learning that would now define an apprenticeship process for direct support. What remains before the field is to translate this architecture into high-quality programs for the preparation and development of direct support practitioners and to identify career paths within direct support that are differentiated by the configuration of skill and knowledge required by different levels and types of direct support practice. The human services field must also learn how to use the message of professionalism to its advantage in marketing the career and field to potential workers.

One day I received a package from Wally's day service. In it was a letter asking me to review the changes to his service plan and sign to indicate my acceptance. Once I started to review the papers, however, I had these intense feelings of anger, sadness, and disappointment. Every change proposed cited his inability to accomplish a task, and the solution was "remove this goal." But there were no substitutions—no other goals were written to accommodate Wally's changing abilities and needs. I was heartbroken! His service providers were telling me that not only were they not going to try, but they were not going to offer Wally anything at all! Of course, I refused to approve such changes and demanded a better approach to supporting Wally through his difficult time. —*Julie*

MYTHS AND MYSTERIES
THAT OBSCURE THE PATH TO QUALITY

Just as the *2001* astronauts on the Jupiter mission confronted the myth of human infallibility when their supposedly reliable computer, HAL, began to act strangely and put the mission in jeopardy, the field must confront the myths that have planted the seeds for the current inadequacies in direct services workforce conditions. Broadly speaking, the conditions of inadequacy are

- Insufficient numbers of qualified candidates available to fill direct support positions in most parts of the country

- Employers' difficulties with retaining direct support staff

- Poor capacity of the direct support workforce to effect the outcomes specified in individual plans

- A disconnect between leaders' shared vision of best practices, including the ethical and philosophical foundations of the work, and the predominant characteristics and competencies of actual direct service practice

- The failure of the publicly funded human service system to support an adequate employer–employee covenant that meets basic cultural expectations for decent wage and work conditions

- Problems with the images of direct support occupational and industry presence in the American economy

- An erosion of service funders', providers', and service recipients' trust in the quality of support

I was recently in Louisiana meeting with numerous people about their state's waivered services. I met a direct support professional who was paid subminimal wages for a good portion of her working hours. She had no paid benefits. Despite this, she devoted her energy to supporting a young mother with a developmental disability and her two sons, both of whom also had disabilities. She helped this young woman buy a home and keep her children at home with her. What testimony to a selfless, committed work ethic! *—Amy*

These conditions should not in any way be considered an indictment of people who fund, develop, and operate services or of the many hard-working men and women who do direct support work. We stand in awe of the difference many practitioners make in the lives of the people they support. It is instead a call to awareness and action to industry stakeholders (e.g., employers, direct support professionals, funders, families, consumers, advocates, policy makers) to recognize how we have contributed to these conditions, how we unwittingly sustain them, and what we can do to rectify them.

Furthermore, these conditions did not simply rise from the dust. They are the legacy of a system that has failed to reform from the inside out. Like HAL in *2001,* many variables have contributed to these less than stellar results. In *2001,* the astronauts struggled with assumptions that ultimately brought about their peril (including the myth of human infallibility). The field has operated under a mythology as well: that there is one way to conduct business, that more money alone will change the current crisis conditions, that no one can change societal perceptions of the value and contribution of direct support work, and so forth. However, during the 1990s as the problems of the direct support workforce intensified, intrepid explorers began challenging this mythology and discovering new and better ways to support people with disabilities.

Myth: Agencies Can Continue to Do Business as Usual and Maintain Quality

There is a growing body of evidence, statistical and anecdotal, that reveals the global connections between a stable and competent cadre of direct support professionals and the quality of life and support experienced by service recipients wherever they live (at home, in community supported living arrangements, or at large intermediate care facilities for people with mental retardation [ICFs/MR]). More research will be necessary to better understand the relationships between specific direct support interventions and service participant outcomes. At the macro level, the first order of concern and the most obvious problems are a result of the fact that there simply are not enough well-trained people to do direct support work.

In a recent evaluation of Home and Community-Based Services (HCBS) waivers in the state of Minnesota (Hewitt, Larson, & Lakin, 2000), it became clear that families were suffering because although they had resources available to them to obtain in-home supports, they could not find people to do the work. Approximately 30% of their support resources were unspent, often leaving these families without the in-home support so critical to family life when a family member has a developmental disability. This evidence is consistent with a national survey that found that more than 84% of direct human service providers reported difficulty with filling staff openings and that across the country, providers are operating with approximately 20% of positions vacant. The same study found that one fourth of the provider community has annual turnover rates in excess of 40% (Reno & Rose, 1999). Hewitt and Lakin quoted staff in one region: "We can't find people to work in the community services we have. I don't see how it is possible to think about bringing 12,000 new people onto the HCBS Waiver" (2001, p. 10).

Another national study of labor conditions in residential settings identified a 25% increase in turnover in private community facilities from 1981 to 1991 (Braddock & Mitchell, 1992). This same study also noted that direct support wages and benefits were significantly better in publicly operated services (with an average hourly wage of $8.72) than in private facilities (with an average hourly wage of $5.97). Conversations with stakeholders across the country brought to light widespread concern that the conditions revealed by these data are a profound deterrent to quality. Under such conditions, staff who are in place must work overtime (Larson, Lakin, & Bruininks, 1998), leading to the kind of fatigue that spawns mistakes such as medication errors and leads to the experience of burnout that renders staff less able to bring enthusiasm and creativity to their labor (Pine & Maslock, 1978, as cited in Hewitt & Labin, 2001). More temporary staff are used under these conditions, putting the people who receive services in the position of relying on strangers who are not familiar with the expectations, routines, and needs of service participants. Likewise, regular direct support staff experience similar stresses when temporary staff cannot understand the people they support and their routines.

At the organizational and systems levels, the fiscal and capacity costs associated with an inadequate workforce are clear threats to quality. When locked into the cost structures of rate setting common in human services, unanticipated costs of recruitment and training of workers, which are estimated at $2,000 to $5,000 per person (Johnston, 1998; Larson, Lakin, & Hewitt, 2002), will come out of the bottom line, affecting both the quality and quantity of service. Using admittedly tenuous estimates of the workforce, the public developmental disabilities system is estimated to lose anywhere from $24 million to $60 million annually. The estimates of $2,000 per person and 725,500 people working in the direct support workforce (excluding personal service) are conservative (Hewitt & Lakin, 2001). Replacing 40% of the workforce (290,000 people) each year costs at minimum $5.8 million and may cost as much as $14.5 million annually. This loss of potential service dollars is staggering but pales in comparison with the human costs experienced by people who may have to tolerate an endless stream of strangers providing "personal" service in the course of a year. A distinct irony in the thriving economy of the late 1990s for human services providers and a tragedy for people who languish on waiting lists for services is the greater availability of funds for services, juxtaposed with the impossibility of spending it on expanding services due to the unavailability of staff. According to Hewitt and Lakin,

> In many ways the development and expansion of community services for persons with developmental disabilities has been a remarkable success... in the sense that there are ever growing expectations that people will enjoy greater freedom expanded option, the full measure of citizenship, inclusion in their neighborhood and acceptance in their community. These successes, however, are fragile. Nothing has made this fragility more evident than the national crisis in providing for an adequate and well-prepared direct support workforce. (2001, p. 13)

Myth: All We Need Is More Money

Stakeholders often say, "We can't do anything about workforce problems until we raise salaries." Although it would be ill-advised to discount the importance of money as a critical factor in the previously described condition, focusing on it exclusively as a key to change is overly simplistic. It is a linear solution to a multifaceted problem. Organizing rallies at the state house to decry the injustice of low wages and the vulnerability of service recipients (rather than undertaking an analysis that will require a response outside of this comfort zone) will not solve the problems.

Although it is true that direct support wages are and have always been low (averaging about $7.00 per hour in 1992 and about $8.00 per hour in 2000), it is also true that some providers do better than others in supporting their employees. Some providers have turnover rates of below 20%, yet others have rates higher than 300%; some providers have vacancy rates as high as 20% and others rarely, if ever, experience a vacancy. What this means is that there certainly *are* organizational practices that do make a difference, even within the reality of low wages.

In our work, we have had the opportunity to work with many community provider agencies to better understand and develop strategies to address their workforce issues related to recruitment, retention, and training. What we have learned is that there are many things agencies can do to find new staff and reduce turnover. In fact, at one agency they reduced their turnover from 300% in 6 months to 0% in 6 months. That tells us that there is no place for the money myth—providers can change practices and can make a difference. —*Amy*

Mystery: Why *Do* We Go to Work?

To debunk the myth of money as a response to strengthening the workforce, it is *very* important to start with a consideration of why people choose to work and why they choose to work in human services. Clearly, given the lower salaries typical of the industry, money is not the primary motivating force behind a human services career commitment. Also, given the limitations on public funds that support most human services, looking solely to wage increases can be a discouraging approach to resolving the problem. Commitment to human services careers and the motivation of others who choose human service careers often starts with a desire to do meaningful work that is of service to those who need more support than others to achieve their dreams.

The commitment to human services that springs from certain life experiences is one of the mysteries of attraction to the field but one that nonetheless has important implications. The human desire to find meaning in work is a powerful motivating force that draws people to enter human service careers, including direct support. Dr. W. Edwards Deming, the pioneer of the Total Quality Movement in the United States, concisely explained this spiritual aspect of work that is seen in the personal search for intrinsically meaningful occupation labor when he said that "People seek joy in their work" beyond the salary to meet their basic needs.

A group of administrators of community-based human service agencies in the greater Boston area invited me to a meeting about workforce issues. In discussing wages, they agreed that there is a "tipping point" below which it is much harder to recruit and retain staff. They pegged this at $25,000 in 1998.

In the autobiography he wrote after the accident that left him paralyzed, Christopher Reeve described his attempt to recruit a therapy aide who provided extraordinary service during his rehabilitation. The aide declined the invitation to work for Reeve despite the generous salary he offered. The man told Reeve that other people needed his services more than Reeve would when he finished his rehabilitation. Money is important, but it isn't everything. —*Marianne*

Myth: People Know Who We Are

In the late 1960s, the special effects and imagery of *2001* were stunning for the time, arousing a sense of wonder and interest in the potential of space travel and what lies beyond the known frontiers. Today, in a world swirling with new technology, services, products, and work opportunities, the human services industry must use its own special effects and imagery in a way that will raise its profile in the world of attractive career choices. If the plea for more money to solve the direct support problems is moved to the background, it may be possible to focus instead on the joy and meaning that individuals seek in their work and to create a career with a future. It is "high touch" instead of "high tech." When direct service work is compared with flipping hamburgers, for example, there is no contest: More joy and intrinsic meaning is found in one direct service job than can be found in the production of a million hamburgers. Although this is intuitively obvious to people in the field, it is harder to convey to potential recruits.

My friends and I lived in a exciting time, coming of age in the late sixties, and each of us had aspirations to make a difference, to contribute to society in some meaningful way. Several of them became nurses—this was a visible, well-defined occupation. I might have chosen that if I could be convinced not to faint at the sight of blood. Eventually, I found my way into human services, but the path was neither clear nor well defined. —*Marianne*

Inducements to enter the human services field must include the promise of a viable career. Candidates should be introduced to the jobs, the job path, and the educational path necessary to thrive in that career. The human services field is part of an intense competition for labor with the rapidly expanding services sector—a sector that is doing a better job of attracting people to their fold. Convenience stores and fast food locations prominently display the management opportunities, fringe benefits, moveable retirement plans, and the relatively short time frames needed to achieve the next step—however advancement is defined.

The potency of images in marketing a profession became clear to me in the early 1990s when I participated in the national movement to develop high-quality practice guidelines (skill standards) for professions that do not require 4-year degrees. I learned more than I care to know about such industries as bioscience, photonics, retail, and hospitality as I worked alongside of representatives of these groups in the effort to develop our respective industry standards. Part of the fun was sharing our "products" with each other. One day, I received a video called "Heavy Metal" from the metal construction group. It was a video about being a welder, and it rocked! It had high production quality, great music, and sexy young men and women welding. It was so persuasive that while watching it, even I wanted very much to be a welder. — *Marianne*

Employers in the human services field should take note of this open invitation to join the team. People want to work for the winning team! How can this image be conveyed instead of the more typical message of charity and sacrifice? One exciting response to these questions is the "Rewarding Work" marketing campaign, a joint effort of the Massachusetts Department of Mental Retardation and the Association of Developmental Disabilities Providers (ADDP). This consortium approach to marketing the direct support role was accomplished by hiring a professional advertising agency to prepare professional advertisements for radio and television featuring direct support work and a toll-free telephone number for inquiries. Another model of the powerful use of polished media to create a compelling message about direct support was developed by Lynn Seagle of Hope House in Virginia. Her very brief advertisements delivered a clever and powerful message about direct support work. Both campaigns were produced by professional advertising agencies and communicate the interest and potential of direct service as a cool career choice.

When the School to Work initiative was launched in 1994, it made sense to talk to national leaders in the area of vocational technical education to generate interest in exposing high school students to human services careers. Their distinct lack of interest was a wake-up call to the need for explicit career paths. (On the plus side, since 1994 there have been a number of successful initiatives with high schools at the local level.) The second wake-up call came in 1999 in a meeting to generate more incumbent worker training dollars for an agency, Lifelinks, that made a significant commitment to employee development. In the meeting, a U.S. Department of Labor representative described direct support as "the secondary labor market," which in their language means dead-end jobs. Direct support is the gateway into human services careers: Most people raise their hand when I ask at conferences and meetings how many people started their work in direct support roles, but this story is never told. —*Marianne*

Myth: People Embrace Change

The effort to strengthen the workforce has also been slowed by the inertia that arises from the fear of change. Such responses are understandable in a world in which things have changed irrevocably so quickly. It is a cyber world where healthy, relatively young retirees seek different lifestyles (which may include a job with meaning and joy) and where young people are often better at meeting on the Internet than in person and find their jobs on-line. Unions are ready to organize to secure improved working conditions; consumers and families press for more say in their lives; waiting lists loom, and prices for fuel, housing, and health care go up. It is no wonder that many would like to return to the good old days.

However, current demographic and labor forecasts show that there is no going back. A powerful trend in the American economy beginning in the 1990s is the enormous expansion of the service sector. Recent data from the Bureau of Labor Statistics indicate that this trend will continue into 2008. During this period, more than half of all new jobs will be created in the service sector, which will require 20 million new jobs by 2008. Human services, representing approximately 6% of this sector of the economy, will therefore need 600,000 new jobs by 2008 in addition to those agencies are presently struggling to fill. This sobering prospect takes on a daunting dimension, given the fact that the population growth is not keeping pace with support needs and fewer people are entering the field.

It is clear that tinkering around the edges will not do the job. The type of shift necessary is what Senge described in his book *The Dance of Change* as "profound change. . . organizational change that combines inner shifts in people's values, aspirations, and behaviors along with 'outer' shifts in processes, strategies, practice, and systems" (1999, p. 15). Without this, it is hard to imagine a system where quality is the norm rather than the exception.

Senge (1999) fully explored the landscape of what it will take to achieve and sustain this kind of change effort. He reminded readers that change is like a seed that bears fruit as time unfolds and with proper cultivation. As in the natural world, profound change invites conditions that both limit and promote growth. The *2001* Jupiter mission had a wayward computer that the crew had to outsmart; the human services field will also need to work hard and smart to dig out of this hole. Leadership is required at all levels, wherever people share the same vision and commitment to high-quality supports for people with disabilities. As Senge defined it, *leadership* is "the capacity of a human community to shape its future and specifically to sustain the significant processes of change required to do so" (p. 16). The next section examines the seeds of change planted by a community of people across the country who share this vision of quality and seek to strengthen the promise of high-quality community support.

EXAMPLES

Along our path, we have learned and benefited from some extraordinary innovators who are confronting the direct support workforce problems with courage and imagination. So many committed, bright, and passionate people across the country have joined with the NADSP to help in resolving these issues. Several of these effective strategies are included here.

STARS in Massachusetts

STARS (Striving To Achieve Responsive Supports) is an on-the-job training (OJT) curriculum for direct support professionals working in community-based supports. Specifically aligned with the *Community Support Skills Standards* (CSSS) (Taylor, Bradley, & Warren, 1996), STARS uses an interactive, experiential approach to assist workers in integrating learning and developing competency for the complex challenges of today's human services environment. Based at the provider agency, STARS is intended to reach the workers who might not initially enroll in postsecondary education or training programs but who desire and require in-depth study of contemporary human service issues and requisite skills. The technical skills of the CSSS, the values inherent in best practices of direct support, and the development of high-performance teamwork skills are the bedrock of the STARS curriculum. STARS is designed to be a low-cost, on-site training course that can be delivered by trained facilitators at individual agencies and through local networks.

STARS began as a local training and development effort in the central region of Massachusetts, with the generous support of the state's Department of Mental Retardation and progressive providers of services in the region. Currently, 4 of the 13 modules of the curriculum have been used in the field. The remaining nine content modules are under development. It is planned that workers will receive a Certificate of Initial Mastery upon successful completion of the STARS curriculum, a critical step toward a voluntary national credential for the direct support professional.

With four modules completed and tested by direct support professionals, agency trainers, and curriculum developers, STARS has been well received and the Policy Advisory Committee is seeking resources to complete the remaining content modules and implement the program throughout the field. In less than a year, the Policy Advisory and Curriculum Development Committees of STARS have

- Developed a schema that maps out the content, structure, methods, and assessment plan of the certificate program

- Developed and piloted 4 of 13 proposed modules

- Trained consortium members to implement the existing modules

- Designed a portfolio assessment process

- Sponsored discussions with key state policy makers in human services and education on how to articulate the STARS Certificate of Initial Mastery with more advanced degrees and certificates

- Developed national interest in the STARS Certificate of Initial Mastery

ELM Homes in Minnesota[1]

Last spring, ELM Homes in Minnesota embarked on a much needed effort to revise the job structure and job descriptions for direct support staff that had not been substantially revised in the 20 years the agency had been providing community human services. A committee, which consisted of direct support staff, frontline supervisors, qualified mental retardation professionals (QMRPs),

---

[1]This section is adapted with permission from *Frontline Initiative*. Author Kellie Miller is the Director of Human Resources of ELM Homes, a residential services agency based in Waseca, MN. You may contact ELM Homes at 14595 Highway 14 East, Post Office Box 489, Waseca, Minnesota 56093, (507) 835-1146.

and administrators, worked to align ELM Homes' direct support professional job descriptions with the CSSS. The new job descriptions include an agency-level value statement for each of the 12 identified competency areas and the corresponding skill standards that all direct support professionals at ELM Homes are expected to exhibit in their work. The skill standards were then divided into three building-block areas by achievement level. The base-level is the Residential Instructor (RI); the mid-level, Advanced Residential Instructor (ARI); and the mastery-level, Certified Residential Instructor (CRI). Accordingly, the pay scales were adjusted to honor job level, seniority, and performance. Work location is also factored into the pay system because the rate structures that ELM Homes negotiates with different counties may vary.

Under the new pay and organizational structures, staff no longer move up through the job levels simply by staying with ELM Homes long enough. They must apply to their supervisors for promotion. The promotion decision is based on an appraisal of job performance, in-service and staff meeting attendance, and personal initiative. Direct support professionals' direct supervisors and program managers (who are QMRPs or designated coordinators) conduct the appraisals. Direct support professionals and their supervisors use a goal setting process for career development to assess areas where improvement is needed. In addition, promotion is not permanent and may even be revoked if performance in the new position is below expectation. However, there is no pressure to move up. Individuals may choose to stay as an RI for their entire employment with ELM Homes if they wish, and this is supported and embraced by the organization. Currently, the certification at the mastery level is an internal ELM Homes process. The agency is excited about the prospect of honoring high-level skill attainment of direct support staff through a national credentialing process. By creating career paths through modified direct support professional job descriptions and pay incentives, this agency has found that their staff are excited and interested in career opportunities and new positions within ELM Homes.

Lutheran Social Services of Minnesota[2]

Lutheran Social Services (LSS) of Minnesota is a large multiservice agency providing services in many regions of Minnesota. The Home and Community Living (HCL) Division provides residential services to 685 individuals with mental retardation or developmental disabilities in 100 settings. In 2000, the HCL division employed 681 direct support professionals and 26 frontline supervisors. LSS implemented several interventions to address its workforce challenges. Major interventions included the following:

---

[2] Reprinted with permission from *Frontline Initiative,* 4(2) (2000). Published by the National Alliance for Direct Support Professionals and the Research and Training Institute on Community Living at the University of Minnesota.

- Using recruitment bonuses to encourage inside recruitment by current employees

- Implementing hiring bonuses in programs with positions that are particularly difficult to fill

- Restructuring salaries for frontline supervisors to increase overall wages

- Revising training for frontline supervisors to provide more training earlier in the employment process

- Training supervisors about effective recognition practices

- Simplifying the staff evaluation form and developing an evaluation calendar to make it more systematic

- Hiring two staff members whose job was specifically devoted to providing staff training

- Conducting quality assurance audits

- Revising and redesigning the policy and procedure manual to incorporate the agency's mission and vision

- Developing a vision statement and a set of core values

In addition to these interventions, LSS developed a comprehensive, realistic job preview (RJP) program to increase the likelihood that recruits were making informed decisions about whether to take a job that was offered to them. In April 2000, a group of 20 supervisors, managers, and direct support professionals met, and the University of Minnesota staff presented a comprehensive overview of how to develop a realistic preview, showed examples of videos that had been developed by other agencies, and shared a chart that detailed the advantages, disadvantages, and design characteristics of various RJP methods. Teams from each region of the state then met to develop an agency plan on how to implement previews in their region. A survey of newly hired direct support professionals was conducted throughout the state to identify the key challenges facing new direct support professionals that should be addressed in the videos. Initially, 11 homes agreed to participate as pilot test sites for the project. An additional six homes heard about the project and also developed their own previews.

Several different types of realistic previews were developed by the pilot homes including:

- Photo preview books (used by 12 sites)

- Formal structured observations (used by 2 sites)

- Structured interview questions (used by 13 sites)

- Informal site visits for all new hires (used by 10 sites)

- Sending job descriptions with all applications (used by 11 sites)

- Including a current direct service provider in the interviews (used by 11 sites)

- Administering a work sample test composed of a structured observation with a worksheet turned in at the end (used by 2 sites)

- Including consumers in interviews (used by 1 site)

- Incorporating the results of a parent survey into hiring practices (used by 1 site)

These interventions were implemented in the fall of 2000 and data about their effectiveness were collected through the end of the Partnerships for Success Project.

In spring 2001, the results of the pilot test were evaluated, and the management team decided to implement realistic job preview interventions statewide. Information about the pilots and the results was shared at a meeting of all supervisors. Minimum standards were set for all sites, including the use of a structured interview for all hiring, requiring a structured observation from all applicants, and developing at least one other form to communicate information about the job to new applicants (e.g., including a photo book, involving consumers). The target date for the realistic previews and structured interviews to be implemented division-wide was August 2001.

The project yielded striking improvements. In 2000, 24 new employees were hired with an RJP in pilot study homes. All of those individuals stayed in their new jobs for 3 months, and 91% were still employed 6 months after being hired. This compares with a benchmark statewide for new employees of 21% leaving in the first 3 months, and 47% leaving in the first 6 months. These findings spurred LSS to implement realistic previews statewide. The hope is that these positive results can be replicated statewide.

Community Supports Program in Minnesota

The Community Supports Program (CSP) for People with Disabilities is a credit-bearing educational program offered through nine campuses of the Minnesota State Colleges and Universities (MNSCU) system. The courses offered in the CSP emphasize building on the strengths and capacities of people with disabilities to maximize community inclusion. The curriculum is designed to train direct support professionals to provide effective residential, vocational, educational, or in-home supports to people with disabilities in their communities, and it meets the competencies identified in the national skill standards for the industry: the CSSS. The program offers several educational awards including a certificate, a specialized diploma, and an associate of applied sciences or associate of arts degree.

The certificate award is aimed at preservice or orientation-level training; however, it is also effective for people with experience in any human service area who want to become more knowledgeable and skilled in community-based, person-centered work environments. Completion of the certificate program is required for participation in the specialized diploma program. It includes three technical courses: Facilitating Positive Behaviors I, Physical/Developmental Supports I, and Direct Support Professionalism. It also includes a general education course related to communication. The diploma program includes advanced coursework in facilitating positive behaviors, person-centered planning, human development, and other important general education areas. In addition, students in the diploma program engage in a work site practicum and choose a specialization such as health, vocational support, or supporting people with challenging behaviors.

The CSP is voluntary and direct support professionals in Minnesota are not required to participate as a condition of their employment. Some students pay tuition out of pocket. Others use money offered by their employer for continued education. The colleges also offer financial aid for eligible students, and there have been some funds available that pay instructor fees and thus waive tuition for students who work in businesses that participate in the grant.

The initial goals of the CSP were to provide high-quality, cost-effective, flexible, and accessible training and educational opportunities for people providing direct support to people with developmental disabilities or related conditions. The program was designed to be delivered in a variety of ways and over varying lengths of time to meet the needs of different learners, including traditional classroom training through academic courses at a local college, interactive television that connects people from across the state, or customized training developed on site at businesses. The program offers for-credit or not-for-credit options.

One incentive for completion of the diploma was created in 1997 when the Minnesota legislature passed a bill allowing people who had completed the CSP diploma and had 2 years of field experience to work in designated coordinator positions. Previously, this position was reserved for people with 4-year degrees only. The newly created position allows for promotion of people who cannot or do not want to complete a 4-year degree program.

The CSP can meet the needs of different types of learners. It can offer experienced staff a chance to learn new skills and hone existing skills while working toward a credit-bearing degree. It can provide an introduction to the skills needed by direct support professionals to high school students or college freshmen. It can be a supplement to the academic career of students in other fields such as occupational therapy, physical therapy, psychology, social work, teaching, and so forth who need to know more about community supports for people with disabilities.

Many students and agencies have shared their stories about the benefits and impact of the CSP. These experiences are about exchanging information on workplace culture and values, sharing new information and skills to be more effective at work, and finding good jobs or being promoted, just to mention a few of the personal and quality outcomes from participating in the program. One of Minnesota's first CSP diploma graduates says that the CSP has had an enormous influence on her personal and professional life. She proudly proclaimed that now she is equipped with the tools needed to provide the support that consumers want and need to reach their dreams.

Careers In Caring in Ohio[3]

In 1995, the Residential Provider Consortium of Cuyahoga County (RPC), a group of 22 major providers of residential services in the Cleveland area, decided to work collectively on their recruitment and retention challenges. The RPC developed a grant funded by the Cuyahoga County Board of Mental Retardation to create an image campaign. The purpose of the campaign was to initiate common efforts by all providers of services to create and disseminate marketing and education material for the mental retardation and developmental disabilities (MR/DD) field. The goals were to attract more potential staff to the residential services industry, create common marketing materials, and perform common advertising with a unified message. The results of the 2.5 years of work resulted in the creation of a marketing video, "Careers in Caring"; common brochure and public service announcements; and common job advertisements that not only created awareness for potential staff but portrayed the industry professions as caring. Research information was gathered for 1 year to better understand the recruitment and retention challenges of the RPC.

From the efforts and research conducted, a smaller group of the RPC decided to launch another initiative in 1998. Calling on the information learned in the Careers in Caring initiatives, the RPC created another concept called the Human Resource Alliance (HRA). The group of agencies in the HRA is smaller (only 8 of the 22 major providers participate), and they planned to hire an experienced human resource executive (as a facilitator) to lead their efforts. This unique collaborative endeavor was aimed at exploring common recruitment efforts, developing strategies that improve retention, developing individual agency recruiting plans, and advocating for common advertising and marketing plans. All eight agencies have experienced a reduction in turnover, an increase in recruitment, and a positive impact on their ability to expand services within Cuyahoga County.

The HRA facilitator works with the executive directors, the human resource staff, and each agency individually to create and implement innovative and creative solutions to the recruitment and retention challenges. Data are collected on vacancy rates, turnover, applicant loss ratios, and applicant–hire ratios and exit interviews. The data for the first year indicates that this model is

---

[3]For more information on this effort and project, contact Tony Thomas in Cleveland, Ohio, at (440) 356-2330.

effective in stabilizing the workforce in participating agencies. The HRA was funded by two grants for 2 years that ended in July 2002.

Lifelinks in Massachusetts[4]

Lifelinks is a medium-sized human services agency providing residential and day support to people with developmental disabilities in Lowell, Massachusetts. In describing their self-directed team process, CEO Yvonne LaGarde said,

> Everything we do begins with the hard work of our people. Increasingly, we're developing new ways to help them help our business as we focus on building not just our financial capital but also our human capital—the intelligence, learning, dedication, and focus of our people.

Lifelinks provides services in an urban "economic opportunity zone," and more than 75% of its employees are African American. Also, Lifelinks is the only agency in the region that supports a self-advocacy group, "OUR CHOICE," and one of two organizations in Massachusetts that has organized parts of its workforce into self-directed teams.

Truly a learning organization, Lifelinks developed a high-quality direct support educational program that culminated in a certificate and 27 college credits, paid for by Lifelinks. These credits are completely valid for the associate's degree in human services offered at Middlesex Community College. Director LaGarde was concerned with achieving higher quality services and vowed to give her staff the tools they needed to achieve quality benchmarks. The program is offered to staff that volunteer and meet entry requirements. It is aligned with the CSSS and was customized, in collaboration with Middlesex Community College, to accommodate the schedules of the Lifelinks employees. Program participants agree to forego raises during the tenure of the program and commit to 1 year of employment beyond graduation. Educational approaches that add value include the use of a cohort model that brings all participants together for several core courses and the use of portfolio assessment.

Some important outcomes of this innovation include a model that was adapted for the statewide direct support professional certification program that is currently offered in collaboration with the community college system and funded by the Massachusetts Department of Mental Retardation. Bringing this program to scale builds capacity throughout the state, and it enabled Lifelinks to join with others to share the costs that were a significant threat to the sustainability of the program. Another fascinating outcome occurred with the adaptation of Lifelinks' methods of organizing work to accommodate the emerging leadership and efficacy of the program graduates. The company de-

---

[4]For more information, contact Yvonne LaGarde, CEO, Lifelinks, Inc., 145 Lexington Avenue, Lowell, Massachusetts 01854.

veloped a self-directed team model led by program graduates. Using "open book" management strategies, the team had access to information about budgets, schedules, and other management tasks in order to assume responsibility and control of the flow and organization of their work and tasks formerly retained by managers. Management and support responsibilities were more carefully defined and divided among team members. Certain responsibilities, such as team secretary, are rotated throughout the team. Employees who have participated in the self-directed team model are enthusiastic about how work feels under the new method and about what they have been able to accomplish, including the development of new job descriptions and methods of peer performance appraisal.

The Massachusetts Department of Mental Retardation Direct Support Certificate Program[5]

The Human Services Research Institute received a grant in 1997 from the National Skill Standards Board to convene stakeholders throughout the state to brainstorm responses to the emerging crisis in recruitment and retention that would utilize national skill standards. Educators, service providers, policy makers, and consumers together evolved a workforce development plan that offered a number of recommendations including the development of a post-secondary certificate in direct support available and recognized throughout the state (Silver & Taylor, 1997). Members of the group also developed a consensus framework for the key characteristics of the program.

These seeds came to fruition in 1999 when the Massachusetts DMR and the Massachusetts Association of Community Colleges collaborated to design and pilot a certificate program in four locations: Northern Essex Community College, Middlesex Community College, Bay State Community College, and Bristol Community College. Each college offered some form of human service certificate program, which they were asked to adapt and align with the CSSS and statewide criteria established by the state's DMR. Candidates are selected on the basis of seniority and other eligibility criteria. The program results in 21 college credits that can be applied to an associate's degree and a certificate in direct service.

The DMR presently funds the certificate program, including tuition and material, and in 2001, the program expanded to eight community college campuses in the state. In addition to the educational incentives of college credit and a certificate award, graduates receive monetary awards, too. Successful graduates receive a one-time bonus of $500 and an annual salary adjustment of $1,000.

---

[5] For more information, contact Stephen Draft, Director of Training, Massachusetts Department of Mental Retardation, 500 Harrison Avenue, Boston, Massachusetts 02118, (617) 727-5608.

CONCLUSION

These monolithic discoveries represent numerous best practice and research-based strategies to address issues of direct support recruitment, retention, and training. They involve large systems interventions such as creating apprenticeship programs and postsecondary educational programs designed to result in career paths for people who enter direct support roles. They also involve agency-based interventions such as improved training, better articulation of job roles and responsibilities, collaborative efforts to find new employees, internal career paths for employees, and a clearer expectation of what the job entails for potential employees.

What these discoveries have shown is that there is not one solution to these immense problems: There are many. These problems are multifaceted and complex as are their solutions. The field must continue in search of additional monolithic discoveries; the road will be difficult, as the challenges of finding new people to work in community human services will continue. Both system and agency interventions must be employed, and continued efforts are needed in order to better understand these workforce challenges, their effect on the people who receive community supports, and their solutions. As the explorers and innovators highlighted in this chapter have shown, with continued collaboration, commitment, and creativity of people, the path to a solution can and will be discovered.

REFERENCES

Hewitt, A., & Lakin, K.C. (2001). *Issues in the direct support workforce and their connections to the growth, sustainability and quality of community supports.* Minneapolis: University of Minnesota, Research and Training Center in Community Living.

Hewitt, A., Larson, S.A., & Lakin, K.C. (2000). *An independent evaluation of the quality of services and system performance of Minnesota's Medicaid Home and Community Based Services for persons with mental retardation and related conditions.* Minneapolis: University of Minnesota, Research and Training Center on Community Living.

Hewitt, A., O'Nell, S., Sedlezky, L., Sauer, J., & Larson, S. (1998). *The Minnesota Frontline Supervisor Competencies and Performance Indicators.* Minneapolis: University of Minnesota, Institute on Community Integration.

Jaskulski, T., & Ebenstein, W. (Eds.). (1998). *Opportunities for excellence: Supporting the frontline workforce.* Washington, DC: President's Committee on Mental Retardation.

Johnston, K. (1998). *Developmental disabilities provider direct service worker study: Results and findings.* Anchorage, AK: Governor's Council on Disabilities and Special Education.

Larson, S., Lakin, K.C., & Hewitt, A. (2002). Embarking on a new century for direct support professionals: 1975 to 2000 and beyond. In D. Crosser, P. Baker, & R. Schalock (Eds.), *A century of concern* (Rev. ed.). Washington, DC: American Association on Mental Retardation.

Larson, S.A., Lakin, K.C., & Bruininks, R. (1998). *Staff recruitment and retention: Study results and intervention strategies.* Washington, DC: American Association on Mental Retardation.

National Alliance for Direct Support Professionals, (2001). *Code of ethics.* Minneapolis: University of Minnesota, Research and Training Center.

Reno, L., & Rose, J. (1999). *Staff recruitment and retention strategies: Results and analysis of the Staff Recruitment and Retention Survey 1999.* Rock Hill, NY: Irwin Siegel Agency.

Senge, P.M., Roberts, C., Ross, R., Smith, B., Roth, G., & Kleiner, A. (1999). *The dance of change: The challenges to sustaining momentum in a learning organization.* New York: Doubleday.

Silver, J., & Taylor, M. (1997). *A plan to enhance the direct support workforce in Massachusetts.* Cambridge, MA: Human Services Research Institute (HSRI).

Taylor, M., Bradley, V., & Warren (1996). *The community support skill standards: Tools for managing change and achieving outcomes.* Cambridge, MA: Human Services Research Institute (HSRI).

CHAPTER 16

Speculation on the Shape of Things to Come

VALERIE J. BRADLEY AND MADELEINE H. KIMMICH

The hallmark of the developmental disabilities (DD) field since the 1970s has been change—change in assumptions about the capabilities of people with disabilities, change in values, and concomitant changes in the nature of supports provided by public DD systems. These changes have inevitably influenced how the system defines and ensures *quality.* In this final chapter, the editors glance into a crystal ball and speculate on the effect that continuing changes will have on the practice of quality assurance and quality enhancement.

Although there is no reason to think that positive reforms will not continue, clouds are on the horizon that suggest an urgency for quality enhancement approaches to be modified, streamlined, and implemented. These observations point to several key challenges for the future.

ENDURING TRENDS

If the past is a predictor of what is to come, then the field can expect that

- Emphasis on individual outcomes and person-centered supports will continue

- Changes in the provider marketplace will escalate (e.g., through financial mergers, the retirement of some "old guard" executive directors) and the basic configuration of provider organizations will continue to evolve, as staff are deployed to dispersed residential and work environments, in which owners and managers can no longer closely oversee their performance

- The system will continue to reallocate resources away from larger group settings toward smaller supported settings

- The gap between those individuals who are receiving comprehensive supports and those who are on waiting lists or have limited "support" waivers will grow

- The staffing crisis will persist, with a consequent diminution of basic protections for individuals being supported

At the same time, the field can expect ongoing changes in quality enhancement, including

- Increased state capacity to ensure quality, spurred by 1) pressures for increased accountability (e.g., from the U.S. Centers for Medicare & Medicaid Services, the media, families) and 2) the advent of new technologies, such as web-based information management, video communications, and so forth

- Movement away from prescriptive program or process standards in favor of more outcome-based monitoring

- Expanding dialogue among states on what is best practice, what is quality, and how to measure quality most effectively

- An increasing emphasis on performance measurement and data-based, data-driven approaches

- Multiplying efforts by public entities and provider agencies to implement quality improvement strategies

PRESERVING GAINS AND MOVING FORWARD

The issues facing the field are not unique to DD services—there is ample evidence from other long-term support systems, such as those for older adults, that resources are being stretched and that some individuals are at risk. The crucial difference is that the DD field values individual outcomes and community participation over custodial aims.

Failure to ameliorate the emerging problems could very well threaten ongoing reform. A serious system failure could lead to a public backlash against individualized living arrangements, with heightened pressure from custodial forces, capped by a drastic reaction by legislators; indeed, if public systems do not plan for the worst, they risk a political donnybrook. The bureaucratic foundation cannot hold unless a basic architecture is in place (e.g., mortality reviews, incident reporting, management information systems).

The trick is to maintain and enhance people's well being and safety (in order to maintain the public trust) while operating a system that is flexible and person-centered. State systems must discover how to protect individuals equally from physical harm *and* from serious infringements on their individual and idiosyncratic preferences and aspirations.

To meet this challenge will be difficult for any organization. It requires keeping two potentially conflicting aims in the forefront—flexibility versus predictable and reliable protections. Both must be present. The freedom to organize flexible supports can only be realized if the public, families, legislators, and people with disabilities are persuaded that the system can be trusted to protect health and safety. This means the system recognizes the difference between normal risk (e.g., crossing a street) and unacceptable risk (e.g., being left unassisted when in severe pain) and takes seriously its role to guard against the latter while allowing the former. Creativity in the crafting of individual supports can only emerge when all parties are convinced that basic safety concerns are addressed. Such a foundation of belief in the ability of the system to minimize risk can and will facilitate individual choice. Dreams of community membership can be attained when one no longer worries about being healthy and free from harm.

CHALLENGES AHEAD

To build a foundation of trust, public officials, families, providers, and people with disabilities will be faced with many challenges, including the following:

- Advocates of community supports need to acknowledge that problems in the performance of some community supports do in fact exist and to take the steps necessary to erect a stronger quality enhancement infrastructure.

- Quality enhancement needs to involve more diverse partners—providers, citizens, families, people with disabilities, state staff—to stretch resources to cover the more numerous and more varied living and working situations.

- Policy makers and practitioners need to mount a serious campaign to train and maintain a competent workforce; this is an issue that grows more urgent every day and that has not been addressed with the gravity and persistence it requires.

- Streamlined quality enhancement systems must be created that are responsive, not cumbersome, and that are simple to implement yet generate a rich picture of services and supports.

- The risk assumed by individuals and families must be minimized to those risks that are part of a normal life, not risks resulting from a failure of public systems to preserve basic health and safety.

- Information that is generated by performance measurement and quality enhancement systems should be broadly available and conveyed in ways that are accessible to a range of audiences.

- Information on the quality of support providers should be used to assist families and people with disabilities to make informed choices.

The first step is to reject the false dichotomy we have created between health and safety on the one hand and personal choice on the other and embrace them all as equally important considerations that are inextricably tied to quality. From there, the delicate balancing act can begin—stretching limited resources to address expanding needs, bringing new technologies into vastly varied organizations, and enticing new professionals into flexibly defined support roles. It is an exciting prospect.

Index

Page numbers followed by "*f*" indicate figures; those followed by "*t*" indicate tables.